SECULARISM AS MISDIRECTION

HEDGEHOG AND FOX

HISTORY AND POLITICS SERIES

"The fox knows many things,
but the hedgehog knows one big thing."

General Editor

RUDRANGSHU MUKHERJEE

Nivedita Menon

SECULARISM AS MISDIRECTION

Critical Thought
from the Global South

DUKE UNIVERSITY PRESS DURHAM & LONDON 2024

First US edition © 2024 Duke University Press
All rights reserved
Printed in the United States of America on acid-free paper ∞
Cover design: Aimee C. Harrison

Library of Congress Cataloging-in-Publication Data

Names: Menon, Nivedita, author.
Title: Secularism as misdirection : critical thought from the
Global South / Nivedita Menon.
Other titles: Theory in forms.
Description: Durham : Duke University Press, 2024. | Series: Theory in forms |
Includes bibliographical references and index.
Identifiers: LCCN 2023037241 (print)
LCCN 2023037242 (ebook)
ISBN 9781478030423 (paperback)
ISBN 9781478026204 (hardcover)
ISBN 9781478059448 (ebook)
Subjects: LCSH: Secularism—Developing countries. | Secularism—Political
aspects—Developing countries. | Women—Developing countries—Social
conditions. | Religion and state—Developing countries. | Political culture—
Developing countries. | BISAC: SOCIAL SCIENCE / Ethnic Studies /
Asian Studies | POLITICAL SCIENCE / Religion, Politics & State
Classification: LCC BL2765.D44 M46 2024 (print) |
LCC BL2765.D44 (ebook) | DDC 211/.6—dc23/eng/20231117
LC record available at https://lccn.loc.gov/2023037241
LC ebook record available at https://lccn.loc.gov/2023037242

Cover photograph by Amar Kanwar

Malathi de Alwis

1963–2021

beloved friend, feminist scholar,
and comrade

Contents

Acknowledgements

FIRST, MY WARMEST gratitude to the larger intellectual community that sustains all of us. In this case, the generosity of spirit displayed by friends and colleagues who readily agreed to read parts of the manuscript or even the whole, taking time from their own insanely busy schedules to scrutinise carefully and offer engaged criticism, directing me to fresh resources and helping to fine-tune or redraft parts of my argument. Never have I felt the truth of this anodyne and familiar phrasing so powerfully; it therefore needs saying that the people I acknowledge below are neither responsible for any errors that remain nor necessarily in agreement with the way my argument plays out. Indeed, at many points in what follows I have felt like adding a footnote such as "X, you will still not agree with this, but thank you for helping me to phrase it less definitively!"

Partha Chatterjee read the manuscript in its earliest iteration, and his encouraging comments both propelled me forward as well as alerted me to gaps and weaknesses requiring further reading and thought.

Humeira Iqtidar read every single word in the spirit of tough love, and her long, insightful, and often critical comments have definitively shaped this book.

Honey Oberoi Vahali and Rachana Johri read the chapter on psychoanalysis, which I presented to them with an unsaid *gustaakhi maaf*. They responded with indulgence, offering wisdom and direction from the deep scholarship in which they are immersed, saving me from some elementary mistakes and driving the chapter in more complex directions.

Kalpana Kannabiran, Rahul Govind, Sanjay Palshikar, and Upinder

Singh read some chapters with a ferocious intellectual and political gaze, and through their own scholarship and the comments they made, enriched several dimensions of my project.

Thank you, Prateek Vijayavargia for enabling access to any material I needed at a moment's notice—through methods I did not enquire further into. (Long live the knowledge commons!)

As I wind up my teaching career and supervise the last six doctoral students before my retirement in a couple of years, my thanks to all the doctoral students I have ever had. Every engagement with each one of you taught me something valuable.

The section on women and land rights in chapter 5 is the latest version of two lectures delivered in 2015—the Nisha Dhanagere Memorial Lecture at Savitribai Phule University of Pune, and at the Institute for South Asia Studies, University of California, Berkeley. Versions of the lectures appear as chapters in Suren Pillay, ed., *On the Subject of Citizenship: Late Colonialism in the World Today*, and Toshie Awaya and Kazuo Tomozawa, eds., *Inclusive Development in South Asia*. The section on Universal Basic Income in chapter 5 was first presented at the South Asia @ NYU Annual Conference in 2017 (Inequality in South Asia), and later at an online seminar in King's College London. I would like to acknowledge the discussions and comments I received at these presentations.

The section on the Sethusamudram Project in chapter 5 is an updated and expanded version of part of an earlier paper in a volume I co-edited with Aditya Nigam and Sanjay Palshikar, *Critical Studies in Politics: Sites, Selves, Power*. The CSP (Critical Studies in Politics) group of scholars and our stimulating interactions in the course of the production of the volume are an important landmark in my intellectual journey.

I started thinking systematically from the global South with a lecture delivered in 2017 in the Pandit Hriday Nath Kunzru Memorial Lecture Series organised by the School of International Studies, Jawaharlal Nehru University (JNU), New Delhi. Subsequently, I taught a course titled "Critical Thought from the Global South," and, in the five or six years since then, have benefited greatly from the highly motivated students who opted for the course; their intellectual curiosity and critical minds pushed and broadened my horizons. The core of chapter 3 is the K. R. Narayanan Memorial Lecture I was invited to deliver at the Centre for Research and Education for Social Transformation, Kozhikode, Kerala, in November 2017, with a somewhat developed version published in the *Economic and Political Weekly* (vol. 54, issue 38, 21 September 2019), and later in a volume bringing together the lecture series titled *Nationhood, Social Justice, and Unequal Transformations: Essays for K. R. Narayanan*, ed. D. D. Nampoothiri, et al. The idea of insurgent constitutionalism in chapter 6 was developed in the Chinta Ravindran Memorial Lecture (2018), and in a presentation at a conference titled "Cultures of the Left inthe Age of Right Wing Populism" organised by scholars of Warwick University and Jawaharlal Nehru University (2019), and also in the Professor V. Aravindakshan Foundation Memorial Lecture (2022).

The collective blog begun by some of us in 2006, Kafila, continues to sputter along, completely unfunded and at the mercy of the constraints of time upon its remaining active members, and has served as a platform that germinates early ideas that sometimes lead to longer articles and books. Many of the ideas in this book too have had their earliest incarnations in posts on Kafila.

Rukun Advani I thank for his editorial skill that saved many an over-academic formulation of mine from certain death. This being a book for general readers as much as for academics and scholars, I have followed his suggestion to stay clear of diacritical marks.

Thank you to Achille Mbembe for enabling Duke University Press to collaborate with the originating publisher Permanent Black, and to Elizabeth Ault of DUP for so enthusiastically shepherding it.

When citing or referring to Japanese, Chinese, Korean, and Taiwanese writers, I have followed the conventions of scholars in the field.

This book has taken shape over a decade that has seen the chaos wrought by India's descent into Hindu supremacist rule, and by the pandemic. It would have been difficult to survive, let alone be productive, without the networks of solidarity and friendship and intimacy that we managed to build and sustain.

My Sah Vikas family—Anindita Bose, Aparna Balachandran, Irfan Zuberi, Kaustav Saha, Madhulika Banerjee, Nagraj Adve, Shahana Bhattacharya, Shaista Anwar—for food and recipes and comfort, for sharing in despair and joy, and for being on call at all times for one another. (Why has the water stopped? Did you know another *dargah* has been demolished?) This has been a security net that envelops with love and information and references on eclectic topics (and cruel mockery when deemed necessary).

Aditya Nigam for the intellectual, political, and emotional journey on which we continue to be companions, for being the sounding board for every idea and passing thought, for reading every word I have ever written with critical care, and for "being there" for me always, regardless of every vicissitude and change.

Shobna Sonpar and Shifa Haq for training my emotional core with loving kindness.

My JNU family—colleagues and friends, our inspiring and courageous students—who continue to stand up against the neoliberal- and Hindutva-driven unravelling of our public universities and continue to pay a price, while drawing strength and courage from one another.

Our friends and students in prison for speaking up against the authoritarian regime. And the tireless, principled lawyers who push back against the destruction of institutions.

To the young musicians and theatre activists (Sanyukta, Anirban and their friends) who taught me, when faced with bleakness and despair, to "start with one corner, keep one little corner clean."

Friendships that have sustained me across distance and across time, seeding my emotions and my intellect, weathering phases of radio silence and every hiccup—Aditi Nigam, Amrita Nandy, Ayisha Abraham,

Chandana Mathur, Dermot Dix, Gautam Bhan, J. Devika, Jamal Kidwai, Janaki Abraham, Janaki Srinivasan, Jinee Lokaneeta, Malavika Rajkotia, Mohinder Singh, P. K. Datta, Rita Kothari, Satyajit Mayor, Shankar Raghuraman, Shipra Nigam, Sneha Banerjee, Shreiya Maheshwari, Sumit Sarkar, Tanika Sarkar, Upasana Garnaik, Urvashi Butalia, Vrinda Grover, Rada Ivekovic, and Goran Fejic.

Ayesha Kidwai, Janaki Nair, Madhu Sahni, Pratiksha Baxi—my daily feminist fix.

Aarti Sethi, Rachana Johri, Sunalini Kumar—who have held my hand and seen me through every cataclysm and celebration.

The wider circles of friendships old and new, of political camaraderie, all of which, I am fortunate enough to say, I couldn't possibly name without writing another book.

Remembering my father B. M. Menon, who passed away in 2010.

And with so much love to my mother Devaki Menon, and to my siblings and niblings—Dilip, Pramada, Lara, Sujata, Naima, Zayan—often taken for granted, but always in my heart.

This book is dedicated to one of my oldest friends whom we lost to cancer in 2021, the Sri Lankan feminist scholar and democratic rights activist Malathi de Alwis. Malathi inspired generations with her passion for justice and the networks of solidarity and friendship she built across continents. I miss her luminous presence in my life.

Introduction

Thinking Secularism from the Global South

I<small>N THE PERFORMANCE</small> of a magic trick, misdirection involves drawing attention away from where the trick is happening to another place, or to other objects that are made to appear more fascinating. In this book I address the manner in which the master discourse of secularism and the grid of meanings it produces effect such a misdirection. The field of meaning that "secularism" invokes structures our vision—making certain objects and features hypervisible while obscuring others that are critical factors in contemporary politics and intellectual production.

What would democracy and intellection look like if we took these factors into account? This is the question that will absorb our attention as we travel this journey together. Lifting this grid, which has long shaped our vision, has been enabled by decades of scholarship from the global South—scholarship that has moved away from the universalising thrust of European Enlightenment thought, opened up its non-European histories, and carefully insisted that all thought emerges from specific spatio-temporal locations.

The perspective I will outline is from the global South and from India, but my attempt will be to open up from this ground and theorise from this location in order to make arguments about secularism and democracy in general. I draw on scholarship and politics in my part of the world to set up conversations with debates on and experiences of secularism globally—much as theorists from the global North, though starting from their own contexts, quite unselfconsciously theorise broadly or imply the universality of their adopted positions.

1

The key difference may be that when we in the global South theorise on the basis of our experiences we rarely assume that our perspectives are universally generalisable and applicable everywhere. At the same time, I believe that a comparative perspective enables conversations across contexts; in such conversations we sometimes hear resonances and sometimes recognise disjunctures—and taken together these enable the mapping of new ground.

This is therefore not a book "about" India but "from" India, reconceptualising some aspects of secularism more generally. A limitation of any comparative theorising exercise across cultural and geographical contexts—especially with the goal of better understanding one's own location—is that the selective study of "other" locations might make the latter seem under-theorised, and under-contextualised in terms of their own dense debates. This is, all the same, a better mode of theorising than simply applying theory—on the assumption of its universality—from the North to other parts of the globe, this having long become a normalised and largely unquestioned mode. By contrast, I see the more implicitly dialogic mode of theorising in the present book as a listening in on conversations elsewhere. This I attempt in order to throw light on our own positions and perspectives, without laying any claim to a full understanding, and in the hope that this theorising speaks to multiple contexts.

I take into account here knowledges that are a form of counter-hegemonic practice. They feed into multiple kinds of resistance to authoritarianism, capitalism, patriarchy, caste, and race domination worldwide. At every point, therefore, resistance is implied in the conversations that are set up in this book.

Thinking from the Global South

The term global South does not here refer to a geographical region, nor to a category within a developmental discourse. It is intended to indicate a space of thought, the possibility of revaluing and learning from speech that exists in the margins, of reworking the co-ordinates of intellectual labour to free ourselves from Eurocentric universalising narratives, and to destabilise the East–West distinction which is routinely made in the context of thought and intellection. Such conceptualisation might make spaces within the geographical global North part of the global South—as, for instance, the thought of African Americans in the United States of America, and of Indigenous people in the Americas and Australia. This would apply also perhaps to some parts of Europe—around the Mediterranean, for example, or parts of Eastern and Central Europe with histories that cut through all neat continental divisions. And, of course, the term global South assumes, to begin with, certain histories of normalised cartography which are challenged by strategies such as "upside down maps." The Argentinian philosopher Walter Mignolo asserts, "I am *where* I think," that is, you constitute yourself (I am) in the place where you do and think.[1] Note that this statement is not a claim to ahistoric indigeneity, authenticity, or superiority vis-à-vis "the West"—a stance very familiar in India from the Hindu nationalist frame-work. Rather, it is an insistence on privileging *location*, a recognition that spatial and temporal co-ordinates inevitably suffuse all theorising. A sensitivity to location invariably leads to a productive contamination of the purity of empty universalist categories with specific histories, thus challenging their claim to speak about everywhere from nowhere, pointing towards unexpected other histories that unsettle the idea of a single point of origin.

The hemispheric divide is bridged by links with the South-within-the-North. Latin American decolonial feminism has found allies in the Latina/x feminist tradition of the United States. Latina/x "symbolically encapsulates identity conditions of migration, immigration, and diaspora to the United States from countries in Latin America and the Caribbean" and can capture a range of identities (e.g. Afro-Latina, Afro-Caribbean, Nuyorican, Xicana).[2] Dalit intellectuals in South Asia have been in conversation with Black politics and scholarship in the USA from the time of the correspondence between B. R. Ambedkar and W. E. B. Du Bois in 1946—when Ambedkar hoped to follow Du Bois

[1] Mignolo 2011: xvi.
[2] Berruz 2018.

in submitting a petition to the UN on the plight of India's Untouchables—down to the present.[3] The Dalit Panther organisation founded in 1972 by Namdeo Dhasal, J. V. Pawar, Raja Dhale, and Arjun Dangle was explicitly inspired by the Black Panthers of the USA; at its peak, for about five years, it provided inspiring and militant leadership to young Dalits.[4] Activists like Thenmozhi Soundararajan, founder of Equality Labs, who studies the practice of caste discrimination among South Asians in the USA, have made explicit connections between Dalit and Black experience. Equality Labs' report *Caste in the United States* was discussed widely among Black audiences.[5]

A more recent alliance is between postsocialist and postcolonial feminisms exploring their "uneasy affinities."[6] On the one hand postsocialist scholars are seen by postcolonial scholars as more aligned with the North; on the other the concept of "postsocialist precarity"— referring to "geo-historical experiences resulting from the dismantling of state socialist modernity and the (re-)incorporation of relatively closed economies into the capitalist neoliberal order"[7]—draws the two closer in their shared critique of imperialism, capitalism, and heteronormativity. Moreover, racism tends to be less visible in the postsocialist imaginary and the conversation with postcolonialism brings the issue of racialised hierarchies into focus.[8]

We can begin to see what thinking the global South involves—the attempt to bring into conversation with one another concepts and categories that have emerged from different spatio-temporal locations is key. This conversation would have to be produced with the sharp awareness of incommensurability, mistranslation, productive misreading, and above all, and always, the awareness of the materiality and politics of location.

The process of engaging with thought from the global South involves

[3] West and Yengde 2017.
[4] J. V. Pawar Interview 2022.
[5] Paul 2018.
[6] Koobak, et al. 2021.
[7] Suchland 2021: 14.
[8] Koobak, et al. 2021.

at least three tasks, each of them addressed in the next three sections. The first is a critique of Eurocentrism which has, as of now, been substantially carried out, with Edward Said's *Orientalism* (1978) as an important landmark. The ensuing section covers this ground and focuses, in particular, on the themes of "Asia as method" and spirituality in decolonial thought.

The second task is to question the West/non-West binary assumed with reference to philosophy, and to unpack and trace the interweaving histories of these two categories of thought.

The third and most critical task is to identify concepts internal to knowledge traditions, think about the extent to which these can travel to other contexts, and to see what productive translations (and mistranslations) can come about.

An important clarification to make is that in this book the word "tradition" is never used as the antonym of "modernity," largely because both terms come under continuous interrogation. I use "tradition" in the sense of continuing practices and knowledges, regardless of whether they have ancient roots or are more recent. Thus, a knowledge tradition could, for example, be scientific or feminist or religious, or have elements of all these. All traditions are living palimpsests through which can be dimly (but sometimes brightly) glimpsed layers of histories, like a fertile undergrowth.

Critique of Eurocentrism

We can briefly define Eurocentrism as a set of assumptions about (i) the universalisability of the European/Western experience, and (ii) the Telos of Progress and History. From this position, the non-West is a place of data and facts which must be excavated and theorised in the "neutral" conceptual frameworks that have evolved in the West. From this point of view, the non-West is either always lacking—modernity is incomplete, secularism impure, democracy immature, development arrested, capitalism retarded—or the non-West can be translated perfectly into Western terms by answering, for instance, questions like "is there 'civil society?,'" "are there conceptions of 'equality?,'" "were there 'liberal' thinkers?," and "what kind of 'modernity' do they have?" Frantz Fanon put it this way: if ever the colonised happen to "arrive," "Everything is anticipated, thought out, demonstrated . . ."[9]

There is of course by now a great deal of self-reflexivity about Eurocentrism among Western scholars: hence, for instance, Charles Taylor's warning against the easy transposing of the state–civil society opposition derived from the experience of Western Europe to other parts of the world, and his proposal to enrich the concept of civil society by including within its purview other forms of state–society interaction in non-European contexts. But—as Partha Chatterjee in his response to Taylor points out—the central assumption of Taylor's proposal continues to be an understanding that "it is only the concepts of European social philosophy that contain within them the possibility of universalisation." Chatterjee's own project, therefore, is to explore the specificity of the European concept of civil society and to try demonstrating the ways in which "that concept could be shown to be a particular form of a more universal concept"; in other words, "to send the concept of civil society back to where . . . it properly belongs—the provincialism of European social philosophy."[10] And, of course, while concepts emerging from Western (Euro-American) social philosophy are assumed to contain within them the possibility of universalisation, the reverse is never assumed. Can, for instance, Nyerere's concept of Ujamaa, or the Mahabharata's trope of Draupadi as the ambiguous figure of assertive femininity, ever be considered relevant in analyses of Euro-American experience? Only Antigone can be made to speak about women and war everywhere.

Asia as Method

One important element of the critique of Eurocentrism has come from the lectures delivered in 1960 under the title "Asia as Method" by the Japanese scholar of Chinese literature Takeuchi Yoshimi. In these

[9] Fanon 2009: 263.
[10] Chatterjee 2010: 275–6.

lectures Takeuchi was concerned with how one could engage with Western theory from an Asian perspective. Taking up the values of freedom and equality as they emerged from Western thought, he recognised the contradiction between these ideals and the imperialist histories with which they were linked. However, rather than simply rejecting these Western ideals he suggested instead that Asia should "re-embrace the West," reassess these values from the outside, and apply Asia's "own cultural values." He noted that "these values do not already exist, in substantive form" but may nevertheless still be possible "as method . . . as the process of the subject's self-formation." He called this process "'Asia as method," concluding that it was "impossible to definitively state what this might mean."[11]

Kuan-Hsing Chen, in his book *Asia as Method* (2010), engages with Takeuchi Yoshimi as well as with Mizoguchi Yuzo's *China as Method*, published twenty-five years after Takeuchi's essay. Mizoguchi Yuzo, in Chen's rendering, rejects Takeuchi's polarising understanding in which Japan "turned direction," gave up its own sense of self, and fully embraced Europe, while China "returned to the core," "resisting Europe even as it constantly tries to overcome it."[12] Mizoguchi Yuzo argues that neither total affirmation nor total negation are possible and that the specific pasts of different societies will condition their present. He used the term *jiti* (base entity) and *muti* (mother's body, or originating basis) to refer to these pasts. Chen sees his own project in *Asia as Method* as developing a theory based on understanding heterogeneous presents through the lens of *jiti* and *muti*.[13]

These concepts are productive beyond the specific context in which Mizoguchi Yuzo developed them. Every moment and space in the contemporary is a knot of intersecting histories and fragments, rooted at different depths, impossible to untangle in the present—they can only be understood *within* and *as* a tangle. The "originating basis" is already variegated and complex, so the invocation of *jiti* and *muti* cannot be

[11] Rojas 2019: 211.
[12] Chen 2010: 247.
[13] Ibid.: 245 and 248 for *jiti* and *muti*, respectively.

a reference to any pure and homogeneous past. Rather, these terms alert us to the view that engaging with the contemporary requires us to accept different elements as having varying resonances and meanings even in the same context, depending on which part of the past's undergrowth we connect to the present.

In his classification Takeuchi Yoshimi had placed India closer to China than Japan, and this seems to me an accurate representation. Several Indian intellectuals had begun articulating a critique of the wholesale adoption of Western thought from the late nineteenth century onwards. In 1954 the *Visvabharati Quarterly*, published by Rabindranath Tagore's university, republished a lecture by Krishna Chandra Bhattacharyya delivered in 1931, sixteen years before India's independence. Titled "Swaraj in Ideas," Bhattacharyya's talk extended the notion of *swaraj* (self-determination) to the realm of ideas.[14] Calling cultural domination a subtle form of political domination, he was nevertheless clear that the assimilation of an alien culture was not necessarily an aspect of subjection, and that in fact the assimilation of new and foreign ideas was probably necessary for progress: "When I speak of cultural subjection, I do not mean the assimilation of an alien culture. That assimilation need not be an evil; it may be positively necessary for healthy progress and in any case it does not mean a lapse of freedom." Cultural subjection happens "when one's traditional cast of ideas and sentiments is superseded without comparison or competition by a new cast representing an alien culture which possesses one like a ghost." The "Indian mind," said Bhattacharyya, has "subsided below the conscious level of culture" for (Western-)educated men; it operates only at the level of family life and in some social and religious practices. Meanwhile,

---

[14] The text of this lecture reappears in a later publication, with "swaraj" spelt as "svaraj." Here the lecture is cited as having been informally delivered in 1928 at a meeting of the students of the Hooghly College, of which Bhattacharyya was Principal, during 1928–30 (Bhushan and Garfield 2011: 103). The *Visvabharati Quarterly* attributes the lecture to October 1931, as part of the Sir Asutosh Memorial Lecture series (Bhattacharyya 1954: 175). I have retained the spelling and date as cited in the *Visvabharati Quarterly*.

Western ideas, "springing as they do from a rich and strong life—the life of the West . . . induce in us a shadow mind that functions like a real mind except in the matter of genuine creativeness."[15]

Bhattacharyya is not arguing for rejecting Western thought, but for Western thought to be *engaged with through* Indian modes of thinking and Indian cultural resources. This is exactly how Naoki Sakai reads Asia as method—as a conceptualisation of agency and subjectivity in critical relation to itself and to colonial modernity—not the valorising of pre-existing "Asian values."[16]

In my view, then, to take Asia as method seriously is to insist on *location*, which is differentially constituted, and rooted in spatially and temporally variegated *jiti*.

Spirituality and Decolonial Thinking

From another part of the global South, Walter Mignolo names as the "Western code" the belief in "one sustainable system of knowledge, cast first in theological terms" and later in secular philosophy and sciences.[17] This system of knowledge is assumed to have been inaugurated by the European Enlightenment. Decolonial thinking counters this idea—that European modernity was the point of arrival of human history—and focuses on the "colonial matrix of power" of which the "rhetoric of modernity" and the "logic of coloniality" are the two sides.[18] Coloniality is a term Mignolo derives from the Peruvian thinker Anibal Quijano, who sees it as a process inaugurated by the European invasion from the fifteenth century of the regions now called the Americas and the Caribbean. Coloniality led to the formation of these regions from kingdoms that existed at the time, and to the massive trade of enslaved Africans. Coloniality is thus constitutive of modernity, its "darker side."

[15] Bhattacharyya 1931/1954: 103–4.
[16] Sakai 2010.
[17] Mignolo 2011: xii.
[18] Ibid.: xviii.

The world around 1500 was "polycentric and non-capitalist,"[19] with several coexisting civilisations—the Ming Huangdinate, the Ottoman Sultanate, the Mughal Empire, the Oyo and Benin kingdoms of the Yoruba nation in Africa, the Incas in Tawantinsuyu, and the Aztecs in Anahuac. At the beginning of the twenty-first century, the world is monocentric, interconnected by a single type of economy, capitalism; the violence of colonial practices has ravaged the world, which is now marked by a diversity of political theories and practices. In between these two scenarios, "modernity" enters as a double colonisation of time and space. A structure of control and management has emerged, of "authority, economy, subjectivity, gender and sexual norms," driven by the exploitation of labour and the expropriation of land.[20]

According to Nelson Maldonaldo-Torres a serious engagement with spirituality is a distinguishing feature of decolonial—as opposed to postcolonial—thought. Mignolo himself is not interested in drawing sharp lines of division between decolonial and postcolonial thought. He sees both as "options" that can coexist, and as having different trajectories in terms of points of origin and linguistic fields, and therefore different areas of concern.[21] But he does outline the "spiritual option" as one of the trajectories that decolonial thinking will have to take seriously in the coming decades as it challenges both secular modernity/coloniality, and also the colonisation of institutionalised religions.[22] Maldonaldo-Torres sees this as a distinctive feature of decolonial thinking for, while postcolonial studies emerge from and are located in the academic field of the secular humanities, decolonial thinking has not been an academic discipline alone: it has included community activists, artists, and scholars critical of modern Western secularism who have drawn from and contributed to religious studies as well.

It is from this perspective that Maldonaldo-Torres reads Fanon as offering a critique of the coloniality of the religion/secularism divide.

[19] Ibid.: 3.
[20] Ibid.: 7.
[21] Ibid.: xxvii.
[22] Ibid.: 33–4.

Rejecting the understanding of Fanon as a secularist philosopher, Maldonaldo-Torres insists Fanon did not believe that overcoming religion is necessary for decolonisation to take place, or that decolonisation would lead to a religionless society. This is reflected, he says, in a paper Fanon co-wrote with an intern, Jacques Azoulay, while Fanon was Director of the Blida Psychiatric Hospital in Algeria. The paper warns psychiatrists and other scientists that while "some conducts, some reactions can appear 'primitive' to us . . . that is only a value judgment, one that is both questionable and bears on poorly defined characteristics." The authors were, in particular, referring to the idea that "genies" (*jinn*) produce madness, a belief prevalent in Algeria.[23] Maldonaldo-Torres concludes that Fanon's "view of the self as a gift and his intersubjective account of healthy individuality and social relations, draw from and are compatible with a large variety of sources, including so-called religious or spiritual formations."[24] Fanon's decolonial thinking should therefore be related to "non-secular or post-secular accounts of reality, including the African diaspora spiritualities that are found in Fanon's own island of Martinique and through the Caribbean, some of which probably informed Fanon's thinking and worldview too." It seems, too, that Fanon is read quite widely as a critic of the coloniality of secularism among militant intellectuals in the Indigenous communities of South America.[25]

In a similar move, but from a position different from that of Mignolo, Achille Mbembe reasserts a "critical and inclusive universalism" as the "latest avatar of a certain tradition of Western humanism." In an interview around his book, *Brutalisme* (2020), Mbembe reflects on the shift that has taken place from the beginning of modernity—when "the sharp separation between the world of humans and the world of objects" was an emancipatory move—to the current moment when what "prevails is the idea that the human is the product of technology" and "[e]verything, including consciousness itself, is

[23] I will engage with this idea at some length in chap. 4.
[24] Maldonaldo-Torres 2022.
[25] Ibid.

being reduced to matter."[26] Mbembe terms this the "new secular religion," counterposing to it the non-dichotomy of precolonial African and Amerindian metaphysics which enables us to "de-dramatize the human/object relationship."[27] At the same time Mbembe is concerned that the "critique of reason" should not become "a war against reason," and it is in this context that he asserts the new critical universalism.

In the present book I attempt to assert multiple notions of reason and unreason, as well as a somewhat suspicious attitude towards universalism. The point, however, that emerges from these different sets of not necessarily congruent arguments is that the idea of "applying theory" produced in one context to "understand practice" in another assumes that "political practice" is "non-theoretical"—completely bereft of any discursive-theoretical content—so that any theory (from the West) can be used to make sense of political practice anywhere. But, as some of us argued in an earlier work, all political practice is always constituted by some form of reflection and thought—theoretical or non-theoretical—and, as we realise today, at least one part of theorisation must be about making sense of "practice" through an understanding of the subject's own world and her categories of thought.[28]

What these layered discussions indicate is that the dichotomies of universal/particular, east/west, and tradition/modernity are articulated in far more complex ways than their invocations often imply.

Unpacking West and Non-West

The second task, also substantially advanced upon, is to go beyond postcolonial critiques of Eurocentrism, and postcolonial theory's object of critique—Empire—in order to unpack "West" and "non-West." Much of modern thought in the non-West has engaged with Western notions and vernacularised them—Sudipta Kaviraj uses the analogy of

---

[26] Mbembe 2022: 129.
[27] Ibid.: 130.
[28] Menon, Nigam, and Palshikar 2014.

speaking English with different accents.[29] But, equally, Western knowledge formations have deep roots in the non-West. In his controversial
book *Black Athena* (1987) Martin Bernal points out that until the
nineteenth century Greek culture was accepted as having arisen from
an incorporation into the Egyptian and Phoenician empires, whereby
Greek culture was undeniably a mixture of European, African, and
Arabic civilisational influences. It was only in the first half of the nineteenth century in Europe that Greece began to be viewed as essentially European or Aryan. This coincided with post-Enlightenment
notions of "progress" as well as the beginnings of institutionalised
racism. During this period a body of scholarship was created which
identified Greece as the cradle of European civilisation. It was intol-
erable in this corpus for Greece to be identified—as it had been for
centuries—as Levantine, or as Mediterranean when the latter de-
noted *all* the territories around the Mediterranean Sea—North
Africa, West Asia, and Southern Europe. Bernal's work came to be
derided as "controversial" precisely because it challenged mainstream
Eurocentric Enlightenment-inflected wisdom, although the attacks
against him were launched on other, ostensibly non-political grounds—
challenging his knowledge of linguistics, his handling of classical
texts, his alleged under-deployment of primary sources, and so on.
Bernal published a definitive response to his critics in 2005, bringing
together essays and replies he had written over the decades, organised
thematically and systematically.[30] He addressed each critique substantially and, in my opinion, his argument stands.

It is a truism now that the supposedly natural division of this part
of the world into continents—Europe, Africa, Asia—is anything but
natural. Spatially, North Africa, West Asia, and Southern Europe are
more contiguous with one another than with other parts of "their"
continents. Moreover, as scholars of Oceanic Studies point out,
oceans have not historically separated pieces of land; rather, they have

[29] Kaviraj 2005.
[30] Bernal 2005.

acted as conduits of communication.[31] In other spheres, too, long hidden or conveniently invisible connections between the three discursively separated continents around the Mediterranean have been made visible. Mahmood Mamdani, when referring to the ways in which knowledge flowed in an earlier age, points out that the graduation gowns seen all over the modern world are derived from the Islamic *madressa* of West Asia. And the early universities of Europe—Oxford, Cambridge, the Sorbonne—borrowed not just gowns but much of their curricula from these institutions, ranging from Greek philosophy to Iranian astronomy to Arab medicine and Indian mathematics: "They had little difficulty at that time in accepting this flowing gown, modeled after the dress of the desert nomad, as the symbol of high learning."[32] When reading Ibn Khaldun's *Muqaddimah*, Mamdani suggests, it may be productive to think of Africa before the Atlantic slave trade in *regional* rather than *continental* terms, involving an imagination that brings together the Mediterranean and West African regions "in a single history," a la Bernal.[33]

We need to recognise and recover what Mignolo calls "decolonial cosmopolitanisms" that go back to the twelfth century.[34] Take for instance Ibn-Rushd (1126–1198), a key twelfth-century figure who developed the Aristotelian distinction between form and matter to assert human free will, which mediates between essence and existence. In the debate between reason and revelation in Islamic scholarship, Ibn Rushd asserted that it was the philosopher, not the theologian, who needed to establish the true inner meaning of religious beliefs in the event of a dispute because of "his ability to deal with doubt, ambivalence and criticality."[35] Between the eighth and fifteenth centuries the Islamic world struggled between faith and mysticism on the one hand, and reason on the other, and eventually Ibn Rushd and the party

[31] Menon, et al. 2022; Hofmeyr 2012; Vink 2007; Ray 2020.
[32] Mamdani 2010.
[33] Mamdani 2012: 2.
[34] Mignolo 2011: 5.
[35] Hoskote and Trojanow 2012: 80.

of reason were set aside. But in twelfth-century Europe Ibn Rushd emerged as the standard bearer of the rebels—they called themselves the Averroists—against Catholic authoritarianism.[36] These were Christian intellectuals who had read Aristotle in Latin translations as well as through the extensive commentaries of Arab Aristotelians, and they made no distinction between Christian, Pagan, and Muslim authorities when arguing points of Christian doctrine. The Church reacted to them with anxiety and brutality through the first half of the thirteenth century, wiping out the mass movement of the Cathars (another sect deemed heretic) while first banning Ibn Rushd's commentaries on Aristotle and then the study of Aristotle himself. However, Ibn Rushd continued to remain a powerful force in the Renaissance.[37] Ranjit Hoskote and Ilija Trojanow have pointed out that while European accounts usually reduce the contribution of Arabic thinkers to European philosophy, treating them as couriers safeguarding and forwarding European philosophical treasures, in fact Arabic thinkers (*falasifa*) were philosophers themselves, not merely translating words but providing erudite commentary and paving the way for critical enquiry.[38]

This story is told very differently by the European scholar Umberto Eco. For him Averroes (Ibn Rushd) is a "blatant example of cultural misunderstanding" because he wrote his commentary on Aristotle's *Poetics* knowing no Greek and "hardly any" Syriac. He read Aristotle, says Eco, through a tenth-century Arabic translation of a Syriac translation of the Greek original. "To increase this mish-mash," he adds, "Aristotle's *Poetics* was accessed in Europe in a Latin translation of Averroes' commentary to the *Poetics* in Arabic."[39] What Eco sees as a mish-mash was a massive and complex project of translation in the twelfth century located on "a bridge between languages" in which texts "began to flow in various directions" among Greek, Arabic, Hebrew, and Latin,

---

[36] "Averroes" being the name for Ibn Rushd in the Christian world.
[37] Hoskote and Trojanow 2012.
[38] Ibid.: 95.
[39] Eco 2003: 85.

and into the emerging languages of Castilian, French, and Italian. "A special process of collaborative translation . . . was developed: usually a Jew (occasionally a Muslim) translated the Arabic text orally into Romance or Castilian, and then a Christian rendered this oral version into written Latin."[40] Jewish interpreters and Latin scribes also translated Greek originals and Arabic commentaries. These twelfth-century translations, cumulatively a massive philosophical project, Eco can only see as a failure.

Jonardon Ganeri outlines the extraordinary ways in which ideas travelled across these spaces: Schopenhauer read the Latin rendering of a Persian translation of the Upanishadic idea that the self is not an object; through Schopenhauer the idea reached Wittgenstein. The Buddha's ideas about the absence of self and emptiness reached China, from where through Jesuit missionaries "they entered that 'arsenal' of the Enlightenment," Pierre Bayle's *Dictionary*, a book "plundered by many Enlightenment thinkers," including David Hume.[41]

An instance of such a transmission from another part of the globe is presented by David Graeber and David Wengrow, who argue that the idea of the desirability of equality was brought to Europe through the encounter of Europeans with the indigenous peoples of North America. Specifically, Baron de Lahontan, a French army officer who took part in several campaigns in Canada in the late seventeenth century, became fluent in the indigenous languages of Algonkian and Wendat, and had several conversations with political figures. Among these was Kandiaronk, a Wendat warrior, strategist, and thinker, four conversations with whom de Lahontan published in 1703. Kandiaronk, who had visited France, offered a severe critique of European civilisation and of the deep inequality he witnessed there. This indigenous critique, as reproduced by de Lahontan, sparked debates and discussions in multiple languages in Europe, fuelling the works of philosophers such as Rousseau.[42]

---

[40] Hoskote and Trojanow 2012: 71.
[41] Ganeri 2007: 7.
[42] Graeber and Wengrow 2021: 78–102.

Evidently, West and non-West (or North and South) are not independent spaces of thought.

"Other" Conceptual Traditions and the Question of Translation

Our third and most important task is to identify concepts *internal* to other knowledge traditions through which intellectual conversations take place. What kinds of debates have happened, and what have been the key issues in them? It is equally important, when doing this, to take care not to treat the non-West as a homogeneous space. It is necessary to recognise and make visible internal structures of power, and voices of dissent and debate within non-Western knowledge formations. In what terms is criticism conducted and dissent expressed within these formations?

The issues of heterogeneity, power, and dissent within the non-West/ global South are not generally addressed by postcolonial or decolonial thinking, where the objects of critique remain empire/coloniality. However, in this book we will look at debates and contentions within the South in order to take seriously the heterogeneity and power relations internal to the South.

Translation as paradigmatic of any conversation, and every act of translation as shot through with power relations—this understanding is now very much part of a certain common sense arising from a formidable body of scholarship. One point of departure from here is in the direction of seeing translation as a hermeneutic project of understanding, an ethical project of destabilising the Self through engagement with the Other. Another is in the direction of recognising constitutive misreading as underlying any project of translation. A third critical aspect of translation is seeing it as a project of rendering things intelligible. What are the limits to this project? Who seeks intelligibility? Who evades it, or simply, in daily quotidian ways, bypasses its operations? Is the quest for mutual intelligibility implicit in all social interaction? But, more critically, is this very assumption of the possibility of mutual intelligibility complicit in projects of power? I will offer one illustration here of heterogeneity within the global South and how translation can act as a mode of exercising power.

In January 2012 the artist Subodh Gupta was one of the performers listed in an evening of performance art titled "Spirit Eaters," organised by Khoj, an artist-led organisation in Delhi. His performance lasted about thirty minutes, during which he remained in the audience. In the video which I saw,[43] the performance began with three men—from their clothes evidently lower-middle class—stepping up to a stage. They did not seem poor but were certainly not of the same class or cultural background as the audience, which was also visible. The three men sat in a row on the floor of the stage, cross-legged, before three steel plates and glasses. (Gupta is best known for enormous art installations using traditional steel vessels.) After they had seated themselves, two other men stepped silently on to the stage, one after the other, to serve on the plates mounds of what looked like beaten rice (*chidwa*) followed by large dollops of curd. The three men sat looking silently at the food for a moment, then raised their voices in an indecipherable chant, then dug their entire right palms into the mass of *chidwa* and curd, lifting huge sloppy handfuls almost up to their mouths, and then let it all drop back onto their plates. At this point one of the men looked at Subodh Gupta in the audience and started to argue loudly in a Bihari accent and vocabulary not immediately comprehensible to the largely non-Bihari audience. From the audience Gupta responded by muttering in Hindi "*chalo shuru karo, shuru karo*" (go on, start off). Once again the chant was resumed by the men on the stage, once again the food taken up to their mouths was dropped, once again there was argumentation, and once again "*chalo chalo, shuru karo*." This process was repeated several times, and it soon became clear that some sort of bargaining was

---

[43] I visited the Khoj Studio, where I was able to see a recording of the whole performance. I am grateful for that opportunity because I missed the live performance, but Khoj is in no way responsible for my interpretation of it. A brief one-minute clip of the performance has been put up by Khoj: https://www.youtube.com/watch?v=T-a7GuSHIYA.

going on. The spokesperson of the eaters demanded, initially, a lakh of rupees for each of them; but gradually, with repeated urgings to continue eating, he came down to a lakh for all three, before finally settling for an even smaller amount—which happened when Gupta appeared to become irritated and said "*toh mat kha*" (well then, don't eat, leave).

The bargaining was amusing and soon engaged the audience, who were laughing at the repartee and who applauded when the eaters lost the battle and started eating in earnest. The man who did most of the speaking for the eaters was flamboyant and good-humoured, and appeared to be utterly relaxed during the performance, while the one who appeared to be the youngest did not speak at all, looking embarrassed and shy.

After the negotiations were done, the remaining eight or ten minutes of the performance were entirely taken up by the men eating silently—very sloppily, using their entire palms (not just the fingers, in the style of most North Indians). They smeared their mouths and moustaches with food, dropping some on the floor and around their plates—first the *chidwa* and curd, and then a succession of huge amounts of rotis, curry, dry vegetable, and sweets. All the while, the upper-class audience, well clad for a Delhi winter, watched attentively, or else with much murmuring and giggling.

The Khoj site describes the performance this way:

> Spirit Eaters explores notions of identity, cultural specificity, aspiration and excess that preoccupy Subodh Gupta's art making. De-contextualizing the presentation of specific cultural practices, Spirit Eaters harks to his childhood experience of watching *kanthababas*, a group of paid, professional eaters in Bihar who rapidly consume vast amounts of food for the appeasement of the souls of ancestors and elders. The performance is simultaneously repulsive, vulgar, amusing and awe-inspiring.[44]

I saw a video of the performance made via two cameras that Khoj used to record the evening, not the performance itself. From detailed

---

[44] Khoj 2012.

conversations with many who did see it live, I gathered that the information above had not been accessed by most viewers before the event, and the general feelings reported were of bewilderment and deep discomfort with the class politics of a performance involving men, clearly poorer than the audience, who were bargained down before they could eat. Many also wondered at the strangely messy manner of eating, so unlike the normal eating practices of most Indians, including the poor. It seemed to many, then, that the performance objectified economic and cultural difference in an elite art space. As one artist, disturbed by the performance, said to me in a personal conversation, "This kind of collapsing of two worlds in a performance space could have been interesting, but the terms of the collapsing are important." She was suggesting, it seemed to me, that there was no mutuality in the collapsing, their world was simply collapsed into ours.

It was only gradually, in newspaper interviews, that the context emerged, and, as the Khoj website later made clear, Gupta had deliberately in his performance—or, one should say, in the performance he produced—de-contextualised the practice of mourning in Bihari Hindu society. The terms "vulgar," "repulsive," "amusing," and "awe-inspiring" on the Khoj website are noteworthy, while another newspaper reported the amount of food consumed as "obscene" and the performance as "simultaneously brilliant and bizarre."[45] RoseLee Goldberg, an American art historian and curator, said in an interview:

> I loved Subodh Gupta's piece. Beginning with physical objects, he brings in the references of rituals, history of class and politics in his work . . . The work was funny and beautiful . . . This is what is performance art. Here is a visual artist who is working in time and space but with such beautiful objects. And whatever he set up for the viewers to see was exquisite—the three eaters, vessels and six screens placed at different places on the terrace for people to watch it comfortably. The angles and the frames showing the hands of the eaters, the lighting . . . it was all really nice. I learnt so much about a place and its culture in just 20 minutes.[46]

[45] Nath 2012.
[46] Tripathi 2012.

What is fascinating in this whole story is the process by which an embedded local practice is decontextualised (and secularised) in a manner that enables it to be translated, or rendered intelligible entirely—and only—in cosmopolitan terms: "obscene" amounts of food, "repulsive," "amusing," "funny and beautiful," "bizarre." What is missing is precisely what Goldberg claims to see—"references of history and class," and specifically because it is de-contextualised. One wonders what she or any viewer learnt about the place and its culture—that was exactly what the performance was *not* about. One did not even learn the names of the performers who enacted a ritual familiar to them, but in a space that was utterly alien, and in a context that could have held no meaning for them. I wondered if they were professional actors rather than traditional *kanthababas*, but had they been actors their names would have been in the Khoj catalogue and website, or they would have been interviewed too. Not one newspaper spoke to any of them—they remain unknowable, except in a language that is ours alone, not theirs. It is because they performed the same role that steel utensils play in Gupta's work that outside of the performance they remain anonymous and unknown.[47]

I should add that Gupta himself had positioned six cameras to record the performance, and in a later interview referred to "Spirit Eaters" as "video art." I can hazard a guess that the video Gupta produced (which I have not seen) will not be a simple recording but an art object in itself which may well escape the terms of my critique.[48] The afterlife of installations and performances as videos, photographic stills, catalogues, and so on is another register of translation that distances even further the "real" objects involved from the contexts into which they were brought by the art work. This can, at least potentially, be a radical move to question context itself, but the initial performance lingers spectrally over all its afterlives.

[47] It is possible that by now their names have been recorded for posterity, but they had not been at the time of the performance, nor for some years afterwards.

[48] "Spirit Eaters" has since then become the title of a catalogue produced for Subodh Gupta's solo exhibition in Switzerland (Hirsch 2013).

What I am trying to argue from the instance above is that we must listen in on conversations *internal* to cultures as well as *between* the West and non-West. Such attention centrally foregrounds the question of language and translation. It is useful here to consider an argument made by Peter Winch, who, writing about the relationship between language and reality, makes a distinction between two kinds of "languages."[49] One is a set of linguistic conventions, such as English, French, and so on. When one knows a specific language and wants to learn another, one remains within the same world, learning English names for the objects and experiences one already knows in French. Thus, when one learns to command, say, in English (to say, "Do this"), one is not learning to command per se. But the differences between the language of science/modernity and those of other worldviews are not of this order. (Winch uses the example of the magic practices of an African tribe, the Azande, as studied by the anthropologist E. E. Evans-Pritchard.) When one learns mathematics, say, or science, one learns a whole worldview, a set of beliefs, of which the language is only an expression. Learning to prove something mathematically is not simply learning a new way of expressing something already known in another language; it means learning a new action that can *only* be performed in that language.

From this perspective we can understand the intellectual predicament outlined by the Guinean scholar Siba Grovogui—that it is impossible to talk in the African languages of many concepts common within the discipline of International Studies, the reason being that these African political societies are radically different. In Guinea, for example, there have been "stateless" or acephalous societies among whom the notion of "Great Power responsibility," for instance, makes no sense. And of course the term "stateless societies" already assumes the modern state to be the norm. Another comparable problem arises in translating across African languages with their different histories.[50]

---

[49] Winch 1987.
[50] Grovogui 2013.

There is also the question of the internal hierarchy of languages. G. N. Devy uses what he calls the "traditional Indian term" *bhasha*—a word deriving from Sanskrit meaning "language"—to refer to modern Indian languages, thus distinguishing them from Sanskrit, which is not the spoken language of any community while being the only language in which Brahminical rites are conducted. So, power relations operate between language communities at different levels—between English and the Indian languages (although English is also one of the two official languages of India); between the claims of Sanskrit—put forward by Hindu nationalism as the oldest "Indian" language—and Tamil, which is claimed to be older;[51] and between on the one hand the *bhasha*s (of which there are many more than the twenty-two state-recognised languages) and Hindi and English on the other.[52] Indeed, as Devy points out, even the Sanskrit heritage has "percolated into the modern Indian consciousness after being filtered through bhasha literature and bhasha culture."[53]

The colonial experience produced one set of complexities; another has been produced by the post-Independence politics of the ruling elites—who have for many decades been English-speaking, and urban upper-class and caste—followed by the rise of the upper-caste and upper-class elites of the Hindi heartland. Positing Hindi as the national language is part of Hindu nationalist politics, and the claim is bitterly contested. Only 26 percent of Indians speak Hindi, and even this percentage is derived by placing under the label of Hindi at least eight full-fledged languages that are claimed to be "dialects" of Hindi.[54]

Similar histories as well as power relations between multiple language communities across the global South are being disentangled,

---

[51] Sulochana 2019. Both these are among the twenty-two languages officially recognised in India.

[52] An analysis of the 2011 census showed that in India there are 121 languages spoken by 10,000 or more people; and that there are more than 19,500 languages spoken as mother tongues: Press Trust of India 2018.

[53] Devy 2009: 52.

[54] *The Hindu* Data 2019.

played out, and lived through. Sri Lanka and South Africa provide just two of many examples.[55]

Translation is thus critical to the enterprise of thinking *from* the global South. Here I use an important distinction made by Anup Dhar in the context of psychoanalysis—between doing psychoanalysis *in* India and doing psychoanalysis *from* India.[56] In my understanding, the first indicates specificity; the second, location. Specificity is important to demarcate, but it must not remain at the level of marking difference from the norm. *From* a location, on the other hand, can be theorised in more general terms, recognising specificity but making comparability key and finding resonances across contexts. Perhaps this is why the Japanese philosopher Naoki Sakai sees translation as having to assume a "heterolingual" mode of address, which assumes a "non-aggregate community of foreigners." That is, translation must assume mutual "foreignness" between two language communities. Rather, what translation tends to assume is a "homolingual" address based on the normalcy of reciprocal and transparent communication in a homogeneous medium. In a heterolingual mode of address, the addressee could respond with varying degrees of comprehension, including missing the signification completely.[57] The heterolingual address thus assumes that every utterance can fail to communicate, because heterogeneity is inherent in every medium, and therefore translation is endless.[58]

All knowledge production must start with one's location, with the questions about the world that puzzle you from your vantage point. A comparative dimension is inescapable—issues in other parts of the world seem at one level familiar to those in one's own, but they get articulated in unfamiliar ways; concerns specific to a location nevertheless resonate, echoing predicaments faced in some other place or at some other time. It is, after all, not just a question of translating words from

[55] Coperahewa 2019 for Sri Lanka; Mekoa 2020 for South Africa.
[56] Dhar 2018.
[57] Sakai 1997: 4–5.
[58] Ibid.: 8.

one language to another, it is about engaging with entire ways of life and modes of thinking arising from different trajectories of time and space.

A striking instance of translation as appropriation is the application of "gender" to African societies, for example.

African feminists have pointed out how Western feminism has universalised the concepts of "woman" and "patriarchy," failing to see the actual, very different structures of societal power in operation. Oyeronke Oyewumi argues that gender as a category did not operate in any significant way in pre-colonial Yoruba and many other African cultures.[59] Western post-Enlightenment philosophy privileges appearance ("seeing"), and therefore the body, and assumes certain structures of social difference based on these. Differences not visible to the eye in the same way are not understood. Oyewumi cites a study on the Ga traders of Ghana that refers to them as "market women," drawing all its conclusions from this foundational premise even when the identity of traders in West African societies is not gender-specific. Through her own work Oyewumi argues that, among the Yoruba, seniority is the defining axis of hierarchy, not gender.

Nkiru Nzegwu, through a critique of Martha Nussbaum and Ifi Amadiume, shows how the "metaphysics of gender" erodes cultural specificity and the historicity of societies such as that of the Igbo.[60] Even Amadiume, a Nigerian scholar—as she struggles to produce a culturally grounded account of the position of women—is caught up in this metaphysics, says Nzegwu. Gender identity in Igbo society, in Nzegwu's account, is "a flexible, fluid, state of being, and is tied to social roles and functions that demand deliberative rationality from females," and here too the principle of organisation is seniority.[61] Nzegwu argues that Nussbaum derives her entire understanding of women and womanliness in African societies by her (mis)reading of some lines from Chinua Achebe's *Things Fall Apart*, while Amadiume too, though

[59] Oyewumi 1997.
[60] Nzegwu 2004.
[61] Ibid.: 563.

much better informed than Nussbaum, even as she recognises the fluidity of gender roles, is trapped in the metaphysics of the binary gender model because she describes non-normative gender roles in binary terms—as for example "male daughters and female husbands."

Another important feminist voice from Africa is Sylvia Tamale, whose *Decolonization and Afro-Feminism* (2020) sees as a key decolonial move the assertion of a reworked Pan-Africanism that is both decolonial and Afro-feminist. Tamale is critical of the Western human rights paradigm based on the fragmented individual. She proposes instead the African philosophy of Ubuntu (from the Zulu language) which thinks in interconnected terms and is better geared to social justice.[62] Ubuntu is far from "I think therefore I am," and is rather "I am because you are"—a person is a person through other people. This idea echoes a theme characteristic of thought in the global South—the discomfort or lack of identification with the individual as assumed by Western modernity.[63] The above is only a brief account of a dense discussion among African scholars, offered here to indicate what it might mean to listen to internal conversations seriously.

Among feminists in Latin America, too, the term "gender" has been seen as problematic, but for a different reason. In an essay on Latin American feminist philosophy and politics, Stephanie Rivera Berruz states that gender entered the region with the translation of Gayle Rubin's scholarship into Spanish. The term was translated into Spanish as *género*, whose direct translation is more akin to "genre" or "species." Latin American feminists have contested the legitimacy of gender as a category of feminist analysis, for they see it as depoliticised and appropriated by states and funding agencies. These feminists have generally used the concept of patriarchy, preferring it because "it offered a framework grounded in ideological and socioeconomic conditions that allowed for articulating the cause of women's oppression."[64] The

---

[62] Tamale 2020.

[63] To this we will return in chap. 4, in our discussion on psychoanalysis from the global South.

[64] Berruz 2018.

interlinked ideas of decoloniality and translation are central to Latin American feminist thought, as translation is "politically and theoretically indispensable for feminist, anti-racist, decolonial, and anti-imperial alliances."[65] Drawing on Sonia Alvarez, Berruz draws our attention to the understanding that difference emerges as a rich terrain from which to engage others. It is evident that this "difference" refers to differences internal to feminism too, not merely between the hemispheres. This understanding involves accepting degrees of incommensurability. However, the idea is not to abandon translation but to "recognize the complexity and diversity of speaking positions with which we engage." The term *transloca* has been coined to indicate both the processes of translation ("trans") and the material effects of location ("loca")—"the transloca highlights multiple dimensions that shape conditions of difference."[66]

Berruz discusses a critical intervention in contemporary Latin American feminisms—a volume in Spanish rooted in decolonial epistemic practices[67]—which "reconceives Latin America as Abya Yala, the term used by Kuna (Indigenous people of Panamá and Colombia) for what colonizers termed 'America'. Abya Yala translates as 'land of full maturity' or 'land of vital blood' and is taken as a methodological starting point for theorising ways of knowing through a decolonial lens."[68] In this understanding decolonisation cannot occur without de-patriarchalisation. The project of decolonial feminisms is not framed by "privileging one category of analysis over another (e.g. race over gender); rather, it proposes a systemic critique focused on the conceptual framework of dominant Latin American feminisms, calling attention to the ways it has reified classism, sexism, racism, and heteronormativity."[69]

[65] Alvarez 2014: 1.

[66] Ibid.: 4.

[67] The Spanish volume is edited by Yuderkys Espinosa Miñoso, Diana Gómez Correal, and Karina Ochoa Muñoz.

[68] Berruz 2018.

[69] Ibid.

To conclude this discussion on translation, we may remind ourselves that translation can work in two ways. First there is the way in which the world has experienced translation since the fifteenth century in the Americas, and since the eighteenth century in other parts of the world—that is, as the process by which the language of the powerful can translate and render legible the languages of the powerless into the terms of the language of power. The other recognises processes under way since the twelfth century in which mutual equality is assumed, and in which there has been both a mutual flow of intelligibility as well as potential misreadings that could be productive. As the discussion in the previous two sections indicates, these two processes are not exclusive and clearly delimited. For when the tangled *jiti* of different spaces and times collides, we cannot say in advance whether power or mutuality will be at work.[70]

Secularism as Misdirection— A Map of the Book

As indicated at the start, this book attempts to show how the smoke-and-mirrors effect produced by the magic term "secularism"—the sound-and-light show that it produces—misdirects us and takes us away from crucial factors, while making certain other objects hypervisible.

In Chapter 1 I start with two key instances of misleading hypervisibility—"religion" and "women." Here I explore the intertwined issues around religion, state, women, and secularism. On the one hand there is the assumption—in debates around secularism in the twentieth and early twenty-first centuries—that a specific field, separate from politics and the state, recognisable as religion, is self-evident, and that modern politics is manifested in establishing a wall between the two. On the

[70] An important intervention in the attempt to start conversations among concepts internal to the global South while simultaneously exploring their potential for travelling more universally is a volume in which twenty scholars from across the world identify concepts in sixteen languages across Asia, Africa, the Arab world, and South America. As the editor of the volume puts it, "They explore the entailments of a word while suggesting that these have implications for the humanities and social sciences everywhere" (Menon 2022: 6).

other hand there is the assumption that religion is made visible primarily on the bodies of women; and that the process of defining religion and religious freedom is to be conducted through indicating specific ways in which women's social status and roles indicate modernity, tradition, democracy, and secularism—or whatever value is at stake in a particular controversy. Both these assumptions are sought to be unpacked in this chapter.

The next two chapters focus specifically on India, hoping to draw out implications for wider contexts. Chapter 2 continues to discuss religion and how it is produced under specific circumstances. By examining ascendant Hindu supremacism as a state project in India, it tries to understand the ways in which the construction of religion functions under conditions of majoritarianism. In addition, three key elements in the co-construction of religion and the state are considered—the Essential Religious Practices test; the idea of religious institutions/deities as juristic persons; and the state's role in managing the finances of religious institutions.

If religion and women are hypervisibilised by the discourse of secularism, other features and objects are rendered invisible. Chapter 3 focuses on one such feature, caste, as it operates in a particular space. Caste, one of the critical elements in this region, is obscured by the celebration and practice of secularism. The chapter examines the millennia-old project of Brahminism in this territory, now called India, of producing a community that abides by the caste system and accepts Brahminism as the dominant ideology. Starting from roughly the Puranas (composed *circa* fourth to eleventh centuries) and continuing into twentieth-century ideologues of Hindutva such as V. D. Savarkar, and further into the Hindutva of the twenty-first century—the rich heterogeneity of beliefs and practices across the subcontinent (those which cannot be classified as Muslim, Christian, Jewish, or Parsi) have been sought to be assimilated into Brahminism, or marginalised, or wiped out.[71] This diversity of practices gets labelled as Hindu only because

[71] "Hindutva" is the self-assumed name of the modern project of Hindu majoritarianism in India. The term simply means "Hinduness" and was used from the nineteenth century to denote a cultural identity. From the 1920s it was popularised by

the legal definition of Hindus is one that gathers up all those who are not Muslim, Christian, Parsi, or Jewish into its fold. Thus, what is often celebrated as the rich diversity, inclusivity, and tolerance of Hinduism is merely the massive and age-old assimilationist project of Brahminism which has still not succeeded in making "Hindus." The grid of secularism that focuses on "religious" identity enables the elision of caste, and via the elision the legal and social normalising of the label "Hinduism." This label enables Hindutva politics to claim Hindus as the majority in India, which is the basis of Hindu nationalist and Hindu supremacist politics. We need to recognise that India is a collection of minorities, not a "Hindu majority" country. This book argues that the modern project of Hindutva is only the current phase of a process that began with the advent of Vedic people into this land mass. Of course, the rise and growth of an ideology called Hindutva in the last hundred years is a new development in the history of Brahminism, and this project has been extensively studied, but in isolation from an older history. Here I focus on Hindutva's continuity with the millennia-old project rather than the breaks. Rejecting the claim of Hindutva that Hindus are the majority requires mainstream Left, secular, and feminist politics to reorient itself through a serious engagement with Dalit Bahujan scholarship and life worlds.

Chapter 4 addresses another element obscured by the grid of secularism—the non-secular self in the global South—non-individuated, non-rational, and drawing on multiple spiritual sources for its sustenance. This chapter takes us on the journey of the modern secular discipline of psychoanalysis in various parts of the global South, and the manner in which it is reshaped here from the lifetime of Freud onwards.

It is interesting to note that although some postsecular arguments draw our attention to psychoanalysis as enabling a questioning of the rationality of political subjectivity, it is only to reassert Freud and

---

V. D. Savarkar as the ideology asserting that the land mass now called India is essentially and eternally Hindu. Hindutva thus refers to the political project of Hindu nationalism in India.

psychoanalysis as expressing some kind of universal human condition. Rosi Braidotti, for instance, sees psychoanalysis as the "missing link" between "feminism, religious activism and the postsecular condition."[72] She draws our attention to two aspects of psychic life that psychoanalysis lays stress on—"the vitality of drives, including the all-powerful death drive, whose entropic force is central to human desire," and "the crucial importance of totemic and iconic figures as fundamental structures of psychic order and social cohesion."[73] This draws all of humanity into one frame, in which radically different philosophies on life, living, death, and afterlife—in the non-Christian as well as other parts of the world—are all assumed to be expressive of the entropic death drive identified by Freud. Totems in Braidotti's reading can be images as wide-ranging as Nelson Mandela, Angela Davis, Elvis Presley, and Princess Diana, all "residues of religious worship practices,"[74] implying both a progression of beliefs in time (from religion to non-religion), and the assumption of an easy legibility for the Western/Northern scholar, across contexts, of all practices of worship involving images and icons.

However, consider another way of thinking across contexts. Writing on the Ayoreo of South America, Benno Glauser points to the intrinsic incommensurability of the two universes—"our knowledge is fragmented, representing a fragmented worldview, we use abstractions that reduce what is being talked about to an object. The Ayoreo discourse in turn always refers to an entire reality in its wholeness, and speaks about concrete events, people, phenomena, very often using images with a sensual quality that abstractions don't have."[75] Glauser finally had to recognise that it was an "absurd pretension" to think that he could write about his conversations with the Ayoreo in methodological terms acceptable to the academy. "We discover that speaking to indigenous peoples forces us to abandon our own method."[76]

---

[72] Braidotti 2008: 10–11.
[73] Ibid.: 11.
[74] Ibid.
[75] Glauser 2011: 23.
[76] Ibid.: 23–4.

Our engagement with psychoanalysis will thus not be reasserting how psychoanalysis speaks to the "human" condition. Through a study of how psychoanalysis was interpreted and how it travelled in the global South, we will find that, in comparison to all the other forms of modern post-Enlightenment knowledge that entered the global South, psychoanalysis was most committed to drawing on specific locations in the project of understanding the self. In doing so, psychoanalysis across the global South offered fundamental challenges to Freud even in his own lifetime, rejecting any idea of a decontextualised human, and often transforming the practice beyond recognition from its incarnation in the land of its birth.

The final element obscured by secular discourse that this book will consider is capitalism, discussed in Chapter 5. The invocation of secularism enables an uncritical acceptance of the violence of capitalism on people and nature as the historically inescapable way into modernity—where religious sectarianism is supposed to no longer hold sway. Disenchanted now, land, forests, rivers, and all of nature are available to be commoditised. This is the journey from the darkness of pagan beliefs and religious sectarianism into the light of secular modernity. Thus, the project of secular modernity emerged alongside capitalist transformation in the West, and in post-Independence India too is intimately tied to a notion of "development" predicated on the large-scale sacrifice of the interests of specific communities in order to serve the greater interest of the "Indian citizen."

Apart from the dispossession of communities from resources and land, a related critical factor obscured by the grid of secularism is that of environment/ecology. Since much of the resistance to capitalist transformation is conducted by indigenous peoples whose lands are rich in minerals, the resistance is often conducted in terms that sacralise nature and draw on indigenous spiritualities. Secular environmentalism is often unable to relate to this mode of resistance to capital. On the other hand in India the political doctrine of Hindutva (as opposed to indigenous and other spiritualities) has a dual relationship to capitalism, as we will see.

Two specific instances from India will be discussed in Chapter 5 to illustrate the larger argument: (a) the controversy over the construction of a shipping canal, the Sethusamudram Project; and (b) the state-led process of ensuring individual land rights for women, now part of a World Bank agenda. I argue that the invocation of land rights for the poor and for women acts as a cover for capitalist transformation of the commons. In India, land rights for women come under the Personal Laws of religious communities, and the boundaries between "secular" capitalism and "religious" personal laws become blurred. There is a wider global recognition of this process too, and we will move outwards from India to get a glimpse of that as well.

The last two chapters map resistances and the assertion of new and other worlds. They look at creative resistances to the anti-democratic and capitalist state, whether by invoking the Constitution (in India and Chile), or through larger global philosophies such as degrowth.

The argument of this book is not that "secularism" should be abandoned, but that secularism is not in itself a positive value and nor is its meaning self-evident. Secularism can serve majoritarian, anti-minority politics, and capitalist transformation, but it can equally be invoked to sustain democratic politics that respects heterogeneity, social justice, and ecological concerns. In India, the understanding of secularism as *sarva dharma sama bhava* alone is legitimate from the perspective that this book adopts, and we see the reassertion of this meaning in militant struggles like the Indian farmers' movement of 2020–1. This movement's central concerns were capitalist transformation of the agrarian sector and climate change, but the questions of caste, gender, and minority rights were also very much in the foreground.[77] We will see how anti-capitalist politics globally inhabits very heterogeneous spaces, facing up to internal dissent and differences that erupt within. These movements coalesce around different kinds of values that are locally produced and inflected but which are, at the same time, in some sort

---

[77] We will not be discussing this movement, but see Sandhu 2021 for a detailed account.

of conversation with one another across the globe. If secularism is invoked at all in these movements, it is never in the sense of separation of state and religion, but in a more people-oriented understanding of how to live with difference. The overriding value being asserted in these movements appears to be democracy, with all its faults. But democracy too is reimagined in more direct terms, distanced in particular from political parties which have over the twentieth century appropriated and ventriloquised "the people."

Is it possible to think of democracy radically differently in the post-Covid twenty-first century? What role does secularism have to play in it, if any? Chapters 6 and 7 will consider these questions and their implications.

1

State, Religion, and the Bodies of Women

THIS CHAPTER ADDRESSES and unpacks two objects made hypervisible by the discourse of secularism—religion and women. I start from the vantage point of India but travel further afield to revisit debates on secularism that, even today, assume a Western perspective as universal. One key component of the argument here is that state and religion are both elements of the political, that they co-constitute each other, and that religion is not a clearly separable self-standing entity.

Globally, in the twentieth and twenty-first centuries, many significant debates and controversies around secularism have circulated around the social roles of bodies marked "women." It is no accident, for instance, that the "Islamic veil," all over the world and including India, has so easily become a sign of the lack of secularism and progressive modern values. In the mid-twentieth century Fanon wrote a famous essay, "Algeria Unveiled," in which he showed how French imperialism produced the veiled Algerian woman as the justification for French intervention—the veiled woman as passive object produced by Arab patriarchy, to be freed by French modernity. However, once Algerian revolutionary women started using their flowing *haik*s as cover while carrying arms and ammunition, the *haik* shifted from being a sign of passivity to a marker of violence.[1] Feminist scholars point out

---

[1] Fanon 1965.

that such controversies referencing modernity often centre on women's bodies precisely because the patriarchal, patrilineal family is at the heart of modern statecraft. Veena Das suggests that once the idea of God had been displaced, secular means had to be crafted to ensure that "the sovereign receives life beyond the lifetime of individual members."[2] This then means the state has a continuous interest in reproduction as well as in the form of the family. In other words, Das suggests that the state has to reimagine its relation to the family in more complex ways than by merely assigning the family to the realm of the private. Whether it is the Islamic veil, or sati in India, or female circumcision in Asia and Africa, women's bodies come to be located in the whirling vortex of patriarchy and imperialism/majoritarianism, and women's resistance comes to be against one or both of these, always walking a razor's edge. Resistance to patriarchy may strengthen the hands of the coloniser or the majoritarian state; and resistance to the state may push women towards greater patriarchal control in their communities.

But while decades of feminist scholarship have established that women's bodies are the site for the performance of both nationalism and community identity,[3] we also need to recognise that within this complex matrix, in some cases, women do exercise agency. It is difficult to imagine women's agency in the context of sati or female circumcision, but with the veil it is possible to find the space to theorise agency. Whether there is pressure to perform femininity through display of the body, or pressure to cover up to protect community honour, the woman's decision to do either will be produced at the juncture of multiple historical processes—imperialism, majoritarian politics, patriarchy, family, misogyny, racism, casteism. And of course in cases such as religiously mandated covering up, or the prohibition on women's temple entry, the woman's interpretation of faith is part of the picture. This chapter will try to open up some of these questions more fully.

[2] Das 2006: 94.

[3] Sangari and Vaid 1989; Yuval-Davis 1997; Mostov and Ivekovic 2004; Boehmer 2005.

Hindu Supremacism
as Secularism in India

In early 2022 our screens filled with images of educational institutions in the state of Karnataka that had barred their gates to women wearing hijab. The ostensible reason was that the hijab violated the uniform which students were expected to wear. Dense with implied violence, these images of a Hindu nationalist BJP-ruled state evoked similar policies by France, the progenitor of a secularism defined as the hard separation of state and religion. We will return to France later, but these images captured in one frozen instant the ideological violence of the Hindu Rashtra (Hindu Nation). Here is the marked and stigmatised Muslim female body exiled from the resources of the nation, kept out by iron gates, to be admitted only on terms set by Hindutva.[4] But let us note that this is not "only" ideological violence, the power of which we have witnessed in plenty since 2014, when the BJP came to power in the Indian general elections. We know the violence that "mere" words from the right quarters can unleash—"love jihad," "*gau hatya*,"[5] and "*kapdon se pehchane jayenge*" (they can be recognised by their clothes)—the last having been uttered by the country's prime minister to make it clear that those who were protesting against the Citizenship Amendment Act (2019) were sartorially identifiable as Muslims.[6] Statements of this variety function as a dog whistle to Hindutva organisations that are emboldened to wreak violence on protesting Muslims. The law—the Constitutional Amendment Act (CAA) 2019—being protested against offers Indian citizenship exclusively to non-Muslims from neighbouring states. It has been very widely understood, and not only by Muslims, as the BJP's strategy to protect the large numbers

[4] See the Introduction for an explanation of the term "Hindutva."

[5] "Love jihad" is the name for the Hindutva campaign against inter-community marriages, particularly of Muslim men and Hindu women. *Gau hatya* means cow slaughter, and this campaign is used to physically attack Muslim traders who work legally with cattle other than cows; it also hits at Muslim livelihoods.

[6] Press Trust of India 2019.

of Hindu Indians in Assam who were unable to prove their Indian citizenship when subjected by the state to register their antecedents in a National Register of Citizens (NRC). The CAA 2019 has been generally interpreted as intending to separate such Hindus—those hitherto uncountable as citizens—from Muslims in a similar situation.[7] The law is among the steps being taken within a process of legally disenfranchising Muslims in India.[8]

As more and more colleges in Karnataka denied entry to women wearing the hijab, and therefore their right to education, the BJP government in Karnataka backed such moves, invoking the Karnataka Education Act of 1983, Section 133 (2) of which states that students must wear a uniform chosen by the college authorities. The government's directive, while invoking this section, added—"clothes which disturb equality, integrity and public law and order should not be worn."[9] The first claim, therefore, is that the hijab violates "uniformity of dress" (hence equality). This is the first level of Hindutva ideology, familiar in India since the 1990s, presenting itself as genuinely non-discriminatory, claiming that it alone is truly secular—hence the insult "pseudo-secular" for those who recognise and accept religious difference. The claim to uniformity in policy was fraudulently demonstrated in some colleges by a few students, male and female, who came wearing saffron shawls—the colour saffron having been claimed by Hindutva as its own—implying that if the hijab was permitted, so should a "Hindu" form of dress. The colleges then, in an ostentatious gesture of even-handedness, banned both saffron shawls and the hijab.[10] However, wearing saffron shawls is not any sort of "religious" or "Hindu" requirement, and groups of students suddenly wearing them to colleges came as stark evidence of political mobilisation by Hindutva organisations. Mohandas Pai, the chairman of Manipal University, said: "A uniform code creates

[7] Chatterji, et al. 2021.

[8] We will return to these protests against the NRC and the CAA 2019 in the last chapter.

[9] Parasher and Vishwanath 2022.

[10] Kidwai 2022.

unity!"[11] In fact, all that a uniform code creates is uniformity. And the norm by which uniformity is created will always be the dominant norm. If everyone has to do or be "something," what will that something be? And who decides what that something must be?

Compulsory uniforms do not create equality or justice. Uniforms are about discipline and the power of an educational institution to control its students and properly socialise them into the dominant norms of behaviour in society. There could be a more positive reading of compulsory uniforms—that they reduce the embarrassment and humiliation of visible class differences at least for the duration of school hours. But this element is not compromised by students wearing the hijab.

Inequality is not produced by difference but by the failure in the public domain to acknowledge the existence of difference. The more important point to note is that the person who is assumed in the abstract to be "the citizen" is already distinguishable, i.e. marked by a particular kind of difference. It is precisely because, by default, the abstract citizen of Europe is assumed to be white, male, and Christian, or in India to be *savarna*,[12] male, North Indian, and Hindu, that the introduction of black, female, or Muslim identities into the mix is so threatening.

In the directive of the Karnataka government it is the invocation of "integrity" and "public law and order" that brings us to the more explicit Hindu Rashtra argument which has emerged more and more in the public domain ever since the carnage of Muslims in Gujarat in 2002, and which has become the dominant discourse through much of India since 2014. No longer claiming to be true secularists, the explicit project now is the building of a Hindu Rashtra which marginalises,

---

[11] Ghosh 2022.

[12] *Savarna* refers to the four castes of the classic caste system in India, which excludes a fifth caste as "untouchable." The former "untouchable castes" are referred to in the Indian Constitution as Scheduled Castes, but the political term adopted by these castes for themselves is Dalit. *Savarna* people are non-Dalit, but internally there are further hierarchies in both sets of castes. *Savarna* is usually used to refer to caste privilege vis-à-vis Dalits, and to dominant castes in general.

assimilates, or physically eliminates minorities and all others who resist it. Revealingly, the Karnataka High Court judgment, while ostensibly upholding the secular principle of hijab as violating the rule of identical uniforms, added that "insistence on wearing of purdah, veil, or headgear in any community may hinder the process of emancipation of women in general and Muslim women in particular."[13] The emancipation of women was not a question the court had been asked to consider at all. The Hindu Rashtra narrative is clearly reflected in the way the Karnataka High Court mobilises constitutional provisions of gender equality to delegitimise Muslim practices.

The "integrity of the nation" demands that all differences be subsumed under a North Indian, *savarna*, masculinist version of "Hinduism," and anything that defies this vision is culpable for the breakdown of public law and order. The responsibility of maintaining "law and order" rests not on those who react violently to dissent and difference, but on those the Hindu Rashtra identifies as dissenters as well as those who insist that their differences with the Hindu Rashtra be noted.

On the issue of the hijab in Karnataka, one kind of voice from among Indian feminists (including mine) defended women's rights to education as well as to their religious beliefs and convictions. Other feminists, though staunchly anti-Hindu supremacist, nevertheless expressed discomfort with religious practices, such as the veil, that they see as patriarchal and discriminatory. From the first point of view, the argument is that the decision to wear or discard the hijab—or for that matter whether women should accept or resist the ban on women's entry into temples—cannot be made on anybody else's behalf, and not even, or specially not even, by feminists. The invocation by the Karnataka High Court of the idea that Muslim women are oppressed into wearing the hijab seems to refer to women's freedom, but, as we know from the explosive expansion of authoritarian Hindutva politics since 2014—from which the Indian judiciary has shown itself as anything but insulated—this politics is very far from endorsing women's rights to dress

---

[13] Singla 2022.

as they wish, love whom they want, marry whom they wish. So, "women's agency" is only a weapon in their arsenal that is used selectively; and the sudden episodic solicitousness that the state shows for Muslim women suggests another move in the overall project of the Hindu Rashtra to establish a Hindu supremacist state.

In any case, as argued briefly above, and in my earlier work,[14] the idea of agency is hardly an easily accessible one. When may women be considered, without the strong shadows of doubt, as victims needing protection? And when, conversely, as active agents engaging with or resisting power and carving out their own spaces? The notion of "choice" is not enough to answer this question; it does not suffice to assume that if people "choose" to do something it necessarily reflects their agency. It is not enough because "freedom of choice" is always exercised within strict boundaries that are non-negotiable—the boundaries that are defined by economic class, by race, by caste, and of course by gender. The freedom to choose is never absolute.

And yet, within those limited boundaries, people do make choices. Amartya Sen puts it in more general terms:

> [N]othing can be more elementary and universal than the fact that choices of all kinds in every area are always made within particular limits. For example, when we decide what to buy at the market, we can hardly ignore the fact that there are limits on how much we can spend. The "budget constraint," as economists call it, is omnipresent. The fact that every buyer has to make choices does not indicate that there is no budget constraint, but only that choices have to be made within the budget constraint the person faces. What is true in elementary economics is also true in complex political and social decisions.[15]

How are we as feminists, to understand these choices without invoking totalising notions such as "false consciousness"?

From the second point of view, for which I will take as a representative instance Noorjehan Safia Niaz, co-founder of the Bharatiya Muslim Mahila Andolan (Indian Muslim Women's Movement), two arguments

[14] Menon 2022: 175–212.
[15] Sen 2006: 5–6.

emerge. First, that the covering of heads or faces by women is not a cultural aspect of the Muslim community alone, and so should not be seen as specific to Islam. Non-Muslim women in North India, too, are expected to observe different kinds of seclusion from different categories of men. In other words, patriarchy is not specific to Islam. The second argument is a stronger one: the hijab is not necessary to being a faithful, practising Muslim. To quote Niaz:

> There are other ways of asserting one's identity. That the hijab is essential to Islam is also a superficial, reductionist understanding of the religion. Islam is not about how much of my head is covered, the length of my sleeve, how long is my abaya. Islam is about equality, justice, wisdom, compassion, prayers, fasting; it's those values that are the basis of Islam.[16]

The problem with this kind of unambiguous feminist articulation is, however, that it is no different from the assertion of the opposite camp, the Hindu Right, arguing that the hijab is not essential to Islam because many practising Muslim women do not wear it. In which case, wearing the hijab is a matter of personal choice—from which it follows that it is legitimate to ban it in educational institutions where students are expected to wear a uniform. This perspective became even more strident in the Indian public domain when the Iranian revolution against the authoritarian regime there took off in 2022—in the Iranian case, rejection of the mandatory headscarf was, as we know, a central demand of Iranian women's resistance to rule by authoritarian Islam.

The only way this conundrum can be unravelled is by recognising that both "women" and "religion" are misleading categories here, and in all such debates. This complex understanding was best articulated in a panel discussion by Iranian women on the forum Jadaliyya, on the ongoing struggle of the Iranian people against a regime in the hands of patriarchal mullahs. They made it clear that the struggle is not against Islam, and it is not about hijab everywhere and at all times. What we are witnessing in Iran, they said, is reflected all over the world, wherever there is resistance to the gendered ways in which all states control populations. This may be by compulsory conscription in wars that people

[16] Niaz 2022.

have no interest in: at the time, Russian men were fleeing their country to avoid military service in Putin's war on Ukraine. Or it may be by making the hijab central to reasons of state—in Iran by compulsory veiling, in France and India by compulsorily unveiling the Muslim woman; or in the USA by denying autonomy over their bodies to women by criminalising abortion. The way in which this panel resituated the hijab issue out of the unquestioned categories of both "religion" and "women" was very productive.[17]

The case reached the Indian Supreme Court, where a two-judge bench delivered a split verdict in 2022, and it is therefore to come up before a larger bench. We will later return briefly to the split verdict, especially Justice Dhulia's judgment.[18]

Another state that banned Islamic headscarves (in 2010) is France, and a comparison of French secularism with Hindutva politics is instructive.

French Secularism as Majoritarianism

France instituted a ban on "conspicuous religious symbols" in public institutions in 2010. This was a coded term referring essentially to the "Islamic headscarf." Scarves worn for other than religious purposes (fashion statement, protection of hairstyle) continue to be accepted. For instance, eleven years after the French ban, as the European Union now considers strict limitations on Islamic headscarves,[19] French style-blogs and magazines continue to promote head-covering scarves worn "like a Frenchwoman."[20] Presumably, this style is meant exclusively to refer to headscarves worn by Frenchwomen who are not also practising Muslims.

Many swimming pools and beaches in France have banned the burkini—a body-covering outfit some Muslim women wear at the beach—sparking protests. One response by municipal authorities in 2019 to the protests and defiance of the ban by Muslim activist groups,

[17] Jadaliyya 2022.
[18] See the next chapter: the discussion on the Essential Religious Practices test.
[19] François 2021.
[20] Images Staff 2022; Chenal 2021.

and by the citizens' rights group called Alliance Citoyenne, was the closure of two swimming pools in Grenoble in southeast France.[21] In May 2021 the city took heed of the continuing protests and permitted swimmers at public pools in Grenoble to use burkinis, but later that month the city's administrative tribunal overruled the decision as contravening "hygiene and security rules." The ban on the burkini was finally upheld in 2022 by France's highest administrative court which, in its ruling, invoked principles of religious neutrality.[22]

Some years earlier, four armed policemen in Nice forced a burkini-clad woman to remove some of her clothing, fining her for not wearing "an outfit respecting good morals and secularism." Meanwhile, the most "conspicuous religious symbol" of all in France, the habit worn by nuns, is not an issue in the French public domain. In response to the Nice incident, many people posted pictures of nuns on the beach to highlight the country's double standards.[23]

In a notable parallel, the BJP chief minister of Uttar Pradesh habitually wears the variety of saffron which identifies Hindu ascetics. Similarly, Sikh turbans were permitted under the rule about uniforms in Karnataka, the state government defining them as a "Constitutional right,"[24] thus reaffirming Sikhs as "Hindus" and making explicit which religious identity works implicitly as the norm in the public domain—and thereby, which is being rendered illegitimate. The more fundamental aspect that underlies this double standard has been made invisible, for built into "secularism" understood as uniformity is the implicit requirement that all citizens adhere to the dominant norm. What is called secularism in France and in Europe generally was achieved in the seventeenth century only after the defeat of rival Christian denominations and diverse cultural practices. The religio-cultural formation that was victorious then attained the status of the "secular universal."

While French democracy enshrines the abstract citizen at its centre, most non-Western postcolonial democracies have intertwined group

[21] Al Jazeera News 2019.
[22] Ataman and Subramaniam 2022.
[23] Campanella 2016.
[24] Kaggere 2022.

identity with individual citizenship. The right to wear a turban or a headscarf to school is in fact precisely the test of secularism in India. By excluding only a Muslim religious symbol, the Hindu Rashtra is making clear that only communities subsumed under the label of Hinduism can claim constitutional rights. This project uses "elimination of difference from Hinduism" to mean "equality." French secularism—and secularism in the European context generally—is thus closer to majoritarian Hindu nationalist politics than to the way secularism has been understood in India as *sarva dharma sama bhava* (the injunction to view all religions as equal) and *dharma nirpekshata* (the state to maintain neutrality between religions).

To conclude this discussion, note that French secularism assumes as normal several dominant Christian and Western cultural norms (both as played out on women's bodies): for instance, nuns' habits, headscarves for non-religious reasons, and body-revealing clothes while swimming (defended on grounds of hygiene as well as religious neutrality, as we saw above). This normalisation makes visible only Muslim practices as defiling the supposedly neutral public domain. In India, Hindutva politics adopts two stances: at times the stance is assertively Hindu majoritarian, at others it claims to defend true secularism as uniformity. The latter stance is entirely compatible with majoritarianism, as we saw in France, for the uniformity that is defended is implicitly ("upper caste") Hindu.

And, finally, the playing out of questions of modernity and secularism on the bodies of women enables the assertion that, in societies in which women and men are equal, the covering of specific parts of women's bodies, or of their bodies in general, is contrary to women's rights— rights which these majoritarian assertions of "secularism" claim to uphold. Thus, the claim to secularism weaponises "women's rights" against the Muslim community.

Secular/Secularisation

The term "secular" arises from the history of Christianity and describes that which is not sacred, or not of the church. The term "secularisation" thus refers to the process by which human activity and knowledge progressively come under the control of scientific rather than religious understanding. Max Weber (1864–1920) termed this rationalisation and intellectualisation characteristic of modern times, "the disenchantment of the world."[25] Jose Casanova distinguishes between three meanings of the term secularisation—the decline of religious beliefs and practices in societies as they grow more modern; the privatisation of religion, seen as a prerequisite for modern liberal democracies; and the separation of secular realms (state, economy, science) from religious institutions and norms.[26]

This differentiating of the sacred from the secular is associated with Europe in the seventeenth century. Talal Asad's well-known argument is foundational for this understanding—that religion as a historical category and a universal globalised concept is a construction of Western secular modernity.[27] Drawing on this, Jose Casanova says there are "multiple and diverse secularisations in the West" associated with fundamental historical differences between different forms of Christianity that are dominant in different parts of the West. For instance, the Protestant reformation was anti-Popish, but not anti-religious, for its purpose was precisely "to bring religion to the world and the world to religion."[28] Separating state and religion thus becomes a particular requirement in such a society.

This process cannot be assumed to have universal validity because in non-Western cultures generally, as Humeira Iqtidar puts it, "there was no hierarchical, structured church that had inherited an empire's state apparatus as the Roman Catholic church had in Europe." The assumed "lack of secularisation" within these societies is therefore not due to "lateness" on their part, it is more simply that "they did not secularise in the way that Europe did because they did not need to."[29] In other words,

[25] Weber [1918] 1946: 155.
[26] Casanova 2006: 101.
[27] Asad 1993.
[28] Casanova 2006: 106–7.
[29] Iqtidar 2011.

the sacred and the secular were not necessarily separate spheres in the context of political rule, but nor were they fused together, as in medieval Christendom. In this sense, a certain separation between them existed already.

It is useful to consider here Aditya Nigam's mapping of relationships between the religious and the political in different historical and spatial contexts. Nigam points out that Kautilya's *Arthashastra* functions with a "secular" notion of statecraft while acknowledging the Vedas as only one of the sources of law.[30] Writers in the early *Arthashastra* tradition exclude the holy Vedas from the class of sciences on the ground that these works are a "superfluity"—or, according to another interpretation, "a hindrance"—in the world of men. The tradition as a whole does not give the same place to Vedic religion in matters of kingship and rule that Christianity does to the Bible and the Biblical tradition in the West. Nigam also draws on Stanley Tambiah's idea of the mandala or galactic polity which underlines the mutual imbrication of religion and political power without there being a fusion; an idea Nigam sees as relevant in the context of traditional polities in South and South East Asia.[31]

Islam had no Church or clergy, and after the first four khalifas the Khilafat and Sultanate were not conjoined. Muzaffar Alam points out that over the Sultanate period of the thirteenth–fourteenth centuries, political power in North India was not based on shari'a law and the actual governing practices of the Sultanate varied a great deal.[32] Thus, although the shari'a was one of the elements legitimising rule, it was only a source of legitimacy, not of power. The state did not impose shari'a through a centralised mechanism, even though at times emperors may have claimed to uphold the shari'a.[33]

In the context of Confucianism and Taoism, Jose Casanova observes that their model of transcendence cannot be called religious in any

[30] The *Arthashastra* is understood by scholars as having been written by multiple authors between the fourth century BCE and the second century CE.

[31] Nigam 2020.

[32] Alam 2004.

[33] I am grateful to Humeira Iqtidar for a very useful discussion on this point.

strict sense, and they have no ecclesiastical organisation. Such religions, which have always been "worldly" or "lay," do not need to undergo a process of secularisation. To secularise is to make worldly, and Jose Casanova's argument is that this process makes no sense in such a context. Rejecting the assumed correlation between modernisation and secularisation, he puts it starkly: "There can be modern societies like the United States, which are secular while deeply religious, and there can be pre-modern societies like China, which from our Eurocentric religious perspective, look deeply secular and irreligious."[34] This broad range of ways in which religion and the state were conceived of shows that the separation of church from state arose out of a specific conjuncture in seventeenth-century Europe. We can discern three broad factors that produced this conjuncture:

(1) the challenge posed to religious knowledge by breakthroughs in science in Europe
(2) the rise of an industrial bourgeoisie which questioned the divine right of kings, opposing the older landed feudal elites that drew on the political and economic power of the Church
(3) fatigue following a century of war in Europe during which Christian denominations clashed with each other for political power.

Multiculturalism

In the twentieth century secularism came to refer, in the West/global North, to two interrelated and sometimes mutually contradictory ideas:

(1) a mode of political organisation in which the state is neutral with reference to all established religions
(2) later in the century, a political practice of the state whereby the rights of minorities in a multicultural society are protected—which involves abandoning a "neutral" stance by the state.

[34] Casanova 2006: 109.

The idea of multiculturalism emerged in the global North—as state policy in Canada in the 1960s with reference to indigenous communities, and in Western political theory in the 1980s. Increasingly, since the end of the twentieth century, multiculturalism has come to refer to religious minorities in Europe, particularly Muslims, and is often counterposed to secularism as state neutrality. However, there have also been arguments which try to show that both secularism as state neutrality vis-à-vis religion, and multiculturalism as the accommodation of religious minorities, are true to essentially liberal principles. The argument then is that conflicts between the two are not general or necessarily fundamental, and that they can be reconciled.[35] On the other hand there are critiques of multiculturalism from feminist theorists such as Susan Moller Okin, who argues that if women are to be prevented from being disadvantaged because of their sex, group rights that permit gender-based oppressive practices should not be accepted.[36] Her position has been criticised from the point of view that it is deeply problematic for "Western feminists to continue to frame questions of cultural pluralism in ways that counter-pose a modern West to a backward set of 'others'."[37] In a volume that brought together several responses to Okin's essay, Bonnie Honig argued that "Okin assumes . . . Western liberal regimes are simply and plainly 'less patriarchal' than other regimes, rather than differently so."[38]

Let us turn now to female circumcision, still widely practised in many communities in Africa and Asia, and sati, no longer generally practised (though the last recorded incident was as recently as in 1987, in Deorala, Rajasthan). Feminists within the affected communities and countries have challenged these practices not on the grounds of accepting or rejecting secularism or multiculturalism, but on the grounds of gender justice—which they see as the state's responsibility to protect. The debates on multiculturalism tend to see communities

---

[35] Lægaard 2017.
[36] Okin 1999.
[37] Kaufman 2002: 231.
[38] Honig 1999: 38.

as constituted by more or less fixed "cultural" boundaries. Not only does such a view reify the boundaries of apparently "naturally" constituted communities, it also fails to take into account the ways in which different identities within communities have independent dynamics in relation to one another. In other words, when it comes to internally discriminatory practices, neither secularism nor multiculturalism as a value is necessary to the insistence that the community can be challenged from within and from without.

Different problems arise in the context of multiculturalism with reference to the Indigenous communities of the global North. Sara Song outlines the critique of multiculturalism offered by First Nations theorist Glen Coulthard, who holds that the politics of recognition underlying multiculturalism can reproduce configurations of colonial power through its focus on reformist state redistributionist schemes—such as granting cultural rights and concessions to aboriginal communities. These kinds of policies fail to confront the structural/economic aspects of colonialism at its roots. Coulthard rejects the assumption that both parties engaged in the struggle for recognition are mutually dependent on one another's acknowledgement for their freedom and self-worth: "the master—that is, the colonial state and state society—does not require recognition from the previously self-determining communities upon which its territorial, economic, and social infrastructure is constituted."[39] Coulthard therefore says that Indigenous peoples should "collectively redirect our struggles away from a politics that seeks to attain a conciliatory form of settler-state recognition for Indigenous nations toward a resurgent politics of recognition premised on self-actualization, direct action, and the resurgence of cultural practices that are attentive to the subjective and structural composition of settler-colonial power."[40] He thus rejects the idea of multiculturalism—the form that secularism often takes in North America—as enabling in any way. Multiculturalist policies, in his opinion, only draw indigenous

[39] Coulthard 2007: 451, cited in Song 2020.
[40] Coulthard 2014: 24, cited in Song 2020.

communities into patron–client relationships with the "settler colonial" state. He emphasises instead, as we saw above, the "resurgence of cultural practices" as a part of "direct action," possibly implying a refusal to be "seen" by the state and what he calls "state society."

These multiculturalism versus secularism debates are meaningful in the contexts discussed above, but irrelevant for India and many other postcolonial states because secularism here was from the beginning posed as the recognition of diversity. To take just one example, in South Africa secularism is understood as protecting the rights of all non-majority groups. According to Justice Sachs, "One of the functions of the Constitution is precisely to protect the fundamental rights of non-majoritarian groups, who might well be tiny and hold beliefs considered bizarre by ordinary faithful."[41] This includes the rights of atheists and non-believers as well as of adherents to indigenous faiths, non-Christian religions, and the various Christian denominations. In both South Africa and India the apartheid and colonial states constructed "religion" and "tradition" in conversation with certain specific groups identified by the state as representatives of "communities" that were assumed to be homogeneous. This was a common feature across Asia and Africa, and hence the communities and practices identifiable and legible to the state today as "religious" or "traditional" are often of recent origin.

Challenges to Secularism as a
Neutral Category

Only in the late twentieth century did it come to be widely recognised that secularism is not a neutral descriptive term with universal applicability, but that it arises from a specific spatio-temporal context. In face of this, Charles Taylor attempted to retain its usefulness by arguing that, despite its specific origins, secularism continues to be relevant for modern democracies everywhere.[42] Even the most diversified

[41] South African Secular Society: no date.
[42] Taylor 1998.

societies can be secular, Taylor suggests—despite differences over religion at the deeper level—by building consensus on a "common political ethic" such as a doctrine of human rights, freedom, and equality. Such a consensus, he says, can be brought about even if there is no agreement about the different sets of (religious/cultural) values in which this ethic is embedded.

But it is precisely the concepts of human rights, liberty, and equality cited as unquestionably valuable by Taylor that have come to be challenged from a variety of perspectives since the late twentieth century— by Marxist and feminist critiques, as well as claims that these values are (Western/Christian) culture-specific. In other words, while the moral basis of these rights is assumed to be self-evident and universally shared, it is in fact highly variegated, even within Western culture itself.[43] It has become evident that, historically, "secularism" was achieved in Western societies only after defeating rival Christian denominations and diverse cultural practices. The religio-cultural formation that was victorious then attained the status of the "universal." What we see today in the West, then, is both a *resurgence* of this suppressed diversity as well as a *new* phenomenon resulting from immigration.

Hindu nationalist politics in India has been pressing an understanding of secularism as uniformity which suits a majoritarian anti-minority-rights politics. A self-critical response from secularists opposed to Hindu supremacist politics has been the acknowledgement that secularism in India has been state-centric and has not engaged sufficiently

---

[43] There is a complex set of critiques of rights discourses that is not simply an endorsement of the traditionalist, nationalist, anti-West critiques of human rights offered by authoritarian regimes. The issue is that rights discourses, as David Kennedy puts it, "occupy the field of emancipatory possibility" and dominate "the imaginative space of emancipation" to such an extent that "alternatives can now only be thought, perhaps unhelpfully, as negations of what human rights asserts—passion to its reason, local to its global, etc." (Kennedy 2001: 250–5). One of my own earlier books, *Recovering Subversion: Feminist Politics Beyond the Law* (Menon 2004), is centrally about the end of emancipatory potential in the language of rights, especially as it plays out in the field of law. My more recent reformulation of this argument will be discussed in chap. 6.

with beliefs and practices on the ground. Secularism has not always been "democratic." Even a strong defender of secularism such as Sumit Sarkar concedes that in India secularism's close association with the "nation-building" project has strengthened its assimilation with "statist endeavours," and to this extent arguments denouncing secularism for being authoritarian and centralist do have a point.[44] Secularism itself, thus, is neither authoritarian nor democratic but can be articulated in either discourse.

Samuel Huntington's "clash of civilizations" thesis argues that current debates over secularism arise from the division of the world into opposing civilisational frameworks, broadly those of the West and Islam.[45] He traces the conflict between "Western" and "Islamic" civilisation to the founding of Islam itself. Thus, what we see today is merely an "ancient rival" reacting irrationally to "our Judeo-Christian heritage" and "our secular present." From this point of view it appears that the contemporary "West" is rational and secular, with its religious heritage lying in the past, while contemporary "Islam" is irrational and trapped in religion. However, scholars have pointed out that the apparent secularism of Western states is normed as Christian. Joan Scott puts it this way: "State sovereignty . . . and Christian practice became inextricably intertwined."[46] To take just two instances, first, observing the weekly holiday on Sunday rather than any other day is Biblical in origin. And second, in many secular states legal access to abortion is curtailed by Christian right-wing values that saturate state institutions. This is so in the USA, and in Ireland which has had a secular constitution since 1973 but where abortion was illegal till 2018. In the USA, many Christian denominations as well as Judaism and Islam, support the right to abortion, so the Supreme Court ruling of 2022 allowing individual states in the USA to make abortion illegal is based on a specific Christian theology alone.[47] The judgment uses the argument that the

[44] Sarkar 2001.
[45] Huntington 1993.
[46] Scott 2018: 18.
[47] Quareshi-Landes 2022.

American Constitution does not protect abortion under the right to privacy guaranteed by the 14th Amendment—as the overturned ruling *Roe v. Wade* had held. Thus the *explicit* argument, as with the hijab ban in Karnataka, invokes not religious faith and principles but apparently "secular" constitutional principles. However, the further explanation by one of the US Supreme Court justices, Samuel Alito, is revealing. He says that the only legitimate unenumerated rights—rights not explicitly stated in the Constitution—are those "deeply rooted in the Nation's history and tradition" and "implicit in the concept of ordered liberty."[48] Abortion is not one of these. Now, "history and tradition" are far from secular and context-free notions; they cannot possibly refer to the multiple traditions that the USA had even at its inception. The argument here is *implicitly* therefore based on a particular Christian view of abortion.

Joan Scott argues that "gender inequality was fundamental to the articulation of the separation of church and state that inaugurated Western modernity."[49] She proceeds to demonstrate how hollow the claims of Western powers are when they invoke women's rights to invade Islamic states, demonstrating conclusively that gender equality would in fact thoroughly destabilise the West's political and social order. Scott's critique of the celebration of secularism *contra* Islam by the West is very powerful, but she relies on the experience of France to conclude that secularism has now been equated with sexual freedom and autonomy (the veil versus the bikini). This, she points out, is deeply problematic because sexual freedom cannot substitute for political and economic equality—which is missing in the West as much as anywhere else in the world.

However, Scott's conclusion that secularism has been equated with sexual autonomy is difficult to sustain even for other parts of the global North, such as the USA, where Christian right-wing-inflected secularism is marked by a strong sexual conservatism, as evident in the positions of state institutions on abortion, contraception, sexuality, and sexual

[48] Brennan Center for Justice 2022.
[49] Scott 2018: 3.

rights. In the global South, too, secularism is not marked by any claims of sexual autonomy.

In India, the secular discourse does invoke women's rights, but these are political and economic rights. What is hidden, however, is how equal rights for women can be a cover for capitalist transformation of the economy.[50] Sexual autonomy is very far from being on the agenda of secularism in India.

The paradoxes of Western secularism are explained in Talal Asad's view by the fact that the emergence of secularism in modern Europe merely shifted the proper domain of violence from religious communities to nation-states.[51] Henceforth, the nation-state would determine the place of religion, and the only legitimate perpetrator of violence was to be the nation-state, whether the violence was inflicted upon its own citizens, upon other nations, or upon colonised parts of the world.

This kind of critique of secularism has also been Ashis Nandy's since 1985. Nandy has developed his views on the striking link between the violence of the modern nation-state and secularism. His argument is that, despite its contradictions, the modern state has succeeded in marginalising all religions, while its own ideologies of secularism, development, and nationalism act as intolerant faiths backed by a coercive state apparatus. He characterises what was called "religious fundamentalism" (or in India, communalism) as a rational and modern project that seeks to control state power. In his view religious fundamentalism is thus a product of "secularisation"—which is as intolerant of the eclecticism of lived religion as is the modern nation-state. Nandy makes a distinction between religion-as-faith and religion-as-ideology in order to argue that a more tolerant society would require the recovery of those resources within religion-as-faith that make it possible to live with "fluid definitions of the self," an idea inimical to both modern state practices and to religion-as-ideology.[52]

While I am in broad agreement with Nandy's argument, I still suggest

[50] This point is discussed at length in chap. 5.
[51] Asad 2003.
[52] Nandy 1985; 1990; 1995; 1997.

we recognise that what we see in India now—i.e. from at least the beginning of the twenty-first century—is not communalism or religious fundamentalism but a triumphant Hindu supremacism. Communalism, a term used by the British colonial government to indicate "the presence in each community of separate collective consciousness as well as of separate collective communal motives,"[53] has become the term to describe conflict between Hindus and Muslims as communities since the colonial period. "Communal" in South Asia has therefore had this negative meaning—as opposed to the positive valence it has in Western political theory, where it denotes "shared by all members of a community." Communalism, its colonial history, and communal violence in India are the subjects of a large body of historical scholarship, of which we may note only two: first, Bipan Chandra's enduring definition of communalism and its history in India;[54] and second, Gyanendra Pandey's account of the construction of communalism in colonial North India, establishing that communalism is a modern phenomenon which came into being along with nationalism, and that colonialism contributed to the making of communalism.[55]

From the 1990s onwards, the advance of Hindu "communalism" lay in this—that it gradually occupied the space of nationalism, while politics based on Muslim identity could only ever be "communal." Hindu nationalism is the agenda of a Hindu supremacist politics, and we can no longer see it as something on par with community consciousness among minorities.

In this context we also need to rethink the terms "religious *fundamentalism*" and "religious *revivalism*." It seems to me that, in all contexts globally, wherever religion is invoked and mobilised in the arena of politics, it is not a "return" to fundamentals or a revival of religious faith but a process of constructing modern identities in the contemporary moment by a selective interpretation from elements within a body of knowledge identified as "religion." This is, of course, to be distinguished

[53] Misra 2020: 30, citing the Kanpur Riot Enquiry Report of 1933.
[54] Chandra 1984.
[55] Pandey 1990.

from the many kinds of spiritual and faith-based practices that do not seek state power or, often, even recognition by the state.

The State Determines "Religion"

Secularism everywhere, both in the West and in India, involves the continuous regulation by the state, largely through the legislature and the judiciary, of what constitutes religious as opposed to non-religious practices and institutions. Sometimes the judiciary has to decide whether freedom of religion impinges on the obligations of citizens to the state; at others it must adjudicate between individual freedoms or individual access to state-mandated benefits which a religious community may refuse on the grounds of its belief. At such times the very idea of what constitutes religion and belief is determined by the state—ostensibly as a neutral arbiter, but in fact always driven by the political forces that control the government or the judiciary. These political forces include the influence of particular groups constituted on the basis of religious identity. There are times when the judiciary and government are not in consonance, at others they reflect the same political beliefs. This state regulation of what constitutes religion is not a perversion of secularism—on the contrary, it is what constitutes the very heart of the practice of secularism. This is why a certain kind of debate on secularism that centres around religious "belief" and its place in a democracy is, in my opinion, misplaced. Secularism is a state practice, it is far from neutral, it tends to reflect majoritarian impulses (including religion-based majoritarianism), and it has nothing to do with the actual religious *beliefs* held by individuals or communities.

Before we look at India, let us consider two of the oldest instances of modern secular polities, both of which uphold the idea of the separation of church and state—the USA and France.

The United States of America

Here the legal apparatus of the state periodically defines what religion is by deciding whether particular forms of public behaviour come under the principle of freedom of religion. From 1890 to 1981, the understanding of what constitutes religion first expanded, then narrowed when faced with various kinds of resistance to state policy on religious grounds. In 1890 religion was defined in terms of believing in a Supreme Creator; in 1961 the US Supreme Court recognised that there are religions which do not have the idea of a Supreme Creator; in 1965, "sincere and meaningful" beliefs were accepted as having the same status as religion. In 1970 this broadened further, merging religion with "deeply and sincerely held moral and ethical beliefs." From this point there was a stepping back, in 1972, to a more exclusive definition of religion, because otherwise it would allow "every person to make his own standards on matters of conduct in which society as a whole has important interests." In 1981 the Court made a distinction between a religious choice and a personal philosophical choice, declining to protect the latter. Chief Justice Warren Burger stated: "Only beliefs rooted in religion are given special protection to the exercise of religion."[56]

The claims from petitioners ranged in these cases from refusing to accept military service to refusing compulsory school attendance. But regardless of the actual decisions, the pertinent point from the point of view of our discussion is that even to ensure a strict separation from religion it is the state that must decide what religion is. And there is a reluctance to accept individually taken ethical decisions as having the status of religion. Religion is a community of belief, as I pointed out earlier, and individually and privately held beliefs are rarely accorded that status.

Apart from adjudicating between religious beliefs and the state, courts are often called upon to mediate between religious communities and individuals. In the US, two key decisions of the Supreme Court in 2020 reaffirmed the rights of religious beliefs of employers over employees laying claim to the law of the land; and, in a third, it broke the wall between religion and state by decreeing that states that aid private schools must include aid to religious ones.[57] These decisions reflect the

[56] Freedom Forum Institute: no date.
[57] Coyle 2021.

growing conservative colour of the US judiciary, which is currently sharply tilted towards a kind of Christianity that is not even the majority Christian opinion in the USA.

France

France was re-established as a Catholic state by Napoleon in 1801 after the French Revolution had instituted church–state separation, and a long journey towards secularisation followed, culminating in the law of 1905 which formally established secularism as the "separation of Church and State." By this law, the state stopped funding religious institutions. It took over and administered all property belonging to institutions of religions that existed in France in 1905, when the law was passed. In the 1920s a process of reconciliation began between the Catholic Church and the French state, with court judgments favouring organised religion, culminating in 1926 when the state reclaimed a role in the process of choosing diocesan bishops.[58] Catholic and Protestant churches and synagogues in the country built before the 1905 law continue to be maintained fully with public expense, while Islam and other religions that entered France later maintain religious facilities at their own expense. From about 2007 a discussion started in France to fund mosques, so the state could both build bridges with the large Muslim minority and regulate Islamic spaces to control radicalism. This discussion was in terms of amending the 1905 law, thus posing Islam as the problematic outsider for whom France would have to sacrifice the precious principle of secularism.[59] The growing presence of Muslim immigrants in France of course links directly to its violent imperial history in Africa, especially Algeria, which is rarely acknowledged in the secular public domain. Thus in France, too, we see how the "separation of state and religion" is a deeply politicised, sectarian, and majoritarian idea, mobilised in different ways at different times.

[58] Betros 2010.
[59] DNA 2015; Alouane 2019.

India

As mentioned earlier, "translations" of secularism in India really express a different relationship between state and religion—very different from European notions of the church/state separation. However, for decades the Indian versions were seen as simply "translating" the English concept of separation between state and religion in some deficient way. This was despite the fact that the Indian versions are actually closer to traditions in the Indian subcontinent where multiple religious and cultural communities have coexisted despite long histories of violence—whether in mutual co-operation, ongoing tension, or by deftly managing conflict.[60] In the Indian subcontinent no philosophical tradition—whether Hindu, Buddhist, Islamic, or Sikh—has seen the state as entirely separate from religion; and yet state and religion have never here been as fused as in medieval Christianity. Recognising these difficulties, the framers of the Indian Constitution decided not to use the term "secularism" at all: it was inserted twenty-six years later through a Constitutional Amendment, at a time when democracy was held in abeyance during the "Indian Emergency" of 1975–7. In political discourse, however, secularism became quite a central category, assuming a self-evident and already accomplished state of being, when in fact the task involved having to learn the entire universe involved in doing things anew. The complicated ways in which Left parties and movements in India have had to negotiate religious and cultural practices—for a long time seen as necessarily regressive—and the new formulations of what secularism can be in the face of the Hindutva onslaught, are indications of the enormity of the task before us regarding knowledges old, new, and reconstructed, and the radically different universes to which languages can give birth. Rita Kothari says "the story of the English word secular is at one level a story of non-translation. It has survived as an English word in Indian languages, with connotations of its own."[61] She may here be touching upon one of the strengths we can draw

---

[60] Discussed later, in chap. 3.
[61] Kothari 2020.

upon to fight Hindu supremacism: i.e. the non-translatability is not a weakness.

Both *sarva dharma sama bhava* and *dharm nirpekshata* imply an imbrication of state and religion, and both expect the state to "see" religion, to recognise it as plural. In addition, the state is expected to be both the neutral arbiter *between* communities as well as the agent of social justice *within* communities. These tensions are evident in the Constitution—which proscribes caste discrimination and ensures temple entry, for example, while simultaneously protecting the right to freedom of religion. This second aspect of the state's self-perceived function—intervening in religious communities to bring about equality—is not associated with secularism in the classic sense; indeed, in the classic sense "religious" is precisely the *opposite* of "secular"; it is what lies outside the scope of secularism. Therefore the interpenetration of state, religion, and religious community-based politics is even more intimate, as well as driven by political compulsions and ideologies. The point is not that the co-constitution of state and religion is somehow illegitimate, but rather that this is the only way in which both emerge.

In an intricate reading of the Taj Mahal as an architectural complex of tomb and mosque, Hilal Ahmed refers to "two kinds of publics" that an iconic photograph of the Taj by Raghu Rai captures—a congregation of worshippers offering prayers at the mosque, "paying no attention to the central building (at least at that very moment)," and a sightseeing crowd which stays at the central building and "seems to follow the given official meanings of the Taj as a world heritage site."[62] From a perspective that privileges the recognised architectural/archaeological/historical values of the Taj, religious worship in its premises appears as an encroachment upon its "secular" space. However, Ahmed suggests that instead of seeing these two publics as expressing a secular/communal or religion/secularism binary, we should see them as expressing two different ideas of secularism. In his understanding, secularisation is not "decline of religious belief" or "shrinking of the domain of religion,"

[62] Ahmed 2013: 71.

but a practice which "influences, shapes and nurtures the everyday acts of the state and modified religiosities of communities."[63] The Taj mosque was part of the Taj monument complex from the beginning, long before the colonial authorities decided to take care of the Taj as a protected monument. Local Muslims continue to worship there and the scope of religious activities has increased over the years. The Archaeological Survey of India draws on two different sets of laws with reference to the Taj—the 1995 Waqf Act, and the 1958 Ancient Monuments and Archaeological Sites and Remains Act. In Ahmed's reading these laws stem from two different conceptions of secularism. The Waqf Act underlines the state's commitment to religious minorities, while the 1958 Act defines the protection of a national heritage as a secular act. Both, Ahmed argues, are equally legitimate forms of secularism. He thus rejects "the polemical claims made by Hindu and Muslim rightists, rigid secularists, and institutions like the ASI or the [UP Sunni Waqf Board], who want us to believe that 'religion' and the 'secular' are essentially fixed and conceptually antagonistic terms." In his words, "the Muslims who offer prayers at the Taj should not be understood as anti-secular; rather, the very act of worship inside a 'protected monument of national importance' . . . signifies an India-specific notion of a secular monument," a "context-specific secular-isation."[64] This reading of worship in the Taj dissolves the binary of law versus culture/religion produced by modern law and the modern state.

One is reminded here of the argument made by Rustom Bharu-cha that the debate for "secularists" is not with the Other, but with "multiple others within our own amorphous constitutency, who can help us to inflect our secular selves."[65] These others are those whose "secular orientations may be diffused, inarticulate or articulated in radically different ways from our own."[66] The horizon within which

[63] Ibid.: 72.
[64] Ibid.: 77.
[65] Bharucha 1998: 26.
[66] Ibid.: 25.

the understanding offered by Ahmed and Bharucha works does not counterpose secular to religious/communal, but attempts to expand the idea of the secular itself to accommodate the "question of faith," as another work by Bharucha is titled.[67] It seems to me that with such an expansion, we step out of "the secular" altogether, giving an old name to a new field made visible by this move.

Let us consider another example—the Jain practice of *santhara*. This involves voluntarily starving to death at a particular stage in one's life. Shekhar Hattangadi arrived at the conclusion—after speaking to scholars, lay adherents of Jainism, and the Jain clergy—that

> a Santhara practitioner relinquishing food and drink voluntarily by this method has arrived at that decision after calm and unruffled introspection, with an intent to cleanse oneself of karmic encumbrances and thus attain the highest state of transcendental well-being. Santhara, for him, is therefore simply an act of spiritual purification premised on an exercise of individual autonomy.[68]

This practice was challenged by a Public Interest Litigation in the Rajasthan High Court in 2006. The ruling given in 2015 was that *santhara* amounted to suicide; not being an essential practice under Jainism, it became a crime under the still operative colonial era Indian Penal Code. On appeal, the Supreme Court stayed the order, thus lifting the ban on *santhara*, but it simply shifted the question to whether "essential and integral parts of a religion can be restricted by the State," asking the Centre and Rajasthan to respond. What remains unexamined is the presumed opposition between the "particularity" of the Jain "religious" practice as opposed to the "universality" of the state's "legal" practice. Shekhar Hattangadi on the other hand, forces us to reformulate this opposition as one between competing particularities:

> the Santhara case serves to emphasize the seemingly irreconcilable difference in perspective on the specific issue of "suicide." In contrast to a

[67] Bharucha 1993.
[68] Hattangadi 2015.

Christian believer who looks upon the human body as a God-given "temple of the human soul" and therefore beyond the realm of wilful and deliberate destruction by any human being, a devout Jain views that same body as a "prison of the human soul," the fulfilment of whose needs corresponds to the accumulation of bad karma. This basic contradiction between a law founded largely on a Christian-inspired bioethic and the essentially Eastern variant of the idea of spiritual advancement through abstinence and renunciation rears its head whenever an ancient religious practice like Santhara collides with contemporary law.[69]

Hattangadi's analysis enables us to see that what is presented as secular law is also deeply rooted in the specific religious worldview of the British. While a Hindutva perspective would then move to replacing a "Christian"-inspired law with a "Hindu" one, what we should recognise rather is that, as Carl Schmitt puts it, "All significant concepts of the modern theory of the state are secularized theological concepts."[70] In other words, any engagement with the state and the law involves engaging with an omnipotent power with its own interests and cultural roots, not a neutral entity.

Let us now turn to two long-standing controversies in India—women's entry into the Sabarimala shrine and the (lack of) a uniform civil code—to illustrate further how majoritarian claims to "religion" get legitimacy, while "other" religions or multiple beliefs and practices within the same "religion" are denied that status.

Can Bharat Mata Enter the Sabarimala Temple?

For Hindu supremacism, while Muslim women are to be "freed" from the veil, Hindu women are to be carefully controlled so that they do not marry Muslims, convert, and expand the population of Muslims in India. Hence the bogey of "love jihad," the supposed campaign of Muslim men to seduce Hindu women, and the violent policing by vigilante groups of relationships between Hindu women and Muslim men.

---

[69] Hattangadi 2015.
[70] Schmitt 1985: 36.

Families in India are already geared to controlling women's sexuality, and now they have the support of such groups.

The chaste and always vulnerable body of Mother India, widely imaged as Bharat Mata, is central to Hindutva politics. Bharat Mata is fair-complexioned, saffron-flag-bearing, ready to bear a thousand sons all eager to protect her honour. Several writers have demonstrated how this image of the Mother, far from being eternal, was constructed in the nineteenth century by the political project of Hindutva;[71] and how this mother can only consider as her sons those defined by Hindutva as "Hindus," never Muslims.[72] This Mother is imagined as a body overlapping with the territory of the nation.[73] Sumathi Ramaswamy recounts the story of how Aurobindo Ghose explained patriotism in 1905: "Do you see this map? It is not a map but the portrait of Bharat Mata: its cities and mountains, rivers and jungles form her physical body. All her children are her nerves, large and small . . . Concentrate on Bharat as a living mother, worship her with nine-fold bhakti."[74] If the Nation is a body—the body of one's own mother—then it precedes its children; or it is constituted by its children, as in Aurobindo's vision (the "nerves, large and small"). From this image follow the implied hierarchies of birth and origin among the children (large and small, older brother and younger brother, sons and daughters). From this follows, too, the idea that the children cannot leave the mother, for that implies amputation, the dismembering of the maternal body, an act that none can survive—neither the mother nor the children. Such emotive imagery prevents recognition of the nation-state as a modern institution emerging *after* "the people," in a process that involves power, the silencing of heterogeneity, and the violence against ethnic minorities that has globally marked the emergence of the modern nation-state system.[75] This mother is the mother who is the nominal head of the

[71] Sarkar 2022; Gupta 2001.
[72] Daniyal 2016.
[73] Ramaswamy 2010.
[74] Ramaswamy 2001: 97.
[75] Mann 2005.

patriarchal household, whose power flows entirely from her maintaining the rules of patriarchy, blood purity, family hierarchies. She acts as the agent of her son or sons as long as she performs these functions. This RSS-constructed *savarna*, North Indian, Aryan vision of the Mother is not the only one on this subcontinent—other, more autonomous, darker mothers are rendered illegitimate in Hindutva discourse.[76] These dark goddesses, fierce and sexual, are disowned by "Hindu" sons. One of the many hundreds of police complaints filed since 2014 on account of hurt Hindu sentiments was in 2022 against a Canada-based filmmaker originally from India, Leena Manimekalai, who shared a poster of her film showing an actor dressed as the goddess Kali smoking a cigarette. It is worth understanding whose religious sentiments could be hurt by this. After all, as many others have also pointed out, Kali is the goddess of destruction and her offerings even today in many temples are alcohol and meat, while in Manimekalai's poster she is merely smoking a cigarette.[77] But the cigarette-smoking woman in Indian popular culture represents a sexually free rebellious spirit, and highlighting that aspect of the goddess is what has hurt her *savarna* Hindu sons—the goddess as sexually free and "immoral."

But even the *savarna* Bharat Mata, though ever fertile, is not considered pure during her menstrual periods. Hindu women do not perform religious rituals while menstruating, nor enter temples, and one temple in Kerala prohibits entry to all women of menstruating age. This temple to the deity Ayyappan, on a peak in a forested hillscape at Sabarimala in Kerala, has been the centre of a legal battle for several years.

The Sabarimala Temple story encapsulates the two themes of this chapter in the best possible way—the manner in which what is termed "religion" is expected to be determined by the state—in this case represented by the court—and how the truth of "religion" is assumed to be discovered etched on the bodies of women. In 2018 the Indian Supreme Court, by a 4:1 decision, declared the ban on women's entry

[76] As discussed in chap. 3.
[77] Sengupta 2022.

into the temple as unconstitutional. But after this order women who attempted the arduous trek up to the temple were physically attacked by men, and finally only two women—a Nair and a Dalit—performed the pilgrimage under police escort.[78] More than fifty petitions seeking a review of the 2018 judgment were immediately filed by various organisations, including a women's organisation of Ayyappa devotees. In 2019 the Supreme Court delivered a judgment, keeping the review petitions pending and clubbing them with several other petitions challenging discrimination against women in religious practices—such as female genital mutilation among Dawoodi Bohras, the entry into the fire temple of Parsi women who have married out of their religion, and the entry of Muslim women into mosques. This hearing is still, despite the passage of years, not yet over, and in the meanwhile the court has ordered that its judgment permitting entry of women into the Sabarimala Temple stands.[79] In 2020, however, the Temple Board which administers the temple declared once again on its portal that all women below fifty years of age would be denied entry, adding this to other Covid-linked restrictions. The Kerala government has not challenged this prohibition.[80]

The dissenting judgment—by the only woman judge in the Supreme Court Sabarimala verdict—is worth a closer look. Justice Indu Malhotra's main argument was that courts cannot impose their rationality on religion and faith.[81] But the Supreme Court judgment had not in fact overturned faith: it had overturned an earlier Kerala High Court judgment of 1991. That High Court judgment was on a petition by a 24-year-old man, Mahendran, and it directed the Sabarimala Temple Trust to prohibit the entry of women of menstruating age (between the ages of 10 and 50) into the temple. Thus, it was the Kerala High Court (the law) that had banned the entry of women, directing the temple trust (the keeper of the faith) to ensure this, and asking the

---

[78] Ameerudheen 2019.
[79] Supreme Court Observer 2019.
[80] Viswanathan 2020.
[81] Suresh 2018.

Kerala government to use the police to enforce the order to ban the entry of women into the temple. The court order specifically said: "We also direct the 3rd respondent, Government of Kerala, to render all necessary assistance inclusive of police and to see that the direction which we have issued to the Devaswom Board is implemented and complied with."[82] It was an appeal against this judgment by a group of women lawyers from the Indian Young Lawyers' Association to which the Supreme Court was responding.

Why was the Kerala High Court order necessary? Because many women were performing the pilgrimage to Sabarimala, especially for the ceremony of the first food given to infants (*choroonu*), but also on other occasions—from the Maharani of Travancore in the 1930s to the young woman whom Mahendran—the petitioner who sparked the Kerala High Court judgment—saw trekking up to the shrine in 1990. By the mid-nineteenth century, according to a British Survey report, it seems an informal ban existed—but that is already well into modernity.[83] Overall, it seems to have been less tradition and more modernity that imposed the ban on women's entry into the Sabarimala Temple. Only in 1972, according to N. S. Madhavan, was a more strict ban sought to be imposed.[84] The ban on women entering the Sabarimala Temple is linked to the gradual Brahminisation of what was most probably in ancient times a Buddhist shrine; and prior to that a Dravidian or Adivasi shrine to a forest god.[85]

This brings us to another of Justice Indu Malhotra's arguments—accepting the claim that Ayyappa worship is a sect, or a separate religious denomination because it follows Ayyappa Dharma, and that it can therefore have its own beliefs and practices, including forbidding women entry into the temple. The judge's agreement with this

[82] *S Mahendran v. The Secretary Travancore* 1991: 45.

[83] The survey report, based on five years of research, completed in 1820, was published in two volumes in 1893 and 1901 (Press Trust of India 2018).

[84] Madhavan 2018.

[85] The possible lineages of the Sabarimala Temple are discussed in chap. 3 as part of understanding the larger process of attempts to assimilate pre-Aryan beliefs into Brahminism.

view can be contradicted by what is historically observable—that is, a non-Brahminical shrine being gradually absorbed into Brahminical Hinduism, thereby losing any claim to be the temple of a separate sect. The push for a ban on women's entry in fact grows stronger with the Brahminisation of the shrine—i.e. the further it moves away from any separate identity that it had.

Justice Indu Malhotra also rejected the plea that excluding women of the ages ten to fifty amounts to untouchability—as Justice Chandrachud had argued in the majority judgment—because, in her view, all forms of exclusion do not constitute untouchability. In addition, she stated that to forbid women entry was not a discriminatory provision because all women as a class were not being excluded, only women of the specified age group were. It is true that untouchability as a practice cannot simply be equated with all forms of exclusion, because the full horror of untouchability—the systematic institutional and cultural dehumanisation of a section of people identified as untouchable by birth—is lost by analogising it with exclusion more generally. However, Justice Malhotra's reading failed to touch upon the significance of the age group excluded—which was on the assumption of menstruation as polluting, and based on the very presence of women of a certain age as threats to male celibacy—the deity Ayyappa being claimed as a Brahmachari (celibate).

First, it is necessary to understand at what point in history menstruation begins to be seen as polluting. This could not possibly have originated with or been practised during the worship of pre-Aryan goddesses of fertility and destruction, and certainly not in the matrilineal communities of Kerala where the onset of menstruation was celebrated like a festival even up to the mid-twentieth century. Menstruation seen as polluting is a consequence of the expansion of Aryan patriarchal religious practices across the subcontinent. What is more interesting here is to consider the fact that, by the nineteenth century or so, the heterogeneous communities labelled Hindus who accepted Brahminism had mostly come to see menstruation as polluting, and certainly by then devout Hindu women stopped entering temples during their periods. Why then was an additional precaution necessary only for the Sabarimala Temple—that no woman of menstruating age should enter it? This would entail the argument that all women within their menstruating age are polluting at all times. Or else the implication is that women are likely to lie and assert they are not menstruating in order to enter the temple. This assumption contrasts with the trust reposed in male devotees. Male pilgrims to Sabarimala are required to have kept a forty-day *vratham* (oath) of celibacy, as well as observe a long list of other kinds of required good conduct prior to the Sabarimala pilgrimage. This is believed without verification. What is evident throughout this process is the powerful misogyny and fear of female sexuality that marks Brahminism.

The very claim that Ayyappa is celibate appears to be a later, twentieth-century addition to bolster the argument against women's entry. As Sandhya Ram puts it, "all of us in Kerala born post-1970s know of this legend solely from a movie titled 'Swamy Ayyappan' which was released in 1975."[86] Once again, therefore, we have here a tradition of modern origin. A corollary worth noting is that transgender people are permitted into the Sabarimala Temple. Neither they nor men are seen to pose a threat to Ayyappan's celibacy. The heteronormativity attributed to Ayyappan—who is believed in one of the stories of his birth to be the progeny of two male gods—is revealing in that it is clearly a modern understanding.[87]

The Supreme Court decision, thus, was not a judicial review of ancient faith, as Justice Indu Malhotra argued, but an overturning of a previous legal interpretation of human, not divinely ordained, practice. This practice—banning the entry of women into the Sabarimala Temple—is of recent historical origin, very probably going back only to the mid-nineteenth century, and even then not stringently enforced.

[86] Ram 2018.

[87] One of the stories of Ayyappan's birth relates to the form Vishnu takes of the enchanting Mohini (related in the *Vishnu Purana*). Shiva is attracted to Mohini, and from their union is born Ayyappan (related in the *Sribhutnatha Purana*). The role of the Puranas in drawing pre-Aryan deities and practices into Aryan deityscapes is discussed in chap. 2.

However, by the time of the Supreme Court judgment of 2019, the Brahminical Hindutva-influenced ethos had acquired enormous clout. This became apparent from the entry into the shrine of just two women—which was treated as a calamity. A WhatsApp message that the Hindu Right circulated after the entry by these two women focused on the "deceitful strategies" the women had apparently used to escape the temple's policing by violent male mobs. In that long rant, one passage stands out: "This is the true nature of our enemy here in Kerala . . . An enemy who does not even have the dignity or courage to enter through the front door, but instead, sneaks in and out of back doors like someone having an ILLICIT AFFAIR [upper case in the original]." An illicit affair with the deity Himself—Bhakti poets have written of the glory of this romance, of the belief that love for God cannot be held within the rigid bloodless bounds set by social norms. Who, then, are the real devotees here?

I have noted earlier that women wanting to enter the Sabarimala Temple were invariably referred to in the media and by political leaders as "activists," whereas the men who explicitly mobilised to prevent their entry physically were called "pilgrims."[88] It seems the legitimacy of faith is permitted only to Brahminical practices, as we have seen from the other instances cited earlier.

It seems worth noting that, during the campaign run-up to the Kerala State Assembly elections of 2021, the BJP made the Sabarimala ban and the ruling CPM's opposition to the ban a major issue. In the end the CPM-led alliance, the Left Democratic Front, won a sweeping victory, while the BJP-led National Democratic Alliance failed to win a single seat. Nevertheless, until December 2022 women have not been permitted entry by the Sabarimala Temple authorities.

The movement for women to enter the Sabarimala Temple can be seen as part of a long history of temple-entry movements by Dalits in Kerala, and more generally in India. References were often made during the Sabarimala controversy to another anti-caste movement in Kerala, the nineteenth-century struggle for dignity by women of the Channar

---

[88] Menon 2019.

caste—now called Nadar, an OBC caste—in Travancore.[89] This move-ment challenged the upper-caste prohibition on lower-caste women covering their breasts and was met with the same violence that women attempting to climb Sabarimala faced two centuries later. Many Chan-nars converted to Christianity to escape caste humiliation. As is widely known, until the nineteenth century not covering the upper body was common across castes and genders in Kerala, until the hegemony of British Victorian morality gradually shamed and "civilised" the upper castes into covering "their" women's breasts. This development was ac-companied by an upper-caste prohibition on lower castes covering their upper body—the intention being to make upper-body covering the exclusive privilege of the upper castes. The right of lower-caste women converts to Christianity to cover their breasts was granted by an order in 1812 by the Resident of the British East India Company, but Chan-nar and Ezhava women who dared to emulate upper-caste Nair women by covering their breasts were attacked, and their schools and churches were burnt as well. Upper-caste violence on the issue and the resistance to it continued until 1859, when, under pressure from the British gov-ernment, the king of Travancore issued a proclamation ensuring the right of lower-caste women to cover their breasts.[90] Caste power clashed against colonial power in the Channar revolts, but we would miss seeing an important dimension if we failed to also notice how colonial power—appealed to by Christian missionaries—normalised the covering of women's breasts as a move from savagery to civilisation, so much so that it was then sought as a privilege by both upper and lower castes.

The Uniform Civil Code

Another long-standing thorny issue, going back to the 1930s, which has reappeared in the contemporary public domain pertains to a "uniform

---

[89] "OBC": Other Backward Class, a state category for castes that are socially and educationally deprived but which are higher in the caste hierarchy than Sched-uled Castes and Scheduled Tribes.

[90] Chandra and Kumaraswamy, no date.

civil code." This invokes the idea of national integration which, it is argued, will be brought about or greatly facilitated by a uniform legal code for all communities, as against the prevailing judicial regime of separate religious personal laws. I have written on this issue at greater length earlier, namely that India's "religious" personal laws, which are more about worldly matters such as property, were concretised during colonial rule and do not embody primordial "religious" beliefs. Feminist analyses, including mine, have highlighted a dimension routinely rendered invisible, i.e. gender justice; and in this context there have been critiques of successive Congress governments that have pandered to Muslim patriarchy.[91] So, here I will address only the most recent phase of the issue.

For over eight decades the women's movement has discussed and debated the desirability and feasibility of a uniform civil code replacing various personal laws applicable to the country's many religious communities. The reason for these discussions has been that all these laws have discriminated against women in relation to marriage, divorce, property inheritance, and the custody of children. Today the feminist movement has ended up posing a simple question—what is the value of the desired uniformity? Is a uniformity in laws desirable for the "integrity of the nation," as some judicial pronouncements have suggested? If so, who exactly is the beneficiary—which sections of the Indian people will benefit from this "integrity of the nation," an abstract concept which is not exactly on top of a woman's mind when her husband throws her out onto the street.

Or are uniform laws meant to ensure justice for women in marriage and inheritance? If so, what would a uniform civil code look like? If it intends to simply put together the best gender-just practices from all the personal laws around, as is sometimes proclaimed by Hindu nationalist leaders, then it must show features that are identifiable as improvements on the current practices of gender injustice. Some of these improving features could be as follows.

[91] Menon 1998; Menon 2012/2022.

First, polygamy and arbitrary divorce as permitted by Muslim Personal Law would need to be outlawed, as they are in Hindu Personal Law. But conversely, as the feminist legal activist Flavia Agnes has often pointed out, a uniform civil code would require the abolition of the Hindu Undivided Family, a legal institution that gives tax benefits only to Hindus, and all citizens of India would have to be governed by the largely gender-just Indian Succession Act, 1925, currently applicable only to Christians and Parsis. Muslim Personal Law is already modern in this sense, since it has since the 1930s enshrined individual rights to property—unlike Hindu law, in which the family's natural condition is assumed to be "joint." In the decades of the 1930s and 1940s, contrary to later discourses about Muslim law being backward, it was Hindu laws that were considered "backward" and in need of being brought into the modern world of individual property rights.[92]

Second, the performance of a Muslim marriage is simultaneously a legally binding contract which protects women better in case of divorce than does the Hindu marriage, which is a sacrament. Therefore, all marriages would need to become civil contracts. Mehr, in Muslim Personal Law—paid by the husband's family to the wife upon marriage—is the exclusive property of the wife and is hers upon divorce, offering her a protection that Hindu women do not have. So, any uniform civil code would need to make the practice of mehr compulsory for all while abolishing dowry.

The patent impossibility of even making such suggestions, leave alone enacting them, arises not from the ideas themselves but from the fact that a uniform civil code has nothing to do at all with gender justice. It has entirely to do with a Hindu nationalist agenda and is one of three long-standing campaign promises of the BJP—the other two being the construction of a Ram Mandir at the site where the Babri Masjid once stood, and the revocation of Article 370 which granted special status to Jammu and Kashmir. A uniform civil code is part of this armoury.

---

[92] We will return to women's individual rights to land as a capitalist agenda in chap. 5.

It is meant to discipline Muslims and teach them—as if they hadn't been taught already—that they are second-class citizens who live at the mercy of "the national race," the Hindus, as M. S. Golwalkar decreed.[93]

So let us pose the question differently: Who suffers in the absence of a uniform civil code? In the current phase of BJP rule (since 2014), gender justice is explicitly invoked by Hindu nationalists while discussing a uniform civil code—specifically for Muslim women, that is, who have long been victims of polygamy and triple talaq. But for decades feminist legal practice has on behalf of countless Muslim women successfully used both the Protection of Women from Domestic Violence Act, 2005—available to all Indian citizens regardless of religious identity— as well as the Muslim Women (Protection of Rights on Divorce) Act, 1986, to deal with polygamy and triple talaq, and to obtain for them maintenance, child custody, and rights to their matrimonial home. In addition, feminist legal activists have used the landmark *Shamim Ara v. State of U.P.* (2002) ruling to buttress their claim that arbitrary triple talaq is invalid.[94]

Moreover, polygamy is not exclusive to Muslims. Hindu men are polygamous too, except that because polygamy is legally banned in Hindu law, wives subsequent to the first wife have no legal standing and no protection under the law. Under shari'a law, by contrast, subsequent wives have rights and husbands have obligations towards them. If gender justice is the value we espouse, rather than monogamy per se, we would be thinking about how to protect "wives" in the patriarchal institution of marriage. "Wives" are produced through the institution of compulsory heterosexual marriage, the basis of which is the sexual division of labour. This institution is sustained by the productive and reproductive labour of women, and almost all women are exclusively trained only to be wives. Thus, when a marriage fails to fulfil its patriarchal promise of security in return for that labour, all that most women are left with is the capacity for unskilled labour. Or they remain trapped

[93] Golwalkar 1939.
[94] Agnes 2016.

in marriage with children to provide for, while men marry again, legally or otherwise, producing still more dependent and exploited wives and children for whom they need take no responsibility. If gender justice is the point of legal reforms, the centrality and power of the compulsory heterosexual, patriarchal marriage, and the damage it can do to women, is what must be mitigated. That then would mean recognising the reality of multiple "wives" as a common practice across communities, and the protection of the rights of all women in such relationships.

A survey conducted by the Bharatiya Muslim Mahila Andolan, a significant voice in the debate, found that more than 90 percent of Muslim women in India want a ban on "triple talaq" and polygamy in Muslim Personal Law. That is, the demand is made within the framework of codifying Muslim Personal Law; it is not made in favour of a uniform civil code, partly because there is no clarity on what a uniform code would look like, but also because that demand comes from clearly Hindutva quarters which have shown their perspective to be one in which both women and minorities are expendable.

The only example of a uniform code in India is the Portuguese Civil Procedure Code (1939) of Goa, which is neither uniform nor gender-just. Marriage laws differ for Catholics and people of other faiths, and if a marriage is solemnised in church then Church law applies—permitting, for example, arbitrary annulment at the behest of one of the parties. The "customs and usages" of the Hindus of Goa are recognised, including "limited" polygamy for Hindus. The positive aspect of Goa's Civil Code is the Community Property Law, which guarantees each spouse 50 percent of all assets owned and inheritable at the time of marriage. However, this provision can be sidestepped in practice, given the power relations in a marriage, and studies show that it has not made any impact on incidences of domestic violence. Clearly, if gender justice is not prioritised, both uniformity as well as its dilution can reinforce patriarchy and majoritarianism.

The woman at the centre of the most recent debate on the uniform civil code—and on whose petition against arbitrary talaq the Supreme Court outlawed the practice in 2019—is Shayara Bano, who had received her talaq by post. She was visible in the media, spiritedly criticising patriarchy in the Muslim community. Revealingly, an interview with her in a national newspaper concluded with a startling question: "What about the 'Bharat Mata ki Jai' slogan controversy?" Ms Bano replied, "I feel all Muslims should say Bharat Maa ki Jai."[95] Does the question not seem irrelevant in the context of Ms Bano's fight for personal justice? What does the compulsory chanting of a Hindu nationalist slogan, "Bharat Mata ki Jai," have to do with a woman fighting patriarchy? But the question does not seem irrelevant at all; it seems to be at the heart of the interview. This alone should alert us to what the demand for a uniform civil code is actually about.

The Indian Supreme Court finally did outlaw triple talaq in 2019, but we must remember it came out of a massive campaign by a grassroots Muslim women's organisation, the Bharatiya Muslim Mahila Andolan (BMMA). Formed in 2007 and with over 100,000 women as members, the BMMA has actively campaigned for legal reforms and was one of the five petitioners in the triple talaq case, besides filing petitions against polygamy. The BMMA has also been pushing for the codification of Muslim Personal Law based on the Constitution and a feminist interpretation of the Koran. The Supreme Court judgment ending triple talaq was thus not a gift of the Modi-led BJP government to Muslim women—as the BJP and the media chose to portray it. The Hindu supremacist move that followed was an additional piece of legislation criminalising Muslim men who give triple talaq. This has taken Muslim marriage and divorce into the domain of criminal law—even as marital rape remains uncriminalised in the country to the detriment of women of all communities. Malavika Rajkotia highlights this contradiction— that it is a crime for Muslim men to unilaterally declare divorce, but it is not a crime for a man of any community to unilaterally force his wife to have sex.[96] This says everything we need to know both about the institution of heterosexual marriage and Hindu Rashtra.

The current position of the BJP, now that triple talaq has been banned and criminalised, is that there need not be a uniform civil code

---

[95] Shayara Bano Interview 2016.
[96] Rajkotia, no date.

at the all-India level; the states can go ahead individually and establish uniform codes since subjects such as marriage, divorce, and property inheritance are on the Concurrent List. Several BJP-ruled states are already preparing to follow up on this.[97] As with anti-conversion laws, which have begun to be enacted by some of India's states,[98] we may shortly see state-level uniform codes that empower Hindu Rashtra, capitalism, and patriarchy.

Religious/Caste/Race Identity and Secular Politics

It has been assumed that the secularisation of society requires the gradual disappearance of all identities other than that of "the citizen"; indeed, that secularisation will be accompanied by this process. If, however, we come to terms with the fact that the unmarked citizen was always implicitly marked in the ways discussed above, there seems to be no way out but to reappropriate the various identities, particularly community identities, that simply functioned underground all the while we thought they were gone. Indeed, many of the political developments globally, of the last two decades in particular, are incomprehensible without a framework that gives visibility to community/caste (and in other contexts race, ethnic, and other) identities.

Fanon charges Sartre with aridly intellectualising the experience of being black in his (Sartre's) essay titled "Orphée Noir" (1948), which served as the preface to a collection of poetry from Francophone Africa. Fanon says that in this essay Sartre presents negritude as "a minor term of a dialectical progression," as merely a transitory stage on the way towards the universal and abstract class identity. "When I read that page," says Fanon, "I felt as if I had been robbed of my last chance . . . Jean-Paul Sartre had forgotten that the Negro suffers in his body quite differently from the white man." The idea that "identity politics" is narrower than another politics which is universal is, of course, the classic act of

---

[97] Anshuman 2022.
[98] Discussed in chap. 3.

power, for universalism is simply a particularism that claims universality. Fanon refuses to accept "that amputation" conducted by Sartre. He experiences himself as black, he lives in a body recognised as black, and he will simultaneously resist the meaning that the world gives to his blackness while celebrating the solidarities it brings him.[99]

The painful dilemma Fanon faced is precisely the way in which the self comes to consciousness in other forms of embodied discrimination—what race is for Fanon, caste, gender, and religious community identity is for Indians. The term "embodied" does not, of course, mean that the body simply exists in nature. The body, in each of these instances, is produced through a network of cultural and material practices. The body that is deemed to be inferior is caught up in the need to recognise its difference from—and simultaneously claim its similarity with—the oppressive identity that marks itself as Self—whether white, *savarna* ("upper" caste), or male. The reinvention of secular politics therefore requires, it seems to me, the recognition, assertion, and reappropriation of various kinds of identities hitherto assumed to be irrelevant—or, rather, that have been thought of as needing to be rendered irrelevant—in a modern democracy. Aditya Nigam terms the reassertion of such identities since the 1980s "the insurrection of little selves" which reflects the global conjuncture of the crisis of modernity.[100]

A significant instance of this phenomenon is the move, discussed above, that the Indian feminist movement has made since the late 1980s, away from the demand for a uniform civil code. What it has instead argued for is to accept that existing religious personal laws have different histories and contexts, and to recognise several other kinds of initiatives towards gender justice, some of which involve reform arising from within communities. This shows awareness of the fact that uniformity does not necessarily lead to gender justice, that community identity is inescapable, and that to reject the homogenising and codifying drive of the modern nation-state—which acts in the name of secularism—is necessary.

[99] Fanon 2003: 70–1.
[100] Nigam 2006: 1.

Similarly, it would be fruitless to try to understand the current impasse in India on the Women's Reservation Bill—aiming to reserve one-third of seats for women in parliament—only in terms of feminism and patriarchy. The resistance to it from OBC political parties can only be understood in the context of the transformation of the Indian polity by non-Brahminical caste assertions through the 1980s. A blanket one-third reservation for women, it is argued, will simply turn the clock back to the pre-1980s situation, when parliament was predominantly "upper" caste. Hence the demand for "quotas within quotas," that is, further reserved quotas for Backward Caste and Muslim women within the one-third. In both cases, the universal unmarked Woman—the subject of the secular women's movement—becomes problematised by other identities of caste and religious community. This is a recognition that has been debated and is now very much at the forefront of feminist politics.[101]

It is increasingly becoming impossible to avoid the recognition that we carry our caste and community identities, whether we want to or not, whether we have rejected them or not. Rejecting their caste identity is not an option for those who are not *savarna*, and those who are *savarna* assume their own privilege in apparent ignorance of caste. It is possible to forget we have a caste only if we happen to be born "upper" caste, whereas a Dalit perforce imbibes that identity with her mother's milk. As for religious identity, for many who never consider themselves Hindu or Muslim or Christian, coming to terms with this inescapable social truth of every person's identity is a difficult process. The fact remains that each one of us who imagine ourselves as "universal" or above the bounds of religion have always been legally Hindu and Muslim and Christian, governed by Hindu and Muslim and Christian personal laws. This is not an identity we can choose to take on or deny, it is an identity that we bear despite ourselves, it hangs from our names, our practices, the way we speak the Indian languages. In the context of the widespread and organised attacks on Muslims that we have seen,

[101] Menon 2004.

especially since 2014, it becomes impossible to ignore and thus all the more necessary to accept the implications of the fact that people are targeted *as Muslims* and in *the name of Hindus*.

A Hindu Left?

Here I wish to distinguish my argument carefully from another though similar kind of argument about religious identities within a secular polity. In a thought-provoking comment on the absence of what she calls the Hindu Left, Ruth Vanita points out that Hinduism may be the only religion in the world today that apparently does not have a Left.

It is true that both Islam and Christianity have had long traditions of feminist and Left interpretations.[102] When it comes to Hinduism, Vanita is right to argue that secular leftism in India contributed to a process of constructing all things Hindu as inherently backward and regressive, thus pushing reformist Hindu organisations with what she terms "left-of-centre" social agendas—such as the Ramakrishna Mission and the Arya Samaj—into the arms of the Hindu Right. She urges the need to make a distinction between an authoritarian Hindu position and a libertarian Hindu position, and suggests that liberal and leftist Hindus should "begin to acknowledge their Hindu identity and speak in defence of Hindu heritage."[103] This text is a brief comment and she does not expand on what Hindu heritage is, but in the recent Introduction to a collection of essays she argues that "Debate about everything, including interpretation of the Vedas, is one of the structuring principles of the epics."[104] She also holds that episodes involving figures like Rama and Dronacharya in which they punish Shudras or Adivasis for daring to try and acquire knowledge are contradictions in or unacceptable aspects of their character, sometimes acknowledged in the text itself.

---

[102] These are too well known and do not need a discussion here, but we could note Mernissi (1975, 2002), Alcoff and Caputo (2011), Gutierrez (1988), and Mahmood (2005).

[103] Vanita 2002.

[104] Vanita 2022: 13.

Vanita's position here could be read as exemplifying that of the many who claim Hinduism as believers, celebrating it as expansive, inclusive, and dazzling in its heterogeneity. I will deconstruct this self-image of Hinduism as capacious and accommodating of dissent in Chapter 3, reading the presence of argumentative or disobedient Shudras, women, and animals differently.

Vanita herself makes no mention in this later book of Hindutva or the Hindu Right, but others who see Hinduism in this way—for example, Shashi Tharoor and Ramachandra Aluri[105]—explicitly reject Hindutva as a narrow political project distorting "true" Hinduism. From Tharoor and Aluri's perspective, Hinduism is internally diverse, respectful of other religions, and fully compatible with the secularism encapsulated by *sarva dharma sama bhava*.

A more complex argument than Vanita's, though also from the position of a practising Hindu whose Hinduism is "deeply nourished by Buddhism," is offered by Lata Mani. She has coined the term "Sacred Secular" to indicate indivisibility, and "the interconnectedness of the sentient and apparently non-sentient."[106] She outlines three key ideas at the core of all mystical traditions (Hinduism, Buddhism, Sufism, mystical Christianity, and nature-based religions), namely, "every aspect of the universe is infinitely alive and endowed with divine consciousness; all aspects of the universe are equally sacred; all aspects of the universe and all beings are intricately interdependent."[107] From this point of view, says Mani, Hindutva and almost all institutionalised religions stand opposed to all spiritual ideals. Spiritual traditions do not come to us pure and untouched by politics or human interpretation, she says, and spiritual practice involves "an inescapably interpretive aspect."[108] She identifies her own position as located within a progressive Hindu space, within and outside the religious establishment, that "has sought to challenge the credibility and authenticity of Hindutva."[109]

[105] See Tharoor (2018) and Aluri (2017).
[106] Mani 2009: 1–2.
[107] Ibid.: 125–6.
[108] Ibid.: 127.
[109] Ibid.

She stresses the essential teachings of love, peace, and unity inherent not only in Hinduism but in all spiritual traditions. In so doing, Mani argues her position differs from the secular position which insists on a separation of religion from politics for fear that their intermingling in the public sphere will undermine the cause of social justice. "Like other cultural practices," says Mani, "religion must be met and challenged in the very places in which it is lived, in the realm of the everyday."[110]

Another kind of argument on this front is made by those who assert their Hindu *community* identity rather than their religious beliefs. This they do, writing in various Indian languages (*bhashas*), precisely to be thoroughly critical of "Hindu heritage," especially its caste and gender oppression. To list just a few:

Volga (*The Liberation of Sita*, originally *Vimukta* in Telugu 2016).

Girish Karnad (*Taledanda* in Kannada, 1989, translated into Hindi as *Rakt Kalyan*).

U. R. Ananthamurthy (*Samskara* in Kannada, 1965).

Vijay Tendulkar (*Pahije Jatiche* in Marathi, better known as *Jaat hi Pucho Sadhu ki* in Hindi, 2017).

Ranganayakamma (*Ramayana Vishavruksham* in Telugu, 1974–6, translated into English as *Ramayana. The Poisonous Tree*).

These are striking instances. These are writers and intellectuals whose engagement with "Hindu heritage"—replete with patriarchal and caste violence—is antagonistic and bitingly critical.

Then there are of course those who have lived from birth with oppression and discrimination because of their caste identity and who therefore see nothing to defend in Hinduism—and indeed question the very assumptions that underlie this umbrella term. The best-known examples of this are B. R. Ambedkar, Bhanwar Meghwanshi, and Kancha Ilaiah Shepherd.[111]

---

[110] Ibid.: 128.

[111] Ambedkar (1936); Meghwanshi (2020); and Shepherd (2001).

And now we must address the inevitable question: if secular-nationalism was normed as *savarna* Hindu in many ways, how is it different from Hindu nationalism? Aditya Nigam offers the answer that, first, secular-nationalism did not see India as Hindu but invoked "unity in diversity"; and second, it contested the "Muslim oppressor" version of medieval history asserted by Hindu nationalism. It drew on "secular ideas of conflicts around class rather than community" and claimed that it was Muslim *rulers* who, like all rulers, tried to expand and preserve their power against the *people* who were both Hindu and Muslim.[112] If the critique of secular-nationalism is that it was culturally Hindu even as it asserted the diversity of India, the critique of Hindu nationalism is of course that it has no pretensions to diversity, homogenises an idea of "Hindu" along *savarna* North Indian masculinist norms, and eliminates the legitimacy of the non-Hindu.

Masculinism is not exclusive, of course, to Hindutva politics. Afiya Shehrbano Zia has focused on masculinism as an aspect of "religious performativity" in the neighbouring regimes of two prime ministers, Narendra Modi in India and the deposed (in 2022) Imran Khan of Pakistan. She compares "the redeemed Sufi masculinity" of the latter with "the ascetic Hindutva one" performed by the former, arguing that the "nativist, capitalist and gender discriminatory regimes" of both states are intolerant of dissent by "subaltern masculinist and feminist politics." Zia concludes that "military-pious-heteronormative masculinity serves to stabilize patriarchy in both 'manly states' and underwrites regional security policies." Both regimes, while performing religiosity, are deeply welcoming of neoliberal capitalist interventions. The dissent against this masculinist vision comes in Pakistan from young feminist voices as expressed in the Aurat March, and from poor and working-class men, gay men, and "transgender celebrities" on apps like TikTok, where the masculinity expressed has a different affect from the misogyny and moral policing on other social media sites.[113] "Religious" masculinist performativity, then, is but one element in a set of very similar state practices when it comes to the economy and patriarchy.

[112] Nigam 2006: 315.
[113] Zia 2022.

Thus far, this chapter has tried to demonstrate how the woman's body as a marker of "community honour" is globally intimately intertwined with state practices and claims to religion. What gets reified as "religion" in secular discourse, such as the law, is in fact an effect of the operation of politics.

Postsecularism Debates in the Global North— Read from the South

I will conclude this chapter with a quick discussion of the "postsecularism" debates in Western philosophy as one kind of response to the global crisis of secularism. This response is internal to the Western paradigm and is largely about recognising the resurgence of religion in the affluent societies of the West. These debates are innocent of any sense of how secularism has travelled in other parts of the world: they tend to reassert new universalisms. Many of their arguments are also focused exclusively on secularism as expressing a relationship between the state and an entity unproblematically called religion.

Secularism, understood as the exclusion of religion from the public domain and the separation of religion and state, has been a troubled idea for some decades now. The German philosopher Jürgen Habermas, generally credited with popularising the term postsecularism, wrote in 2008: "A 'post-secular' society must at some point have been in a 'secular' state. The controversial term can therefore only be applied to the affluent societies of Europe or countries such as Canada, Australia and New Zealand, where people's religious ties have steadily or rather quite dramatically lapsed in the post-War period."[114] Such societies now find they have to adapt to the fact that religious communities continue to exist in a context of ongoing secularisation. Postsecularism, then, appears in this debate to be a narrow term reflecting on "religion"— understood to be a self-standing entity referring to faith—and its relationship to the state/public domain. In this vein, Habermas argues that "three overlapping phenomena converge to create the impression

[114] Habermas 2008.

of a worldwide 'resurgence of religion': (a) the missionary expansion (b) a fundamentalist radicalisation and (c) the political instrumentalisation of the potential for violence innate in many of the world religions."[115]

The first is the advance of "the orthodox, or at least conservative, groups within the established religious organizations"; the second, the growth of "fundamentalism," which involves "rigid moral conceptions and literal adherence to the holy scriptures"; and the third is illustrated by "the mullah regime in Iran and Islamic terrorism" which are "merely the most spectacular examples of a political unleashing of the potential for violence innate in religion." Habermas adds: "Often smouldering conflicts that are profane in origin are first ignited once coded in religious terms. This is true of the 'desecularisation' of the Middle East conflict, of the politics of Hindu nationalism and the enduring conflict between India and Pakistan and of the mobilisation of the religious right in the United States before and during the invasion of Iraq."[116]

In light of our discussion on the layers of complexity the term secularism involves, both in its place of origin and elsewhere, Habermas' understanding appears thin. The reference to "the Middle East" for West Asia, normalising the point of view from Europe, is the least problematic aspect. He suggests that conflicts that are profane (secular) in origin are "ignited" once coded in religious terms, as if these are two separate stages in the development of conflict. The purpose of this chapter has been to demonstrate that what is called "religion" is nested in specific historical developments in different parts of the globe, that it is not a self-evident category. This has been established for decades by scholarship both in the North and the South, to some of which we have referred. To show no awareness of this scholarship, and to continue to think of religion as some sort of primeval belief that can "ignite" secular conflicts, is not useful. The three examples Habermas gives—Israel–Palestine (without naming them), Hindu nationalism, and India–

[115] Ibid.
[116] Ibid.

Pakistan—are all better understood in terms of the modern nation-state system, and its violence and ethnic cleansing, rather than in terms of the "resurgence of religion" in secular modernity. The Christian right in the USA, too, is a modern politically right-wing mobilisation, not a return to religious fundamentals. As mentioned earlier, fundamentalism is a misleading term, which Habermas uses too, meaning "literal adherence to the holy scriptures." But none of the expressions of religious or spiritual belief in the political domain are in fact invoking the unquestionable fundamentals of scriptures; rather, the scriptures in almost all such cases are deeply internally contested.

Habermas outlines the debate in the West as one between secularists and multiculturalists, suggesting that each in their own way—the latter arguing for the preservation of cultural identity, the former for the enforcement of shared citizenship—are in fact accepting "the indispensability of including all citizens as equals in civil society." He concludes that the democratic state must engage with "the polyphonic complexity of the diverse public voices," particularly religious traditions, which possess the power "to convincingly articulate moral sensitivities and solidaristic intuitions," and which offer resources for "the generation of meanings and the shaping of identities."[117] However, as we saw in our discussion on multiculturalism earlier in this chapter, there are feminist and Indigenous voices that have challenged both ends of this polarity even in the "affluent countries" Habermas is talking about, making it impossible to sustain this distinction.

Two other key figures in the postsecularism debates are Charles Taylor and William Connolly, who shift the focus from religion to pluralism and offer more complex visions of postsecular societies that give space to religion and faith in the public domain. Taylor proposes to replace the model of "separation of state and religion" with the model of diversity, the focus of which will be "the correct response of the democratic state to diversity."[118] Connolly proposes "a regime of deep, multidimensional pluralism" in which participants from "multiple

[117] Ibid.
[118] Taylor 2011: 36.

minorities" bring into the public realm different aspects of "their own existential creeds and ontopolitical stances"; they then "recoil back relationally on those existential stances," acknowledging without resentment "the legitimate contestability of this creed in the eyes of others." Connolly terms this as "double-entry pluralism," which is deep because "it reaches into the spiritualities and creeds of participants, rather than trying to quarantine them."[119]

While both Taylor and Connolly take the idea of postsecularism in more productive directions than Habermas, what is noticeable among all three is a disinclination to address heterogeneity inside the spaces identified as "non-secular"—diversity, pluralism, and multiple minorities are all assumed to be internally homogeneous. The dimension of power—both in the public domain where these collide, as well as inside these spaces—remains untheorised. Second, the manner in which the public domain has already constructed some practices as spiritual/religious, as opposed to secular, remains unconfronted, such that it appears the only challenge to secularism comes from spirituality. And third, it seems in such perspectives unquestionable that secularism is valuable in itself but can be enriched by an acknowledgement of deep plurality.

All three assumptions seem untenable in light of the unpacking of the idea of secularism in this chapter. Here I recollect Hilal Ahmed's delicate and nuanced reading of the photograph of the Taj Mahal, indicating the density of the interplay between secular and religious publics. And I will conclude with another such reading of a public event in Kolkata, the Durga Puja, by the art historian Tapati Guha-Thakurta.

The Durga Puja of Kolkata has now been included in UNESCO's Intangible Cultural Heritage of Humanity list, partly due to Guha-Thakurta's painstaking chronicling.[120] "Can a festival of a goddess be secular?" asks Guha-Thakurta about this collective public worship

---

[119] Connolly 2011: 651–2.
[120] UNESCO 2021.

which she describes as being simultaneously "Kolkata's biggest public art event."[121] The Durga Puja of Kolkata has over time become, she asserts, "the constitutive ground in the dismantling of boundaries between artistic, religious and secular practices."[122] The depiction of the goddess and her environs in the hundreds of neighbourhood *pandals* of Kolkata involves artistic practices varying from a replication of the Bhurj Khalifa Tower in Dubai and the Sistine Chapel in Italy, to directly political depictions of Durga and her family as people disenfranchised by the NRC and as migrant labour desperately trekking back home after the grotesquely short-notice lockdown that was declared during the Covid pandemic.[123] Guha-Thakurta tracks the shift from the thirty-four years of Left Front rule in West Bengal, during which the state government maintained a distance from all religious events, to the stance taken by the party currently in power (since 2011). The current regime in West Bengal is equally strongly opposed to Hindutva politics, but it has made this festival the platform of its cultural politics, in which "the 'secular' translates into an act of inclusiveness of other communities to present a non-communal, culturally inclusive identity of the Durga Puja."[124] At least two conceptions of the secular can be discerned here—distance from religion and *sarva dharma sama bhava*. In addition, there is the notion of the secular as expressing the values of "social empathy and political protest,"[125] and through the devotional space of the puja, the "secular" and the "religious" become inextricably mutually implicated. At the same time, each can be seen to render the other inadequate—the Durga Puja is inadequately secular because the goddess Durga remains the central protagonist; and the Puja is inadequately religious because of the trespassing of worldly issues into it. Guha-Thakurta's conclusion is that over the long period of its history, the festival has "opened up a domain of social affect and

[121] Guha-Thakurta 2022: 260.
[122] Ibid.
[123] The plight of migrant labour during Covid is discussed in chap. 5.
[124] Guha-Thakurta 2022: 272.
[125] Ibid.: 278.

transaction where the normative, institutional categories of the 'religious' and 'secular' can neither fall comfortably in place nor be set off in opposition to each other."[126]

Although both Ahmed and Guha-Thakurta are theorising specific instances, I suggest that there are sufficient such instances globally which permit a more granular and grounded understanding—beyond the postsecularism debates—that deconstructs the binary of "secular" and "religious."

---

[126] Guha-Thakurta 2022: 289.

2

Hindu Majoritarianism and the
Construction of Religion

THIS IS THE FIRST of two chapters in which I focus on the Hindu
supremacist project in India which has worked within the state–
religion nexus to normalise Hindutva and Brahminism as
Hinduism. Here I analyse the contemporary moment; in the next
chapter I will explore its long-term historical dimensions.

The Hindu Rashtra as a State Project

After the 2014 election victory of the BJP-led National Democratic
Alliance (NDA), the creation of a Hindu Rashtra in India is now an
explicitly state-led project. So we need to think of the situation differently from positions expressed in debates of the 1990s, when the state
project was secularism.[1] In addition, two familiar strategies of coun-
tering Hindutva—along the lines of there being a "true" Hinduism,
and of criticising the Left's disdain for the religiosity of the masses—
are no longer useful, as these arguments miss the point altogether.[2]
Religion or religious beliefs are not what are at stake now, if they ever
were. The term Hindutva is no longer sufficient to describe the ideology
that drives the Indian state. Hindutva—Hinduness as political identity—is indeed the ideology of Hindu nationalism, but the emphasis
has shifted away from the *samrasta* which meant a gradual assimilation

---

[1] Bhargava 1998; Madan 1998; Chatterjee 1998.
[2] Mehta 2020; Yadav 2020.

91

of the "lower" castes and the non-Hindu other. While the project of accommodating the former continues—in tension with another strand of Hindutva that is deeply violent in relation to Dalits, as we will see—with reference to the latter what has emerged now is the naked face of the political project of Hindu supremacism in institutions of the state.

Yvonne Tew uses the term "stealth theocracy" in the context of Malaysia to describe "the fundamental alteration of a constitution's secular character through informal change by judicial and political actors, rather than through formal mechanisms like constitutional amendment or replacement."[3]

While the term "theocracy" is misleading for India because there is no one clergy behind Hindutva—its fountainhead being a non-religious majoritarian political organisation, the Rashtriya Swayamsevak Sangh (RSS)—Tew's argument about the transformation of a democratic polity "by stealth" is instructive.

While the politics of the Hindu Right has been on the ascendant since the 1990s, few scholars of India could have imagined it would be possible to so dramatically accelerate the pace of the RSS's explicit Hindu Rashtra agenda—i.e. the establishment of a Hindu supremacist state—after 2014, when the BJP came to power. The pedal was pressed down even more after May 2019, when the party was returned with an absolute majority of its own, its clout substantially enhanced by the parliamentary seats of its allies.

The moves towards the establishment of a Hindu Rashtra have taken place at three levels: first, institutionally—for instance, within months of the 2019 election victory, by amending the Constitution to abrogate Article 370 on Kashmir and splitting the state into three parts; and by passing the Citizenship Amendment Act 2019; second, "by stealth"— via controlling the media, the courts, and the state governments by money power, political intimidation, and co-optation; and third, by unleashing on the ground,[4] and in social media,[5] people incited

---

[3] Tew 2018: 31.
[4] Ali 2020.
[5] Chaturvedi 2016.

(sometimes trained and sometimes paid) to carry out violence by word and action. For all its claims to be a cultural and educational organisation, the RSS is a political organisation; it is not a religious body; it is non-elected; and it does not represent the vast bulk of those who would define themselves as Hindus. The RSS has never contested elections. Its stated goal is to establish a Hindu nation that will exclude those who are not Hindu from citizenship rights. The project is both exclusionary—of Muslims, Christians, Parsis, and Jews—and assimilationist in claiming as Hindu all those who are not Muslim, Christian, Jewish, or Parsi. The current Indian prime minister and home minister are both proud members of the RSS, several of whose leaders have for long and publicly admired the Italian Fascists and seen Hitler's treatment of the Jews in Germany as a model to follow. The RSS runs a paramilitary force which has informally but publicly worked with the police in several states since the Modi-led regime came to power in 2014.[6] It influences multiple organisations that are encouraged to perform acts of violence against non-Hindus and non-conforming Dalits and women.[7]

Many argue that this moment in India is simply business as usual, that most Indians—Dalits, Adivasis, the poor, and of course Muslims—have lived under an undeclared Emergency ever since Independence. But this is a mistaken analysis—like an orthodox Marxist analysis which sees no difference between the liberal democratic state and the fascist state because both are capitalist. There is a specificity to this moment that we must recognise, arising from a process set in motion in the 1990s.

[6] TNM Staff 2020; Verma 2021.

[7] All this is too well established to expand on here, but see Dhirendra K. Jha (Jha 2021) and Marzia Casolari (Casolari 2000) for a detailed discussion of RSS antecedents and its devotion to fascism; Christophe Jaffrelot (Jaffrelot 2021) for a thorough examination of the latest of "three ages of Indian democracy" as he puts it, that is, the age of Hindu majoritarianism and the key role played by the RSS in this; and Subhash Gatade for a sharp analysis of the first five years of Modi's rule (Gatade 2019). Also see the classic study by Paul R. Brass (Brass 2003) of how RSS and organisations linked to it form "institutionalised riot systems" capable of producing anti-Muslim violence at any point.

Since the 1990s, it appears to have become common knowledge that the RSS has steadily increased its reach over individuals in state institutions, the police, and the bureaucracy. In states where the BJP is in power, the RSS has a controlling influence, if not direct control, over the state government. Gradually, since the BJP first came to power in 2014, and especially since May 2019, an atmosphere of fear has shrouded the minorities, Muslims in particular, through a nexus between state governments, the police, and what the Indian media calls "anti-social elements." RSS members have been appointed as public prosecutors in trials relating to anti-Muslim violence, ensuring that those among the accused who are Hindus are acquitted.[8] Only in the states in which the BJP is in power did the nationwide protests from the beginning of 2020 against the CAA supposedly "turn violent." This is because the police come under the control of state governments, except in Delhi, where the Delhi Police are under the central government. Fact-finding investigations by citizens' groups and journalists, both in Delhi and Uttar Pradesh (the latter under a hardline BJP chief minister) suggest possible police complicity with RSS activists and local "anti-social elements" in incidents of stone-throwing from within anti-CAA demonstrations, and arson on public property during protests.[9] In Delhi, moreover, the violence was exclusively in the seven constituencies (out of seventy) that the BJP won in the state assembly elections of February 2020,[10] and journalists' reports strongly indicate the police's complicity with pre-planned assaults.[11]

A common feature of such violence which apparently just "breaks out" is that it is followed by massive and violent state reprisal against Muslims—in the shape of mass arrests, brutal beatings in police custody, and the denial of bail. In UP, the state government also levied huge amounts as "compensation" on those it accused of the destruction

[8] Khetan 2020.

[9] Vij 2020; Karwan-e-Mohabbat 2020.

[10] The Aam Aadmi Party won that election and is currently running the government in Delhi.

[11] Ellis-Petersen and Rahman 2020.

of state property; the accused were mainly prominent Muslims, but some very poor. Some of them were under preventive house arrest during the time the protests "turned violent."[12] Journalists have reported in detail on this reign of terror that the police unleashed on Muslims in UP.[13]

Although there is a long history of police brutality and what are euphemistically termed "police excesses" in independent India—and not only against Muslims, as one reading list testifies[14]—I suggest that three features constitute specific transformations to the Indian political system by the proponents of a Hindu Rashtra.

First, *there is now a formal dispossession and disowning of the Muslim.* The Sachar Committee Report showed that Muslims show up even lower on most socio-economic indicators than historically marginalised communities among the Scheduled Castes and Scheduled Tribes.[15] Attacks against Muslims have often happened before, also mostly by RSS-linked or influenced groups, but at least formally all communities have been seen and treated as constitutionally equal.

This formal equality for Muslims has been jettisoned. Ali Khan Mahmudabad terms this the shift from marginalising Muslims to "a lethal combination of political, institutional, legal, economic and social exclusion."[16] The direct targeting of Muslim lives and livelihoods has been mainstreamed. Existing laws against "cow slaughter" have been activated and new laws passed which provide cover for police and vigilante attacks on all cattle trading. The threat of lynching and arrests enables an extortion network by RSS-linked groups like the Bajrang Dal, which—as Niranjan Takle found when he did an undercover sting operation in Gujarat—has taken protection money to permit the cattle business.[17]

[12] The Polis Project 2020.
[13] Ellis-Petersen 2020.
[14] EPW Engage 2019.
[15] Sachar 2006.
[16] Mahmudabad 2020.
[17] Takle 2019.

The passing of a law criminalising triple talaq—i.e. the unilateral divorce permissible by husbands under Muslim Personal Law—immediately after the Supreme Court declared the practice invalid in 2019 has worked as another signal by the state and its supporters to Muslims that they are to be disenfranchised in multiple ways. Already, Muslim men are incarcerated vastly disproportionately to their share in the population—as are Dalits and tribals.[18] This law can only increase the disproportion. Men deserting wives is not a religion-specific practice, but only Muslim men who desert their wives can be charged with this crime.

The Supreme Court has played its part, ending the long-standing dispute over the Babri Masjid in 1992 by declaring the demolition of the mosque to have been a criminal act. Despite this, it asked for the site to be handed over to the Hindu petitioners and moreover asked the government to set up a trust for the construction of a Ram Temple.[19] In effect, the verdict by the highest court of the land is an acknowledgement of Hindutva criminality, followed by a judicial enforcement of Hindutva aspiration, and an acceptance of the Hindu supremacist project. The court's justification for what has seemed to many an inexplicable process of reasoning is perhaps laudable, namely the need to arbitrate decisively and end a hitherto unending dispute with major political ramifications. What is of larger consequence for my purposes here is, as outlined above, the end result of that justification. There have been a series of similar accommodations of Hindutva by courts at different levels, orders that protect the BJP;[20] orders stepping delicately back from addressing Hindu patriarchy while coming down hard on Muslim patriarchy;[21] orders penalising dissenters against Hindutva and crony capitalism.[22]

The most important landmark in the formal disenfranchisement

[18] Joy 2019.
[19] India Today Web Desk 2019.
[20] News Desk 2020.
[21] Menon 2019a; Munoth 2017.
[22] PTI 2020a.

of Muslims is, of course, the CAA, which excludes Muslims alone from being able to claim refugee status in India. The state has declared this is a forerunner to a National Register of Citizens (NRC) which will identify "illegal immigrants." The Indian home minister has spelt out a "chronology" from the CAA to a National Population Register (NPR) to the NRC, making it clear that the CAA is intended to protect all non-Muslims from being seen as of illegal status after the NPR and NRC have been conducted.[23] After nationwide protests erupted, Prime Minister Modi claimed that the NRC was not being contemplated.[24] Yet, within three months of that assertion, the government reiterated to the Supreme Court that "preparation of NRC was a necessary exercise for any sovereign country for identification of citizens from non-citizens, and to deport or expel illegal migrants."[25]

What this will inaugurate is the large-scale formal disenfranchisement of Muslims. It will also almost certainly equally affect Dalits, the poor in general, and individuals within other minorities who are unable to produce documents—all such citizens, many of them born in India and with no connection to any other country, are sought to be removed from Indian electoral rolls and deprived of citizenship. It has been pointed out *ad nauseam* that the very possession of documents is a luxury which the majority of Indians do not have—migrant labour, women who upon marriage move to their husbands' villages, the poor who have no means of protecting documents from rodents, floods, fires; trans- and intersex children abandoned by their families; queer people who run away from home to escape violence; sex workers.[26] But not all such "doubtful citizens"—a category introduced by the NPR—will be placed in detention centres. Nor will all of these be Muslims—because as of now there simply isn't the space to accommodate all Muslims and

[23] Krishnankutty 2020.

[24] Varma 2019.

[25] Rautray 2020. For a detailed account of "the contemporary regime of citizenship" as structured around the CAA, and present and past changes in the citizenship law, see Roy 2022.

[26] Special Correspondent 2020.

non-Muslims who fail the NRC test. In effect, the NRC can if properly executed only ensure that the entire country will become an informal detention centre, with vast masses of the population excluded from electoral rolls, living in fear and uncertainty, and at the mercy of extortionists and blackmailers. Many of these undocumented people, made homeless non-citizens by the only country they have known, would simply be collateral damage—because the NRC's target is the Muslim.

Systematically, during the pandemic-related lockdown, extensive arrests, mainly of Muslims, were made of those involved in the peaceful anti-CAA protests. During the protests the entire country was electrified, in part because it was not only Muslims who were protesting.[27] Arrests, or even the removal of protest sites over the initial phase of the protests, were ruled out as likely to cause major embarrassment to the government because of the sheer scale and media visibility of the state oppression of citizens that would have been involved. But once a "public health" claim became possible with Covid for the suppression of dissent, protest sites were violently dismantled by the police and thousands of arrests ensued.[28] In effect, the lockdown served as a political emergency in which democratic rights were suspended. In Delhi in February 2020, as noted above, there was a planned attack against Muslims in the few constituencies won by the BJP.[29] It was Muslims whose lives and property were largely affected,[30] and yet Muslims were also those who were arrested in the largest number.[31] This repression continues unabated on an almost daily basis.

Second, *Hindu Rashtra functions through controlled chaos.*

Unlike the manufacture of organised "communal riots" in the earlier phases, which had beginnings and endings, what has been unleashed

[27] See nrcprotest.in.

[28] Ameen 2020.

[29] A very considerable majority was won by the Aam Aadmi Party, which is currently therefore the party in power in Delhi.

[30] Ellis-Petersen 2020a.

[31] Pal 2020.

since 2014 is a lynch-mob culture which produces a state of continuous turbulence, threat, and terror.[32] Violence can now be sparked anywhere by an activist or two of a Hindutva organisation, drawing in a larger crowd which recognises that it can participate in it with impunity, enjoy the violence, and record it. This new kind of violence targets not entire communities but individuals. And, each time therefore, the authorities maintain that each such particular act was not a casteist or communal incident but simply an aberrant criminal act. Each one is argued as an independent law-and-order issue to be dealt with, or ignored, separately.

The impunity for such actions is such that it psychologically compensates young unemployed subaltern men for their utter lack of power in the system, and for the crashing economy. The lack of work and income is overcome for a short period by the heady rush of stopping a random middle-class man and forcing him to say "Jai Shri Ram"—the salutation demanded from all as obeisance to Hindutva's preferred deity, Lord Ram. In one such case the man happened to be a Hindu doctor,[33] but there have been innumerable horrifying incidents of Muslims being forced to chant Jai Shri Ram, then thrashed, tortured, and sometimes killed. Acts of violence against Dalits too have gone up in number and intensity since 2014.[34] This lynch-mob culture taps into Hindu caste society's deep reserves of belief that violence is justifiable when directed against Dalits and women, and Hindutva's supremacist politics has unleashed it from repressed interiors into the open.

The massacre of Muslims in Delhi in February 2020 and in UP in early January 2020 was of the older, more established kind—organised targeting of Muslim homes, businesses, persons—systematic and planned in advance.[35] While the older model of sudden systematic attacks continues, the maintenance of a constant state of controlled chaos

[32] Tripathy 2019.
[33] Jaleel 2019.
[34] Saaliq and Bose 2018.
[35] Tripathi 2020.

and an atmosphere of intimidation, especially for Muslims, is the default condition now. Though not always directly connected with the RSS, this complete breakdown of norms is a feature made possible by the RSS takeover.

Third, *there is now an unprecedented crackdown on dissent and control of media organisations.* Dissent, even by private individuals on social media, and freedom of expression and critical thinking in universities and other spaces have been so thoroughly subjected to harassment that this amounts to state intimidation of a kind never experienced before. Individuals are mostly targeted through police complaints and court cases by supposedly private individuals, but the fact that police and courts take such complaints seriously is an indication that they enjoy the regime's backing.[36] In an extraordinary move, the government banned two TV channels for forty-eight hours for "being critical of RSS" and for "siding with one community" in their coverage of the Delhi violence of 2020.[37] That is to say, these channels had failed to show one of the two acceptable narratives—namely, either that "both sides are to blame," or that Muslims alone were responsible for the violence. More important, however, was the fact that "being critical of the RSS" was explicitly stated as a reason for the ban. The order was withdrawn after strong protests from sections of the media, but the heavy hand of the RSS on the reins of India-as-Hindu-Rashtra became starkly apparent. The censorship of opinion is completed by a debilitation of the media, which has been intimidated or bought over, so that self-censorship often obviates the need for RSS or government action.[38] A spate of vicious online attacks by Hindu right-wing trolls on anti-establishment stand-up comics, and threats of arrest to such people critical of the current regime, have led to public apologies by many of them.[39] The suicide of a young Hindi film actor was weaponised by this troll army and the BJP into an onslaught against the Bombay

[36] Agrawal 2020.
[37] Kaushik 2020.
[38] Goel and Gettleman 2020; Human Rights Watch 2022.
[39] Express News Service 2020.

film industry, hitherto a space of syncretism from which prominent Muslim figures and strong voices have emerged opposing the Hindu Rashtra.[40]

While the suppression of dissent happened during the Emergency of 1975–7 too, that was a period of less than two years of a declared "Emergency" by the state, so that the abrogation of civil rights was formally made known to all. By contrast, we are now almost a decade into an undeclared war—which has included assassinations—on dissent against the state, sometimes carried out by anybody whose "sentiments are hurt," as well as by armed Hindutva terrorists.[41] While the Emergency produced a polarisation of state versus citizens, the Hindu Rashtra has created a situation of molecular everyday violence against clearly targeted communities. This is, as Christophe Jaffrelot characterises it, an "authoritarian vigilante state."[42]

These three features, inextricably tied to a specific kind of nationalism, are what mark out the Hindu Rashtra from business as usual. Each feature has shown ways for marking out the nationalist from the antinationalist—inflected over the past three years through the pandemic—and each is explicitly geared towards establishing Hindutva's supremacy.

Does the ascent of Hindu Rashtra indicate the will of the people? The BJP did come to power through two successive elections. However, doubt has been cast on the "massive mandate" argument as the Election Commission of India (ECI) appears over several instances to have been protective of the ruling party while being quick to act on opposition party leaders, raising serious questions about its impartiality.[43] In addition, two legal changes in 2017 tilted the financial balance decisively in the BJP's favour. First the limits on corporate donations to parties and candidates, which was earlier 7.5 percent of their profits, has been removed to allow unlimited corporate funding.

[40] Menon 2020.
[41] Yogesh 2018.
[42] Jaffrelot 2021: 349.
[43] IANS 2019.

And second, the BJP has legislated electoral bonds into existence, and these allow anonymous funding to political parties through banking channels. The BJP has, according to one estimate, received about 95 percent of the approximately twenty billion rupees of funds generated through electoral bonds until 2019.[44]

Well-documented doubts have also been raised about the functioning of Electronic Voting Machines (EVMs).[45] None of these uncertainties have been cleared so far: the ECI has either given "vague" replies to the Supreme Court,[46] or petitions regarding these in court are pending.[47] A Right to Information (RTI) application by Venkatesh Nayak revealed that the computer chips used in EVMs are not One Time Programmable, as claimed by the ECI, which means that they can be reprogrammed, but no further action has been taken on this crucial information.[48] There have been allegations of a connection between a company favoured by the Gujarat government under Chief Minister Modi, and one of the companies that manufactures EVM microchips for India.[49]

The BJP's second-term victory has in particular come under question. A series of Right to Information (RTI applications) in 2019 by Manoranjan Roy regarding the number of EVMs produced by the only two companies that have the licence to do so (Bharat Electronics Limited and Electronics Corporation of India Limited), and the number of EVMs received by the Election Commission of India (ECI), revealed major discrepancies—there were 190,000 "missing" or unaccounted for EVMs between those produced and those received by the ECI. Roy filed a Public Interest Litigation in the Bombay High Court but this case has not moved forward since then.[50]

[44] Bhushan 2019.
[45] Agarwal 2019; Menon 2019; Nair 2019; Statement 2019.
[46] Legal Correspondent 2019.
[47] ANI 2019.
[48] Nayak 2019.
[49] JKR Staff 2017.
[50] Ramakrishnan 2019a; Ramakrishnan 2019b.

The questions that therefore remain pending are: Where are these missing EVMs? What are they being used for, and by whom?[51]

Broadly speaking, then, what we are facing is a fascist transformation of the polity through state institutions. The police, the judiciary, the Election Commission, and the media have been made pliant or intimidated instruments in the project. While Hindutva has produced ground-level transformations as well, these are temporary and dependent on the power and reach of the regime. The real transformation that has taken place is at the level of a subversion of institutions. We cannot take for granted any longer that India is the democracy that it was before 2014, and that all elections here continue to reflect the will of the people.

The Majoritarian Politics of Numbers and Religious Conversions

Hindu supremacist politics tries to ensure its relevance by constantly invoking the bogey of minorities becoming the majority through rapid breeding and conversions. An example of the first claim is the statement by a prominent Hindutva activist urging Hindus to give birth to

---

[51] The controversy over whether elections are any longer free and fair is hotly debated even within the camp of opponents of Hindu Rashtra. In the period 2020 to 2022, the BJP has lost some state elections (Kerala, Bengal, Delhi), which is seen as vindicating those who hold that elections still reflect the people's votes. However, in these states other parties were in power and it could be said the reach of the BJP was limited. Other state elections have been won, contrary to every political prediction, with razor-thin margins (Bihar, Goa). Gujarat of course which the BJP has controlled for decades, was a landslide victory. Each of these elections could be explained within the framework of the argument that there are serious anomalies in the election process now, from voting, to counting, to the noting of results on the ECI's website. There are reports, confirmed by the ECI in response to RTIs, of "malfunctioning EVMs" from different states (Agarwal 2022), despite the draconian Rule 49MA of The Conduct of Elections Rules which criminalises "false" reporting of the malfunctioning of Electronic Voting Machines and Voter Verified Paper Audit Trails. There are also reports of the unauthorised movement of EVMs during elections (Pandey 2019; Mirror Now 2022). The concern therefore is also

more children to avoid India becoming an Islamic country.[52] This fear is invoked relentlessly despite recorded evidence that there has been a significant decline in fertility rates across religious groups, with Muslims recording the highest drop.[53] Religious conversions have long been on the agenda of Hindu nationalism because of the perceived danger of "Hindus" losing majority status. Attempts to pass a national anti-conversion law in 1954 and 1979 failed because of stiff opposition in parliament. In 2015, after the BJP came to power at the Centre, the union law ministry circumvented the problem by declaring that since "law and order" is a state subject under the Constitution, state governments can enact such laws. Locating religious conversion as a "law and order" issue presumes a public dimension to conversion and criminalises it pre-emptively—though to convert is fundamentally a private decision affecting only the individual or groups concerned.

Some states enacted such legislation many years back: Odisha (1967), Madhya Pradesh (1968), Arunachal Pradesh (1978), Chhattisgarh (2000 and 2006), Gujarat (2003 and 2006), and Himachal Pradesh (2006). After 2015, many other states did so too: Uttarakhand (2018), Jharkhand (2017), Karnataka (2021), and Haryana (2022). In 2020 Uttar Pradesh passed an ordinance, the Prohibition of Unlawful Conversion Ordinance, which was replaced by an Act in 2021.[54] Karnataka's legislation, titled Protection of Right to Freedom of Religion Act (as many of these are), makes it a cognisable and non-bailable offence to "convert or attempt to convert, either directly or otherwise, any other person from one religion to another by use or practice of force, undue influence, coercion, allurement or by any fraudulent means or by any other means or promise of marriage; nor shall any person abet or conspire such

---

about the complete lack of transparency of the process which the EVMs make possible. We cannot go into the details of this argument here. Suffice it to say that I am among those who believe that concerns about these anomalies remain unaddressed by the government and the courts.

[52] PTI 2022.
[53] *The Hindu* Data 2021.
[54] Rao 2022.

conversion."[55] The Karnataka Act is particularly draconian because any-body can accuse a person who converts of having been converted fraud-ulently, after which the burden of proving that the conversion does not come into the prohibited categories lies upon the accused.

Tamil Nadu in 2002, and Rajasthan in 2006 and 2008, also pas-sed similar legislations but the first was repealed in 2008 in the face of protests, and the Rajasthan bills lapsed because they did not receive the assent of the governor of the state and the president of India—the Congress-led United Progressive Alliance being in power at the Centre.

The laws passed in Himachal Pradesh, UP, and Uttarakhand include conversions relating to marriage—a marriage can be declared void if it was solemnised for the sole purpose of conversion, or alternatively if a conversion was done solely for the purpose of marriage.[56] All these laws criminalise conversions conducted through force, fraud, or in-ducements—but the terms are not defined and therefore open to in-terpretation. The BJP's election manifesto of 2004 refers to "promises of social or economic benefits" as fraud and coercion.

What can religious conversion by coercion possibly mean? It is clear that conversion "by the sword" is not an issue today. And if this had ever been practised in India with any seriousness, Muslims would not be a mere 14.23 percent of the Indian population after centuries of rule by dynasties that practised Islam. After two centuries of British colonial rule, Christians are less than 3 percent of the country's popu-lation.[57] The fears and anxieties around claims of forced conversion to

[55] DNA 2021.

[56] Mathur 2020.

[57] Religious conversions were always complicated by multiple factors that went beyond "religion." One fascinating example is offered by J. Devika in the context of the Christian fisherpeople of Vizhinjam in Kerala: "The people of these villages were converted 'from above'—through the order of the local Hindu Raja who sought the support of the Portuguese in the petty struggles of local Hindu powers at that time [c. 1532]. Francis Xavier entered the scene [about a decade later] at a time when the struggle between these powers to control the lucrative pearl fisheries on the southern coast had heightened . . . The fisherpeople were asked [by their Raja] to obey Xavier like they would obey their Raja. . . ." Devika 2022.

Christianity and Islam that suddenly appear from the 1920s have to be seen in light of the politics of numbers in the emerging nation-state that wanted to claim a Hindu majority. These claims were amplified without evidence by nationalist leaders such as Gandhi and Nehru. Abhinav Chandrachud, in his well-researched book, cites only these two leaders' statements for multiple claims of forced conversion to Islam from the 1920s to Partition.[58] Other scholars have looked more analytically at these anxieties rather than treated them as facts. Gandhi was concerned with losing "untouchables" from the Hindu fold, even terming Christian evangelical work as "anti-national."[59] In the Constituent Assembly, Hindu lobbies portraying Hinduism as a non-proselytising religion pressed for a ban on conversion, fearing that Hinduism would be overtaken by Islam and Christianity. In this matter, Hindu nationalists and Gandhi spoke in unison.[60]

It is certainly likely that some forced conversions did take place during communal violence under colonialism, and one may find some evidence of these in the work of historians of specific regions in various languages. For example, after the Mappilah Rebellion in Kerala in the early 1920s, during which such instances of forced conversion to Islam were claimed, the Arya Samaj is said to have conducted *shuddhikaran* (reconversion ceremonies) as well.[61] Chandrachud also refers to a claim by the Meo community (largely resident in Haryana and Rajasthan) in 1948 that 20,000 of them had been forcibly converted to Hinduism.[62] What is revealing is that such claims of forcible conversion come into being only with the emergence of the politics of the nation-state in the early twentieth century. In the violent outbreaks that marked the run-up to Partition, and during the traumatic transfer of populations, there were certainly forced conversions

[58] Chandrachud 2021: 58–63.

[59] Frykenberg 2003: 7–8.

[60] Viswanathan 2007; Bauman 2008.

[61] Both claims are made routinely with no evidence on Hindutva sites. For example, here: https://aryasamajkerala.org.in/congress-and-gandhi-jis-silence-on-moplah-riots/.

[62] Chandrachud 2021: 60.

to both religions and the Nehru–Liaquat pact was signed in 1950 expressly addressing this; both nation-states were equally anxious about majorities and numbers.

However, violent forced conversions are not the issue in post-Independence India, as is evident from anti-conversion laws that focus on undue influence, allurement, promise of marriage, and other non-coercive routes to conversion. The Niyogi Commission of 1954, set up to look into Christian missionary activities, noted no instances that can be described as coercion. Its report noted "illegitimate methods" used by missionaries on the "ignorant" and "illiterate aboriginals and other backward people," such as

> offering allurements of free education and other facilities to children attending their schools, adding some Christian names to their original Indian names, marriages with Christian girls, money-lending, distributing Christian literature in hospitals, and offering prayers in the wards of indoor patients. Reference was also made to the practice of the Roman Catholic priests or preachers visiting new-born babies to give "*ashish*" (blessings) in the name of Jesus, taking sides in litigation or domestic quarrels.

There were also "claims of abduction of women and children" and "recruitment of labour for plantations in Assam or Andaman as a means of propagating the Christian faith."[63] That missionaries did recruit labour for tea plantations during the colonial period is an established fact.[64] It is likely that such connections still exist, but the Niyogi Commission Report cites "claims" of abduction with no further corroboration or detail. Also, it seems more likely that already converted tribals and other local people may have been induced to work in tea plantations to escape grinding poverty at home, even though conditions of labour in tea plantations are notoriously exploitative until today.[65] But the conditions of work of tea plantation labour were, of course, of no concern to the Niyogi Commission.

[63] Niyogi Committee Report 1956: 3.
[64] Chatterjee 1986.
[65] Sharma 2018.

A study of the Niyogi Report by Chad M. Bauman notes that many of the most anti-Christian testimonies recorded by it were provided by upper-caste Hindus; none of the testimonies, with one or two rare exceptions, were subjected to cross-examination; and "whereas most of the Christian claims of harassment were dismissed outright by the Committee as spurious and baseless, the Hindu testimonies were largely accepted at face value by the Committee."[66] Indeed the following statement in the Niyogi Report indicates that most witnesses were not Christians complaining of being fraudulently converted but non-Christians expressing suspicions: "There was a general tendency to suspect some ulterior political or extra-religious motive, in the influx of foreign money for evangelistic work in its varied forms."[67] The Report concluded that large-scale Christian evangelism intended to "take advantage of the freedom accorded by the Constitution of India to the propagation of religion, and to create a Christian party in the Indian democracy on the lines of the Muslim League ultimately to make out a claim for a separate State, or at least to create 'militant minority'."[68] Here, finally, the fear of the Hindu majority nation-state is revealed. Numbers are central to the fear.

The question is, why is conversion due to promises of social or economic benefits fraudulent? If Dalits or tribals convert to Christianity, Buddhism, or Islam in the hope of, and lured by, economic benefits such as jobs, schools, health facilities; and social benefits such as dignity and self-respect, how is that fraudulent? After all, people pray for material benefits even from the gods of their ancestors. The unquestioned foundation of the entire discussion are two assumptions: first, that converting from one religion to another is essentially wrong, an act requiring justification; and second, that the state can legitimately override such a decision taken by individuals on the presumption that it was not taken freely.

The public delegitimising of religious conversion uses the justifica-

---

[66] Bauman 2008: 15.
[67] Niyogi Committee Report 1956: 3.
[68] Ibid.: 60.

tion of the abstract citizen presumed by secularism, a supposedly autonomous individual with a private religious identity whom the state protects (even against herself) with such laws. The Niyogi Committee Report explicitly cites the secularism of the Indian state while asserting that "the State will not allow its citizens to do whatever they please in the name and under the guise of religion. Article 25 itself specifies the limits within which religious freedom can be exercised."[69] The implication is that the religion into which one is born is natural and unquestionable, and the state can demand justifications from the citizen for choosing to exit it.

But of course the real reason for the Hindu Right's obsession with conversion has nothing to do with religious belief. The creation of a birth-based political majority is crucial for the project of Hindutva and for its definition of Indianness. If "others" turn into the majority, the easy coinciding of Hindutva and Nation falls apart.

Saumya Uma and Niti Saxena argue, in the context of the UP Anti Conversion Ordinance of 2020, that the law passed to control interreligious marriage (which Hindutva politics calls "love jihad" conducted by Muslim men) gives the government the power to scrutinise every religious conversion undertaken for marriage, even if with the informed consent of the individuals in question. Thus, another layer of control is added to the already existing powers of the community and family over marriages that are self-chosen, especially by women, and which do not observe the limits set on caste and religious identity. Uma and Saxena argue that if the goal is to prevent non-voluntary conversion upon

---

[69] Ibid.: 134. The Niyogi Committee Report is fascinating for the way in which it conflates (a) US and British imperialism with Christian evangelical viewpoints, and (b) all of the latter, despite the internal differences between them evident in the Report itself. The Report also draws in every belief and utterance of Christian organisations based in the USA and UK, including their anti-communism, to indicate hostility towards newly independent nation-states: "the aim of accelerating the process of proselytization is the following . . . to resist the progress of national unity in the colonial countries after their independence. That can be gathered, as pointed out in the *New Statesman and Nation*, dated November 26th, 1955, from the 'rival' Russian policy of strengthening the nationalism of these countries." Ibid.: 59.

marriage, procedures under the Special Marriage Act, 1954, should be streamlined, allowing for interreligious marriages without religious conversion.[70] The reason they say this is because in fact the Special Marriage Act is severely circumscribed in practice by local authorities who often insist that a public notice be posted, parents be informed, and so on.[71] Uma and Saxena are thus highlighting the fact that the agency of the converting person would be better protected by ensuring the proper execution of the Special Marriage Act rather than through anti-conversion laws. The subversion of the former as well as anti-conversion laws in fact serve the same purpose—that of constraining self-chosen marriages that breach rules of caste and religious community endogamy.

The point is that majorities in a democracy cannot be birth-based but should be seen to emerge contingently around different issues. A permanent birth-based majority is the very antithesis of democracy, for it is based on two problematic assumptions—that a small group claiming to represent that majority can permanently direct public policy, and that the birth-based group is homogeneous in its interests. A majoritarian politics is entirely directed towards shoring up both these assumptions and attempting to silence any questioning of them.

An insightful analysis regarding the importance of numbers in modern democracy is offered by Humeira Iqtidar in a deeply engaged comparative study of the thought of the Hindutva ideologue V. D. Savarkar and his contemporary Abul A'la Maududi, one of the most influential "Islamic and Islamist thinkers" of the twentieth century. Having initially identified as an Indian nationalist, by the late 1920s Maududi began to see the anti-colonial struggle as distinct from nationalism. Having understood the relationship of European nationalism to a majority/minority framework, he became deeply critical of nationalism, being anxious over Muslims becoming a permanent minority in an independent Hindu-majority Indian democracy. A more fundamental objection Maududi had to nationalism was that he saw Islam and nationalism as mutually contradictory, because Islam deals with "man as

[70] Uma and Saxena 2021.
[71] Ahsan 2021.

man"—i.e. all of humanity is invited to join Islam on the basis of justice and equality and there can be no distinction on the basis of race or nation. Nationalism, on the other hand, tends towards imperialism because those who are not members of the nation in a state cannot be considered equals. Iqtidar says that Maududi distinguishes between two types of nationalities: "political nationality," under which "different nations live within a political entity, participate in it, and continue their differences, debates, and contestations with each other"; and "cultural nationality," where there is "homogeneity of religious identity, thought, and sentiments; kinship and marriage relations; and habits and practices." He did not think that, given the differences among Hindus and Muslims in India, the situation was right for cultural nationality, although political nationality could work. Maududi carved out a space between on the one hand nationalist Muslims who supported the Congress as Indian nationalists, and on the other Muslim nationalists who supported the Muslim League. In Maududi's view, says Iqtidar, the only point in making a separate nation was to set up an Islamic state, "one where Allah's sovereignty over law-making would be recognized explicitly and no laws would be made in contravention to the framework of Islamic justice." A secular Muslim nation-state was therefore not one Maududi thought had any meaning, but he moved to Pakistan because he thought the possibilities of the kind of Islamic state he had in mind were greater there, given the larger percentage of Muslims in the population.[72]

Iqtidar compares the views of Savarkar and Maududi on religion and nation and points out the key difference: Savarkar's enthusiastic acceptance of a modern nation-state based on Hindutva, as opposed to Maududi's distrust of nationalism and his belief in the ideal of an Islamic state open to all humans and based on the principles of Islamic justice—not a nation-state in which Muslims would be a permanent minority, nor a Muslim-majority nation-state which was secular. I see also an important similarity in their thinking: both Savarkar and Maududi kept the meaning of Hindutva and Islam as wide as

[72] Iqtidar 2021: 122–8.

possible, with one caveat each. For the former, Hindutva included all who would accept India as their sacred land, and for the latter Islam included all of humanity who accepted Allah's sovereignty. Iqtidar points out the other significant similarity relevant for our argument above: "Both Savarkar and Maududi are responding to, and taking for granted, a structural imperative within democratic politics: the importance of constituting a majority."[73]

In India as a representative democracy, therefore, religious conversion matters not to believers in the community being exited, but to Hindutva politics that sees such exits from "their" community into a rival community as an act of secession reducing the claimed Hindu majority.

"Reconversion" and "Inter-denominational" Conversion

Hindutva claims that Hinduism is a non-proselytising religion and so needs to protect itself from other, marauding, religions. But, at the same time, the RSS and Vishva Hindu Parishad (VHP) conduct conversions to Hinduism of Muslims and Christians, especially focusing on Adivasis and Dalits. Such conversions are called "reconversions" (*ghar wapsi*, or homecoming) because the claim is that everyone in "India" was "Hindu" before waves of conversions by Christians and Muslims. This claim underlies the implied exemption of conversion to Buddhism under these laws, although conversion to Buddhism, according to Rakshit Sonawane, has "continued intermittently on a smaller scale in several states, involving SCs, STs and a section of the erstwhile Shudras (modern-day OBCs)."[74] The inspiration, of course, is B. R. Ambedkar, who converted to Buddhism in 1956 in a mass conversion ceremony alongside thousands of Dalits, asserting that he would not die a Hindu. The Hindutva project of claiming all non-Muslim, Christian, and Parsi communities as "Hindu" has meant an ambivalent attitude to conversions

---

[73] Ibid.: 129.
[74] Sonawane 2022.

to Buddhism. Some state laws (in Rajasthan and Arunachal Pradesh, for instance) seem to exempt "reconversions" to "native" or "original" faiths from their prohibitions, while in the Gujarat law of 2003 an exemption was proposed in 2006 for "inter-denomination" conversions within the same religion, with Buddhism and Jainism being defined as denominations of Hinduism. However, the Buddhist and Jain communities objected strongly to being subsumed as denominations of the Hindu religion and the state government withdrew the amendment.[75] Interestingly, when Ambedkar converted, Savarkar refused to accept Ambedkar's act as a conversion, describing Buddhism as a "Non-Vedic sect within the Hindu fold."[76]

The anti-conversion Ordinance of UP (2020), now a law, was denounced by some Buddhist organisations as an attempt to stop Dalits from converting to Buddhism. It was promulgated soon after the rape and murder of a young Dalit woman in Hathras in UP, in reaction against which 300 Dalits converted to Buddhism.[77] However, a newspaper report on 145 cases booked within nine months of its promulgation showed that no one was arrested for the attempt to convert to Buddhism, and the overwhelming majority arrested were Muslims.[78]

Harish Wankhede argues that within the Hindutva discourse "Buddhism has been appropriated as an integral part of greater 'Indic Civilization'," and therefore the Buddhist conversion movement is not considered a threat. Further, he says Hindutva forces assertively appropriate "crucial Dalit-Bahujan icons and underplay the fierce ideological antagonism that the early Dalit movement had against the Hindu social order."[79]

This hitherto accommodative stance towards Buddhism was, however, not in evidence after a mass conversion to Buddhism organised

[75] Law Library 2018.
[76] Sukhdeve 2020.
[77] Venugopal 2020.
[78] Rashid 2021; Taskin 2021.
[79] Wankhede 2022.

by the Buddhist Society of India in October 2022, in which Rajendra Pal Gautam, a Dalit minister of the Aam Aadmi Party (AAP), a Buddhist himself, participated. Along with others he recited the twenty-two vows given by Ambedkar on the day of his own conversion, formally giving up worship of Hindu deities. The BJP lodged police complaints against both Gautam and the AAP chief minister of Delhi, Arvind Kejriwal, for hurting Hindu sentiments and insulting Hinduism. Gautam apologised and resigned as minister.[80] Some Buddhist organisations wrote to the President of India criticising Gautam and claiming Buddhism did not have an antagonistic relationship to Hinduism.[81] Conversely, many commentators in the media, some of them Buddhist, defended the event and the vows.

This event and its fallout indicates that Buddhism will only be accepted by Hindutva on condition that Buddhism itself accepts a "denominational" status within Hinduism. This project is part of a larger long-standing one—that of producing "Hindus" as a homogeneous majority comprising all non-Muslims, Christians, and Parsis. This project has largely failed to achieve its objective on the ground, though it has the full backing of the law and the state.

What this account of Hindutva on the ascendant in India seeks to establish is that the manner in which what is called religion is deployed, made visible and naturalised needs deconstruction.

Let us now consider three aspects of the state–religion relationship in India, namely the Essential Religious Practice test; religious institutions as income-generating entities; and religious institutions/deities as juristic personalities.

Essential Religious Practice

Since the 1950s Indian courts have held that only the practices "essential" to a religion will be protected under the religious freedoms guaranteed by the Constitution. Thus, these courts have routinely used the

---

[80] Harad 2022.
[81] Bhattacharya 2022.

Essential Religious Practice (ERP) test to decide faith-based disputes. The Supreme Court has held that the essential part of a religion refers to the "core beliefs upon which a religion is founded" without which the "nature of the religion will be changed."[82] Whether a particular practice—such as the hijab—is compulsory for the practice of that faith thus becomes central to the decision. For example, in the Karnataka High Court decision on the hijab, wearing the hijab was deemed not to be an essential religious practice, and therefore students could be asked not to wear the hijab wherever a uniform was mandated.

Umang Poddar, tracing the emergence of the ERP test, noted that it was initially devised by the courts to distinguish between what is secular and what is religious in the religious domain, as Article 25(2)(a) gives the government power to regulate or restrict "secular activities which may be associated with religious practice." The very idea that there can be secular practices within the field demarcated as religion, and that the state can identify these, should tell us something about the way in which the discourse of secularism continuously produces "religion."

In 1954, when the Supreme Court first used the term "essential part of a religion," it was to separate an "essentially religious" activity from a secular activity in a case that involved the government's control over temples. Here the court gave the power to the religious denomination to decide what would constitute an essential practice. But gradually the ERP test expanded into the court itself determining the practices "essential to a religion." In order to arrive at this the courts started looking at texts and the practices themselves to determine if a religious practice was "essential." As Gautam Bhatia puts it, "essential" has gone from qualifying the nature of the practice, i.e. whether it is religious or secular, to qualifying its importance within the religion, i.e. from whether something is essentially religious to whether it is essential to the religion. This is a drastic shift which makes India's courts arbiters on theological matters.

[82] Poddar 2022.

In 1959 the sacrifice of cows for Bakr-Eid was determined not to be essential for the practice of Islam, and laws banning cow slaughter were upheld. Since the question had arisen in the context of conflict with the Hindu practice of worshipping the cow, logic would suggest that worshipping the cow should also have been put to the ERP test. Is worship of the cow an essential practice within Hinduism? This question has never been considered by the courts.

Another notable instance dates to 1994: while deciding on the acquisition of property in and around the site of the Babri Masjid, the Supreme Court said that a mosque is not an essential part of Islam and prayers could be offered anywhere, even in the open. But this could be said of Hindu prayers as well, which can happen in homes or halls or spaces that are not temples.

Some other instances: in 1983 a court ruled that the performance of the Tandava dance in public was not essential to the Ananda Margi sect of Hinduism; in 2018 a court decreed that barring entry to women at the Sabarimala Temple was not essential to Hinduism or to the worship of Ayyappa, the deity at Sabarimala. A dissenting judgment held—as discussed in detail in the previous chapter—that Ayyappa worship constituted a distinct denomination and that the restriction placed on women of a particular age group was an essential part of that sect. A review of the Sabarimala verdict from 2018 is pending before the Supreme Court. Given the length of time many difficult cases have remained in limbo before the Supreme Court, the ERP test will, at some indeterminate point in the future, be reopened.

The ERP test has come under criticism from legal scholars and judges themselves, for the reason that it makes secular courts enter areas of theological dispute; that the test is arbitrary in its application and that it is not based on the Constitution.[83] To this list of objections the law scholar Gautam Bhatia adds that the ERP test negates individual agency in refusing to recognise religious freedom and choice within a religion, and thereby legitimises religious compulsion. Bhatia holds that better tests to apply would be arguments about freedom of speech

[83] Venkatramanan 2022.

and the right to privacy and freedom of conscience, which would respect individual agency better.[84]

It is instructive here to revisit Supreme Court Justice Sudhanshu Dhulia's judgment in the Karnataka hijab case (discussed in the last chapter). Setting aside the Karnataka High Court's ban on the hijab, Justice Dhulia rejected the Essential Religious Practices test as the basis for his decision in this particular case. He held that what is at stake is an individual's freedom—to wear the hijab—against the state's restriction on her freedom. Justice Dhulia held that the ERP is inapplicable here because there are in every religion different views on what religious doctrine truly means. His judgment thereby admits the legitimacy of dissent both to state law as well as to the dominant voice in religious communities. Bhatia points to the importance of this argument on account of the fact that the ERP doctrine erases the very possibility of religious dissent and religious pluralism. "It requires the Court to make a determination that a particular doctrine is 'essential' to a religion or not, and in doing so—inevitably—the Court relies upon the dominant viewpoints within the religion (by looking at religious books, the opinions of 'authorities', and so on)."[85] Justice Dhulia's judgment foregrounds both the freedom to interpret religion and the dignity of the individual, which contrasts with the "discipline" upheld by Justice Gupta's judgment upholding the hijab ban. It can only be hoped that Justice Dhulia's rejection of the ERP in this case will lead to a more fundamental rethinking on the legitimacy of the ERP test itself.

Religious Institutions as Income-generating Entities

The other way in which state and religion are intertwined is through the Indian state's administrative control of major temples through temple trusts, and over mosques through the Central Waqf Council, established by the Central government, which co-ordinates Waqf boards

[84] Bhatia 2022a.
[85] Bhatia 2022b.

set up by state governments. In 2021 it was reported that the BJP government in UP planned to bring in an additional new law to regulate temples, mosques, and churches, and to keep a tab on donations to these.[86] On the other hand, in 2022 the BJP chief minister of Karnataka announced a planned bill to free Hindu temples from government control. Both decisions reveal the financial aspects of religious institutions, with some sort of internal debate within Hindutva between more and less government control over such revenues. The most explicit political economy-based argument for freedom of Hindu temples from government constraints is that market structures yield the most efficient outcomes, and "temple-based institutions can create pseudo-market structures." Under the current dispensation, "ossified government structures" managed by "overburdened bureaucrats" are a disincentive for temple management which could otherwise exercise "the freedom for creative use of funds that could benefit Hindu society at large."[87]

Abhinav Chandrachud has tracked the history of state control over religious institutions in India from the colonial period when the East India Company took over the administration of religious institutions, just as earlier rulers had done. Under pressure from Christian missionaries, who objected to the government's connections with "heathen" religions, the British government handed over the management of religious institutions to Indian trustees. However, when Indian legislatures came to power in the twentieth century, they restored the state control of Hindu temples. In 1926 the Madras legislature enacted a Hindu Religious Endowments Act that sought to reintroduce state control over temples, and this law survived till soon after Independence.[88] A reviewer of Chandrachud's book, Suhrith Parthasarathy, suggests interestingly that as the colonial government ceded control over temples, dominant communities within Hinduism began to appropriate religious foundations and trusts, and that it was in order to circumvent this that state control was sought to be restored.[89] This

---

[86] Srivastava 2021.
[87] Shastry and Ananthkumar 2022.
[88] Chandrachud 2020: 22–3.
[89] Parthasarathy 2020.

introduces a dimension that goes beyond the secularism/religion binary, of the state having to arbitrate between rival claims to assets of a religious community.

Chandrachud implies that colonial secularism was in some sense "hard"—involving the strict separation of state and religion—born out of "Christian evangelical revulsion towards Indian religions," and therefore this kind of secularism was not practised by the colonial state at home. But this hardness is also by implication purer, for Chandrachud then characterises the post-Independence Indian state as adopting "soft" secularism, introducing God in oaths to be taken by public officials, "entangling" itself in the administration of Hindu temples to prevent corruption. The Indian state "abandoned" Queen Victoria's proclamation asking government to stay aloof from religion,[90] and the Establishment clause—akin to the one in the first amendment to the US Constitution—was dropped during discussions on the Indian Constitution, although a formal state religion was not established either.[91] In his opinion, these moves led to the "disintegration" of the secular state in India long before the rise of the Hindu Right.[92]

However, the rich and fascinating detail with which Chandrachud invests his study of several specific issues—the evolution and practice of laws on cow slaughter, religious conversions, separate electorates for Muslims, the administration of Hindu temples, and the taking of oath by public officials—in a sense undercuts the hard/soft argument about secularism with which he attempts to bind his material. If a colonial state is more "properly" secular in the colony than in its democracy at home, then evidently the term secularism itself needs to be interrogated. Chandrachud's book is in fact a fine illustration of the argument I am attempting to make here—that the term "secularism" acts as a misdirection, structuring the field in such a way that both secularism and religion become reified, making some objects hypervisible while rendering others invisible.

[90] Chandrachud 2020: 15.
[91] Ibid.: 23.
[92] Ibid.: 15.

Religious Institutions/Deities as Juristic Personalities

The third important aspect of the state–religion relationship we will discuss here is that Waqf boards and Hindu deities are "juristic persons" that can acquire, hold, and dispose of property. While Waqf boards, as we saw above, are state-instituted groups of individuals with clearly explicated norms of functioning, decision-making, and accountability who function as such in the legal domain, Hindu deities as juristic persons require humans to act on their behalf. These humans are self-appointed, or appointed by organisations with no public accountability. The human is designated legally as the "Next Friend" and in some cases an additional argument is made—such as that the deity is a minor, as was made for instance in the Ayodhya case where the idol is Ram Lalla, or Rama as a baby.

How the "Next Friend" status is appropriated is a political game worth understanding, especially when no court seems to question claimants to this status.[93] In the Ayodhya case, three individuals with close links directly either to the RSS or to the VHP—the two often work in tandem—took on this role one after the other. In 1989 Deoki Nandan Agarwal (VHP vice president), after retiring as an Allahabad High Court judge, and having collected data, including revenue records, claiming to prove that the land belonged to Ram Lalla, filed a writ petition at the Allahabad High Court's Lucknow bench seeking his own appointment as Ram Lalla's *sakha* (friend); Agarwal acted as Ram Lalla's "Next Friend" throughout his life. After his death in 2002 T. P. Verma, a retired history professor at Banaras Hindu University, got himself appointed the next *sakha*. In 2008 Verma applied for retirement in court, citing ill health and age. Triloki Nath Pandey (organisational secretary of the VHP) then took charge as the Ram *sakha* in early 2010.[94] Thus, this position of "Next Friend" has been appropriated by the RSS/VHP, and no court has challenged the claim.

---

[93] De 2010; Menon 2010.
[94] Srivastava 2010.

With this we enter a domain in which it becomes clear that courts in India, from the lower courts to the Supreme Court, have gone beyond delineating religion from non-religion and have instead become participants in the process of establishing a Hindutva agenda. The Ayodhya judgments after the demolition of the Babri Masjid, both of the Allahabad High Court (2010) and the Supreme Court (2019), even while recognising the illegality of the demolition and of the insertion of idols at the mosque while it stood, handed over the site for the construction of a Hindu temple. This has led to an increase in Hindutva's claims to other mosques and monuments that, by Hindutva assertion, stand on the sites of temples; and, ignoring the 1991 Act, courts continue to give space to these claims.[95]

Rahul Govind has outlined the emergence of the idea of the Hindu deity as a juristic person and the role it has played in the Ayodhya judgment. The idea is a result of colonial jurisprudence and has no basis in traditional Hindu law. Govind shows that it emerged in the context of disputes over the right to the immoveable and moveable property of the temple, which included offerings and gifts to the temple/deity. In the traditional (pre-colonial) Hindu Mimamsa conception, Hindu deities could not hold property, and *shebait*s (temple managers) had a proprietary right over the temple lands and properties. In the colonial period, particularly during the nineteenth century, many legal disputes arose regarding the *shebait*'s right to alienate/rent the properties of the temple. Colonial Hindu jurisprudence evolved the idea of the juristic person of the deity in an attempt to regulate the properties of the temple and prevent mismanagement of temple properties by *shebait*s. This also enabled the worshipping Hindu community to lay claim on managing the properties of temples, which became subject to a legal regulatory framework.

In pre-colonial traditional Hindu jurisprudence a public or a worshipping community had no rights to the temple, whose proprietary

---

[95] Places of Worship (Special Provisions) Act, 1991, protects the status of places of worship as they were on 15 August 1947, thus prohibiting any further claims of one community to another's place of worship citing ancient history. This Act is currently under challenge in the Supreme Court.

rights rested with *shebait*s and priests who were clearly demarcated by caste—they could only be Brahmins. Thus, when the Hindu scriptures are cited in claims over mosques—in order to prove that the properties of the temple are perpetual and do not suffer from adverse possession and limitation—this refers, as Govind points out, to the proprietary rights of the *shebait* and/or Brahmin priests, not to a broader community of worshippers. Nor does the Hindu scriptural literature show any reference to a "Next Friend" who can represent the Hindu deity.

All of this, Govind points out, was affirmed in the 2019 Supreme Court judgment on Ayodhya.[96] The judgment said: "The recognition of juristic personality was devised by the courts to give legal effect to the Hindu practice of dedicating property for a religious or 'pious' purposes. . . . By stating that the artificial person created is in fact the owner of the dedicated properties, the court guarded against maladministration by the *shebait*."[97] Further, the court affirmed the illegality of both the placing of idols under the central domes of the Babri Masjid in 1949, as well as its "desecration" in 1992.[98]

Regardless, the Supreme Court recognised the juristic personality of Ram Lalla, even though there existed no evidence of an original deed of endowment—which by the court's own understanding was required. The verdict awarded the title to the deity, Shri Ram Virajman. The complete doing away by the Supreme Court of the requirement of an original title deed/endowment in recognition of the juristic personality of Lord Rama has become the basis, argues Govind, for the reiteration of such claims in various other places, including Kashi, Mathura, and the Qutub Minar complex: "It is ironic that juristic personality which was a judicial device evolved to protect temple property from the internal mismanagement of the *shebait* and others has now been turned into a mode for appropriating the religious places of worship of other communities, which have an undisputed legal standing."[99]

---

[96] *M Siddiq v. Suresh Das* 2019.
[97] Ibid.: 161–2.
[98] Ibid.: 755.
[99] Govind 2022.

Global Hindutva

Hindutva is now a global phenomenon, and one of the key projects of Hindutva in the global North is to present Hindutva as coterminous with Hinduism—as a belief protected by the multicultural norms of these countries. This enables Hindutva organisations abroad, as within India, to claim that any critique of Brahminism, caste discrimination, or patriarchy within communities identifying as Hindu is an expression of "Hinduphobia." These Brahminical organisations and related individual voices claim co-victimhood with anti-semitism.[100] Their resonance with the Zionist strategy of conflating anti-Zionism with anti-semitism is evident, even though, ironically, the political ideology they support in India, as mentioned earlier, draws explicit inspiration from Nazism.

Caste hierarchy and caste violence is foundational to Hinduism.[101] Caste discrimination and harassment are equally widespread among Hindus in the USA, as has been meticulously documented by Equality Labs' Thenmozhi Soundararajan.[102] As expected, this report has been received with outrage by the Hindu American Foundation. Attempts to include discussions of caste discrimination and patriarchy within Hinduism in textbooks in the state of California represent an ongoing battle for at least a decade, with Hindutva organisations claiming that such discussions lead to prejudice against Hindus. Fairly recently, these organisations have succeeded in getting some textbooks removed, alongside some references to untouchability which they claim are derogatory to Hinduism.[103]

The argument made by Hindutva activists in the US is that, as South Asians, Hindus "share in the burden of being brown in America. We also stand out for our 'foreign' languages, foods, cultures, and religious traditions."[104] Their argument is that to bring up internal oppression based on caste and gender, or to criticise Hindutva for being anti-

---

[100] Banerjee 2021.
[101] As we shall see at greater length in chap. 3.
[102] Soundararajan 2020.
[103] Thaker 2018.
[104] Shukla 2018.

Muslim and anti-minority in India, further stigmatises an already stigmatised singular community of Hindus in the USA. These claims
by Hindutva organisations in the global North to respect and protection[105]—on the grounds of being a stigmatised minority in the
North—are made even as they financially and politically support a
regime in India that explicitly stands for at best a degradation in status
and at worst the complete elimination of minorities. It has been noted that the term "decolonisation" is widely in use within right-wing
Hindu spaces "to defend state-sanctioned discrimination against
minorities and mute discussion of atrocities, all while claiming a position of vulnerability."[106] This statement refers to US-based Hindu nationalist groups, but indeed "decolonialising" and "decolonial" is used
to buttress the Hindu supremacist project in India too—to project it
as anti-colonial and therefore progressive. Dheepa Sundaram argues
that Hindu nationalist groups in the US "capitalize on anti-racist discursive models, decolonial language, as well as the liberatory structures of Black and Indigenous futurisms to characterize Hindutva
ideology as a modern, anticolonial resistance movement." But the
actual politics of these groups, says Sundaram, "undermine anti-racist
solidarity and decolonial efforts in the US and transnational contexts"
and in effect promote a neocolonial politics.[107]

Of course, there are also democratic organisations and voices of
South Asians in North America and Europe that are opposed to Hindutva, some claiming Hinduism, others emerging from broader Left
and queer feminist traditions.[108] One of the organisations critical of
Hindutva while claiming Hinduism is Hindus for Human Rights, whose
mission statement says: "We advocate for pluralism, civil and human
rights in South Asia and North America, rooted in the values of our

---

[105] Including in Australia and Canada, for example; see Grewal 2022 and Wyeth
2022.

[106] Sundaram 2022.

[107] Ibid.

[108] For a few of their names, largely located in the USA, see Priyadarshini 2020
and Statement of Support 2021.

faith: shanti (peace), nyaya (justice) and satya (truth). We provide a Hindu voice of resistance to caste, Hindutva (Hindu nationalism), racism, and all forms of bigotry and oppression."[109]

What this chapter has tried to establish through a study of the Hindu supremacist project in India and elsewhere is further illustration of the argument in this book about the co-constitution of state and religion. We have seen in this chapter that the state in many instances is constituted by religion just as much as religion is constituted by the state. I have tried to show, moreover, that the construction of religion will always be such as to advantage the dominant voices within a community, and under majoritarian conditions to advantage the majority community.[110]

[109] Hindus for Human Rights, no date.

[110] For a detailed and analytical study of the transformation of India in less than ten years under the Hindu supremacist project led by Narendra Modi, see the incisive and insightful book by Christophe Jaffrelot, *Modi's India: Hindu Nationalism and the Rise of Ethnic Democracy* (Jaffrelot 2021).

3

The Failed Project of
Creating Hindus

IN THIS SECOND OF two chapters focusing on the Hindu supremacist project in India, I explore the attempt going back millennia
to construct a "Hindu" community. The old project has had to
be resumed and reconfigured in the modern context of nations and
nationalism precisely because it has failed to achieve its objective on
the ground even in the modern era, despite the backing of law and
the state. The two chapters preceding this have addressed two objects
made hypervisible by the discourse of secularism—religion and wom-
en. In this chapter we will confront a category that has been rendered
invisible by this discourse—that is, caste.

Savarkar's Imagined Hindu Nation

The two interrelated ambitions of Hindu nationalist politics since the
late nineteenth century have been to claim a homogeneous Hindu
majority going back to time immemorial, and to produce the Muslim
as the perpetual outsider and enemy Other. Both these ambitions
are manifest in V. D. Savarkar's *Essentials of Hindutva* (1923).[1] As he
puts it there, "Moreover everything we have in common with our

---

[1] To address one strand in Savarkar's thought relevant to the argument in this
book, the discussion here is based mainly on Savarkar's key text defining Hindutva.
Savarkar's larger body of work is well discussed in Vinayak Chaturvedi, *Hindutva
and Violence: V. D. Savarkar and the Politics of History* (Chaturvedi 2022).

126

enemies, weakens our power of opposing them. The foe that has nothing in common with us is the foe likely to be most bitterly resisted by us . . ." Savarkar dwells on the "necessity of creating a bitter sense of wrong invoking a power of undying resistance . . ." The resistance he passionately advocates, however, is not to the British colonial state ruling India at the time, but, first of all to Buddhism, through whose "opiates of Universalism and non-violence" India lost the faculty of resisting invaders. Worse, foreign invaders favourably inclined to Buddhism would "find secret sympathisers among Indian Buddhists all over India . . ."[2]

"Dark hints abound in our ancient records," says Savarkar, to show that "some foreign Buddhistic powers had actually invaded India with an express national and religious aim in view." He then cites from the *Bhavishya Purana* and provides references to "Buddhistic forces" from Japdesh, China, and Shymadesh (*sic*—his term for Siam, modern Thailand) led by "Nyanapati, the king of the Huns" who fought a war on the "Aryadeshajas." These invaders were heavily defeated and forced to renounce all "ulterior national aims against India."[3] He adds: "Buddhists as individuals had nothing to fear from India, the land of toleration, but they should give up all dreams of endangering the national life of India and her independence."[4] None of these phrases appear to be directly from the available translation of the *Bhavishya Purana* but are paraphrased by Savarkar; and the last sentence is entirely his addition.[5] The available versions of the *Bhavishya Purana* are based on a printed text published during the British colonial era. This Purana is widely acknowledged by scholars to be a composite text put together over a period extending from 500 CE to modern times. The Puranas as a whole are understood to be a living and developing tradition, not written texts fixed in a distant past.[6] The earliest parts

[2] Savarkar 1923: 12.
[3] Ibid.
[4] Ibid.: 13.
[5] *Bhavishya Purana*: no date.
[6] Rocher 1986: 53.

of the Bhavishya Purana may have been composed between 500 and 1200 CE but there is no lower limit to the later parts of it.[7] Therefore, what are claimed as the *Bhavishya Purana*'s predictions—about, for example, the Prophet Muhammad and Jesus Christ; or of historical accounts such as the Huna invasion which Savarkar refers to as "Buddhistic"—were in fact produced somewhere between the thirteenth century CE to as late as the nineteenth century.[8] In other words, the "predictions" in this work pertain not to what the future holds but are about historical episodes that have occurred in the past.[9]

Returning to Savarkar's *Essentials of Hindutva*, then, and setting aside anachronistic references to India, China, and Japan in ancient times, before these had emerged as nation-states, the inconsistencies in Savarkar's claims deriving from the *Bhavishya Purana* are worth considering. He says, as we saw above, that "Buddhistic" territorial ambitions in India were roundly defeated in ancient times, and yet he believes Buddhism continued to have the philosophical power to be "disastrous to national virility."[10] In fact, he believes Buddhism rendered "India" vulnerable to "Mohammedan invasions" centuries later.[11] Again, what we do know from the historical scholarship is that the Huns (or Hunas)—the name given by ancient Indians to a group of Central Asian tribes who, according to Savarkar, led the "Buddhistic" invasions—were unlikely to have been Buddhists.[12] D. N. Jha argues that the Huns/Hunas destroyed Buddhist monasteries and centres of learning in Gandhara in the northwestern part of the Indian subcontinent, which they occupied by about 465 CE. The Hunas were ultimately defeated by a coalition of Indian princes in 528 CE and driven out of India.[13] What the historical

[7] Hazra 1940: 188.

[8] Hiltebeitel 1999: 217–18.

[9] I will return to the Puranas in some detail later to discuss the accepted scholarly understanding on dating and authorship of these ancient texts.

[10] Savarkar 1923: 9.

[11] Ibid.: 10.

[12] Coins dated to the Hunas show images of the bull, seated goddesses, and a trident. Handa 1981. While these may not reflect "Hinduism" as Savarkar comes to think of it by the twentieth century, they are not symbols related to Buddhism.

[13] Biswas 1971; Hasan 1999; Haywood 2002.

scholarship affirms, contra Savarkar, is that the Hunas did not enter the subcontinent as an alliance of "Buddhistic forces." Furthermore, we know that it was Buddhism which had been under attack, from around the end of the reign of Ashoka (third century BCE), and that these attacks were by Brahminical forces.[14] D. N. Jha offers what he calls a limited survey of the desecration, destruction, and appropriation of Buddhist stupas, monasteries, and other structures by these forces. In his argument there was a Brahminical onslaught on Buddhism during the post-Mauryan period, especially under the Brahmin ruler Pushyamitra Shunga. Sanchi, an important Buddhist site since the time of Ashoka, has yielded archaeological evidence of the vandalisation of several edifices during the Shunga period. Jha offers similar evidence from several other sites of present-day Brahminical temples—for instance, Bhuteshwar and Gokarneshwar in Mathura—to argue that they were Buddhist sites in the ancient period. In present-day Sultanpur district, forty-nine Buddhist sites seem to have been destroyed by fire in what the archaeologist Alois Anton Führer terms Brahminism's "final victories over Buddhism."[15]

In other words, Buddhist sites and monuments were destroyed by Brahminical forces, by the Hunas, and even by Jains in some places in present-day Madhya Pradesh. It must be clarified that this historical evidence may not have been available to Savarkar. However, the central fact about Savarkar is his interest in writing histories of Hindu valour with scant regard for evidence that could counter his claims. Like other nationalist writers of the period, he was making an ideological argument that cited "history," but this was a purposive history looking selectively at the past largely to make an argument about the future—about what "India" could become by emulating heroic Hindus

[14] According to Ashish Kumar, an inscription found at Kura in the Salt Range mentions the construction of a Buddhist monastery during the reign of the Huna king Toramana. So Buddhism, although under attack, was not entirely wiped out in the region under the Hunas. See Kumar 2021.

[15] Jha 2018: 95–107. Jha's argument regarding the violent end of Buddhism (as opposed to it fading away due to lack of royal and affluent patronage) is contested by historians, but in light of the other material surveyed in this chapter I find Jha's argument convincing.

of the past. In this kind of endeavour Savarkar was not alone: M. K. Gandhi's *Hind Swaraj* is a good example of the same basic strategy of valorising "India's" glorious past, though Gandhi did not take recourse to history. Moreover, Gandhi's vision of India's past and future was neither "Aryan" nor explicitly Hindu, and the future he envisaged was diametrically opposed to Savarkar's vision.[16] Invoking a nation going back thousands of years is a basic nationalist strategy from eighteenth-century Europe onwards, and we see this in Jawaharlal Nehru's *Discovery of India* too. The kind of future nation imagined on this basis is where nationalisms differ.

For Savarkar, thus, the first enemy of Hindutva is Buddhism, because it taught and instilled defeatist values. Yet Buddhism can still be assimilated into his idea of what belongs to Bharatvarsha (India) because its founder was born within the domain defined as Bharatvarsha. The real and lasting enemy then, is Islam, forever the outsider against whom the "bitter sense of wrong," earlier alluded to, must be cultivated. It was in the "prolonged conflict" against "Arabs, Persians, Pathans, Tartars, Turks, Moguls"—all seen as "Muslim" even though each regime violently displaced the last, and even though each dynasty in power worked closely with non-Muslims—that "our people became intensely conscious of ourselves as Hindus and were welded into a nation . . ."[17]

Compare how Savarkar writes about the "Mohammedan invasions" with how he discusses the advent of the Aryans and their expansion: "The intrepid Aryans" who "lighted their first sacrificial fire on the banks of the Sindhu . . .," their "adventurous valour that propelled their intrepid enterprises."[18] They could no longer be "cooped" up within "the narrow compass of the Panchanad"—Savarkar's Sanskritised name for Punjab.[19]

---

[16] See Chaturvedi 2022, passim, for the ways in which Savarkar used history to arrive at his idea of "Hindutva."

[17] Savarkar 1923: 19–20.

[18] Savarkar 1923: 4.

[19] Ibid.: 6.

The vast and fertile plains farther off stood out inviting the efforts of some strong and vigorous race. Tribe after tribe of the Hindus issued forth from the land of their nursery and led by the consciousness of a great mission and their Sacrificial Fire that was the symbol thereof, they soon reclaimed the vast, waste and but very thinly populated lands. Forests were felled, agriculture flourished, cities rose, kingdoms thrived—the touch of the human hand changed the whole face of the wild and unkemp [*sic*] nature.[20]

Unlike many later proponents of Hindutva who insist that the Aryans were the original inhabitants of the subcontinent, Savarkar did not reject the Aryan immigration thesis. On the contrary, he claims them proudly as valorous adventurers from outside whose "foremost band" made the banks of the Sindhu "their home."[21] He is proud to claim them as the ancestors of "Hindus"; they were intrepid—an adjective he uses many times for them—and they established "colonies."[22]

But who were the original inhabitants of the region's forests, and of the vast lands described by Savarkar as "waste," "wild and unkempt," and "thinly populated," which the early Aryans colonised? Against whom did the early Aryans have to be intrepid and valorous? Savarkar leaves this crucial question unasked; we will return to it later.

At this point we might like to consult a contemporary historian who is more forthright about the violence involved in this expansion. The entire process, Upinder Singh shows, is drenched in violence: the Vedic world is "pervaded with conflict, war and violence. . . . In the hymns of the *Rigveda*, the people who call themselves the *aryas* battle fiercely and incessantly among themselves and against other people they call *dasas* and *dasyus*."[23] The *aryas* see themselves as cultured, civilised people, while the *dasyus* include specific named tribes.

Savarkar proceeds to build a narrative that conflates Hindu—the Arabic pronunciation for Sindhu, meaning the river Indus—with the

[20] Ibid.
[21] Ibid.: 4.
[22] Ibid.: 6.
[23] Singh 2017: 22.

religious community called Hindu from approximately the nineteenth century onwards, thus implying a Hindu community that went back millennia. He also Sanskritises Hindu*stan* (from the Persian *stan*) to Hindu*sthan* (from the Sanskrit *sthan*). Both *stan* and *sthan* are cognates deriving from proto Indo-Iranian and Indo-European roots, but the name given to this terrain by outsiders was Hindustan, not Hindusthan. This community called Hindu was, according to Savarkar, not based on *Hinduism*, which was concerned with religious beliefs and practices, but on a historical cultural identity he called *Hindutva*, based on race and originary geographical location within the boundaries of this land—"Hindutva embraces all the departments of thought and activity of the whole Being of our Hindu race."[24] Suresh Sharma points out that this distinction Savarkar made between religious practices and a geographical region was imperative if he wished to define Hindus monolithically, as a singular and unified community, which it is not and has never been. Sharma states that any such attempt would invariably have got caught up in "sectarian schism." [25]

Savarkar proceeds to claim the unitary identity of this community from time immemorial, citing a number of common features that distinguish it from the Other. First, the language, which he calls Hindusthani: "Hindusthani is par excellence the language of Hindusthan or Sindhusthan." This language was "the medium of expression throughout India" centuries before the advent of British rule: "a Nanak, a Chaitanya, a Ramdas could and did travel up and down the country. . . teaching and preaching in this tongue."[26] On what basis does Savarkar claim this? There is in fact no evidence that these fifteenth- to seventeenth-century saints spoke "Hindusthani." Nanak and Ramdas preached in Punjabi and Marathi, respectively. Guru Nanak is said to have known Persian and to have rejected the Sanskrit and Arabic used by Hindu and Muslim clergy.[27] Chaitanya's teachings have been

---

[24] Ibid.: 4.
[25] Sharma 1996.
[26] Savarkar 1923: 18.
[27] Singh 2019.

recorded in Sanskrit by his disciples, and biographers have claimed he spoke several languages, including Pali, Prakrit, Arabic, and Persian, and of course Early Bengali and Oriya.[28] But he could not have spoken Hindust(h)ani for the simple reason that no such language existed in his time.

So, what exactly does Savarkar mean by "Hindusthani" when there was no such language in the period he asserts it was spoken? The language called Hindustani (without an h) is a mixture of Prakrits—which were vernacular Middle Indo-Aryan languages that were used in the Indian subcontinent from around the third century BCE to the eighth century CE—Sanskrit, a substantial Persian and Arabic vocabulary, and Khari Boli which was one among several Indo-Aryan dialects. This Hindustani is understood to have developed between the seventh and thirteenth centuries CE, being carried to various parts of the subcontinent by administrators of successive governments in Delhi—which Savarkar would categorise as Mohammedan—and by traders, artisans, and other itinerant communities. If Savarkar really believed Hindustani served as a link language, then he would have to acknowledge its—and the subcontinent's—highly syncretic culture. But since in his view "everything we have in common with our enemies, weakens our power of opposing them," it is necessary for him to forge a new language lineage. This he does by conflating "Hindusthani" and Hindi, the latter having become by the early twentieth century the supposedly pure Sanskrit-based language of the Hindus. From claiming Hindusthani as the language par excellence of Hindusthan, Savarkar elides to the declaration that therefore the attempt to raise Hindi to "the pedestal of our national tongue is neither new nor forced."[29]

What is clear from Savarkar's sense of the language communities of the subcontinent is the aspiration to set aside all evidence of diversity in a community he calls "Hindu" and somehow construct a simplified narrative of unity and singularity. The subcontinent's language

[28] Sen 2019.
[29] Savarkar 1923: 18.

diversity having been reduced to an imagined Hindusthani spoken by Hindusthanis, he then assumes a neat fit between language and religious community with confident assertions such as this: "Let the work of Kamba, the Tamil poet and, say, a copy of Hafiz be kept before a Hindu in Bengal and if he be asked, 'Which of these belongs to you?' he would instinctively say 'Kamba is mine!'"[30] Would a Bengali claim a Tamil poet as his own over a Persian? Unlikely, to say the least, since Tamil is alien to Bengal whereas Bengali is replete with Persian words and Persian influence. Persian was in fact the official language of Bengal for 600 years until the British changed it to English in 1836, and over 1822–3 Ram Mohan Roy ran the pioneering weekly newspaper *Mirat-ul-Akhbar* which was neither in Bengali nor English but in Persian. Savarkar is arguing a point about sensitivity to poetic language on the assumption that what matters to the Bengali Hindu is not the poetry of her language, Bengali, but the religion of the poet she is reading, Hinduism.

Merely to travel across India in Savarkar's time as much as now, a century later, would force the recognition that "religious" identity is everywhere inflected by regional and linguistic identity, so that the Bihari Muslim and the Bihari Hindu, for example, can relate to each other in multiple ways while finding their religious counterparts in, say, Kerala, alien. The histories of Islam in these regions are independent of one another, with many regional rituals carrying distinctly regional flavours; and what comes under the umbrella term "Hindu" varies even more radically, as will become more and more clear.

Savarkar's second claim, again reductive and intent on singularity, is that "Hindus" are all people of one race or *jati*. All Hindus, says Savarkar, claim "to have in their veins the blood of the mighty race incorporated with and descended from the Vedic fathers, the Sindhus."[31] He asserts that there has been extensive interaction between castes—"a common flow of blood from a Brahmin to a Chandal."[32]

[30] Ibid.: 35.
[31] Ibid.: 30–1.
[32] Ibid.: 31.

Living in the early twentieth century Savarkar could not have been unaware of the powerful prohibitions on inter-caste mingling and dining, let alone intermarriage, for he himself had spoken up strongly against such prohibitions elsewhere while discussing the "seven shackles" of Hinduism.[33] Clearly, his project is political and ideological—that of claiming the prior existence of a community he was in fact trying to construct.

We in the twenty-first century have an advantage, though, because we know from a study analysing genetic material from seventy-three Indian population groups that, over 4000 years ago (c. 2000 BCE), there were two genetically separate populations based in North and South India.[34] These populations (Ancestral North Indians and Ancestral South Indians) were already the product of earlier migrations, beginning with the early migration of anatomically modern humans (*Homo sapiens*) from Africa, some 55,000 to 45,000 years ago, and then, to quote Tony Joseph, "the farming-related migrations from West Asia that probably occurred in multiple waves after 10,000 BC, or the migrations of Austro-Asiatic speakers such as the Munda from East Asia the dating of which is yet to determined, and the migrations of Tibeto-Burman speakers such as the Garo again from east Asia, the dating of which is also yet to be determined."[35] These migrations entered the subcontinent from multiple directions and settled, so that by 2000–1500 BCE they had become stable in the North and in the South.

From about 1500 BCE there began a widespread intermingling of populations which even included the most isolated groups.[36] This

[33] "Seven Shackles" is a compilation on the site Savarkar.org of relevant sentences translated from the Marathi writings of Savarkar between 1927 and 1937 that criticise caste orthodoxy (see Bibliography). Vikram Sampath (Sampath 2018) refers to a 1931 essay by Savarkar titled "Seven Shackles of Hinduism" but the reference he gives is to this compilation. I have been unable to locate an essay by Savarkar with this title in English. Vinayak Chaturvedi too discusses Savarkar's views on caste and intermarriage but not by citing "Seven Shackles" (Chaturvedi 2022: 191).

[34] Moorjani, et al. 2013.

[35] Joseph 2017.

[36] Moorjani, et al. 2013.

coincides with the immigration into the subcontinent of Indo-European language speakers who had split off around 2000–1600 BCE from the Iranians.[37] Subsequently, Indo-Aryan groups are thought to have moved to the Levant (the Mitanni), the northern Indian subcontinent (the Vedic people), and China (the Wusun).[38] Scholarly opinion now holds that these were migrations, not invasions, and the theory of Aryan invasions into India has long been rejected. The fact that the Indus Valley Civilisation declined around the same time as the Indo-Aryan migrations into India was seen by some scholars as indicative of an Aryan invasion, but archaeological evidence from bodies buried in the top layers showed no indication of violence in the Indus Valley Civilisation. The current understanding is that there were multiple factors for the decline of that developed urban civilisation which operated in various parts of a vast Harappan culture zone. One of these could be some natural event or process, such as flooding, or the shifting or drying up of water sources.[39]

The intermingling of populations is thought to have continued from 1500 BCE up to the first century CE.[40] Then, from about the first century CE, several subgroups of the mixed population stopped marrying outside their group, and genetic indicators show that these populations became frozen. The genetic evidence therefore suggests that once the caste system was established and had begun to spread as a social practice, endogamy became the norm: "Thus, India experienced a demographic transformation during this time, shifting from a region where major mixture between groups was common and affected even isolated

[37] Lubotsky 2020.

[38] Beckwith 2009.

[39] Witzel 2005.

[40] Moorjani, et al. 2013. The details of the timing, routes, and archaeological markers of Aryan migrations are the subject of intense debate among historians. Moreover, historians using textual sources are joined by scientists using DNA evidence, as with Moorjani, et al. So, while flagging the fact that different kinds of knowledges are attempting to map histories of caste, in this chapter I follow the trajectory of one broad kind of argument drawing on different sources, for which the details of the internal debates and disagreements are not really relevant.

tribes such as the Palliyar and Bhil, to a region in which mixture was rare."[41] In other words, once "the Brahmin and the Chandal," as Savarkar puts it—alluding to the caste system—became established, from the beginning of the Common Era at least,[42] there was in fact, contra Savarkar, no question of blood flowing between castes, not even in Savarkar's own time, as he knew. Today, there is evidence of genetic admixture of a much broader kind which Savarkar, even had he been aware of it, would not have acknowledged because what it shows is that it was not "Hindus"—those in his understanding that comprise the entire non-Muslim population—who shared a pure ancestry with the Aryans. It shows, rather, that all South Asians are descendants from a hybrid mix which started with the earliest humans out of Africa, moving on to South Asian hunter-gatherers, Iranian hunter-gatherers, and Central Asian steppe pastoralists as well as Austroasiatic and Tibeto-Burmese-speaking people. There is thus strong scientific evidence from the developed sector of gene studies to show a large and varied contribution to the genetic pool in this region.[43]

Third, Savarkar's claim that all forms of religious practice other than Islam and Christianity are naturally "Hindu"—"Sanatanists, Satnamis, Sikhs, Aryas, Anaryas, Marathas and Madrasis [sic], Brahmins and Panchamas—all suffered as Hindus and triumphed as Hindus"[44]—is not tenable. Savarkar's animus in this text is not against the British Empire but against Mohammedan rulers, against whom "we" united as Hindus. But the idea that Brahmins and Panchamas (the fifth caste or "outcastes") suffered alike under "Mohammedan rule," or that Sikhs and "Madrasis" shared a common identity at any point in the history of the

[41] Ibid.: 429.

[42] Historians in fact hold that the textual evidence of untouchability is much older than this. And that how exactly the caste system worked with regard to marriage and interdining, etc., is more clear vis-à-vis the Brahmins and Chandalas than in relation to intermediate groups. Even the early history of caste is thus indicative of Brahminism, whereas Savarkar pronounces confidently that it did not exist.

[43] Reich, et al. 2009; Narasimhan, et al. 2019; Basu, et al. 2016.

[44] Savarkar 1923: 20.

subcontinent—these are fantastical claims that remain mere assertions serving the purpose of solidifying a highly unwieldy and heterogeneous community. Savarkar claims that "the majority of the Hindus subscribes to that system of religion which could fitly be described by the attribute that constitutes its special feature, as told by Shruti, Smriti and Puranas. . ."[45] Knowing full well that this definition will reduce the total population of "Hindus" down to a tiny minority, he performs a sleight of hand by adding the term "Sanatan Dharma," which he offers as an encompassing form of Hinduism to all others—"Avaidik brethren," the "heterodox"—who would otherwise be "relegated to the non-Hindu pale":

> [T]here are other Hindus who reject either partly or wholly the authority—some of the Puranas, some of the Smritis, and some of the Shrutis themselves. But if you identify the religion of the Hindus with the religion of the majority only, and call it orthodox Hinduism, then the different heterodox communities being Hindus themselves, rightly resent this usurpation of Hindutva by the majority as well as their unjustifiable exclusion.[46]

The term "Sanatan Dharma" has emerged from Brahminical texts such as the *Manusmriti* and the *Bhagavata Purana* to refer to supposedly eternal and universal values such as honesty, mercy, and so on. But it is invoked in different contexts to mean quite different things. It acquired new life in the nineteenth-century Hindu nationalist project of reform, revival, and unification when it began to be deployed to indicate an eternal Hinduism, a non-sectarian and pan-Hindu identity.[47] This is exactly how Savarkar uses the term. However, no such all-inclusive Sanatan Dharma existed as a religion, then or now: it is simply the invocation of a goal, a dream of the Hindu nationalist to eliminate all difference in Dalit Bahujan and Adivasi communities and discipline them into the Brahminical framework. Indeed, the reverse meaning

[45] Ibid.: 39.
[46] Ibid.
[47] Zavos 2001.

was also being asserted in the nineteenth century, even as traditional Hinduism faced a challenge from reformist movements like the Arya Samaj. That is, the term "Sanatan Dharma" or "Sanatani" Hindu was a self-definition among those opposed to the Arya Samaj and reform, and who observed the orthodoxy/orthopraxy of caste. In this intra-Hindu debate the Sanatani Hindus presented themselves as the majority.[48]

A third meaning of Sanatan Dharma emerges from Ramakrishna Paramhansa and the Ramakrishna Mission. Their definition of Sanatan Dharma, while claiming to be closer to true Vedanta, sounds more like a secular acceptance of multiple practices and beliefs—including non-Hindu streams[49]—than Savarkar's "Sanatan Dharm," which is a Brahminical assimilative project.

Savarkar did not invoke Sanatan Dharm for an orthodox defence of caste, he used the phrase in the reformed pan-Hindu sense.[50] Yet he did also repeat the Sanatani claim that the orthodox were in the majority among the "Hindus." In fact, as we will see later, the majority of the people defined as Hindus consist of those whom Savarkar describes as heterodox. Ever since the label "Hinduism" emerged in the nineteenth century, communities forcibly assimilated by nationalist politics and the Indian state under that label, far from demanding inclusion within the label—as Savarkar claims—have each demanded recognition as a separate religious community. Savarkar lists Sikhs, Lingayats, and "several Samajis" who would "deeply resent" being told that they are not Hindu.[51] This is very far from being the case

[48] Ibid.: 110–11.

[49] Samrat 2021.

[50] One of the "seven shackles" of Hinduism, according to Savarkar, is *shuddhibandi*. This refers to the orthodox Sanatani resistance to the Arya Samaj's programme of *shuddhikaran* (purification) which converted non-Hindus, "lower" castes, and Adivasis to Hinduism. *Shuddhibandi* was the orthodox, Sanatani rejection of any conversion whatsoever to the Hindu fold. Savarkar disagreed with the Sanatanis on this. For an account of the clash between the Sanatanis and the Arya Samaj on this issue, see Zavos 2001: 117–19.

[51] Savarkar 1923: 40.

because, like many originally breakaway, reformist, and dissenting sects such as Buddhism, those of the Lingayats and Sikhs have long claimed they are not Hindus precisely because their very raison d'être is opposition to aspects of core Hindu practices such as caste. Sikhs may be defined by Indian law as "Hindu," but this legal definition is constantly contested in the public domain as well as in courts.[52] Sikhism's claim to be an independent religion, like that of the Lingayats, has a history going back to the nineteenth century, when the label of Hinduism began to emerge.[53]

Savarkar claims that "we" Hindus have feasts and festivals, rites and rituals in common—Dasara, Divali, Rakhibandhan, Holi: "the Rakhi day would reveal to you every Hindu soul from the delighted damsel of Punjab to the austere Brahmins of Madras tying the silken tie..."[54] This is not even true for all *savarnas* who consider themselves Hindu, let alone for the Dalit Bahujan and Adivasi communities. What is regularly apparent in Savarkar's assertions about Hindu unity is incorrect claims disguised as facts. His constant effort is to construct a monolithic entity called Hinduism which he can simultaneously map perfectly onto a unitary India that is always already Hindu.

Neither Holi nor Rakshabandhan is observed in the South of the subcontinent. Rakshabandhan, the celebration of ties of sisters with brothers, has a particular significance only in the North, where marriage is not only virilocal but where women, once married, break all formal ties with their natal families in order to properly "belong" to the man's household. Thus this festival is an annual opportunity for married women to visit their natal homes. In the communities of the South, exogamy is not so strictly enforced, and an annual day to mark the brother–sister bond is therefore unknown. There are also unrelated, older, Vedic rituals around this time of year in various parts of the country, such as Brahmins changing their "sacred thread" and Brahmins going from home to home tying sanctified

[52] PTI 2013; Brar 2019.
[53] Jones 1973.
[54] Savarkar 1923: 36.

threads on wrists of members of those households in return for gifts and money.[55] In contemporary times Hindutva has started introducing Rakshabandhan as a "Hindu" festival—in Kerala, for example, in a highly politicised and polarising move, exactly as was Savarkar's.[56] This attempt to introduce a North Indian festival as "Hindu" is perceived in Kerala as an aspect of North Indian and Hindi dominance.

Dussehra (Dasara), too, is not celebrated in the same way nor for the same reason in the different Indian regions. The defeat of Ravana by Rama is an occasion in some places; the defeat of Mahishasura by Durga in others; in the hills, local gods are worshipped; and in the three southern states of Tamil Nadu, Andhra Pradesh, and Karnataka Dussehra is marked by a festival of dolls. In Chhattisgarh Dussehra is the worship of nature and of Devi Danteshwari, the presiding deity of Bastar, concluding with *muria durbar*, a conference of tribal chieftains.[57] What this range of deities and rituals involved in both Raksha bandhan and Dussehra indicates is the existence of a pre-Brahminical festival linked to the seasons which has over the centuries been sought to be assimilated into Brahminical narratives, but never very successfully.[58]

Nor are "Hindu" and "Muslim" as radically contrary as Savarkar portrays them. The instances of an intermingling of "Muslim" and "Hindu" practices, even well into the twenty-first century, are common. For instance, Onam in Trissur (Kerala) has a Muslim connection, with the *pulikkali* (tiger dance) on the fourth day having probably been brought in by the Muslims of Tamil Nadu, where this performance is a feature of Muharram.[59] *Pulikkali* may have been part of an indigenous culture pre-dating Islam as it is not a feature of Muharram observations in other parts of the country. Similarly, the deities of

[55] Duane 1963; Gnanambal 1969.

[56] Puzhakkal 2020.

[57] Sahaney 2022.

[58] It is well known that the assimilation of pre-existing practices and beliefs is also a feature of both Christianity (King 1949/50) and Islam (Goitein 2010).

[59] Saktidharan 2019: 28.

both Jagannath in Odisha and Ayyappan in Kerala have Muslim dev-otees/friends,[60] at whose shrines pilgrims to these temples pay their respects.[61]

The assimilative political project of Hindutva has of course had its successes. The larger identity of Hindu has generally become nor-malised, especially as it is the only "religious" identity offered by the state to those who are not Muslim, Christian, Jewish, or Parsi. Another important aspect of this success is highlighted by Chinnaiah Jangam, writing about the dense universe of debate, thought, and political action of Dalit intellectuals in the early twentieth century. During the modernist "Hindu" reform movements of the early twentieth century, many Dalit intellectuals and activists were strongly influenced by the modernist drive towards "hygiene" and therefore urged their communities to give up "unclean" practices—such as the consumption of meat and liquor, as well as animal sacrifice.[62] These were of course, as I have argued here, pre-Aryan customs now considered in the Brahminical understanding to be simply "backward." Jangam tracks a later shift in the thought of some of these intellectuals as they became sceptical of the caste-Hindu reformist agenda. Nevertheless, the claim of all "untouchables" to be "adi-Hindu," that is, primordial Hindus, and demanding to be re-corded as such in the colonial census in Hyderabad, was one of the significant positive responses to the Brahminical assimilative pro-ject in the twentieth century.[63]

Jangam's work alerts us to the heterogeneity of Dalit intellectual and political publics, even as we focus on the wider resistances faced by the assimilative project: one, a refusal by some communities to accept the umbrella label "Hinduism"; and the other, the defiant assertion by var-ious communities of their Hinduness, despite not conforming to Hin-dutva's homogenising claims, for example by their being meat-eating

[60] The spellings "Ayyappa" and "Ayyappan" are both used. I have used Ayyappan throughout.

[61] Hans 2017; Ameerudheen 2018.

[62] Jangam 2017: 110–16.

[63] Ibid.: 143–5.

and even beef-eating, as in Kerala and Bengal.[64] An instance exemplifying both these reactions is the legal attempt by the Ramakrishna Mission in 1980 to be defined as a non-Hindu minority, a claim turned down by the Supreme Court in 1995.[65] All the same, today the Ramakrishna Mission expresses its meat-eating Hinduness as different from the Brahminical vegetarian variant of Hindibelt Hindutva, even as it accepts Islam and Christianity equally as paths to God.[66]

Clearly, Savarkar's effort to render Indian heterogeneity into a "Sanatan Dharm" retrospectively named "Hindu" runs repeatedly into deep water. His struggle must be understood as part of a massive project of attempted assimilation that goes back to the Puranas—an enterprise that has been forced to continue well into the twenty-first century precisely because it has been a continuously failing project.

The Puranas

A quick note on the dating and authorship of these ancient texts may be in order. The available manuscripts of ancient texts such as the Ramayana, the Mahabharata, and the Puranas are best understood as palimpsests, through the fabric of which can be glimpsed transmissions over millennia—starting with oral versions transcribed by many people over time, added to, edited, amended, and so on. Start and end dates attributed to such texts indicate the earliest and latest possible points of composition/addition, calculated on the basis of internal and external intertextual references, as well as, in some instances, evidence from material culture, as for example in Patrick Olivelle's introductions

---

[64] According to the National Family Health Survey (2019–21), 77 percent of Indians eat chicken, fish, and other kinds of meat (Newsclick Report 2022). This obviously includes a large number of people classified as Hindus, including Brahmins in Bengal and Kashmir. One of Hindutva's planks is to push vegetarianism as the Hindu way of life. This is fiercely challenged by many communities which, nevertheless, lay claim to being Hindu.

[65] AIR 1995: 2089.

[66] Samrat 2021.

to the *Arthshastra* and the *Manusmriti*. Scholars also hold that the Puranas and epics would not have begun as books intended for reading, they would originally have been "more accurately described as performances, intended to be seen, heard, and enjoyed."[67] Eventually, over centuries, they also took shape as written manuscripts.

To illustrate how intertextual references work in this context, we can go back briefly to the *Bhavishya Purana*. Records of land grants of the fifth century CE quote verses which occur only in the *Padma*, *Bhavishya*, and *Brahma Purana*. On this basis it was assumed that these Puranas are from earlier than the fifth century CE. However, other scholars argue that these verses were being simply quoted by these Puranas from the even earlier Dharmashastras, i.e. the *Padma*, *Bhavishya*, and *Brahma Purana* are quoting earlier texts, and the land-grant inscriptions too could be quoting the Dharmashastras, not these Puranas. Sections of the surviving manuscripts that are dated to be older are thus judged to be partly borrowed from other texts such as the *Brihat Samhita* and the *Shamba Purana*.[68] The dating of ancient texts is a highly contested field, but some arguments—those backed up by scholarly rigour—are more convincing than others.

When it comes to the authorship of these ancient texts, in most cases even when authorship is often attributed to a single name there is not likely to have been some single individual author—as is the case with more modern texts that have historically identifiable authors. Each ancient text as now received represents layers of variously authored materials that have been gathered into a single unit over the centuries. Moreover, as Velcheru Narayana Rao tells us, in this tradition the authorship of a text is not intended to inform us about the actual producer of the text but to indicate the status of the text. The texts of the highest authority are deemed above human authorship—for example, the Vedas. "Texts of the next level of authority are composed by a superhuman, and therefore infallible person"—for example, Vyasa. After this come *kavya*s, texts composed by humans blessed

---

[67] Matchett 2005: 129.
[68] Winternitz 1981: 526.

by Sarasvati.[69] Elsewhere, Rao explains: "If a text changes its meaning, the author changes as well. A story told about the author is part of the text, which signals among other things the status of the text, and the way it is to be read and received." Referring to two different biographical stories about Valmiki, for example, Rao says that the biography depends on how the text is being read. If the Ramayana is being read as a Bhakti (devotional) text, the author is Valmiki—the low-caste dacoit who reached the righteous path with Brahmin instruction and did meditative penance while an anthill rose around him. If the author is Valmiki as the sage who uttered the first Sanskrit *shloka* ever—while cursing a hunter for killing the *krauncha* bird, leaving its partner bereft—then the Ramayana is being read as a political text prescribing exemplary behaviour. Thus, according to Rao, the "author" of an ancient text is determined by the mode of reading and by the reader.[70]

Because of these factors, many such ancient texts are "polysemic," and in them, as Upinder Singh puts it, "multiple ideas, sometimes contradictory ones, jostle with each other within a single text." An additional factor she points out is that, in the ancient intellectual tradition of the subcontinent, even as vitriolic debate goes on between systems of thought that view themselves in oppositional terms, "*within* traditions, what is visible is the tendency to juxtapose different views rather than to reject or replace them."[71]

Keeping in mind this backdrop on dating and authorship of ancient texts, we can revert to the dating of the Puranas, which pose particular problems because in their oral forms they go back to well before the Common Era. It is also important to note that, within the Puranas themselves, this kind of question about dating is irrelevant, for it is asserted that they all come into being at the same time as a result of Vyasa's work in each *dvaparayuga*.[72] Given all of these caveats,

[69] Rao 1993: 93.
[70] Rao 2019.
[71] Singh 2017: 9.
[72] Matchett 2005: 132.

the consensus among scholars is that the earliest Puranas have been compiled in the fourth–eighth centuries, and the latest from the eleventh to the eighteenth centuries.

What are the developments prior to this? Starting with the arrival of the Indo-Aryan people in around 1500 BCE, there is evidence of a period showing rituals and practices that can be deemed part of the Vedic religion. The Purusha Sukta in the *Rig Veda* describes the varna order, with Brahmins at the head and Shudras at the foot.[73] B. R. Ambedkar termed the Purusha Sukta unique among other cosmogonies in the world for several reasons: first, that "though the existence of classes is the de facto condition of every society, nevertheless no society has converted this de facto state of affairs into a de jure connotation of an ideal society." The Purusha Sukta is the only instance in which "the real is elevated to the dignity of an ideal," sanctioned as divine and sacred. Further, the scheme of caste hierarchy given by the Purusha Sukta is unique in giving "the de facto state of class composition a legal effect," and finally, although other societies have assumed that people find their own place in classes, and the relative importance of classes changes, being "determined by the forces operating from time to time," the society shown in the Purusha Sukta "has an official gradation laid down, fixed and permanent, with an ascending scale of reverence and a descending scale of contempt."[74]

There is a debate on whether the Purusha Sukta is a later interpolation—which would imply that caste is not sanctioned by the Vedas—but this is irrelevant for our purposes because what is uncontested is that Brahminism emerges from the Vedic religion and is fully established by the early centuries of the Common Era. Brahminism is understood here as an ideological formation that involves (a) exaltation of the four Vedas; (b) the hierarchy of the four varnas, and the assertion of Brahmin superiority; (c) worship of the trinity of Brahma, Vishnu, and Shiva; and (d) the theodicy of karma and rebirth as foundational

[73] Jamison and Witzel 1992: 48.
[74] Ambedkar 1946.

to and justifying the varna order. (Buddhism and Jainism too subscribe to the last belief but they rejected the other three, and therefore their belief in rebirth is not linked to a justification of the varna order.) Thus, although Brahmins were not a homogeneous group (specialists in Vedic learning were at the top; then there were temple priests, and many other occupations, including landowners and kings); and though philosophically there were internal debates among different schools, the four features identified above form the core of Brahminism as an ideology.[75]

By the time of the written Puranas, there are many passages in which "the rules of varnasramadharma are set out firmly and clearly, sometimes introduced by the idea that this is what God wants."[76] Of course, the norms of varna-dharma are laid out not only in the Puranas but in the Dharmashastra, where varna is taken as the fundamental basis of social organisation. All other social groupings are explained through the theory of the mixture of varnas. The genetic evidence discussed above also suggests that by this time the segregation of castes had been more or less accomplished.

The Ramayana and Mahabharata reach their latest incarnations between the fourth century BCE and the fourth century CE, by when Brahminism had established itself as a powerful new ideology. Meanwhile, Jainism and Buddhism emerged approximately between the seventh and fifth centuries BCE as dissenting voices against Brahminism.

The centuries in which the Puranas emerge are thus marked by an enormous socio-cultural churning in which Brahminism faced resistance and challenges. In the background is the series of invasions in the period c. 200 BCE to 300 CE from the northwest—Indo-Greeks, Sakas,

---

[75] "Brahminism" is also spelt "Brahmanism." However, some descriptions of Brahminism in philosophy encyclopaedias not only spell it as Brahmanism, but link it to both Brahma the creator and Brahman—meaning ultimate reality—in many schools of ancient Indian philosophy. There are also accounts that state Brahminism/Brahmanism is a precursor to modern Hinduism, assuming a teleology posited *by* Brahminism. All of these are problematic assertions and this chapter will not be engaging with them except to mark their existence.

[76] Matchett 2003: 141.

Parthians, Kushanas—which are partly responsible for the anxieties visible in Brahminical texts regarding fears of *mlechchha* rule. Then there were the challenges on the one hand from organised dissenting religions like Buddhism and Jainism, and on the other, even before these emerged, from the vast sea of heterogeneous practices and beliefs of non-Aryan peoples who continued their relatively autonomous existence within the territorial boundaries of the subcontinent. The Puranas, it has been cogently argued, were meant to draw these multifarious beliefs into the web of Brahminism through narratives linking local deities with the Aryan trinity: Narayana Rao terms the Puranas "Brahminic ideology" functioning to "puranize the folk tradition."[77] He says that, like any new emergent power seeking to control the present by recasting the past, Brahminism sought to create new ways of perceiving the past. This process involved transforming even the concepts of time and space, so that Brahminism attempted to override "folk" conceptions of these—just as, later, British colonial modernity overrode Brahminical notions of time and space. Thus, India still has three ways of conceptualising time and space: "low-caste, non-literate people have a folk concept... upper-caste Sanskrit-educated Brahmins have a Puranic concept ... and Westernised educated Indians have a modern concept of time/space."[78] Folk time is "repetitive and regenerative" and analogous with the agricultural seasons, while Puranic time "deteriorates."[79] Each of the Four Ages (*yugas*) is inferior to the previous one until the final dissolution with *pralaya*, and then a new cycle starts.

Rao illustrates the "ideological change" that a folk story undergoes when it is puranised; he does this by comparing a folk tale—which he gathered in Andhra Pradesh through interviews with folk singers—to its version in the *Skanda Purana*. The story comes from the Komati caste, a trading caste which was once of low status. In the folk version Kanyaka, their caste goddess, is a young virgin who is the chief player, making decisions for herself as well as for the caste. The Puranic version

[77] Rao 1993: 89.
[78] Ibid.: 88.
[79] Ibid.: 88–9.

of the folk tale about the origins of the Komati caste places this caste within the Vaishyas. Thus they are in this world for a predetermined purpose and in accordance with a divine scheme—they do not merely exist as profit-seeking traders. In the Puranic version, which in this way raises the caste status of the Komati caste, Kanyaka is replaced by a Brahmin priest as chief actor who is obeyed by all the Vaishyas, and Kanyaka herself is merely a chaste woman obeying the commands of the priest and her family.[80] In Rao's words, "Vast bodies of folk/regional stories, events, legends, and histories have been incorporated into the Puranas along with prescriptive codes of behaviour appropriate to people of different stations of life. Such incorporation has made a Brahminic interpretation of the material possible without necessarily erasing local colour and regional flavour."[81] However, not all Brahmins are ready to accept the Puranic project of giving "Shudra" castes a higher caste status. Manoj Mitta writes about a suit filed in 1817 by Komatis (Comatis) in a district court of Madras Presidency, against Brahmins who refused to perform religious ceremonies for Komatis "in the language of the Vedas." The implication was that Komatis are Shudras, not Vaishyas, and therefore undeserving of this honour, and the case was finally decided in favour of the Brahmins after nearly three decades, in 1845.[82] What this indicates is that, well into the modern era, the effort of some Puranas to incorporate some non-Brahmins into the coveted "upper" castes was not always successful in the face of Brahmin resistance. In other words, the Brahminical project of creating Hindus has been resisted even from within.

The Puranas underwent a major shift with the emergence of Bhakti saints.[83] In fact the mode of Purana composition changed significantly

[80] Ibid.: 90–2.

[81] Ibid.: 92.

[82] On the grounds that Brahmin refusal did not constitute a rights violation. Mitta 2023: 82–3.

[83] Bhakti (devotion) refers to the form of worship inaugurated by individual devotees through personal devotion and by claiming a direct relationship to a chosen deity, and rejecting the caste system and Brahmins as a conduit to the divine. Its earliest beginnings are traced to the Tamil country around the sixth century, and

after Bhakti emerged. While the earlier Puranas were informative and instructional, the Bhakti Puranas "create an atmosphere of participation in religious ecstasy."[84] It is clear that the Brahminical ideology was also attempting to incorporate Bhakti into its fold.

This "mass assimilation of local cults into the Puranic fold" was managed by linking them in some way or the other to Shiva or to an incarnation of Vishnu.[85] According to Vijay Nath, who attempts to connect the Puranas to historical developments, there are three dominant cultic streams in the Puranas—Vaishnavism, Shaivism, and Saktism—and their growth and development were directly related to their success in assimilating and absorbing countless local cults and deities. Many of these were taken to represent multiple facets of the same Aryan god. Thus, Vishnu "came to subsume such independent cults as Jagannatha of Puri, Venkatesvara of Tirupati and Narasimha of Srisailam . . . or in the case of Shiva, who became associated with countless local cults by the mere suffixing of Isa or Isvara to the name of the local deity, e.g. Bhutesvara, Chandesvara, Hatakaesvara."[86] There are also stories that link tribal communities to the puranic world: for instance, Vishnu in his incarnation as Narasimha fell in love with and married a girl of the Chenchu tribe, and this tribe regards Narasimha as their son-in-law.[87] Tribal gods such as the primeval fish, the toad, and the boar that were common to many tribal creation and evolution myths "graduated into incarnations of Vishnu."[88] The avatars of Vishnu incorporated pre-Aryan deities and totems as well as the anti-Brahminical Buddha.

What is noteworthy though is that these folk traditions and stories also survive in their originary non-puranic form well into the late

---

it has fifteenth- to sixteenth-century manifestations in North India. Bhakti poet-saints expressed radical views challenging gender, caste, and class norms, as well as the ossified rituals of organised religion. See Ramanujan (1973) for translations of some Bhakti poetry, and Hawley (2015) for an analytical study of how the idea of a Bhakti "movement" came to be constructed in the nineteenth century.

[84] Ibid.: 99.
[85] Nath 2009: 23.
[86] Ibid.
[87] Ibid.
[88] Sakthidharan 2019: 10.

twentieth century—as when Velcheru Narayana Rao met Komati folk singers and heard the story of Kanyaka from them. As we will see later, there is a seething "outside" to the Puranas that keeps bursting forth with fresh life even millennia after the Puranas were composed to contain subversive anti-Brahminical forces.

The Puranas really continue the project begun by the Mahabharata and the Ramayana of knitting non-Aryan people, beliefs, and practices into the Brahmin fold and disciplining them into Brahminism through different kinds of narratives.[89] Citing the Mahabharata, Upinder Singh draws our attention to the idea that the victory of the Pandavas was not just a scramble for power but "necessary for the creation of a new righteous world order from the annihilation of an older one." After Parashurama wiped out all the Kshatriya men, Kshatriya women approached ascetic Brahmanas to renew their line; a new breed of Kshatriyas was born and the varna order restored. But the asuras, defeated by the devas, took birth in many forms on earth—as animals, humans, even kings, and the devas too took birth in different forms to defeat them again.[90] The Mahabharata also lays down norms for appropriate violence by Kshatriyas to establish civilised norms and to end the uncivilised violence of *dasyus*.[91] Rama as maintainer of the varna order under Ram Rajya, and the punishment he metes out to a Shudra, Shambuka, for reciting the Vedas, is exemplary.

Padmanabh S. Jaini argues that this is the very reason the Jaina Puranas are written around the ninth century CE—to counter "the

[89] Such projects of the appropriation and assimilation of religious diversity into a hegemonic unity by dominant elites is of course far from unique to the Hindu puranic tradition, being visible in the histories of emergence of dominant religious traditions everywhere, as noted earlier for Islam and Christianity. For one of the most persuasive histories of an analogous process in modern South Asia, see Harjot Oberoi's fine study of how the Khalsa Panth roped a variety of sects and cultic practices into what is today recognisable as Sikhism: Oberoi 1994. However, what is critical in the context I discuss here is the modern linking of this process of assimilation of only some traditions to a nation-state project that specifically excludes others—which are treated as inimical and unacceptable.

[90] Singh 2017: 62.

[91] Ibid.: 76.

Brahminic attempt to appropriate such worldly heroes as Rama and Krishna, sanctify their secular lives and set them up as divine incarnations of their god Vishnu."[92] The Jaina Puranas integrate these two heroes into the Jaina tradition, rejecting as false the Brahminical appropriation of them as avatars of Vishnu and subordinating them instead to their own Tirthankaras. The Jaina Puranas also find a place for the Pandavas who, at the end of their lives, become Jaina monks. There are passages in the *Bhagavata Purana* and the *Shiva Purana* that "openly use invective against Jaina holy men and their teachings" in response to such retellings.[93] The Jaina Puranas thus show a counter-assimilative tradition performing the same exercise with pre-Aryan deities and cults as the Brahminical Puranas—though of course they pertain to the efforts of a much smaller community.

Later regional and caste Puranas of the twelfth to the seventeenth centuries CE contain origin myths of specific castes. In a study of two caste Puranas of Gujarat, Veena Das shows how, through the insertion of a myth of divine intervention by a Brahminical god, such Puranas ascribe a higher status to the particular castes they eulogise in order to contradict the low status traditionally ascribed to their occupations. The purpose of such Puranas was quite worldly—to establish social status before the ruler: "The myths of origin along with other such evidences were submitted by the caste groups who wished to be considered for a particular rank in the caste or varna hierarchy, then the evidences would be interpreted by the King or his learned Brahmins and ideally the decision was given on the basis of these interpretations of the evidence."[94] Later, these Puranas were submitted for the same purpose to the British census operations of 1901 and 1911. The later Puranas thus became part of claims to power and social status within the Brahminical *varnashrama* framework.

On the other end of the power spectrum are "outcaste Puranas" such as the *Jambava Purana*, which is the *kula purana* of the Madigas, an outcaste community. Priyadarshini Vijaisri, in her magisterial study

[92] Jaini 1993: 208.
[93] Ibid.: 245.
[94] Das 1968: 155.

of the still vibrant ritual tradition around the clan goddess Matangi (also known as Matamma) of the outcaste Madigas, shows how outcaste ritual specialists are "awe-inspiring, feared and . . . revered as representatives of the goddess."[95] The *Jambava Purana*, from which this tradition is drawn, claims the status of a Purana "to authenticate its sacrality" while counterposing itself to the Brahminical Puranas.[96] What makes it significantly different from the latter is that it is "uniquely contemporary" because the sacred oral narratives preserved on palm leaf are narrated by storytellers at the time of worship every year and are thus subject to "constant radical interpolations."[97] The origin of untouchability is traced not to some innate impurity but to death and sacrifice in order to resolve a question of righteousness.[98] Providing a deep study of the rituals, Vijaisri argues that Brahminism fails to subsume the power of the fearsome goddess: "Strikingly, the physically and mentally awesome demonstrations of ritual behaviour recreate fear and destabilize hegemonic values in the rituals of possession . . ."[99] In these rituals the Brahmin is not pre-eminent, and the entire village community collectively participates in a ritual space which is "transfigured into the field of divine lethal power; it also constitutes a renewed bond of unconditional submission to the outcaste clan goddess."[100]

In short, the Brahminical Puranas have been far from successful in containing and assimilating the multitudes of the Other that lie outside its fold. It has needed in the past, as it does now, to resort to institutionalised violence to keep the resistance to it in check.

The Violence of Brahmin Expansion

The expansion of Brahminism, as with any other such grand transformative project—for instance, capitalism—is partly brought about by

[95] Vijaisri 2015: xiv.
[96] Ibid.: 193.
[97] Ibid.
[98] Ibid.: 194.
[99] Ibid.: 225.
[100] Ibid.: 228.

the hegemonic transformation of the sphere of ideas and partly by the violence of the state. But in relation to both capitalism and Brahminism the latter factor, state violence, is rarely addressed. It is perhaps further evidence of the massive ideological sway of Brahminism that the advance of northern "Aryans" into the South of the subcontinent, the eastward expansion and triumph of Brahminism, and the decline of Buddhism within most of India are all generally written about, even in reputable works of history, as a pacific, normal, and non-violent process that occurred quite naturally and inevitably. The bulk of histories of the past two millennia in the subcontinent seem from their combination of avoidance, elision, and erasure of social and political violence to almost suggest that the first entry of such violence into the subcontinent happens because of "Muslim" invaders.

Let us consider, as one instance, the elegant argument made by Johannes Bronkhorst.[101] The first part of his argument is an interesting counter to the accepted scholarship on Buddhism and Jainism—which holds that these religions emerged in the context of Brahminism and in opposition to it. Bronkhorst says an increasing number of scholars have come to believe that the non-Brahminical Shramana movement developed independently, east of the confluence of the Ganga and Yamuna rivers, in an area he calls Greater Magadha; meanwhile, Vedic-Brahminical culture remained to the west of this riverine confluence. Bronkhorst's view is that Brahminism initially belonged to a geographically limited area in the middle and western parts of the subcontinent's North. Subsequently, over the period between *circa* the fourth century BCE and the sixth century CE, we see Alexander's invasion culminating in the unification of much of the North under the Mauryas, and then a series of invasions after the Mauryan Empire collapses. Over this period, says Bronkhorst, Brahmins faced slaughter and extinction. As a result, "Brahmanism as an institution was under threat; it either had to face disappearance or reinvent itself."[102] Brahminism, which he calls a socio-political ideology, did the latter, and spread eastwards on the

[101] Bronkhorst 2016.
[102] Ibid.: 3.

subcontinent, and eventually over an immense geographical area from Vietnam and Indonesia to the western frontiers of the Indian subcontinent.

This socio-political ideology had a fixed social hierarchy, at the top of which were Brahmins claiming exclusive possession of spiritual knowledge and power as well as statecraft. Retaining the elaborate sacrificial heritage of the Vedas—which had come to include different forms of religious practice—was part of their hegemonic strategy for paramountcy.[103]

Setting aside the debate on whether the Shramanic traditions developed independently of or in opposition to Brahminism, let us consider Bronkhorst's argument on "how the Brahmins won." He believes the "incredible success of the Brahmanical vision of society and politics" was "not the outcome of political conquest or colonization," nor of religious conversion. Brahminism was not primarily a religion, it was "a socio-political ideology with a variable religious dimension." Rulers who adopted it did not necessarily convert from one religion to the other.[104]

What meaning Bronkhorst attaches to "political conquest" and "colonization"—when denying that these processes were involved in Brahminisation—is not clear. For instance, he says that much before royal land grants to Brahmins, Brahmin villages appear to have existed—"they somehow created villages for their own exclusive use."[105] He then cites Witzel's telling of the story of King Mathava the Videgha from the *Satapatha Brahmana* to establish that this does not refer to conquest or "military expansion" but to "Brahmanization" and "Kshatriyization" through carrying the sacrificial fire to "the marshy country of the East."[106] How Brahmins "somehow" created villages exclusively for their own use without what is inevitable within such colonising processes everywhere—the threat and use of force when required—is

[103] Ibid.: 3–4.
[104] Ibid.: 4.
[105] Ibid.: 406.
[106] Ibid.

not addressed by Bronkhorst. What does an eastward expansion of Brahmins accompanied by armed Kshatriyas imply for earlier inhabitants of these areas? Historians of ancient India, especially Dalit Bahujan intellectuals, have been asking this question for a while. The assumption that these areas were *terra nullius*—lands belonging to no one—to which the sacrificial fire could just be peacefully carried is startling and highly counterintuitive.

Bronkhorst notes that royal courts played a central role in the spread of Brahminism, though the process here differed from the expansion of Christianity in the West, which too was promoted by monarchs. Brahminism was introduced in "numerous kingdoms of relatively limited size" and the rulers of these did not have to convert. But is conversion not an irrelevant factor here? There is no disagreement that Brahminism permitted many kinds of practices and beliefs as long as the superiority of the Brahmins and their Vedas was accepted, making "conversion" irrelevant to the success of their expansion. The logical question is: Why did the rulers of these small kingdoms accept Brahminism? Bronkhorst's explanation is basically that the Brahmins deployed eschatological strategies inspiring human awe for divine commandments based on storytelling skills that were unbeatable and irresistible. Powerful Brahminical figures dominated the stories told in the Sanskrit epics and elsewhere, legitimising the caste-based hierarchy with Brahmins, and "the special powers that inhere in Brahmins," positioned on top.[107] The Brahmins, in his view, won because they won over a series of small monarchs. They did not need to win wars over the rulers of these small kingdoms into which they spread because they had a convincing rhetoric. They produced stories that persuaded ruling elites of their superior knowledge and possession of magical powers to which they had sole access.[108] For instance, in the Brahminical telling even the Mauryan Empire, "which the modern historian may think of as a disaster for Brahmanism," had been created by a Brahmin, Chanakya, who was also the author of the

[107] Ibid.: 409–10.
[108] Ibid.

Arthashastra. This telling thus conveyed the idea of immense advantage to kings who appointed Brahmins as their chief advisers.[109]

In this context, Patrick Olivelle's dating of the *Arthashastra* helps us see the Brahminical appropriation of this text more clearly. Olivelle locates the Brahminical version as the latest: whereas the oldest layer of the text, the "sources of the *Arthashastra*," dates from the period 150 BCE–50 CE, the next phase of the work's evolution, the "Kautilya Recension," Olivelle dates to 50–125 CE. In this phase a historical person with the name Kautilya composed a work with a title that was probably *Dandaniti* (Policy of Punishment) which remains the core of the *Arthashastra*. The final version of the text is what Olivelle calls the "Shastric Redaction," namely an elaboration of Kautilya's text by many authors between 175 and 300 CE. This version Brahminised the text and established the role of a Brahmin, Chanakya, as the real source of power in the founding of the Mauryan Empire. Olivelle and other scholars thus believe that the *Arthashastra*'s defence of the caste order is a Brahminical insertion woven into the earlier layers of the text in this later period, and that Chanakya and Kautilya are not the same person.[110]

The greatest triumph of Brahminism was the establishment of the Brahmin as being above all punishment or regulation, and thereby permanently worthy of protection by the king. Priyadarshini Vijaisri, in an exploration of the significance of the concept of *matsyanyaya* through a study of the Niti texts, the Dharmashastras, and select *parvas* of the Mahabharata gives us a fascinating account of the establishment of the Brahmin as the "weak" person who must be protected from cruel and ruthless predators. What emerges from these texts, she says, is that the idea of "sacrifice" is made the embodiment of the natural law sustaining the cosmic order, which in turn makes it the "imperative duty of the king to ensure by all means the continuous performance of sacrifice (and distribution of gifts to the brahmanas)." Those who do not adhere to the maintenance of sacred fires and sacrificial rites are regarded

[109] Ibid.: 411.
[110] Olivelle 2013.

as wicked, thereby making it permissible for the king "to take away the wealth from irreligious people" and, rather than amassing wealth in the treasury, to give it to "those who are good and know well the science of virtue." All the clusters of "weak" persons listed as deserving protection have "one constant presence, i.e. the Brahmin," who, unlike the other categories in these clusters—for example women—are beyond sin: "even a despicable Brahmin must be honoured." Thus, in the conception of *matsyanyaya,* says Vijaisri, "'weak' as a category becomes a cryptic code for the imperilled Brahmin."[111]

We have seen that Bronkhorst focuses very substantially on the realm of hegemony in ideas, suggesting there were no material dimensions in the triumph of Brahminism. How plausible is such an argument? It assumes the existence in relation to Brahmin narratology of high levels of receptiveness in a very large swathe of courts and kings. The persuasiveness of even the best-spun yarns has to be seen in the context of who they were spun for—rulers lacking monopoly over violence whose survival depended on suppressing rebellion and brigandage as well as the effective use of force against neighbouring principalities. No one in the ancient world ruled without the backing of arms. Moreover, the displacement of one social group from positions of material power by another cannot but involve some form of power struggle. Therefore it is difficult not to be sceptical of Bronkhorst's over-reliance on ideological persuasion when accounting for Brahminism's expansion. What is obviously more credible is the argument that, as with capitalism, the spread of Brahminism had to do with both the normalisation of a new social order through narratives, stories, philosophical exegeses, and state patronage, as well as the use of force and violence when necessary to establish a new order in the face of stiff resistance.

I have earlier examined the construction of hegemony in the puranic literature; now I will move to the available scholarship on the expansion of the Vedic people outward from the northern region called Aryavarta, bearing Brahminism as an ideology and socio-economic

[111] Vijaisri 2023.

practice. From records of land grants and stone inscriptions, scholars see Brahmin migration going back at least to 400 CE.[112] In other words, from about the fifth century CE to the eleventh there were large-scale migrations of Aryans/Brahmins to the regions that are now Bengal, Assam, Odisha, Gujarat, and Maharashtra, as well as to the South along the western coast.[113] These migrants brought with them new farming techniques, Shudras to perform manual labour, and their Brahminical religion—which included the *chaturvarna* caste system. Kings granted them land and were, additionally, expected to protect them and grant them privileges. Lands granted to Brahmins were of course those that had once belonged to the original inhabitants, and it was from them—the dispossessed—that the kings were expected to protect the Brahmins.

In Kerala the establishment of temples from the ninth to the eighteenth centuries further secured Brahminical power. These temples were central to the economy. Some of them extracted taxes, developed into centres of political activity, and were entirely controlled by Brahmins.[114] In Karnataka, temple-centred religious practices inundated the agrarian landscape in the eleventh and twelfth centuries, and temples were built at a "feverish pace" by "Rulers and chiefs, merchants, peasant proprietors and other elites."[115] The emergence of temples all over the subcontinent after this period brought new forms of worship into existence, which involved the central role of the Brahmin priest, gifts to him, and an entire political economy that developed around the temple.

So, to return to Bronkhorst's question: How did "Brahmins win"? It is impossible to answer this question without confronting the issue of violence.

Upinder Singh shows "a certain level of consensus on the Kshatriya–Brahmin relationship in the ideology and practice of state power" which

[112] Witzel 1993: 267.

[113] Witzel says, in fact, that "they [the Brahmins] have been on the move ever since our oldest testimony, the Ṛgveda! How else was the brahmanization of the whole of India possible?" Ibid.: 266.

[114] Veluthat 2013.

[115] Devadevan 2016: 26.

had emerged by the middle of the first millennium CE and gradually spread across the subcontinent. This was enabled by the movement of Brahmin ideologues to royal courts, though Brahmins as such were a heterogeneous group and had no institutional organisations. "[I]t was the wide circulation of *sastric* knowledge, literary works and epic traditions that offered powerful templates. . . for the construction of royal ideology." Apart from court patronage, grants of villages to learned Brahmins "were also important nodes in the spread and increasing influence of Brahmanical culture"—a process that Singh terms "Brahmanization."[116]

The eastward expansion of Brahminical culture is linked to the idea of Aryavarta, whose boundaries constantly shift across different texts. This term, Aryavarta, also has a social dimension: the *Vishnu Dharmasutra* describes lands where the varna order is not established as the lands of *mlecchas*, implying that Aryavarta refers to lands where the Brahminical caste order has been established. The idea of Aryavarta suggests "a potential spatial incorporation of the forest people into an expanding Brahminical universe," while the term *mleccha*—indicating both tribals and foreigners—with its origins in later Vedic texts indicates the cultural segregation of the latter.[117] Thus, Upinder Singh says that "early Vedic texts contain the ideas of extensive conquest, political paramountcy and empire."[118] She points to unequivocal evidence that "Vedic ritual represents a masculine martial ideology that justified, promoted and directed violence against people outside the tribe."[119]

Later, in the second century BCE, a Brahmin commander of the Mauryan forces, Pushyamitra Shunga, established the Shunga Empire after a military coup against the last Mauryan king. Pushyamitra is said to have performed the Ashvamedha, "a complex and violent Vedic sacrifice" in which a sacrificial horse was allowed to roam for a year, accompanied by armed men who battled all who impeded its progress.

[116] Singh 2017: 219.
[117] Ibid.: 376–7.
[118] Ibid.: 23.
[119] Ibid.: 24.

The horse symbolised the establishment of royal dominion by armed force over new lands. In the Buddhist texts Pushyamitra is said to persecute Buddhists, and, while the extent of his cruelty is debated among historians, there is no doubt about Pushyamitra's rule as indicative of a Brahminical reaction against Mauryan patronage of Buddhism and Jainism.[120] This coup and the subsequent rule of Pushyamitra Shunga, and the violent restoration of the caste order that followed, is described by Ambedkar as the Brahminical counterrevolution.[121]

The violence of the Brahmin–Kshatriya alliance is directed at all outside the tribe, but at forest people in particular, because theirs are the lands to be annexed and tamed. A variety of ancient texts describe common forest huntsmen as violent, uncultured, and lowly, even as they extol the royal hunter. Between 600 BCE and 600 CE the relationship between the state on the one hand and on the other "the wilderness" and its inhabitants—human and non-human—is one of "exploitation and violence."[122] The expansion of agriculture, and the setting up of cities and states is a continuous process of either outright violence displacing tribal and forest inhabitants or carried out through the threat of violence against them. The great ancient empires and kingdoms of the subcontinent coexisted with "vast forest tracts where the writ of the state did not run smoothly or run at all."[123]

The performance of sacrifices, central to the Vedic religion, "was associated with the settlement" of these wild areas.[124] Carrying the sacrificial fire into new frontiers of marshland and forest was not possible without violence and conquest, for the sacrifice was a demarcation of the separate spheres of village and forest. It protected the village from the

[120] Ibid.: 95.

[121] The text in which B. R. Ambedkar discusses this is titled *Revolution and Counter Revolution in Ancient India*, compiled from scattered material by the editorial committee of his Collected Works. This was published in 1987 in Volume 3 of his *Collected Works*, by the Government of Maharashtra. See Ambedkar 1987.

[122] Singh 2017: 370.

[123] Ibid.

[124] Ibid.: 373.

forest, asserted the superiority of the village, and "drew the forest into its orbit by propitiating and encompassing it."[125]

The accounts of forest people in the Puranas are also revealing. Most of the Puranas describe their contents as having been narrated by a bard to sages in the Naimisha forest in the course of a 12-year-long sacrifice. The forest chiefs are never mentioned. These chiefs were not considered rulers by the political texts either but recognised as a political force that kings had to deal with.[126]

One tribal group that does find mention in the Brahminical texts is that of the Nishadas, who are placed outside the caste system but who are likely to have been a political force to be reckoned with.[127] In the Mahabharata Ekalavya, betrayed by Drona, is a prince of the Nishadas. In a later episode the Pandavas escape from a house which was meant to be set on fire while they were sleeping. They set fire to it themselves, leaving in it Duryodhana's man and a Nishada woman and her five sons whose burnt bodies are later presumed to be those of the Pandavas and Kunti. But there is also a good and wise Nishada king, Kapavya, who has protected Brahmins and taught his people to respect and fear Brahmins.[128] We also find in the Ramayana that Guha, a Nishada king, is Rama's loyal friend; and Shabari, a tribal woman, is Rama's devotee.

In the Mahabharata "the forest is not just the antithesis of the kingdom; its violent decimation forms the kingdom's formation."[129] The Adi Parva describes the destruction of the forest of Khandavaprastha which the Pandavas burn down to build a city. Historians see this as "an epic rendering of an actual historical process—forest clearance as a precursor to city and state formation." There is no mention of people, but the vegetation, flora, and fauna are all exterminated in the horrific fire: animals that jump out to escape are cut to pieces with a sword by

[125] Ibid.
[126] Ibid.: 377.
[127] Ibid.: 378.
[128] Ibid.: 405–7.
[129] Ibid.: 400.

Arjuna, who, laughing, flings them back into the fire.[130] We can only imagine what was done to the human inhabitants of the forest.

The "insertion of oases of Brahmanical culture" into forests through land grants involved "conflicts with forest dwellers and a fracturing of their livelihoods, habitat and culture." But, as we have seen with figures like Shabari and Kapavya, forest dwellers are not only to be "subordinated and eliminated, but also incorporated and assimilated."[131] In fact, Brahmin/Kshatriya rulers apart, even Buddhist rulers were clear about subjugating the forest people, at least some of whom seem to have been in a continuous state of armed insurrection. Ashoka's *dhamma* is compassionate towards all, including animals, but the emperor threatens to use force against recalcitrant forest people.[132]

The "victory" of Brahminism was thus brought about by a Brahmin–Kshatriya alliance that involved a continuous project of hegemonisation—backed up by the violence of the state and rulers. However, is it a victory at all if the project of building one "Hindu" community based on the Brahminical *chaturvarna* system is never complete, and if violence is required even now, in the twenty-first century, to ensure compliance?

Who Are Hindus?

All strands of nationalism, including the anti-Hindutva mainstream ones, have unquestioningly accepted that what could be termed a "Hindu" community actually existed. B. R. Ambedkar seems the first and more or less sole modern intellectual to have had the perspicacity to declare that Hindu society is a myth. He pointed out that the name "Hindu" was given by outsiders to refer to all those who lived this side of the Sindhu river. Such people had no common name for themselves since they did not perceive themselves as a single community. Ambedkar asserted that "Hindu society as such does not exist. It is

---

[130] Ibid.: 401.
[131] Ibid.: 459.
[132] Ibid.: 388.

only a collection of castes."[133] Thus the much older term "Hindustan" for the land southeast of the Sindhu or Indus river is not the same as the label "Hindu" which emerged in the late nineteenth century as the name given to heterogeneous communities of people supposedly practising a single religion.

Scholars such as David Lorenzen have contested this claim, pointing out that, well before 1800, European scholars resident in India "had identified Hinduism as a set of diverse but identifiable set of beliefs and practices clearly distinguished from Islam."[134] These identifiably distinct practices are—exaltation of the four Vedas, the four varnas, and the trinity of Brahma, Vishnu, Shiva; of goddess worship; of the theory of the four yugas; and of the theodicy of karma, transmigration, and rebirth.[135] One can readily concede Lorenzen's claim because the point is not that there was no identifiable community with this set of beliefs and practices; the point is that this community was not coterminous with all those who were not Muslim. The religion described here is Brahminism, and all communities that are not Muslim or Christian cannot be pigeonholed under the undoubtedly convenient but essentially reductive umbrella term "Hinduism." Further, goddess worship is also more complicated, as we will see, for it has an independent existence outside of Brahminism and takes radically different forms among Dalit Bahujan and Adivasi communities. These goddesses cannot be conflated with those that are the spouses of male gods in the "Hindu" model. In other words, while it is possible, as Lorenzen does, to identify a community by specifying a set of common beliefs and practices across diverse groupings, that community is not so much "Hindu" (as the term has emerged since the nineteenth century) but Brahminical, and all the remaining communities that were "not Muslim" did not necessarily follow these Brahminical beliefs and practices.

The use of the label "Hinduism" retrospectively is misleading—for instance, Jamison and Witzel use the term "Vedic Hinduism," even as

[133] Ambedkar 1936.
[134] Lorenzen 2006: 13.
[135] Ibid.: 14.

they concede it is a contradiction in terms.[136] Romila Thapar uses the term Puranic Hinduism to differentiate it from the earlier Vedic Brahminism. However, she also uses the term Puranic religion to refer to this amalgam of Vedic Brahminism interwoven with local deities and aspects of Shramanic religions, thus drawing a large following from castes lower in the hierarchy. However, Thapar says that Puranic Hinduism continued to be the religion of the upper castes while the lower castes had a more local and regional focus.[137] Thus, it seems Puranic "religion" rather than Puranic Hinduism would be a more accurate rendering in Thapar's own terms, and it also appears to continue to be Brahminical. It would seem that the Vedic religion was gradually replaced by a Brahminism which included the project of the Puranas, even as, outside both of these, hundreds of other beliefs and practices continued to proliferate, which Brahminism continuously tried to co-opt in its millennia-old project.

Manu V. Devadevan examines the debate on the origins of Hinduism between what he terms the "constructionist" position—that Hinduism was constructed during the colonial period under British influence, or even invented by the British; and the "primordialist" position—which holds that Hinduism existed in India long before the arrival of the British. In the constructionist camp he places Robert E. Frykenberg, John Stratton Hawley, and Christopher John Fuller. In the primordialist camp he places Brian K. Pennington, David N. Lorenzen, Thomas R. Trautmann, and Wendy Doniger.[138] Devadevan holds, persuasively in my opinion, that both approach Hinduism with an "essentialist bent of mind," taking "religion as an always-already formed entity, with an essential core of its own."[139] The first position, he says, seems to suggest that other religions like Islam and Christianity were not constructed, while the second sees an unbroken line in identifiably "Hindu" practices from the nineteenth century to the primordial past. He says that

[136] Jamison and Witzel 1992: 3.
[137] Thapar 2020: 92–3.
[138] Devadevan 2016: 2–5.
[139] Ibid.: 7.

his own account is only "*a* prehistory and not *the* prehistory of Hinduism," as indicated by the geographical limits and the select traditions he has chosen for analysis.[140] Hinduism indeed began to be imagined at a pan-Indian level only in the nineteenth century. Neither the word Hinduism nor its variant in any Indian language existed before 1816. When the word Hindu is used prior to this date, in some cases it indicates the geographical entity, but for the most part it indicates a non-Muslim: "it is not an autonomous or internally constituted marker of identity," unlike other religious identities that "can produce self-descriptions without invoking the other."[141] That is, while all identities (not just religious identities) are constructed through a mode that involves positing an internal self and an external other, religions other than Hinduism do have internal reference points to indicate what that self is. Hinduism does not have this internal dimension which can be seen as its self-description or its conception of itself because the teeming heterogeneity of communities it seeks to define as "Hindu" prevents the identification of any feature that can internally fix what "Hindu" means.

Devadevan argues that religious identities emerged as such only around the eleventh and twelfth centuries as a result of transformations in political economy. Prior to this, a person was identified as belonging to a particular religion only if they had been initiated into it as a renouncer of worldly life or as a worshipper. "Worshipping a deity was simply a part of everyday life," like eating rice or living in a thatched hut. These were not markers of identity. Nor was religious identity conferred by being born to parents who professed a faith: "Even the son of the first Tirthankara had to *become* a Jaina. He could not be *born* as one."[142] Moreover, the religious identities that do come into being from the eleventh century onwards were Shaiva, Vaishnava, or Jaina, not "Hindu." Thus, the term "religious conversion" is misplaced for the preceding period because Ashoka or Nagarjuna, for instance, did not "convert" to

[140] Ibid.: 9.
[141] Ibid.: 10.
[142] Ibid.: 19.

Buddhism, they were initiated into another order. It was the emergence of temple-centred forms of worship that led to the transformation of religious identities during the eleventh and twelfth centuries.[143]

Devadevan concludes that the theory and history of Hinduism and its practice were brought into existence by "the upwardly mobile, literate and mostly male intelligentsia" of the nineteenth century. The lower rungs of the middle class, the lower classes, and the peasantry were not part of this enterprise.[144] That the classes and castes which constructed the idea of Hinduism were *savarna* is not posited by Devadevan, but that would indeed have been the caste composition of the classes he describes. His claim—that "Only now are we witnessing the real beginnings of Hinduism as faith, canon, practice and identity"[145]—is my sole point of disagreement with his prehistory of Hinduism. As I have argued here, it seems clear that the modern Hindutva project to construct one homogeneous Hindu community is as contested and resisted now, in our time, as the broader project of Brahminism has been since the time of the Puranas.[146]

Colonial governmentality was responsible for two developments in this broad arena. It first constructed a monolithic Hindu community and then proceeded to fracture it. The idea that India consisted of mutually exclusive, internally homogeneous religious communities was concretised first by colonial census officials who developed methods to classify the Indian population from the late nineteenth century onwards, whereby all communities that were not Muslim, Christian, or Parsi were categorised as Hindu. Ram B. Bhagat shows that, in ad-

[143] Ibid.: 35.

[144] Ibid.: 178.

[145] Ibid.: 182.

[146] Andrew J. Nicholson (2010) argues that the idea of the unity of Hinduism is neither ancient nor imposed by outsiders, but rather a conviction that dates back to the fifteenth and sixteenth centuries. He studies the commentaries of Vijnanabhiksu on Samkhya philosophy to make a case that a unified Hinduism was emerging at that time. However, as argued here, the use of the label "Hinduism" is anachronistic for this period. What is emerging as a unified set of thought and practices is essentially Brahminism.

dition, after the censuses of the nineteenth century, colonial officials also started producing a discourse in which the Hindus were seen as the majority community threatened by the growth of the "minorities," this idea growing into a larger project once Hindu nationalists saw its potential as an asset for political mobilisation.[147]

Colonial power soon realised that using the census to construct a homogeneous majority had been unwise. In the census of 1911, therefore, its provincial superintendents were asked to enumerate "genuine Hindus" by eliminating as Hindu some castes or tribes through a ten-point test. Groups were not to be classified as Hindu if they

   i.   Deny the supremacy of the Brahmans

   ii.   Do not receive the mantra (sacred words and phrases having mystical effects) from a Brahman or other recognised Hindu Guru (religious teacher)

   iii.   Deny the authority of the Vedas (ancient Hindu religious texts)

   iv.   Do not worship the great Hindu Gods

   v.   Are not served by good Brahmans as family priests

   vi.   Have no Brahman priests at all

   vii.   Are denied access to the interior of ordinary Hindu temples

   viii.   Cause pollution a) by touch, b) within certain distance

   ix.   Bury their dead

   x.   Eat beef and do not revere the cow.[148]

By these tests, large numbers earlier classified as Hindu now failed to be classifiable as Hindu. For example, in the Central Provinces and Berar alone a quarter of the persons classified as Hindus denied the supremacy of the Brahmins and the authority of the Vedas; more than half did not receive the mantras from a recognised Hindu guru; a quarter did not worship the great Hindu gods and were not served by Brahmin priests; a third were denied access to temples; a quarter caused pollution by touch; a seventh always buried their dead; half did not regard cremation as obligatory; and two-fifths ate beef. Moreover,

[147] Bhagat 2001.
[148] Census of India 1911. Cited in Bhagat 2001: 4354.

in India the social and cultural practices of Hindus and Muslims are not entirely separable. The 1911 census reported that "there are many so-called Hindus whose religion has a strong Muhammadan flavour."[149] This last feature continues into the twentieth century; its continuation into our own time has been well documented by Shail Mayaram for the Meo community.[150] P. K. Datta argues that this move in the 1911 census was intended to fracture the "Hindu" community by caste in order to isolate the upper castes who had threatened British power during the Swadeshi movement of 1905. Not surprisingly, Hindu nationalists such as Madan Mohan Malaviya and Lajpat Rai challenged the results of this census as an attempt to make Hindus "politically impotent."[151]

The fact seems therefore to be that these caste communities, even as they were not Muslim or Parsi or Christian were indeed not "Hindu" either. In the longer-term process of political assimilation and the operation of modern governmentality which had fixed slots for "religious identity"—into one or the other of which each individual needed to declare she fitted—many individuals earlier belonging in fluid ways to these communities would necessarily have needed to describe themselves as Hindu because no other option was available. To such non-voluntary categorisation there has been resistance. In the aftermath of the 1911 census and subsequently there have been sporadic attempts by communities defined as Hindu to claim an independent identity—these, more often than not, being then thwarted legally and politically.[152]

By the time of Independence it had become clear that "Hindu" could not be defined in any consensual and uniform way that referred to common practices or beliefs. The Constitution, therefore, in Explanation II to Article 25(2)(b), states that "Hindus shall be construed as including a reference to persons professing the Sikh, Jaina or Buddhist

[149] Ibid.

[150] Mayaram 2017.

[151] Datta 1999.

[152] Some of these attempts are referred to in this chapter and elsewhere through the present book, passim.

religion." Later, for the purposes of the Hindu Code Acts of 1955–6, the term "Hindus" was declared to include "a Virashaiva, a Lingayat or a follower of the Brahmo, Prarthana or Arya Samaj." Evidently, even this did not cover the hundreds of other belief systems in the subcontinent, so the next category was simply "any other person domiciled in the territories to which this Act extends who is not a Muslim, Christian, Parsi or Jew by religion, unless it is proved that any such person would not have been governed by the Hindu law or by any custom or usage as part of that law." The burden of proving oneself as not Hindu is thus upon the person who does not belong to the other four listed communities. The umbrella meaning given to the term "Hindus" by the Constitution has thereby brought into one box a wide variety of practices, many of which had in fact emerged as dissenting heterodox critiques of Hinduism-as-Brahminism—such as Jainism, Buddhism, and Sikhism. Court judgments too have asserted the capacious character of "Hinduism," thus defining and establishing this category in the course of denying claims by different groups to be a non-Hindu minority. The case of the Swaminarayan sect is revealing. It denied Dalits entry into its temples, claiming that it permitted entry on the basis not of caste but of membership of its *satsang* (spiritual community). This claim was accepted in court in 1951, but the Bombay Act of 1956 threw open all places of worship to "all classes and sections of Hindus"—carefully avoiding the term "caste," as Manoj Mitta points out.[153] As appeals against the Swaminarayan dispute mounted and reached the Supreme Court, the matter was finally settled in 1966 with Chief Justice P. B. Gajendragadkar declaring Hinduism to be uniquely inclusive, encompassing a wide diversity of gods, beliefs, philosophies, and practices, thus emphasising that the Swaminarayan sect was "Hindu" and came under the Bombay Act of 1956. Analysing this judgment, Mitta points out that Gajendragadkar did not touch on Hindu beliefs on caste and untouchability as a contradiction to this view of "Hinduism" as capacious and accommodative. He could avoid this discussion

[153] Mitta 2023: 446.

because, unlike Sanatanists who cited scripture to deny Dalits entry into their temples, the Satsangis claimed distance from Hinduism.[154] This 1966 definition of Hinduism by the Chief Justice, paradoxical though it was in the context of the Swaminarayan sect, is an important landmark, reinforcing the idea of a "Hindu majority."

In this context, the parliamentary debates over the Hindu Code Bills (mentioned earlier) are revealing, and yet another instance of the assimilative drive of Hindutva. Under the legal definition of "Hindu" have been lumped a large number of heterogeneous communities with diverse practices—whether or not they called these practices Hindu or thought of themselves as Hindus. These were communities with matrilineal inheritance practices; communities in which women had the right to divorce, remarry, and remarry when widowed; communities with widely varying forms of the marriage ceremony. Feminists argue that one of the goals of the Hindu Code Bills was to bring about uniformity among these practices as a national integration measure rather than to endow women with rights.[155] Uniformity conceived as a measure that empowers women is deeply problematic. Madhu Kishwar has shown how the Hindu Women's Right to Property Act, which was passed under British rule in 1937, while establishing a Hindu widow's right to her husband's property, worsened the situation for Jain widows when applied uniformly to all communities classified as "Hindu"; the Jain widow was much better provided for under customary law. The "reformed" law worked to her detriment because of a blind application of the principle of uniformity to all believed to be Hindu.[156]

Heterogeneous practices were also disciplined in other ways: the Hindu Marriage Act of 1955 set up norms for the dissolution of marriage that were more stringent than those practised by many communities and castes. While in its final form the Act permitted communities to retain their customary forms of divorce, customs as defined by the Act had to meet the test of not being "immoral" or "opposed to public policy."

[154] Ibid.: 447–8.
[155] Parasher 1992.
[156] Kishwar 1994: 2151.

Whether they met these criteria depended on how judges ruled when a case came up. Thus, on later occasions a caste custom which permitted a woman to leave her husband and remarry without his consent was adjudged void on account of being deemed immoral; another which permitted the dissolution of a marriage by either spouse on payment of a sum of money fixed by the caste was adjudged void as being opposed to public policy.[157] Even while permitting customary law some leeway, jurisprudential applications and requirements kept custom tightly within the bounds of North Indian *savarna* morality. Invariably, practices that differed from the upper-caste North Indian norm were either not considered at all or rejected, with only one kind of practice being enshrined as truly Hindu and Indian. Kishwar quotes the following exchange in parliament during a debate on the Act:

> To Mukut Behari Lal's assertion that no Hindu parent would want to inherit a daughter's property in the event of her death (an argument against property rights for daughters), L Krishnaswami Bharathi asked, "Why not, why not, what's the harm?"
>
> In response another MP, Bhargava said—Perhaps my honourable friend comes not from India but from some outside country.
>
> Bharathi—I come from south of India . . .
>
> Bhargava—In India no father or mother will ever think of receiving anything from the daughter.
>
> Bharathi—That may be so in the Punjab.
>
> Bhargava—It is so in the whole of northern India . . .
>
> Therefore the entire fabric of the rules of devolution is based on anti-Hindu ideals.[158]

Another instance of such disregard for practices that did not match *savarna* North Indian norms is visible in S. P. Mukherjee's mocking comment when speaking against making divorce less complicated: " Somebody said . . . that South India was specially progressive and many of the laws we are considering are already in existence there today. I say, good luck to South India. Let South India proceed from progress to progress, from divorce to divorce why force it on others who do not want

[157] Ibid.
[158] Ibid.: 2155.

it?"[159] Of course, the reverse was what happened—the Hindu Code reforms eventually did force *savarna* North Indian norms on all those labelled "Hindu," whether they wanted it or not.

The sense of entitlement that Hindutva proponents have to what they call India is such that they genuinely believe the rest of the population resides in the country as their tenants, and that they themselves are very generous landlords. For instance, during incidents of racist attacks on Africans in Delhi in 2017, when India was being rightly criticised as racist, Tarun Vijay, former editor of the RSS journal *Panchajanya* and a leading RSS ideologue, said in an international news channel: "If we [Indians] were racist, why would we have the entire South? Which is you know . . . completely Tamil, you know Kerala, you know Karnataka and Andhra. Why do we live with them? We have blacks, black people all around us."[160]

In recent years Lingayats, who have for long been subsumed under Hinduism, have reasserted their old claim that they are not Hindus. This claim is at least eight decades old—they had asserted their separate identity even while the Constitution was being drafted. Lingayats are followers of the twelfth-century social reformer Basavanna who rebelled against Hinduism and all its tenets. He rejected the authority of the Vedas and Upanishads, he rejected caste, idol worship, and "the authority of Sanskrit," instead giving ritual and religious primacy to Kannada.[161] Linked to the Lingayat claim is that of Veerashaivism, which, although it has its roots in the Vedas, worships no god other than Shiva and claims to be a sub-sect of Lingayats with antecedents preceding Basavanna. This sub-sect can be found spread across the southern states. Lingayats and Veerashaivas both claim minority status, which was granted to them in 2018 by the Congress government in Karnataka. The opposition BJP in the state termed the decision an attempt to divide the Hindus. Later that year, in a successful appeal to the Karnataka High Court, the BJP government at the Centre stated that it had

[159] Ibid.: 2150.
[160] Press Trust of India 2017.
[161] Lankesh 2017.

rejected the recommendation of the state government to grant religious minority status to the Lingayat and Veerashaiva communities. The Centre reiterated that "these communities are part of the
Hindu religion and do not form another religion of their own."[162]
What better evidence could there be for a new variant of the ancient
Brahminical drive to appropriate and assimilate? When Lingayats
claim minority status they are accused of "dividing Hindus." Surely
a conundrum here must be recognised: if Lingayats are already Hindu, then it is Hindus who are dividing Hindus. Why is the claim of
Lingayats to be not Hindu not acceptable? To whom is it not acceptable? The answer has always been obvious while not being allowed
the visibility it deserves: It is not acceptable only to the politics of
Hindutva. For ordinary people who have for legal reasons and census
reasons and reasons of state been positioned under the umbrella term
"Hindu," only their own practices and labels attributed to themselves
matter, not whether or not others accept this label for themselves.

Hindutva is the modern politics of the nation-state in which it is
essential to establish that "Hindus" are a majority—the foundation of
its *national* culture. This myth is sustained by the legal definition that
all communities that are not Muslim, not Christian, and not Parsi
are Hindu. If Lingayats were allowed a legally valid identity separate
from "Hindu," it would lead to many other communities demanding
the same—and then Brahminism would just be one among many
minority religions on the subcontinent.

To summarise: what then, is the difference between Hindutva and
Hinduism? In one familiar formulation, "Hindutva" is the modern political ideology that tries to produce and control a nation-state predicated
on one identity, "Hindu," as the only pure Indian identity. "Hinduism"
on the other hand is a set of heterogeneous religious beliefs and practices. In addition, I have argued that while an identifiable community
with specific beliefs and practices can be termed "Hindu," this is only
one specific form of belief and practice, namely Brahminism. Not all

---

[162] India Today Web Desk 2018.

the other communities that are not Muslim, Parsi, or Christian can be brought under this umbrella term.

"Hinduism," the way it has come to be used over the twentieth century, then, is merely a label that enables the Hindutva assertion of an eternal identity, claiming its own narrow idea of Hindus as the majority in India by assimilating multiple and often contradictory practices into its reductive embrace. Simultaneously, practices contradictory to Brahminism—meat-eating, for example—are sought to be erased. Thus the term "Hinduism" also functions to discipline the diverse practices of castes and communities into a single and narrow Hindutva vision—North Indian Brahminical/*savarna*, and masculinist.[163] Evidently, twenty-first century Hindutva does not even recognise the significance of their founding father Savarkar's strategy of offering Hinduism even to those who do not accept the Vedas and Brahminism. Instead, violence is freely used against those who do not comply with Sanatani norms. As the many instances discussed so far demonstrate, this is precisely because not even a small percentage of people pushed into Hinduism by Hindutva necessarily identify either with Hinduism or with Hindutva.

Adivasi-Dalit-Bahujan Counternarratives to Hindutva

Some fascinating revisionist accounts of popular Hindu festivals emerge from the perspective of Adivasi-Dalit-Bahujan communities. These are not really "revisionist," they simply bring to the surface older histories that have long simmered below the skin of mainstream *savarna* Hindu society and are now breaking through Hindutva narratives from within.

[163] We need not go into different strands of Hindutva ideology here. Suffice it to say that Savarkar, who represents a modernist strand, was sharply critical of caste, did not promote vegetarianism, and in "Seven Shackles" provides strong statements of modernist distaste at orthodox Hindu beliefs. The form that Hindutva has taken is not therefore strongly Savarkarite, although he is genuflected to as the originator of Hindutva.

The Ambedkarite intellectual Kanwal Bharti reminds us that the myths behind almost all Hindu festivals as told in the Puranas involve the defeat of the asuras (demons) by the devas (gods)—whether Dussehra, Diwali, Onam, or Holi. The devas he identifies as Brahmins, and the defeat of the asuras is the defeat of anti-Brahminical and pre-Brahminical ways of life and religious practices—in forests and outside centres of established kingdoms. Very often this defeat is by trickery—of Mahabali by Vamana, of Ekalavya by Dronacharya—and by the co-opting of willing elements in these non-Brahmin societies—of for example Vibheeshana and Prahlada.

Bharti retells the story of Holi to illustrate this claim. The pre-Hindu spring festival of Holi has a later Hindu mythology that draws it into the Aryan configuration of a perennial deva–asura confrontation. Prahlada, the pious son of the asura Hiranyakashipu (himself pious, but too arrogant for the gods), is sought to be killed by his own father in various ways because he has become a devotee of Vishnu. One of the ways is by getting Hiranyakashipu's sister, Holika, Prahlada's aunt, to sit with her nephew in her lap in the sacrificial fire, for she has a boon—that fire will not burn her. Her boon fails, Prahlad survives by chanting Vishnu's name, and Hiranyakashipu is slain by Vishnu in the form of Narasimha. On Holi, effigies of Holika are burnt to symbolise this defeat. But what was it a defeat of? In Kanwal Bharti's telling, Prahlada turns to the Brahminical religion while Hiranyakashipu and Holika continue to fight Brahminism.[164]

A similar reversal is effected for Onam by reading it through Dalit and Adivasi narratives. Onam is the festival associated in Kerala with the annual return of the beloved and good asura (daitya) king Mahabali to meet his people. Vishnu, in his avatar as a dwarf Brahmin, Vamana, has tricked Mahabali into exile in the netherworld (*patalam*) and usurped his kingdom. But upon Mahabali recognising Vamana as Vishnu, he does not protest and accepts his exile. For this he is permitted to return once a year to see his people.

[164] Bharati 2016.

Mahabali's power as a symbol of non-Brahmin identity is acknowledged by Jotirao Phule, the nineteenth-century philosopher and anti-caste activist. In his important work *Gulamgiri* (Slavery; 1873), Phule
wrote of Mahabali as a "strong and valiant King" who was "a friend of
the downtrodden," and Vamana as "mean, cunning, treacherous and
ungrateful." *Gulamgiri* was a secularised reading of Puranic stories that
inverted the deva–asura hierarchy.[165]

Telling the story of Mahabali from two perspectives, the tribal
and the *savarna*, Vinod Kottayil Kalidasan offers us another layer. In
the standard telling, Mahabali's reign is said to have been marked by
the characteristics associated with modern democracy and socialism.
Mahabali traces his ancestry to Prahlada and is himself a devotee of
Lord Vishnu. The god Indra becomes jealous of the growing reputation of Mahabali and calls upon Vishnu to intervene, who does so in
the form of Vamana, later graciously permitting Mahabali's annual
return. This myth, drawn from the Puranas, is seen with some variations
in other parts of India as well as in Thailand, Trinidad, and Malaya.[166]
Although the story of Mahabali (or Maveli) has been promoted by Left
and democratic forces in Kerala as the return of a non-Brahmin king
and the celebration of his just reign, Kalidasan argues that this myth
remains inside the caste-Hindu frame as it "requires a mode of submission" to the "Aryan colonization of South India."[167] This is effected
by Mahabali's devotion to Vishnu and his calm acceptance of his exile,
and by the graciousness of the Lord who does not kill him and permits
his annual return. Some contemporary images of Mahabali even show
him as a fair-skinned, portly, middle-aged man wearing a *poonul* (the
Brahminical sacred thread), thus completing the erasure of Mahabali,
the wiry-bodied brown-skinned non-Brahmin.

There is another myth about the origin of Kerala, which is entirely
Brahminical and involves Parashurama, a Brahmin, as the founder of
sixty-four Brahmin villages, who then goes in search of a Kshatriya to rule

[165] Omvedt 2008.
[166] Kalidasan 2015: 105.
[167] Ibid.: 107.

over them. This is the myth associated with many rulers of Kerala even up to the early modern period—among the Zamorins of Calicut, for example. At the top of the social order "there was always the figure of the Brahmin deciding or consecrating the sanctity of the title," and this is the right asserted by Vamana too.[168] According to Kalidasan, the mainstream telling of the story of Mahabali thus remains within this paradigm. Nevertheless, the project of Brahminising the Mahabali narrative is an unstable one and struggles to succeed even in the twenty-first century. For example, in 2016 the BJP home minister Amit Shah greeted Kerala on Onam by calling the festival "Vamana Jayanti"—the day Vishnu was born in his avatar as the Brahmin Vamana – thus relegating Mahabali to the margins and making the Brahmin the centre of the festival. This caused an uproar in Kerala.[169] The furore has not deterred Hindutva forces continuing since then to claim Onam as Vamana Jayanti, although this Brahminical framing of Onam has little credence in Kerala.

In contrast to the mainstream telling of the Onam story, Kalidasan narrates stories by Adiya and Paniya Adivasis from the tribal regions of Wayanad in the Western Ghats. In the first, the Adiyas were not slaves to begin with, they lived under the just guidance of their tribal elder Mavelimantu. Three lords entered the village and beat Maveli to death, usurped the land, and imposed the caste system on the people. The second has two princes stealing soil from Maveli's land under their fingernails and later using this soil to control his entire kingdom. The third tells us that Maveli was tricked by a Brahmin landlord (Thampuran), but not, unlike in the Vamana story, with supernatural feats. They play a game weighted against Maveli, and he and his people are enslaved forever. In the fourth story, three Brahmins attack Maveli with weapons and bring a violent goddess, Malu, to subjugate the people, divide them into castes, and enslave them. This last story resembles the defeat of the "demon" Mahishasura by Durga, which we will be touching upon later.[170]

[168] Ibid.
[169] Harikrishnan, et al. 2016.
[170] Kalidasan 2015: 111.

Kalidasan draws our attention to the way in which these Adivasi tellings of the story of Mahabali/Maveli involve no supernatural elements and no redemption. There is no return of the just king and the enslavement is eternal. This is in fact the historical reality of the Paniya and Adiya castes of Wayanad, who became agrestic slaves to the feudal lords—Brahmin and non-Brahmin—who took over their lands, and who bought and sold them like animals well up to and for many decades after 1947. "The enslavement was physical, sexual, cultural, economic and spiritual."[171]

M. B. Manoj, in an interview to *Dalit Camera*, says that if you read Onam through the eyes of Dalits the festival loses its natural association with Malayali identity. In fact, he says, "Onam is a black day for Dalits, a day of murder, even as it is a day of happiness for the upper castes."[172] From this perspective the coming of Onam also marks the coming of the caste system and slavery to Kerala. Manoj speaks of Dalit folk songs that criticise the upper-caste nature of Onam and its vegetarianism, as well as songs that criticise the temple-entry proclamation of Kerala. There is a realisation among Dalits, says Manoj, that Onam is a celebration of the murder of their king by the upper castes. As part of this realisation, Dalit movements—and especially the Indian Dalit Federation—have observed hunger strikes during the Onam festival. Manoj remembers participating in one of these hunger strikes in Idukki town in Kerala during his college days. He stresses that most Dalits, tribals, and backward castes eat meat during Onam and their cultures fall outside the cultural milieu of Onam.

The practice of offering meat, tobacco, and alcohol to non-Aryan deities continues to this day in many parts of the country, including Kerala, where "deities like Chathan, ancestor Mutthappans and mother goddesses like Kali and Kurumba" receive such "impure" offerings.[173]

However, the drive to assimilate such shrines into Brahminism and extinguish their previous identity is ongoing well into the twenty-first century. O. B. Roopesh has written about "templeisation," a process

[171] Ibid.: 112.
[172] Manoj 2012.
[173] Sakthidharan 2019: 99.

he describes as one of "converting myriad forms of worship places like *kavus* (sacred spaces near traditional homes of various non-Brahmin and Dalit caste communities in Kerala), to the Hindu (or Brahminical) temple form."[174] Sakthidharan says that all over Kerala, Tamil Nadu, and Karnataka deities made of sand and lime have been replaced by granite ones that do not dissolve in the rite of ablution. Uncovered sacred groves of local goddesses have "been Aryanised and have become Hindu kshetrams (temples) of Kali, Durga or Bhagavati, with their upper-caste priests and tantris."[175]

The Sabarimala Temple episode discussed in detail earlier is a perfect example of this templeisation drive. There is sufficient historical evidence to suggest that Sabarimala was a Buddhist shrine, and that Ayyappan was Nilakantha Avalokitesvara depicted in the Buddhist Puranas. The chant of Sabarimala pilgrims, *Swamiye sharanam Ayyappa*,[176] echoes the Buddhist chant *Buddham sharanam gachhami*. Rajeev Srinivasan suggests that prior to its Buddhist incarnation the temple was an early Dravidian Shaivite centre and has thus been a sacred spot for three to four millennia.[177] He cites Devakumar Sreevijayan who has an interesting perspective on the myth of Ayyappan as the son of Vishnu and Shiva—that this suggests an assimilation of Ayyappan into Brahminism through a reconciliation between Shaivites and Vaishnavites. Unlike other parts of the South, therefore, where the two were often in conflict, Kerala has typically seen harmony between them.[178]

Jitheesh P. M. has surveyed scholarship on the origins of Sabarimala and Ayyappan and finds it is difficult to establish Ayyappan in the Puranic texts, and nor is his worship found north of the Vindhyas. However

[174] Roopesh 2018.
[175] Sakthidharan 2019: 102.
[176] The chant specifically has "Ayyappa," not "Ayyappan."
[177] "Dravidian" has specific linguistic and ethnic connotations which I will not get into. Suffice it to say that Dravidian refers to non-Aryan people thought to be inhabiting the peninsular part of the subcontinent long before the advent of the Vedic people.
[178] Srinivasan 1997.

he finds non-Brahmin influences on the historical evolution of Sabarimala. The relationship of Ayyappan with the horseman god Ayyanar of Tamil Nadu is one such influence. According to T. A. Gopinatha Rao, whom Jitheesh quotes: "Ayyanar is basically a village tutelary deity, worshipped by the lower castes. There are iconographical similarities between the two deities and etymologically too it appears to be feasible."[179] It is these layered histories of tribal, non-Aryan, Dravidian, and Buddhist divinities that the templeisation of Sabarimala seeks to erase.

There are also existing temples to the anti-heroes of the Mahabharata in at least two states, Uttarakhand and Kerala. In Uttarakhand, some villages worship the Kauravas as their ancestors and there are temples to Duryodhana in several places. This practice is being replaced by mainstream "Hindu" beliefs in current times, such as the claim that the temples to Duryodhana are actually to Someshwar or Shiva.[180] Nevertheless, they continue to exist as temples to Duryodhana.

In Kerala there are temples to Duryodhana and Shakuni; in these there are no idols and the worship is conducted by the Kurava tribe. Legends link the visit of Duryodhana to these places during the exile of the Pandavas, and he is remembered as a noble prince who did not observe caste restrictions and worshipped Shiva. The place of worship is a raised platform at which devotees can submit to a divine power of their own understanding. The priests here are from the Kurava community, a hunting-gathering tribe of the southern part of the subcontinent who in the Sangam period ruled the mountains and were considered warriors. Gradually subjugated, these forest people were labelled Criminal Tribes by the British colonial government and are now Denotified Tribes living in penury over many parts of South India. The absence of an idol at these temples indicates pre-Brahminical forms of worship drawn into puranic narratives through the link, interestingly, to Duryodhana, not the Pandavas. Nandi, Shiva's bull, is installed at the Malanada Duryodhana temple in Kollam

[179] Jitheesh 2018.
[180] Aswal 2016; Ramanan and Ramanan 2017.

District on the stone platform—where it is not Nandi who is worshipped but the stone platform itself, called Appuppan or "grandfather."[181] These temples still flourish, worship is conducted at them, and the main offering is liquor.[182]

"Appan" could indicate Buddhist influence too, as we saw above. Buddhism entered Kerala around the third century CE, very much before the Aryan expansion southward. The *kavus* (sacred groves) that existed in several regions of Kerala were at one point, it is believed, Buddhist shrines. These sacred groves were also educational institutions and martial training centres known as *kalari*. Almost all these sacred groves have been converted into temples. Kerala's Buddhist heritage until the tenth century, followed by the disappearance of Buddhism, also indicates the takeover and possible destruction of Buddhist shrines and practices by Brahminical forces. However, there are traces of this memory in several sites—for instance at the temples to Ayyappan and Duryodhana discussed earlier. Another instance is the Kiliroor Kunnummel Bhagavathy Temple, dedicated to a goddess but with a sculpture of Buddha within a shrine devoted to Krishna. The idol termed Krishna, however, resembles a Yogic Avalokitesvara in *padmasana*. According to Ajay Sekher, "The Krishna shrine is in Gaja Prishta architectural style (that resembles the bottom of a standing elephant), a style that is commonly found in ancient Buddhist temples. This shrine faces the east and the northern door is designated for Sri Buddha but remains closed."[183]

Most places of worship in India are palimpsests reflecting and refracting layers of history and myth, and the Hindutva project of claiming Brahminical deities as the original or only divinities at non-Aryan, Dravidian, and Muslim places of worship is part of the violent political project of eliminating the diversity of this terrain and re-forming it as Hindu Rashtra. Recognising such entangled histories, Parul Pandya Dhar asks us to consider perceiving "a mosque as a kind of temple,"

[181] Santhosh 2018; Neelakantan 2013.
[182] *Mathrubhumi* 2022.
[183] Sekher 2011.

citing the twelfth-century *Jayaprichchha* and the fifteenth-century *Vriksharnava*—architectural treatises (*vastu-shastras*) from western India—in which "a mosque is called a 'Rahman-Prasada' or 'Rahman-Suralaya' (Temple of Rahman)." This synthesis of Arabic and Sanskrit to give the mosque a new name, says Dhar, "expresses how Hindu–Muslim pasts were perceived by brahmin writers of these *vastu-shastras* and by local building communities in Gujarat."[184]

The entry of "northern" gods to the South has been extensively tracked by scholars. George L. Hart points out a key difference between southern indigenous practices, in which power emanates from everyday objects, and northern practices in which power is summoned from another world, as in the *Rig Veda*. In the South, the priests were of the lowest classes, and southern indigenous sacred power was closely associated with death, as many of the gods worshipped were spirits of dead heroes—men and women. The new gods therefore had to both "remain entirely separate from the dangerous (and impure) forces that pervade the South Indian countryside—but at the same time, they had to be accepted as sacred and efficacious."[185] This is why the same deity often has varying natures and histories at different sites. For instance, Murukan (or Subramanian) in Tamil Nadu is worshipped by Hindus partly as Shiva and Parvati's son, and partly as an independent deity, while the same deity is worshipped as Katargama in Sri Lanka by Hindus, Buddhists, and the indigenous Vedda people. In this context the work of Malathi de Alwis and Sharni Jayawardena on the Hindu-Buddhist cult of the goddess Pattini (as Sinhala Buddhists know her) and Kannaki/Kannagi (as invoked by Tamil Hindus) is relevant. Their work ponders on the complex nature of idealised womanhood: on the one hand Pattini/Kannaki is revered as a chaste and loyal wife, but on the other held in awe for her violent, vengeful, and destructive power.[186] One can see here the familiar modes of incorporating and domesticating pre-Brahminical deities into the Aryan pantheon.

[184] Dhar 2022.
[185] Hart 1979: 30.
[186] De Alwis and Jayawardene, no date.

Dalit Bahujan Adivasi Goddesses

In the Ramayana and Mahabharata the presence of powerful women who must be killed, maimed, and humiliated has been remarked upon by feminists from Irawati Karve to Nabaneeta Deb Sen and Uma Chakravarti.[187] Surpanakha in the Ramayana, for example, has been read by many feminist scholars as a woman unashamed of her own sexual desire who was never taught that she must be passive and submissive—she must learn that lesson brutally by having her nose cut off by Rama's brother Lakshmana. That these are women of communities we would today describe as Dalit-Bahujan-Adivasi has also been noted. Uma Chakravarti reads Valmiki's Ramayana as a reconstruction of multiple elements of stories circulating across South and South East Asia into a particular narrative whose aim is to establish a new norm over the variegated practices of the land—the Aryan, patriarchal, patrilineal order of sexuality and property.[188] Thus, the southern people of Lanka, where women were freer, have to be subjugated and taught proper codes of sexual conduct, the people of the forest (the Vanaras) are pacified into the Aryan king's loyal army, and Sita is instructed in the dangers that lie in wait on crossing the limits set by the Lakshman Rekha.

As Kanwal Bharti reminds us, the young princes of Ayodhya, while in exile, travel deep into forests, establishing by armed force Aryan Brahminical rule over the original inhabitants—asuras of various kinds— who are killed for disturbing the austerities and ceremonies that sages insist on performing in their forests. Why are the Brahmin sages entering these forests without the permission of the original inhabitants in the first place?

Or take the story of Mahishasura and Durga, which at one level is yet another account of the defeat of Adivasis by Brahmins using trickery. But a feminist reading produces another level of complexity. While the defeat of the demon Mahishasura by Durga is the occasion for one of the most important Hindu festivals, Durga Puja, the journal *Forward Press* had for some years been reporting on Mahishasur Puja

---

[187] Karve 1967; Sen 1997; Chakravarti 1983.
[188] Chakravarti 1983.

in eastern India by Adivasis and publishing images of Mahishasura. For this it faced police raids and ultimately closed down its print version.[189] The fact is that Mahishasura has for long been worshipped by Santhals and other tribal people across the swathe of the tribal belt in Central India.[190] The Asur tribe of Jharkhand of over 10,000 members is classified as a "Particularly Vulnerable Tribal Group" by the Indian government, and their language, spoken by some 7000 individuals, is described by UNESCO as "definitely endangered." The Asurs, who claim ancestry from Mahishasura himself, believe that the birth of Durga from the conjoined powers of Brahma, Vishnu, and Shiva was a "crooked conspiracy" hatched because their king Mahishasura was blessed with a boon by Brahma that no man or god could kill him. The more traditionally inclined members of asuras therefore even choose to completely isolate themselves and mourn Mahishasura's death during the period of the Durga Puja.[191]

The Santhals of Bengal, too, have their own story about Mahishasura. He was their Raja Debi, defeated by trickery using a woman named "Durga" sent by the gods. The Santhal musical genius Bajar Hembrom described the origins and meaning of the Dashoi festival, which Santhals observe on the last day of Durga Puja in this way:

> *The Dashoi dance is on the last day of Durga Puja. You worship Durga. We search for, we still search for, our lost Raja Debi. You call him Asur.*[192]

It is clear that the mythology is a deep sorrowful acknowledgement of the dispossession of adivasis from all that was once theirs—*jal, jangal,* and *jameen*—rivers, forests, and land.

It was learnt in 2016, when a concerted attack by the BJP on Jawaharlal Nehru University (JNU) had just begun, that Dalit Bahujan students of JNU had been celebrating Mahishasura for some years. At this the minister for education at the time expressed shock in

---

[189] Dayal 2016.

[190] Ranjan 2016.

[191] Pandey and Biswas 2016.

[192] As related to Kunal Deb and translated by Madhushree Mukherjee: see Mukherjee 2015.

parliament, terming it "demon worship," which she simultaneously labelled "anti-national." The conflation of the Nation here with North Indian *savarna* Hinduism, and simultaneously an ignorance of or contempt and hatred towards alternative traditions of worship, could not be clearer.[193] Hindutva is shamed and embarrassed by the practices of communities that it terms "Hindu" for its purposes, and its attempts to "reform" such practices into the rigid North Indian upper-caste version is key to the Hindu nationalist project of consolidating "Hinduism."

The role of Durga here as a mere "seductress" makes the story more complicated. Who is this Durga? Is this the same deity worshipped by *savarna* Hindus? In the words of Mrinal Pande:

> Durga's historical origins are embedded firmly among the indigenous pre-Aryan cultures of India. The Vedic tradition has no goddess similar to Durga, the warrior goddess. The early Puranic references to Durga. . . associate her with the Sabara tribals residing among the Vindhya mountains. This was initially an intractable area described as. . . hard to access—*Durgen gamyate*, hence the name Durga. The mountainous region with thick forests and inhabited by wild tribes and animals, was peripheral to civilised society. . .
>
> The first images of Durga—armed to her teeth—slaying Mahishasur, a semi-male buffalo, begin to be visible throughout India around the fourth century CE. Her festival held at harvest time, the precursor to today's Durga Puja, also associated her powers of fertility with not so much the womb, but vegetation (as Shaakambhari). Motherhood of the genetic sort was not her priority and as an armed warrior and protector of men and women, it became entirely appropriate that this combative Durga be kept energised with blood offerings and wine as vital nourishment for her body and soul. . . [T]his extremely powerful, militant armed goddess arrived as Durga, the mainstream Hindu goddess of peasants and traders, only during the medieval period. Thus, in many respects, the Durga of the Puranas since the very beginning negates the misty-eyed and maternally inclined Mata Rani model being defended so fiercely by bhakts today.[194]

So Durga never gets fully domesticated as Shiva's wife Parvati and retains these fierce, unpredictable, untameable elements.

[193] Pareek 2016.
[194] Pande 2016.

The second element in the Adivasi telling that clearly is also an attempt to recover Adivasi masculinity from its defeat by Brahminism is that of Durga as a mere agent of Brahminism, a "seductress." From Mrinal Pande's account it is clear that the Durga of Mahishasura myth refers not to the general principle of female power but to the specific Brahminical goddess worshipped as Durga.

There are other, more ancient visions of female power in this land than the RSS Bharat Mata—black goddesses who pre-date the patriarchy normalised over centuries by Aryan migrations from the North— potent, mysterious forces that offered their devotees annihilation, blood, and rage. One historical reading of such black goddesses of the southern part of the Indian subcontinent is offered by Lynn E. Gatwood, who makes the argument that the wild, independent, sexual tribal goddesses of pre-Vedic times were domesticated and tamed by Brahminical priestly classes in the process of pacification of the non-Aryan peoples of the South.[195] They were domesticated by being "spousified"—they were installed as the wives of Aryan male gods. In addition we see the domestication of other kinds of divinities with complex histories of formation—also black, some ancient forest gods, many non-human—such as Ganesha, Ayyappan, Skanda/Subramanian—they become the children of these newly formed conjugal couples. The libidinal excess that cannot be contained in these narratives escapes into myths such as the birth of Ayyappan from Shiva and Vishnu—the latter in the temporary form of the beautiful goddess Mohini, born from his thigh, after he returned to his male form. However, the shrines to these deities continue independently and have a clear presence in the cosmological landscape, attracting large numbers of worshippers. Wild undomesticated goddesses are still present as living principles—Ellaiyamman, for example as well as Sheetala Mata, who protects children from smallpox. As Vidya Dehejia puts it:

> She is encountered in manifold guises. In a simple wooden shrine in the town of Chhatradi in the Himalayan foothills she stands as a glowing brass

[195] Gatwood 1985.

image, smooth and sensuous, adorned with jewels and silks. On a hilltop near Guwahati . . . worshippers invoke her presence in the simple form of a cleft in a natural boulder, filled with water from an underground spring . . . She is a bizarre fiendish figure riding a wild ass with a third eye in its flank in Tibet; in southern Madurai she is a dark stone figure concealed beneath crown, jewels, silks and flowers. And in the numerous villages of the Indian subcontinent, she is little more than a vermilion smeared stone or mound of earth.[196]

D. D. Kosambi, writing about mother goddesses in villages all over Maharashtra, shows how some of them represent Dalit Bahujan figures such as a "red-daubed female in relief," who represents a *teli* woman (of the oil-vendor community) killed by a stray bullet, and who would not let her community sleep in peace until worshipped. Others are tribal goddesses, such as "a remarkable primitive and dangerous mother goddess Satavi" who has nothing to do with Sati, he says, which is also the name in Marathi for an unpleasant harridan. Bolhai is another tribal goddess who has not been Brahminised, beyond being labelled a sister of the Pandavas, to whom blood sacrifice is made, and who sets out on a two-month hunting trip every winter, symbolised by a palanquin procession. None of these ancient goddesses have a male consort—they are mothers, but unmarried. The next step in history, says Kosambi, is to marry them to a male god. His argument is that in tribal societies knowledge of the father of the child was irrelevant. Although his book appeared in 1962, goddess worship of this kind embodies living traditions even today, in the twenty-first century.[197]

Into this picture must also be brought Putana, a bad mother, the asura woman who tried to kill the baby Krishna with milk from her poisoned breasts. The baby suckles the life out of her, and her body is cut into many pieces and burnt outside Gokul. While her body was burning, the fragrance of *agar* filled the air. Because the Lord himself had fed on her milk, she was redeemed. An interesting aside about Putana is that texts such as the *Garga Samhita* and the *Brahma*

---

[196] Dehejia 1999: 13.
[197] Kosambi 1962.

Vaivarta Purana reveal her to have been the daughter of Mahabali in a previous birth, seeking revenge for the treacherous murder of her father by Vishnu, of whom Krishna is an avatar.[198]

Such counternarratives seem to redeem asura "wickedness" and re-fashion asuras as characters with more complex motivations than simply "evil hating the good," which is the narrative that Hindutva has sought to popularise since the nineteenth century. The Puranas were a much more complex and sophisticated project of assimilation than nineteenth to twenty-first-century Hindutva—the latter being a narrower, more immediate political project, while the former tradition is not limited by the immediate needs of a political creed. Moreover, because Hindutva is a modernist project tied to defining "nationhood," it is primarily interested in cultural homogenisation, which was not the burden of the Puranic project of assimilation. Given these differences, and given the fact that even the Puranas could not succeed in enveloping the diversity of beliefs and practices on the subcontinent, it is no surprise that modern Hindutva still struggles to establish its legitimacy and is in its current in carnation having to resort to rule by diktat via repressive state authoritarianism.

Returning to the Putana narrative, the image in puranic narratives of the good son—who can bring about the salvation of his wayward or wicked mother by killing her—is fascinating and recurrent. Another such story is that of Renuka and Parashurama, her son (an avatar of Vishnu) who beheads her for momentary lack of attention towards his father, her husband. Renuka, it should not surprise us, is the Sanskrit name given to an ancient pre-Brahminical goddess, Yellamma. A deity of fertility, there is archaeological evidence of a temple to Yellamma from the Chalukyan period (eighth to eleventh centuries CE) in present-day Karnataka; there are even earlier signs of human habitation going back to the third century BCE, from which period her worship could date.[199] Yellamma, worshipped today, is linked to Brahminism through being identified as Renuka, mother of an avatar of Vishnu. Among the stories

[198] Herbert 1996.
[199] Yoffee 2007.

through which the link is made is one in which Renuka, running to escape Parashurama, takes refuge in a Paraiyar (Pariah) village. Paraiyar are an outcaste hunting-gathering community. A Paraiya woman tries to save Renuka from Parashurama but he beheads them both, and later, when his father grants him a boon enabling their revival, the heads are transposed—the Dalit goddess thus has the head of the Paraiyar and the body of the caste-Hindu woman. The ancient worship of an outcaste Yellamma is by this rhetorical strategy drawn into the Brahminical frame. However, a subversive element has attracted attention too: "the head that symbolises power/knowledge of the Brahmin . . . is replaced with the head that signifies the power of the Paraiyars (brute mundane power) in the realm of the material. . ."[200]

Delegitimising the mother as well as matrilineal kinship and support structures is a common theme in the epics and Puranas as a whole, with the key villain often being the maternal uncle: Shakuni in the Mahabharata, and Kamsa in the story of Krishna. The establishment of patrilineal primogeniture—the eldest son of the ruler being always inheritor of the throne—as an inviolable right is central to the story of both the Ramayana and Mahabharata. Mothers are generally noble but some mothers precipitate calamitous events through their greed for power and their bid to reject patrilineal primogeniture—as Kaikeyi does in the Ramayana: even her loyal maid Manthara, who accompanies her from her natal home and represents the mother's family, is portrayed as the very epitome of sly evil. Endowing legitimacy to new patriarchal norms is quite patently a prime function of these narratives.

Hinduism and Hindutva

The recovery of *older* and *other* narratives that *savarna* Hindu society remained unaware of tells us that the domestication of the goddess

---

[200] Clarke 1998: 35–53. The worship of Yellamma has many other complex dimensions such as its link to the devadasi practice but we will not go into them here.

and the pacification of non-Aryan peoples was never completely successful; indeed, the project of homogenising and subjugating pre-Aryan deities and practices remains incomplete to this day. What lies outside the boundaries keeps fracturing what is sought to be termed "Hinduism." The simplistic Hindutva narratives forged in the late nineteenth and early twentieth centuries, with their black and white asuras and devas, continually come up against those posed by alternative narratives and historical memories that either robustly survive or visibly persist.

The evidence of this subversive persistence comes in many shapes and forms, one of which are the asura kings Ravana, Hiranyakashipu, and Mahabali. All three are revered as scholars, and as devout, even noble figures by otherwise devout Hindus who worship Rama and Vishnu. The town of Mandsaur considers itself the birthplace of Mandodari, Ravana's wife, and here about two hundred families see themselves as the descendants of Ravana. In the Vidisha, Ratlam, and Indore districts of Madhya Pradesh, Ravana is a local god. There are temples to Ravana here, and his effigy is never burnt on Dussehra. Ravi Ranka, a cloth merchant in Mandsaur, explained this to a journalist: "We remember Ravana for his knowledge of all the Vedas and his devotion towards Shiva. Burning his effigy is seen as a sign of disrespect towards him and so 'Ravana *dahan*' is never done in this town . . ."[201]

Although Ravana is sought to be brought within the Brahminical fold by being enshrined as a devotee of Shiva, the narrative of a Hindutvavadi Ramayana is sharply disrupted by rendering Ravana as a hero. Many Valmiki communities of North India (who are former untouchable castes, constitutionally Scheduled Castes), revere Ravana and avoid looking at Ravana *dahan* during Dussehra.[202] There have been protests against Ravana *dahan* (the burning of Ravana's effigy) by the Bhartiya Dalit Panther Party in UP, the organisation which organised a *mela* celebrating Ravana in 2014.[203] The Gond tribe, which had

[201] Agnihotri 2016.
[202] Zee News 2011.
[203] TNN 2014.

ruled almost the entire hilly region of Central India from the fifteenth to the eighteenth centuries, believe Ravana was their king—called Gade Raja. In the 1970s there was a Gond movement demanding that the symbolic slaying of Ravana during Dasara be stopped.[204] Ravana Mahotsavs are still held by Gonds in several districts of Maharashtra. These protests and demands are ignored, for only one kind of "religious sentiment" is permitted by the state as "Hindu"—that is, Brahminism. In July 2017 the Supreme Court dismissed a Public Interest Litigation to stop the burning of Ravana effigies on Dussehra, the plea being that the burning was environmentally hazardous and hurt the sentiments of certain groups. The Supreme Court cited freedom of religion as enshrined in the Constitution while dismissing the PIL. The protests, however, continue. In 2016 when the villagers of Bisrakh (near Delhi) were about to instal Ravana's idol in a newly renovated Radha Krishna temple, vigilantes from a Hindu right-wing organisation burst in and broke the idol. Bisrakh is believed by its inhabitants to be the birthplace of Ravana.[205] In 2018 a Dalit organisation, the Bhim Army, objected to burning Ravana's effigy and demanded that violators be booked under the SC/ST Act.[206] The young and charismatic Dalit leader who was one of the founders of the Bhim Army, and who has been arrested several times, has taken the name Chandrashekhar Azad Ravan. He often holds up a Hindi copy of the Constitution at protests, thus bringing together in his persona two counternarratives to Hindutva—a Dalit challenge to the Ramayana and an assertion of constitutional morality.[207] Similarly, the highly influential founder and spiritual head of the Adi Dharam Samaj, a spiritual community of Valmikis, calls himself Darshan Ratan Ravan.

These kinds of politically conscious rebellions against the Ramayana are seen going back almost a century in the campaigns that were

[204] Rashid 2015.

[205] *Hindustan Times* 2016.

[206] Haygunde 2018.

[207] "Constitutional morality" as an ethical basis for political action will be discussed in chap. 6.

publicly launched by Dravidian movements and leaders like Periyar in the early twentieth century. Periyar famously garlanded the portrait of Rama with slippers and broke an idol of Ganesha (known as Ganapathi in the South).[208] Such rebellions are now widespread across communities and regions, posing fresh challenges to Brahminical hegemony well into our own time.

Shiva himself, whose devotee Ravana is meant to be, contains within himself multitudes and has never been successfully disciplined into a clean living, fair-skinned Aryan god—he remains Shiva, the dreadlocked ascetic, Shiva the tantrik for whom cemeteries are a playground, Shiva who consumes marijuana and plays Holi with the ashes of freshly burnt corpses. A traditional and popular Holi song celebrates this macabre Holi—*Shivji khele masane mein Holi*—sung by, among others, most famously, Channulal Mishra of Banaras.

In May 2022 a Delhi University professor, Ratan Lal, was arrested for a satirical and mocking Facebook post casting doubt on the validity of the object claimed to be a shivaling found at the Gyan Vyapi Mosque in Banaras.[209] Professor Ratan Lal responded with an interview:

> *Shivji hamare hain, vo toh dalit hain, picchdon, adivasiyon ke devta hain, kale kaloote, aise saamp lapete hue, bhang vung, jangal . . . adivasi ke poore roop hain voh.*

> (Shivji is ours, he is a Dalit, he is the god of the marginalised, of Adivasis. Black, with snakes wrapped around [his neck] *bhang* [cannabis], jungles—he is the very picture of an Adivasi.)

[208] Geetha and Rajadurai 2008: 291. This book on the Non-Brahmin Movement also discusses the specific critique of religion as such (not only of Brahminism) offered by Periyar and the Self Respect Movement (ibid.: 291–5).

[209] Mohan 2022. Hindutva politics claims pre-existing temples at sites of iconic mosques. The Babri Masjid at Ayodhya (demolished by Hindutva groups in 1992), the Gyan Vyapi Mosque in Banaras, and the Shahi Idgah in Mathura are the holy trinity at the top of their agenda. Their claims about pre-existing temples are made on the basis of dubious archaeological arguments listing "Hindu" features and artefacts at these sites, when such features are as likely to indicate syncretic styles of architecture.

He went on to add that given how many temples are built atop destroyed Buddhist temples and *viharas*, "my sentiments are also hurt, return my Buddha to me."[210] As a Dalit himself, Ratan Lal claimed both
Shiva and Buddha as his own, rebuffing Hindutva's Hinduism.

There is a debate, however, on whether Shiva can be claimed as a
pre-Aryan deity. The art historian Y. S. Alone holds that the worship
of Shiva and Vishnu was a post-Buddhist Brahminical phenomenon
in ancient India, and that even though one Shaivite sect, the Kapalika,
was described as untouchable, most Shaivite sects, e.g. the Pashu-
pata, were Brahminical, and in competition with Buddhism and Jainism. Visual imagery from eastern India shows an ongoing feud between the Buddhists and the Shaivites, and Shaivite Tantrism saw
Tantra as a means of protecting Brahminism from Buddhism. While
Shudras have been drawn into the worship of this Brahminical deity
Shiva, Dalits and Adivasis were never part of these worship practices.
Alone also rejects the idea that the epithet *shamshanvasi* (one who
resides in a cremation ground) for Shiva indicates Shiva's Shudra or
Dalit origins, for many Hindu crematoria, even in villages, are not
open to Dalit and Adivasi communities. Alone sees the attribution of
Dalit or Adivasi origins to Shiva as part of the process of the assimilative politics of Brahminisation/Sanskritisation. He suggests that
the process continues well into the twentieth century, when tribal
craft traditions began to be shaped by urban caste-Hindus, leading
to tribal craft practices producing images of Brahminical deities.[211]

Thus there are claims and counter-claims swirling around these deities well into our day. Krishna, incorporated as an incarnation of Vishnu,
is another possibly pre-Aryan deity who is not quite tameable—the
dark-skinned Yadava with multiple adoring women surrounding him
might indicate another instance of the incorporation of pre-Aryan,
more sexually free elements into Brahminism.

The villagers of Dronagiri in the Uttarakhand Himalaya will not
worship Hanuman for he defaced the mountain they worship by

[210] Lal 2022.
[211] Alone 2022.

breaking off an entire side of it. This happened when Hanuman was dispatched to pick the *sanjivani-booti* herb to revive Lakshman.[212] Nabaneeta Dev Sen tells us about songs sung by women in rural Bengal which berate Rama for abandoning Sita: *"Ram tomar buddhi hoilo naash"* (Ram, you lost your mind) they sing.[213] What is presented by Hindutva forces as "insulting" to Hindu gods and goddesses is in fact the modern re-enactment of a much longer cultural struggle of the subjugated to reclaim their own icons and cultural space.

At this point I would like to add another layer to the reading of the Puranas offered here, drawing connections between "myth" and "history." These connections are not intended to be direct, there is no implication that myths "reveal history not known from other sources or confirm known history"—as Sanjay Palshikar puts it—identifying this tendency as "part of a materialist paradigm of history."[214] Palshikar's own project is to identify the "text's scheme of evaluation *in its own terms.*"[215] He studies the evolution of the term "asura" as expressing a form of evil in the Bhagavad Gita and in many Puranas, while in earliest references in the Rigvedic texts, the term is used more in the sense of "lord" or "leader."[216] He is interested in examining how the epithet "asura" (demon) gradually acquires the meaning "evil" even while retaining the contradiction of having noble characteristics (we have discussed Mahabali for instance, and some versions of Ravana); and how this epithet then became a more general signifier, applicable to other groups, for example, Muslims in medieval inscriptions and kaavyas, and in histories of that time written in the colonial period.[217] I think the kind of scholarship Palshikar practises is valuable, and part of an honourable scholarly tradition that resists reading ancient texts through the lens of the present, or anchoring such texts in "known history." However, I don't think

[212] Pande 2016b.
[213] Sen 2021.
[214] Palshikar 2014a: 27.
[215] Palshikar 2014b: 38; italics in the original.
[216] Ibid.: 32.
[217] Palshikar 2014a: 31–8.

the scholarship discussed here contradicts Palshikar's project: the two are complementary. My own argument, drawing on both, does not claim to reveal history; rather it draws connections with persisting and still-evolving "myths" and the contexts in which they emerged, as well as with the multiple ways in which, in the present day, they play a living part, being claimed and disowned by different groups. If Palshikar shows us how the term "asura" can travel across time from the Rigveda to the nineteenth century and down to today by analysing its journey across texts, it helps us locate its capacity to affix itself to some groups and not others, and to understand what that signifies for contemporary politics.

The point that I have emphasised throughout this chapter is that the tremendous heterogeneity of beliefs and practices discussed is not an illustration of the capacity of "Hinduism" to be accommodative, or of its putative capacious, generous, all-inclusive nature—as we have been wont to imagine. The Ramayana and Mahabharata are not ur-texts, of which there are multiple "versions"; rather, these epics are attempts to contain countless deities, beliefs, and practices and discipline them into Brahminism. Our perspective on this robustly surviving heterogeneity must be reshaped by Dalit Bahujan and Adivasi scholarship which enables us to see that "Hinduism" is in fact merely the label produced by Hindutva in order to assert an eternal identity, and to assimilate, discipline, and render invisible the subversive churning and seething going on outside.

Brahma Prakash says the difference between Hinduism and Hindutva is not that Hinduism is good, Hindutva bad. The differences lie, he argues,

> in the ways they disclose themselves. Hinduism maintains pretensions, Hindutva is flat . . . When it comes to caste hierarchy . . . if Hinduism is cunning, Hindutva is crude. What Hinduism does with its 'accommodating ideology', Hindutva does . . . by othering! What lower castes were to Hinduism, Muslims are to Hindutva. One maintains its ideology through hegemony, the other wants to maintain it by brute force . . .

In his opinion Hindutva is not dangerous for Hinduism; in fact it has given "a new lease of life to Hinduism which was facing a crisis from its lower castes . . . Hindutva is a general manifestation of Hinduism in a neoliberal regime. We can say that Hindutva is not an aberration. It is the religion in its true sanatani sense."[218] I would only add a brief observation to Prakash's statement: where he holds that "Hinduism maintains its ideology through hegemony" while Hindutva "wants to maintain it by brute force"—I would say that while the latter is true, brute force played a key role in establishing the former too. This is what this chapter has tried to show.

The failure of this millennia-old project to present Brahminism as a single religion called Hinduism from the nineteenth century—a project ongoing in different forms from the Puranas to the twenty-first century—is evident from the increasing violence required to establish it as the only acceptable form of religious practice. Widespread physical attacks against Muslims and Dalits, as well as against nonconforming "Hindus," are carried out by independent actors even while state institutions—the government, many court judgments and the police—act in concert both to repress dissent and to produce the new normal of India as Hindu Rashtra. Modern Hindutva is not so much a mass movement as a state-led project behind which lies the shadowy power of the RSS, and of the many small and large outfits which owe allegiance to it, formally or informally.

There is no single majority religious community in India. Hindutva is the latest stage in the millennia-old attempt to produce one.

[218] Prakash 2022.

4

The Self and Psychoanalysis from
the Global South

THIS CHAPTER addresses another element obscured by the grid of secularism—the non-secular self in the global South, non-individuated, non-rational, and drawing on multiple spiritual sources for its sustenance. Here I focus on psychoanalysis in order to consider the role that "secularism" plays, both as norm and as active shaper of lives and selves in our worlds. From this perspective, psychoanalysis is an exception to other bodies of modern knowledge and other disciplines—which have tended to interpret their societies in their own terms.

A brief digression is necessary here: this chapter is concerned with psychoanalysis, not with the discipline of psychology. The latter, as a field of experimental study, is seen as having begun in 1854 in Germany, when Gustav Fechner created the first theory of how judgements about sensory experiences are made and how to experiment on them. In 1879 the first psychological laboratory dedicated exclusively to psychological research was founded, also in Germany. Psychology thus, like the other social sciences, seeks objective and scientific analyses of the human mind. Psychoanalysis, on the other hand, has from the early twentieth century undermined the idea that human nature is essentially rational. Some overlap of the two (psychoanalysis and psychology) may happen in the course of this chapter, but my focus is on psychoanalysis. Therefore I will not be discussing the Indian Psychology Movement and the Manifesto on Indian Psychology (2002). One of

198

the originators of this movement and manifesto, Ramakrishna K. Rao, says it "refers to a system/school of psychology derived from classical Indian thought and [is] rooted in the psychologically relevant practices such as yoga prevalent in the Indian subcontinent for centuries."[1] My earlier chapters have questioned the idea that the Indian subcontinent has any homogeneous and unchanging traditions over centuries; and in this chapter too I will critically consider such assumptions in the scholarship on psychoanalysis.

Of all the forms of modern secular knowledge that entered the societies of the global South, psychoanalysis appears to have been the one most confidently taken over by its practitioners who translated and located it into their own contexts, from where they successfully drew on non-secular and spiritual resources to address malaises of the self. Of course, a parallel process has also continued—the one more familiar to the rest of the social sciences and humanities—of seeking to translate indigenous notions of self and other into the terms of European psychoanalytic theory.

Psychoanalysis came to our societies in the early twentieth century—like other modern European forms of knowledge—as secular and modern. As Edward Said puts it, "Freud's awareness of other cultures . . . is inflected and indeed, shaped by his education in the Judaeo-Christian tradition, particularly the humanistic and scientific assumptions that give it its peculiarly 'Western' stamp."[2] Although Freud was concerned with what stands outside the limits of reason, convention, and consciousness, says Said, the Other thus outlined is always an Other recognisable mainly to readers well acquainted with the European canon deriving from Graeco-Roman and Hebrew antiquity.

When looking at the scholarship on how psychoanalysis entered and was received across many societies of the global South from the early twentieth century onwards, what is interesting for the outsider to the field is how practitioners and theorists immediately draw its two

---

[1] Rao 2014.
[2] Said 2014: 12.

key ideas—the role of the unconscious and of myth in self-making—into the dense *jiti* of their own locations.[3] This secular, modern mode of interpreting the self with its claims to universality is transformed by traversing these diverse landscapes: practising psychoanalysts and psychotherapists in India, Egypt, Morocco, Japan, China, and other parts of the global South translate, read, and practise psychoanalysis through different languages, traditions, myths, and spiritual practices.

The two key reasons for this difference are, first, that the process of secularisation that had "disenchanted" the public domain in Europe—banishing religion and myth into the realm of the "private"—had barely begun in these parts of the globe in the early twentieth century; even today it is contested at every stage. Self-construction in these locations therefore draws on the kinds of resources that any secular form of knowledge would either assimilate or not recognise.

Second, the emergence in the North of the heterosexual nuclear family as the only legitimate type of family was a process that colonial regimes introduced in the South over the twentieth century. But again this has not been a fully successful venture anywhere in the South—or even among people of colour in the North. Thus the key assumptions of Freud and psychoanalysis that arose from particular forms of the family in the West/North did not necessarily hold in these other contexts. In effect, practising psychoanalysts in the South encountered very different modes of self-formation from those outlined by classical psychoanalysis in Europe. However, it is also important to note that in all these contexts in the South it appears that psychoanalysis has been adopted and adapted by the more dominant, hegemonising, local tradition. Thus the heterogeneity of the *jiti* that psychoanalysis enters is often lost to it; but today, in the twenty-first century, that internal heterogeneity of the global South is also speaking up from the heart of psychoanalysis itself.

Clearly, there are three significant processes at every location: the translation of psychoanalysis into location-specific contexts; the translation of the local self into Western psychoanalysis; and internal

[3] The concept of *jiti* has been discussed earlier, in the Introduction.

clashes between hegemonic and counter-hegemonic traditions, encountering each other in several ways. I will attempt to map some of the predominant ways in which these three strands of responses to psychoanalysis from the global South intersect with one another in different locations.

Ideas of the Self

So what is this thing we now call the "self"? Philosophical traditions globally have had different notions of the self, but it has been argued by the Sri Lankan anthropologist Gananath Obeyesekere that it is useful to mark the break that Enlightenment thought institutes. The idea of the human actor as a person, as a carrier of essence, roles, rights, and responsibilities is a social and philosophical creation that has long and multiple histories, differing across time and space. The idea of the post-Enlightenment Self, on the other hand, implies a self-evident internal substance upon which it is possible for the Self itself to reflect. European languages have hundreds of self-referents, whereas many non-European languages have only a few. This does demonstrate that Western society possesses "a language rich in critical self-reflection," but, says Obeyesekere,

> reflection on the self is only one aspect of reflexivity; I can reflect on life, on my body, or on philosophical and existential issues as I can on myself. 'Within this fathom-long sentient body I postulate the world, the arising of the world, the cessation of the world, and the path leading to the cessation of the world.' This is critical reflection of a Buddhist sort without the postulation of a transcendental ego or self. Buddhists have a well known meditation text, Satipatthana Sutta, 'awareness of mindfulness.' This 'awareness' is not directed to the self, but, on the contrary, to its non-recognition because of its nonexistence. With different language games, you can have different forms of reflexivity.[4]

Thus, philosophical traditions globally have had different notions of the self, but the break that Enlightenment thought institutes is the idea

[4] Obeyesekere 1990: 246.

of the human as individual and of separate personhood. This European post-Enlightenment idea of the self also implies a gradual progression of the person, a "growing up" of her to the status of an "individual." The process is a concept naturalised across various discourses in the course of modernity—law, modern religion, philosophy, and psychoanalysis. This variety of individuation is experienced by people either as something real, or as a frustrated inability to become properly individuated. My argument is that this process—which is now commonly assumed to be a natural process of growth of each person into a properly individuated selfhood—is distinctive to Western modernity. The key notion central to Western modernity that has enabled the "common sense" assumption outlined above has been the putting into place of a specific notion of the individual—that "I am" this body and that "my self" stops at the boundaries of my skin. This seems an entirely natural identification of selfhood to the modern mind, but it is in fact only about 500 years old and has specific cultural moorings in the experience of the West. It is tied to the material destruction of premodern communities and their livelihoods. In non-Western societies this notion of the individual, separate from all other individuals and comprising the unit of society, is still not uncontested since communities continue to play an important part in their lives. At every level, in non-Western societies, there remains a sense of the self that is an amalgam of individuated bodies and collectivities of different sorts. Individuation—the process of recognising oneself as primarily an individual—is therefore always in the present continuous tense, as it were, than a completed process in our part of the world.

A remarkable insight on the polarity assumed between modern and pre- or non-modern notions of the self can be found in A. K. Ramanujan's brilliant essay, "Is There an Indian Way of Thinking?" (1989), in which he defines the non- or pre-modern as context-sensitive and the modern as context-free. He shows how, in the context-sensitive ("premodern") Indian way of life, the context-free (the "modern") becomes simply yet another context. That is, people simultaneously live within multiple contexts, in which the modern is just another context.

What is understood to be universal modernity, sweeping everything before its path, becomes in India merely one of many contexts within which people work, and between which they seamlessly move. Ramanujan's theoretical innovation lies in stepping away from the field of dichotomised modernity/tradition, rational/non-rational, as well as the notion of "alternative" modernities that leaves normative modernity unquestioned. I push his argument further, suggesting that his framework is not just a unique Indian phenomenon but has theoretical purchase globally. Consider, for example, the computer programmer anywhere in the world (context-free in the space of her work) observing a religious fast, whether for Lent, Navratri, or Ramzan (involving context-sensitivity)—this is an instance of Ramanujan's insight about the nature of the self.

If we take this insight as going beyond Indian specificity, then for most people living in the global South (including the South within the North) the everyday would involve continuous acts of translation between context-free and context-sensitive aspects of their own selves as well as the selves of others. This would happen, first, voluntarily—as in everyday acts of communication and dialogue, or indeed in the breakdown of communication and dialogue; or in seeking to make oneself visible to the state for various purposes. And it would happen, second, involuntarily—as when one is translated into terms legible to the more powerful, whether to the state or to other sections of society.

The idea of the self as an atomised individual does not come "naturally" or easily to people in the global South. Reading feminist or Dalit or African-American autobiographies, for instance, one is struck by the co-production of selfhood along with that of community identification (of women, caste, or race). Viewing the autobiography or memoir as a modern literary form predicated upon the sense of an individuated self that emerged with modernity, it might seem that the very idea of "Dalit memoir" or "feminist memoir" is a contradiction in terms.[5] At

[5] The nature and emergence of individual subjectivity in the early Indian autobiography and memoir is the central subject of Arnold and Blackburn, eds. 2004; and in relation to Kerala, of Kumar 2016.

one level, perhaps not, because Dalit and feminist philosophy are quintessentially modern, with their ferocious critique directed precisely at modernity's failure to deliver on its promise of the universal, emancipated individual. But at another level there could be a contradiction, since the Dalit and feminist claim to individual autonomy is accompanied by an insertion of the individual self back into a radically reconstituted or newly created community. The story of self-emergence then, in all these cases, is inextricably linked to narratives of collectivities rather than individual selves.

The self-evident nature of the self, in other words, is a very provincial idea originating from the core of Western thought since Descartes. Even Freud—Obeyesekere points out—who deconstructed the Cartesian primacy of consciousness, did not question the self-evident nature of the self. "Normally," wrote Freud, "there is nothing of what we are more certain than the feeling of our self, of our ego."[6]

Whereas for a Buddhist, this is not so easy, for the fundamental tenet of the doctrine is that of *anatta* or "no-self." Obeyesekere quotes from the *Teachings of the Buddha*: "Consider all substances, can you find among them any enduring 'self'? Are they not all aggregates that sooner or later will break apart and be scattered?"[7]

In a later work, Obeyesekere develops the idea of it-thinking as opposed to a thinking-I, a form of cognition he terms passive cerebration or passive cognition. These terms imply that "the unconscious *thinks*, but in a special way." He is inspired in this by the Buddha who "discovered the foundations of his epistemology through meditative trance" but then reworked them later in "more rational and philosophically profound form" in his discourses.[8] He suggests that "passive cerebration" opens the way for "a futuristic neurology that can link the phenomenology of visions with the workings of the brain, without reducing one to the other."[9] As Obeyesekere puts it, he is the product of two Enlighten-

[6] Cited by Obeyesekere 1990: 240.
[7] Ibid.
[8] Obeyesekere 2012: 4.
[9] Ibid.: 7.

ments, the European and the Buddhist: "One cannot live *without* Reason, and one cannot live *with* it either, at least in its exclusionary Enlightenment or Euro-rational sense."[10] His idea of the self is best approached, in his view, by "neuro psychoanalysis," which bridges the gap between phenomenology and neurological science. To him the connection between the Buddha and Freud is clear: "The Buddha's spiritual experience entails the furthermost development of the kind of 'thinking' that Freud formulated in the dream-work."[11]

Obeyesekere's reading of psychoanalysis through the "two Enlightenments" is a fascinating example of the first kind of response I listed at the beginning of this chapter—that is, the translation of psychoanalysis into location-specific contexts. According to Honey Oberoi Vahali, comparing Buddhism and psychoanalysis we may note that the focus of Buddhism is the moment by moment flow of consciousness, while the focus of psychoanalysis is the emergence of affects from the depths of the unconscious. In many Southern cultures the two have existed together rather than one or the other being considered to be prominent, particularly as Buddhism concedes to an experiential self.[12]

It is important not to think of non-individualised, non-conscious notions of the self as pre-modern, implying something that lies in the past. These multiple notions of selfhood are very much co-present in the contemporary moment. Radhika Govindrajan, for instance, has written about "interspecies relatedness" in non-urban communities of the hills of the central Himalayas in India.[13] Her ethnographic work, conducted over the early years of the second decade of the twenty-first century, tracks the complex relationships of rural farming communities with animals that they live with or treat as predators. Cattle, goats, dogs, bears, pigs, monkeys, leopards—the lives of humans are "knotted," as she puts it, with these other species, in love and desire, as well as in violence and fear. Love does not preclude violence, as with ritual animal sacrifice,

[10] Ibid.: 4.
[11] Ibid.: 37.
[12] Personal communication.
[13] Govindrajan 2018.

for example. A young woman fantasises about romantic and loving sex with a bear, and in this region folk stories about sexual relationships between bears and humans are common. Animals are equally agential in these relationships—a cow falls ill when her loving owner is forced to sell her; a goat treats the woman who helped her give birth as a second mother; a pig is in a "domestic but not domesticated relationship" with his owner.[14] A mother consoles an 11-year-old daughter whose dog has disappeared, probably carried away by a leopard, saying that everyone has to leave their family one day, just as she will when she gets married.[15] Govindrajan reflects on the parallel between "kin relationships frayed and raveled by marriage" and the snapping of bonds between dogs and their families when they are snatched by leopards. "The lives of dogs," says Govindrajan, "are related to the lives of both humans and leopards, but the full realization of one form of relatedness entails the violent erasure of another."[16] This is one kind of porous notion of the self with which people live. However, the incursions of the modern state and the cultural hegemony of the global North can bring about distinctive transformations.

An interesting instance of how the norms of "modernity" reconfigure notions of the self is offered by the British journalist Poppy Sebag-Montefiore, who writes about changing notions of legitimate public touch in China. In the late 1990s, when she started living there, she noted that it was common to be touched in different ways by perfect strangers in public:

> Touch in public, among strangers, had a whole range of tones that were neither sexual nor violent. But it wasn't neutral either. At times, yes, you'd be leaned on indiscriminately because of lack of space, or to help take some weight off someone's feet. Yet at other times, you'd choose people you wanted to cling to, or you'd be chosen. You'd get a sense of someone while haggling over the price of their garlic bulbs and you'd just grab on to each other's forearms . . . Touch was a precise tool for communication . . . If the state was like an overly strict patriarch, then the nation, society or the people

14 Ibid.: 6.
15 Ibid.: 176.
16 Ibid.

on the streets were the becalming matriarch . . . [U]sually touch was like a lubricant that eased the day-to-day goings-on and interactions in the city . . .[17]

When she returned to Beijing in 2008, a modern city had replaced the city she knew; it had been physically transformed in the run-up to the Summer Olympics that Beijing was hosting. Among the changes that had been brought about were strictures on certain forms of behaviour—"spitting, disorderly queuing, indiscretions of the body"—policed by volunteer elders seated in public places.[18] But while old forms of touch were being stigmatised, touch was now becoming both privatised and sexualised. Another kind of touch was now considered legitimate: "The younger generation now performed a newly liberated sexuality on the streets . . . sometimes with gestures that resembled the globalized, romantic Hollywood way."[19] Even in reflexology clinics where—as with other forms of China's traditional medical practice—touch is central, Sebag-Montefiore found that the masseur wore plastic gloves. Meanwhile, the new practice of psychotherapy was becoming popular, and she notes the irony of the shift from healing through touch to a form of healing "with strict boundaries against physical contact."[20]

The issue of location may be flagged here before we move further. In India, the self inescapably bears caste identity, and touch is intricately circumscribed between castes even today. The potential for unregulated touch in India, unlike in China, is not therefore great. While it may be possible in modern anonymous spaces where caste identities are unknown, even in such spaces, as in a reflexology clinic, the name will reveal the caste identity, and the context-free suddenly becomes, as Ramanujan points out, just another context: consider for example the practising of caste discrimination among Indians working in perhaps the most ultra-modern of modern contemporary spaces, the Silicon Valley.[21]

[17] Sebag-Montefiore 2019: 18–19.
[18] Ibid.: 24.
[19] Ibid.
[20] Ibid.: 25.
[21] Chakravarti 2020.

In the sections that follow, I discuss some predominant strands in the narratives of psychoanalysis in China, Japan, Morocco, Egypt, India, and some other places. I cannot hope nor intend to cover the entire field of psychoanalytic scholarship and thought in and from these countries. There will also be some reflections on psychiatry in certain contexts, because although as forms of knowledge and practice the two are very different (psychiatry being pharmacologically oriented), I found some of the critical scholarship on psychiatry by psychoanalytically oriented scholars relevant to understanding the "non-secular" self in the global South.

Psychoanalysis as Culture: China, Japan, and Buddhism

Sebag-Montefiore suggests a shift in the Chinese context from a (non-modern) self whose physical boundaries are porous to all, to a (modern) self whose physical boundaries are inviolate to all but one romantic partner. But the further reference to the growing popularity of psychotherapy, enabling the "inner self" to be accessed legitimately by a trained professional, reflects what researchers have called a "psycho-boom" in the first decade of the twenty-first century in China. This involves a "surge of popular interest in psychotherapy as well as the infiltration of related ideas and values into the cultural sphere."[22]

China is an interesting instance to begin tracking psychoanalysis in the global South because of its very specific history of the Communist state's extreme hostility to the idea of taking individual minds and lives seriously. Thus, between 1949 and 1976 all branches of the discipline were under heavy censorship and opprobrium. But prior to 1949, and after the end of the Cultural Revolution in 1976, especially at the beginning of the 2000s, the interest in psychoanalysis/psychotherapy was extremely high, growing into the psycho-boom referred to above. It seems to me that China may best exemplify the second process identified at the beginning of this chapter, wherein the indigenous

[22] Huang and Kirsner 2020: 7–8.

self is enthusiastically and creatively interpreted through Western psychoanalytic theories. Indeed, once psychoanalysis gains legitimacy, Confucianism and Taoism are invoked as having a particular affinity towards psychoanalysis because of specific features inherent in these philosophies. It is suggested that there is "a cultural aptitude for the psychodynamic modes of thought, its dialectics, the co-existence of contradictions, the suspension and collapse of linear time categories, that allows Chinese students and candidates to 'take to' and understand analytic thought and practice." It is expected by Western scholars that "the Chinese will, in the tradition of their rich and ancient intellectual heritage, develop a form of 'Chinese psychoanalysis' which will synthesise the Western psychoanalytic schools and teachings with uniquely Chinese tempers, flavours, registers and characteristics."[23] In a similar vein there is a significant and enthusiastically received book applying Western psychoanalytic thought—a Lacanian framework in particular, especially through Zizek's reading—to contemporary Chinese thought and political discourse.[24]

Or take the widely studied Sang subculture among Chinese youth, which is dated to about 2017. This expresses "an inchoate feeling of loss."[25] The basic meaning of "sang" is "to lose something through death, and hence it is associated with mourning and related moods of dejection and depression. Sang culture is immediately ironic, since the young peo ple are 'mourning' something they have never had"; and, as is common today, a consumer culture has grown up around "sang."[26] An important analysis of this and similar counter-success trends among Chinese youth by Liu Xinting finds Zizek's reading of Lacan a useful framework to read this, emphasising that it is not resistance in any sense but merely a way of finding momentary pleasure (*jouissance*) in the pain of the moment.[27]

[23] Loewenberg 2020.
[24] Wu 2014.
[25] Tan and Cheng 2020.
[26] Ge and Ownby 2020.
[27] Xinting 2020.

In an earlier historical moment, though, there was a more located engagement with psychoanalysis. Jingyuan Zhang's study covers the period 1919 to 1949 and states that by 1929, "amid extended argument and controversy, psychoanalysis had become an established field of study in the human sciences."[28] In 1929 Freud wrote to Zhang Shizhao, a former minister of education then touring Europe. While the letter to which he was replying is not on record, Freud's response suggests that Zhang asked him about his knowledge of Chinese practices—such as foot binding that Freud had written about—and informed him of his intention to introduce psychoanalysis to China (which Freud encouraged). Freud refers to China or Chinese culture four times in his entire oeuvre, says Jingyuan Zhang, the subjects being foot binding as fetishism, a book on Chinese ways of interpreting dreams, and the Chinese script and language. In his reply to Zhang Shizhao, Freud explained that he got his information about China from the *Encyclopaedia Britannica.* But Jingyuan Zhang thinks Freud's information on China went beyond the superficial. He believes that from Freud's argument that dream interpretation must be based on context—as happens with meaning in the Chinese script—"Freud considered the Chinese language itself to be a model for his own interpretative strategies."[29]

Interestingly, while Loewenberg sees Chinese philosophy as attuned to psychoanalysis, Jingyuan Zhang suggests that Freud's philosophy of dreams was shaped by his understanding of the structure of the Chinese language. The first suggests a Freudian Confucius, the second a Confucian Freud![30]

In the late 1930s, a psychoanalytic culture emerged briefly around the figures of Bingham Dai (Dai Bingyeung), a native of China who returned in 1935 after studying in the USA, and Adolf Storfer, Freud's

[28] Zhang 1992: 6.

[29] Ibid.: 9.

[30] After writing this, I came across the phrase "Confucian Freud," the title of a lecture by Howard Chiang (https://www.freud.org.uk/event/the-confucian-freud/) at the Freud Museum, London, on 16 February 2022. Unfortunately the lecture is not publicly accessible so I do not know in what sense the term is used by Chiang.

publisher, who came to China in 1939 to escape anti-Semitism in his home town Vienna. They met and interacted briefly in that year, after which Dai left in the same year, and Storfer in 1941 because of the Japanese invasion.[31] After a doctorate in sociology from the University of Chicago, Dai started analysis as a part of learning more about interview techniques, and trained with Leon Hall who was being supervised by Karen Horney. Thus Dai's training was not in the Freudian frame, and, like his mentors, he sought to understand personality not exclusively in terms of intrapsychic tensions, but in their social and cultural contexts. Earlier intellectual influences on Dai included Rabindranath Tagore and the *Bhagavad Gita*. But the "most profound effect on him" was produced by Liang Shu Ming's *Eastern and Western Cultures and Their Philosophies* (1922). Liang, a Confucian scholar, believed in a return to Confucian ethical values, most importantly "the principle that in the flux of life all elements are bound together harmoniously and are best expressed in the concept of *jen* (benevolence)."[32] Liang held that the critically rational mind fostered by Western science would threaten all values. Therefore, learning should not be only focused on the intellect but also on moral values. Based on these principles, Liang set up a small "commune-cum-academy."[33] In the spirit of the early sages, students and teachers lived together and kept watch on one another's moral failings. Students also kept diaries giving free expression to their feelings. It was to this short-lived experiment that Dai came. He had been informally counselling students on his return to China but here he adopted the more systematic format of Liang. However, unlike Liang he departed from strictly following Confucian ideology and tried to acquaint students with different schools of philosophy. In much later work he drew parallels between his psychotherapeutic approach and his religious background. He suggested that the Zen concept of selflessness was a primary goal of psychotherapy, "in the sense of being involved

[31] Blowers 2004.
[32] Ibid.: 96.
[33] Ibid., citing Alitto 1986.

in an ongoing task or interpersonal relationship. without being fetter-ed by compulsive egoistic concerns."[34] The reference to "selflessness" here appears to be about the Buddhist concept of non-self (or *anatta* in Pali), and Dai's suggestion that the Buddhist goal of attaining un-derstanding about the non-self is also the goal of psychotherapy is quite striking.

Huang and Kirsner, in an essay tracing the history of psychoanaly-sis in China, tell us that in the 1910s and 1920s psychoanalytic work was translated into Chinese—although the translation of Freud's *Interpretation of Dreams* "reinterpreted the sexual references or re-moved them completely."[35] Freudian ideas percolated into the culture through general literature as well. Psychoanalysis was also taken up by members of the "Creation Society" in the struggle against Confucian ethics, which emphasised balance and harmony, while psychoanalysis was seen to help understand "the 'discomfort' of the human being in his culture."[36]

Thus, until 1949 psychoanalysis had a "respectable though not stun-ning" influence in China, but the Japanese invasion, the civil war be-tween Nationalists and Communists, and the Communist victory put an end to organised interest in psychoanalysis for the next thirty years.[37]

In the restructuring of institutions after the Communist revolution, psychologists and social workers were expelled from the mental health system, psychology was transformed into a research-oriented discipline, psychiatry was restricted to asylum-like institutions, and psychotherapy was disparaged because of its Western origins and "idealist" (as opposed to materialist) disposition. Between 1949 and 1965 only a handful of psychiatrists and psychologists were permitted to experiment with psy-chotherapy, and only in "ideologically unproblematic" ways focused solely on curing neurasthenia, then the most prevalent neurotic disorder in China.[38] During the Cultural Revolution (1966 to 1976) mental

---

[34] Ibid.
[35] Huang and Kirsner 2020: 4.
[36] Ibid.
[37] Ibid.: 5.
[38] Ibid.

health problems were dismissed as the consequence of "wrong politics" and bourgeois influences, to be resolved by socialist re-education.
Psychology and kindred approaches were attacked as pseudoscience.[39]
After the death of Mao in 1976 and denunciation of the Cultural Revolution, psychiatry and psychology "turned to the West, especially the
U.S., as the source of knowledge and the model to emulate."[40] However, at this time psychoanalysis—as prior to 1949—continued to have
influence mainly in the cultural domain, barely existing as a clinical
practice.

The 1980s were marked by what was called "Freud fever."[41] Many
more of Freud's works became available in translation, both those that
had already been translated as well as new translations of others. Influential psychoanalytic thinkers in general were also widely read in translation, including Carl Jung, Alfred Adler, Erich Fromm, and Karen
Horney. Two key figures in the field of psychoanalysis/psychotherapy
in the 1980s and 1990s were Tseng Wen-Shing (1935–2012) and Zhong
Youbin (1925–2009). Tseng studied in the USA in the 1960s and
then emigrated there, returning from the 1980s to visit China regularly as part of WHO programmes, coming to be renowned as a psychotherapy teacher. His position was that "psychoanalysis was useful
for understanding psychopathology, but as a treatment modality
should be adapted to the needs and habits of Chinese people."[42] Tseng,
it appears, saw psychoanalysis as the frame in which "Chinese needs and
habits" should be accommodated.

Zhong remained all his life in China, living through the Cultural Revolution and personally experiencing its violence on intellectuals. His
approach seems different to Tseng's in that it was inflected by a socialist
understanding. In 1989 he published "a highly influential" monograph
titled *Chinese Psychoanalysis*, "the case vignettes presented in which
showed that his treatment combined psychoanalytic explanations
and socialist practices. After taking a detailed life history and making

[39] Ibid.: 6.
[40] Ibid.
[41] Ibid.
[42] Ibid.: 7.

sense of it using a psychoanalytic framework, Zhong would urge the patient to accept how ridiculous and infantile his or her symptoms were—a recognition that led to their relinquishment."[43] Both evidently treated Western psychoanalysis as the interpretive frame through which Chinese particularities were to be viewed—quite unlike Dai.

The beginning of the 2000s saw the neoliberal transformation of China, producing a class of people who were wealthy and "interested in Western-style products and services." The search for meaning in life "became a pressing issue after material needs were fulfilled." Psychotherapy now found a place along with "a variety of religious, spiritual, and traditional Chinese practices."[44] The state was actively interested in mental health and a government certification of 2002 produced a new mental health sector composed exclusively of private practitioners of psychotherapy, with only a fraction of the practitioners having formal training in psychiatry or psychology. What was practised was largely psychotherapy, but the term was generally conflated with psychoanalysis. Highly influential "foreigner-taught programs" (Germany, Norway) imparted professional training. The most influential however is the China American Psychoanalytic Alliance (CAPA), formed in 2008, which used Skype to conduct training and analysis at a distance. It thus appealed directly to potential candidates who were trained entirely in English-language classes by American teachers, and has a very strong presence in China today. The International Psychoanalytical Association (IPA) too has had a China committee since 2008.

Since then the field has expanded further and become more professionalised. It has also gone digital, in keeping with the general expansion of digital technologies in social relationships in China. As the interaction with the international psychoanalytic community deepens, there has been a surge of publication projects "usually led by foreign analysts who are heavily involved with the development in China. Contributors include foreign analysts and, to a smaller extent, their Chinese colleagues."[45] There has also been a flood of translations of psycho-

---

[43] Ibid.
[44] Ibid.: 8.
[45] Ibid.: 13.

analytic works into Chinese, but very little writing on the practice of psychoanalytic psychotherapy in China, or on "the kinds of experiences [that] are revealed and made sense of through such kinds of therapeutic process." The reason for this, say Huang and Kirsner, is that psychiatry and psychology journals only accept articles that adopt mainstream research paradigms in their disciplines, and case studies are absent. However, even though they are not much into publishing, Chinese therapists do make presentations on their clinical experiences at conferences in China.[46]

Perhaps there is more going on at the level of practice which will be accessible even to a Chinese literate public only when these accounts are written up analytically. But even at this peak of the psycho-boom in neoliberal China, in which the Chinese self is rendered legible in Western psychoanalytic terms, rich philosophical reflections continue trying to put Freudian concepts in conversation with indigenous ones. Tao Jiang, for example, in his contribution to a volume on the reception of Freud in China,[47] reads Freud's unconscious together with a Weishi Buddhist notion of "the storehouse consciousness" articulated by Xuanzang, coming to the conclusion that the two are based upon radically different notions of personhood.[48] Xuanzang, as an orthodox Buddhist, believes in the no-self, and the attachment to a substantive self is "the hurdle that needs to be overcome through rigorous meditative practices in order to reach awakening."[49] For Freud, the ego is under assault from the unconscious world as well as the external world, and "the strengthening of the ego is essential to restoring the psychic order in psychoanalytical practices."[50] Jiang intends through this study to question the way Freudian theories of the self have become normalised.

Coming now to Japan, it is noteworthy that the inaugural moment in China was also deeply marked by Japanese influence, as Chinese translations of psychoanalytic literature were often from Japanese

[46] Ibid.
[47] Jiang and Ivanhoe 2013.
[48] Jiang 2013.
[49] Ibid.: 290.
[50] Ibid.

translations. In the second decade of the twentieth century, most works on psychology were translated into Chinese from Japanese. A series of publications in 1912 introduced psychoanalysis to Japan, and over 1929–36 more than twenty books by Freud were translated into Japanese. There was also a psychoanalytic institute in Tokyo at that time.[51]

Ohtsuki Kaison is believed to have written the first article on psychoanalysis in Japanese in 1912, entitled "The Psychology of Forgetting," and published in the psychology journal *Shinri Kenkyu*.[52] In the second decade of the twentieth century there were two views on psychoanalysis in Japan. Marui Kiyoyasu, trained in neurology in the USA, returned to teach in 1918. At this time Japanese psychiatry was influenced by German thought, which emphasised biological causes as the reason for personality problems and prescribed pharmacological treatments. American psychiatry, by contrast, emphasised environmental causes and psychotherapy. Blowers and Chi suggest that his American training made Marui more open to psychoanalysis, and he set up a department of psychiatry in Tohoku University that taught depth psychology.

The resistance to psychiatry came from two sources—the German-trained psychiatric establishment, but more significantly from our point of view from Morita (Shoma) Masatake, "whose therapeutic system for dealing with psychoneuroses was strongly influenced by Buddhist thought. For Morita, neurosis was the result of an overconcentration of the self to the exclusion of objects and events external to the person, with the result that it interrupts the 'smooth flow of normal life'."[53] This recalls Bingham Dai's reference to non-self as the very goal of psychoanalysis. Morita, however, seems to have counterposed the two, feeling that "the clues to uncovering the mind's faults and providing their cure lay in experiential accounts." Psychoanalysis, he held, did not produce the patient's own sense of overcoming the problem.[54]

[51] Zhang 1992: 40.
[52] Blowers and Chi 1997: 115.
[53] Ibid.
[54] Ibid.: 116; Taketomo 1990: 961–2.

One of Marui's senior students, Heisaku Kosawa, took note of Morita's criticisms and started rethinking the conceptual framework for psychoanalysis in Japan. Kosawa met Freud in Vienna, underwent three months of personal analysis there, returning in the 1930s to Japan. Throughout the 1930s and 1940s, Kosawa and Marui were the leading, if opposed, figures in the field. Kosawa was deeply influenced by the Jodo Shinshu (True Pure Land) sect within Japanese Buddhism. In his practice he noted that, compared with patients in Europe and America, those in Japan tended to relate easily to the mother–child relationship, and that the fundamental conflict often seen in such relationships was the child's ambivalence towards the mother. Kosawa's significant contribution was a theoretical paper, titled "Two Kinds of Guilty Consciousness (Ajase Complex)," challenging a fundamental premise of Freudian thinking. He proposed an "Ajase Complex" based on his version of the Buddhist story of King Ajase (Ajātasatru in Sanskrit), who ruled in the Ganges area over 494–62 BCE. Kosawa sent a German translation of this paper to Freud but received only a brief acknowledgement.[55] As with Girindrasekhar Bose of India, Freud did not take kindly to attempts to locate psychoanalysis "elsewhere," or to retune its essential elements, although he expressed pleasure at the "proud conquests" psychoanalysis had made overseas.[56] Kosawa's Ajase is drawn from a character found in two Buddhist texts—the *Nirvana Sutra* introduced to Japan between 700 and 1000 CE, and the *Kyogyoshinsho*, a text by Shinran Shonin (1173–1262), a celebrated Japanese priest. Kosawa questioned the universality of the oedipal myth in psychoanalysis, drawing on the mutual dependency in Japan between mothers and their children. The myth of Ajase centres on Ajase's lifelong dependence on his mother, whom he initially targets with hostility, but with whom he is eventually contented because of her undying affection.[57] Kosawa's use of the story shows it exemplifies for him the

[55] There is reference to a favourable reply from Freud, but it is missing: see Taketomo 1990: 971.

[56] Letter to Marui, cited by Harding 2009: 73.

[57] Blowers and Chi 1997: 119.

fundamental issues that arise with the very fact of birth itself. As further worked upon by his student Keigo Okonogi—who would go on to develop the psychical consequences of this structure—the originality of the Ajase Complex lies in its themes of matricide and "prenatal rancour" (from the Buddhist concept of *mishoon*, or resentment towards one's origins, an idea intimately linked with reincarnation), in contrast to the Oedipus Complex, which emphasises incestuous desire and patricide.[58] As Blowers and Chi put it:

> The mother wishes both to have her child and kill it, her ambivalent feelings arising out of her desire to exercise power over its life and death and the paranoid fear of retaliation that a projection of this desire onto the child brings in its wake. On the other hand the ambivalent feelings of the child arise out of an idealisation of the mother as a love object and the knowledge that she is capable of killing it.

Kosawa's Ajase Complex may have been the first written attempt at an Asian cultural variant on what, for Freud, was a universal mechanism.[59]

Kosawa took on as his last patient in the early 1960s a famous novelist and political activist, Harumi Setouchi, who later became a Buddhist nun. By then Shin Buddhism had permeated his therapeutic approach. Rather than attempt to mingle psychoanalysis and Buddhism at a conceptual level, he sought, as he told another of his clients, to "do psychoanalysis in the spirit of Shinran," a reference to Shin Buddhism's thirteenth-century founder.[60]

The opposite trend in Japanese psychoanalysis, that of reading Japanese society through Western psychoanalysis, may perhaps be exemplified by Yaekichi Yabe, who went on to found the Japanese Psychoanalytical Association. Yabe had been told that Freud thought *Beyond the Pleasure Principle*—one of the first of his works to be translated into Japanese—"too daring" for Japan. This work deals with Freud's exposition of the "Nirvana Principle," or death instinct, and

[58] Okonogi 1979.
[59] Blowers and Chi 1997: 119–20.
[60] Harding 2018.

Yabe's explanation to Freud, when he met him, was that the ideal of life tending towards death was a Buddhist idea; and since Buddhism influences Japanese thought, "an understanding of psychoanalysis might be easier through this book." Freud was delighted by the explanation, as reported by Yabe.[61] There is a clear parallel with a similar claim discussed earlier in the Chinese context—that Taoism and Confucianism are predisposed to psychoanalysis.

Psychoanalysis as Culture: Arabic and Islam

It has seemed to many scholars that Freudian psychoanalysis universalises as a human condition what is essentially a narrowly parochial experience, that of (male) European modernity. A significant text in the field is Fatima Mernissi's essay on the Muslim concept of active female sexuality. Mernissi begins by comparing the Christian concept of the individual as torn between two poles (good and evil, flesh and spirit) to Islam's "more sophisticated theory of the instincts," which she sees as being "more akin to the Freudian concept of the libido."[62] Islam views raw instincts as energy which takes good and bad forms only in and through the laws decided by a social order. In the Muslim order, it is not necessary for the individual to eradicate these instincts but to harness them to serve the purposes of the Muslim order.

Mernissi offers a comparison between Imam Ghazali and Sigmund Freud on female sexuality, showing that while Ghazali, writing in Persia in the eleventh century, believed he was attempting to reveal only the true *Muslim* belief on the subject, Freud, at the triumphant inception of modernity in Europe, could claim the authority of Science to elaborate not just a theory about European sexuality but a *universal explanation of the human female*. Mernissi argues that in comparing Freud's and Ghazali's theories we should be aware that we are in fact comparing the two cultures' different and parochial conceptions of sexuality, not a universal theory (Freud) with a particular one (Ghazali).

[61] Blowers and Chi 1997: 121.
[62] Mernissi 1987: 29.

Ghazali sees female sexuality as active, dangerous, and destructive to the Muslim social order, and the work of civilisation is to control this power.[63] However, he does not see male and female sexuality as polarised, but as "partaking of and belonging to the same kind of sexuality." He uses the same word for the female as for the male reproductive element—*ma* or water drop—and sees both as actively and equally involved in reproduction.[64] Ghazali also grants the female equal capacity for sexual pleasure. Her ejaculation, as he sees it, is a slower process than the male's and to withdraw from her before she has "reached her pleasure is harmful to her."[65]

Freud, writing in Europe after two centuries of transformations that had reshaped notions of sexuality there, offers the novel contribution to Western contemporary culture that sublimated sex is the source of civilisation itself. But although Freud reinstates sex as the foundation of civilised creativity, Mernissi argues that he polarises male and female sexuality as based not on anatomical differences but on the notion of the active nature of male sexuality and the passive nature of female sexuality. In other words, although Freud moves away from an anatomical conceptualisation of sexuality positing a fundamental bisexuality to humans, he nevertheless equates masculinity with activity and femininity with passivity. Moreover, Freud's theory of female sexuality is based on the castration of the phallic features of the female and the elimination of clitoral sexuality.[66] Mernissi concludes: "By contrast with the passive Freudian female, the sexual demands of Imam Ghazali's female appear truly overwhelming and the necessity for the male to satisfy them becomes a compelling social duty."[67]

From Mernissi's complex reading of the two thinkers what emerges is not a valorisation of the Muslim as opposed to the Freudian view of sexuality, but an understanding that patriarchies and misogynies can

[63] Ibid.: 33.
[64] Ibid.: 36.
[65] Cited by Mernissi 1987: 37.
[66] Ibid.
[67] Ibid.: 38.

arise from entirely differing grounds. Thus, because of the fear of the sexually rapacious woman, Moroccan folk culture is "permeated with a negative attitude to femininity" and "the Muslim social order faces two threats: the infidel without and the woman within."[68] Of course a Freudian perspective of passive femininity can equally arrive at such an understanding—that femininity is destructive to the social order – but Mernissi's argument is that Freud and Ghazali arrive at this understanding from entirely opposite assessments of female sexuality.[69]

Freud and psychoanalysis found their place in Arabic as a language and a culture in the 1940s. Psychoanalytic terms were confidently translated into Arabic. Omnia el Shakry observes that the key term of reference for psychoanalysts working in Arabic was never the ego but "the polysemic Arabic term" *nafs* (soul, spirit, psyche, self).[70] Thus, psychology was *ilm-al-nafs*, the science of the soul. The psychologist Yusuf Murad introduced the Arabic word *al-la-shu'ur* for the unconscious into the language in the Egyptian *Journal of Psychology* in 1945. He drew from the twelfth-century Sufi philosopher Ibn Arabi— "redolent with mystical overtones" as El Shakry puts it—for the term was used by Ibn Arabi to refer to the "incommensurability and alterity of God."[71]

Freud's thought travelled widely in Egypt, and though never treated as the source of an unchanging truth, says El Shakry, was seen as a "multivalent tradition" acting as one resource for "broader Arabic debates surrounding the status of the unconscious in psychic life."[72] In

[68] Ibid.: 40, 41.

[69] Fatima Mernissi's work is seen by some scholars as having moved from "secular" feminism to "Islamic" feminism. The former refers to her earlier work using a postcolonial feminist critique to address what she saw as the misogyny of Islam; while her later work focuses on Islamic texts (the Quran and the Hadith) to uncover more positive understandings of women and femininity that have become perverted or misrepresented over time. The essay comparing Ghazali and Freud, cited here, is seen in this framework as part of Mernissi's "earlier" secular feminism: Rhouni 2010.

[70] El Shakry 2017: 14.

[71] Pandolfo 2018: 3.

[72] El Shakry 2017: 1.

the Arab world the new science of the self in the mid-twentieth century drew from Freudian and other psychoanalytic traditions, but equally from classical Islamic thinkers like Al Ghazali and Ibn Arabi, who were in fact not unknown to Western psychoanalysis. El Shakry points out that Lacan had referred to Ibn Arabi several times, and aligned his own position with Ibn Arabi's mysticism as opposed to the rationalism of Ibn Rushd (Averroes).[73] The intersection of Sufism and psychoanalysis has long been of interest among Arabic scholars, particularly the "medical-spiritual tradition of the *nafs*" in therapeutic practice by Quranic scholars.[74]

El Shakry draws our attention to a revisiting of the link between psychoanalysis and Islam by contemporary scholars who read Ibn Arabi's rendition of the Quranic story of Abraham, where Abraham takes a dream to be a divine commandment. Ibn Arabi says that Abraham was mistaken in taking the vision literally, for "every dream demands a transposition or interpretation."[75]

The contemporary Tunisian analyst Fethi Benslama cautions that Ibn Arabi's unconscious is not the Freudian unconscious; rather it is "the spiritual veiling and unveiling of the multiple forms of man."[76] But El Shakry uses the idea of "epistemological resonance" to draw parallels between Ibn Arabi's thought and modern psychoanalysis in the latter's rendering of ideas such as the unconscious (which has resonances with Freud) and the imaginal world or *hadrat al-khayal* (which resonates with Lacan's Imaginary).[77] Here I recall a trajectory discussed at length in the Introduction: when we come across resonances between on the one hand Western thinkers since the seventeenth century and on the other much earlier thinkers from the global South, it is facile to assume that the latter somehow "anticipated" ideas of the European Enlightenment. My contention, in agreement with that of Martin Bernal and

[73] Ibid.: 8.
[74] Pandolfo 2018: 3.
[75] El Shakry 2017: 9.
[76] Cited in ibid.
[77] Ibid.

others, is that there had long been a shaping flow of ideas from the global South to Europe centuries before the European Enlightenment.

In the context of psychoanalysis. Stefania Pandolfo puts it this way:

> The family relationship . . . between the psychoanalytic and Islamic traditions . . . digs its roots into the intercultural exchanges around the thought of the trace and the intermediate realm of imagination *(mundus imaginalis/alam-al-mithal)* and the problematic of divine manifestation and prophetic knowledge . . . [T]he intercultural exchanges that contributed to the psychoanalytic conceptual archive have been shown to be much wider than the Arabo-Greek connection, crucially including Persianate and Perso-Indian traditions . . .[78]

Pandolfo reminds us that Freud, in his understanding of dreaming and the unconscious, borrowed from "Aristotle's theory of the memory trace" and "from ancient Byzantine and Arab treatises of dream interpretation," among others, which he sees as prefiguring his own theory of regression in dreams. And, as discussed in the Introduction, Aristotle's work was first translated with commentary into Arabic by Muslim scholars; and then from there translated into Latin. Thus, Arabic influences on Freud and Lacan and the affinity that twentieth-century Arabic scholars felt for psychoanalysis should not surprise us.

Scholars such as El Shakry and Pandolfo do not therefore view psychoanalysis as simply yet another technology of the late colonial state or of postcolonial nationalism, although El Shakry concedes that psychological theories did sometimes perform the service of "disciplinary projects and prescriptive visions of the postcolonial subject."[79] In contrast to Fethi Benslama, then, whose caution about reading Ibn Arabi alongside Freud we noted earlier, and who sees psychoanalysis and Islam as being mutually ignorant of and even hostile to each other,[80]

[78] Pandolfo 2018: 11.

[79] El Shakry 2017: 15.

[80] In part because Freud was a Jew and "the Muslim world rejects everything Jewish" and also because psychoanalysis is seen by Muslims as fostering atheism: Benslama 2006.

El Shakry traces "historical interactions, hybridizations, and intercon-nected webs of knowledge production between the Arab world and Europe."[81] She points out that Yusuf Murad's confident translations often returned to classical Arabic texts and holds that these terms were therefore often closer to the German spirit of Freud's terms than the standard English translations—for instance, *nafs* for psyche, *al-ana* for ego, and *al-ana al-a-'la* for superego.[82]

Interestingly, both El Shakry and Pandolfo see psychoanalysis in the Arab world as pursuing a project similar in spirit to that of Frantz Fanon. Lewis Gordon draws our attention to Fanon's recognition of the limitations of psychiatric approaches to social alienation. Gordon sees a parallel between Freud's prognosis at the end of *Civilization and Its Discontents*—that for a normal subject to be also a healthy one the abnormal society would have to be transformed—and Fanon's at the end of *Black Skin, White Masks*—that in a colonised society "cohe-sion and alignment would require making the patient, in reality, ab-normal."[83] However, we must note that, unlike Freud, who assumed a universal human condition, Fanon saw colonialism as a specific con-text that shaped the understanding of self and other; he approached psychoanalysis as a resource for reconstituting the psychic interiority of the colonised subject.

In El Shakry's reading Fanon is reflected in Yusuf Murad's "integrative subject as an agent of synthesis" in post-War Egypt.[84] Pandolfo draws on Fanon's figure of the "agony of culture: a cultural tradition reduced to the status of a living ghost" and hears resonances in the spiritual practice of the Quranic therapist, an imam who has been the main in-terlocutor in her ethnography over many years.[85] The latter's concept of "soul choking" (*tadyik al-nafs*) invokes for her Fanon's depiction of agony, even though it is drawing on a specifically Quranic idea of the

---

[81] El Shakry 2017: 11.
[82] Ibid.: 23.
[83] Lewis 2015: 79–80.
[84] El Shakry 2017: 25.
[85] Pandolfo 2018: 6.

constriction and expansion of the *nafs* in response to God. The resonance with Fanon here lies in the imam using "soul choking" to refer
to a disablement of the soul in contemporary existential and political
trauma, produced by the violence of the state and "the mass pull
towards undocumented migration."[86]

Psychoanalysis as Culture:
A "Hindu" Landscape

An interesting experiment was conducted by a young psychoanalyst,
Dev Satya Nand, between 1942 and 1944 in Punjab. Sarah Pinto
offers us a fine and textured reading of this case study self-published
in 1947 and titled *The Objective Method*. In this he analysed the daydreams of a 21-year-old woman, whom he calls Mrs A. The doctor was
Christian, Mrs A. a recently married Hindu upper-caste woman, and
their sessions could have taken place in Amritsar or Lahore. Mrs A.
was not his patient, but a friend who had agreed to help with his experiment to test his new vision of dream analysis in which he would help
her enter, while awake, into *samadhi* (a state of concentration). He
was certain that this method using "Oriental" concepts was more in
tune with Indian reality than those of Freud and Jung.[87] Using the concepts of "dream smudges" and "dream spaces," he "parsed" the daydreams,
says Pinto, in "the familiar way psychoanalysis has of inviting the past
into the future."[88] In her sessions Mrs A. spoke often about Hindu Socialism, which Satya Nand "saw as an original and exciting vision, both
for its own sake and for the ways in which it might demonstrate that
dreams and their analysis are creative pathways to the new, not just point-
ers to what has already been or lay within."[89] Mrs A. talks about and
identifies in different ways with the epic heroines Shakuntala, Draupadi, and Ahalya, and thinks of the Pandavas in exile as performing

[86] Ibid.: 6–8.
[87] Pinto 2019: 1–2.
[88] Ibid.: 1.
[89] Ibid.: 5.

"cooperative farming" with the villagers in their places of exile. Satya Nand saw these stories as universal rather than as a purely Hindu vocabulary, and indeed in his understanding what made his technique Oriental was also what made it objective. *Samadhi* was the foundation, in his understanding, for a "better, stronger science," while Freud's free association was unscientific because it could not access "the whole truth."[90] As Pinto puts it, "Mrs A.'s Hindu Socialism, a 'new thought' representing 'new values,' was for Satya Nand the 'solution' to the case, the interpretation of the dream, and also its creative product."[91]

Sarah Pinto's close reading of Satya Nand's text shows us that he went beyond simply asserting a non-Western or local idiom of the self, but rather, with Mrs A., suggested these idioms had universal validity. Pinto adds that Mrs A. as analysand was "active" and "contentious" and challenged Satya Nand's ideas. Thus, Pinto finds there is "less of a sense of a singular, masculine, authoritative voice" and more of a sense of figuring things out together, and the whole exercise is very different from the way Freud worked.[92] Although Satya Nand's book fell into obscurity—partly perhaps, Pinto says, for its idiosyncrasies and dense writing style—Pinto's own accidental access to it through a doctor who drew her attention to it, and her careful reading, offer us a rich resource for thinking about how the secular body of knowledge called psychoanalysis entered different *jitis* and was shaped by them.

Indian psychoanalysts have long struggled with what they see as the difference between Indian and Western patients when it comes to becoming proper masculine subjects. Sudhir Kakar says that when reading early Indian case histories he was struck by the fluidity of patients' cross-sexual and generational identifications.[93] His argument is that the hegemonic narrative of Hindu culture, as far as male development is concerned, is neither that of Freud's Oedipus nor of Christianity's Adam. One of the more dominant narratives is that of Devi, the great

[90] Ibid.: 12.
[91] Ibid.: 63.
[92] Pinto 2020.
[93] "The Maternal Feminine in Indian Psychoanalysis," in Kakar 1997.

goddess, especially in her manifold expressions of mother in the inner world of the Hindu son. Further, myths in India are not "vestiges of infantile fantasies of whole nations," as for the European Freud, but vibrantly alive, with their symbolic power intact. Kakar tells a familiar story of Skanda (Subramanian) and Ganesha, sons of Parvati and Shiva, competing to win a fruit offered by their mother as a gift to whichever of them raced around the universe first. When Skanda triumphantly returned after circumnavigating the universe, he found Ganesha ensconced at his mother's feet, eating the fruit—he had circumambulated his mother, worshipped her, and declared, "You are my universe." Furious, Skanda rushed away to an inaccessible mountain top, to which an annual pilgrimage is conducted to this day.

Kakar's point is that Skanda's punishment is exile from the mother's bountiful presence, and the reward is the promise of functioning as an autonomous adult man. Ganesha remains an infant, and his reward is to never know the pangs of separation from his mother—and the fact that Ganesha's lot is considered superior to Skanda's is "perhaps an indication of the Indian man's cultural preference in the dilemma of separation-individuation."[94] Thus, even while remaining within the framework of Freudian psychoanalysis, with its implied oedipality, Kakar enables a deconstruction of the universality assumed by psychoanalysis for itself.

An interesting counterpoint is raised by Rachana Johri, whose feminist psychoanalytical work focuses on the mothers of daughters in northern India. These are missing figures in the epics and Puranas, and in contemporary times, within cultures of overwhelming son preference, they feel a lack of entitlement to the status of mother. Mothers' love for their daughters was accompanied by anxieties of impending loss (through virilocal marriage), Johri finds, and they have guilt-laden fantasies that the daughters will never leave home, even as consciously they prepared daughters with varying degrees of harshness to ready them for the departure.[95]

[94] Ibid.: 80.
[95] Johri 2010.

Girindrasekhar Bose, who founded the Indian Psychoanalytical Society in 1921, wrote to Freud to say that "my Indian patients do not exhibit castration symptoms to such a marked degree as my European cases. The desire to be a female is more easily unearthed in Indian male patients than in European . . . The Oedipus mother is very often a combined parental image, and this is a fact of great importance . . ." Freud, in responding to Bose, acknowledges the difference in *Indian* patients from what he assumes to be the human norm, but advocates the need not to reach hasty conclusions on the basis of Indian experiences. It seems to me that Bose could legitimately have asked Freud not to reach hasty conclusions on the basis of his own limited experiences of European patients. Sudhir Kakar, drawing our attention to this correspondence between Bose and Freud, noted that the relationship Bose invoked in his analytic encounters was in fact the *guru–shishya* (teacher–student) tradition that would be immediately familiar to any Indian patient.[96]

Ashis Nandy sees Freud as having an ambivalent relationship with the European Enlightenment, to which he was already an Other. However, Nandy argues that Freud's project of attempting a new concept of self was relevant in India only for a small minority of modernising elites who had internalised Victorian moral codes.[97] This project was one that attempted to accommodate an underside repudiated by two centuries of European modernity—a "more real" self operating according to principles the "apparent self" knew nothing about, or rejected as immoral. Nandy reminds us that psychoanalysis and other sciences came to India neither through apolitical cognitive choices nor through some sort of cultural diffusion, but through the colonial project of civilisational transformation which was attempting to devalue all surviving native systems of knowledge. The science of psychology was one of a series of techniques that sought to retool Indians into a prescribed version of the nineteenth-century European.[98]

[96] "Encounters of the Psychological Kind," in Kakar 1997.
[97] Nandy 1995b.
[98] Nandy 1990: 139.

However, while this was the way British practitioners approached the Indian self,[99] Nandy says it was not true for Indian practitioners like Bose. For one thing, because of organisational and logistical reasons, the formal technical requirements of psychoanalysis were often diluted, which allowed some space for it to find local roots. For another, Bose wrote extensively in Bengali on India's sacred texts and epics, in which he developed notions of the "Indian" self, but in these, says Nandy, he was relatively "low-key" in invoking psychoanalysis—as against in his writings in English. He did not use psychoanalysis to demystify Indian culture and, on the contrary, used Indian cultural categories like *guna* (quality), and *atma* (self) as all-pervasive in nature, thus attempting to "domesticate psychoanalysis for Indians."[100] Nandy thus argues that Bose in his Bengali writings is trying to "locate contemporary psychology in the Indian experience and to legitimise the discipline as a natural out-growth of traditional knowledge."[101]

An interesting argument Bose makes in a Bengali essay is that the idea of the unconscious unburdens the individual of the need to believe in superstitious emanations, such as ghosts. Nandy suggests that this is not a move to secularise the Indian world, for the unconscious is compatible with spirituality, but invokes a non-superstitious, higher, more abstract form of spirituality.[102] We will see how this distinction between superstition and a higher spirituality has globally shaped "traditional" practices of healing of the psyche as they enter a postcolonial world in which the context-free seeks hegemony. In response to modern and secular psychotherapy/psychoanalysis, modernising elements emerge from heterogeneous local practices and beliefs, denouncing the latter as superstition. Wherever collaborative practices have been attempted, traditional practices that distinguish themselves from superstition are the ones that the secular practice of psychotherapy tends to tie up with.

[99] Hartnack 1990.
[100] Nandy 1990: 122.
[101] Ibid.: 126.
[102] Ibid.: 128–9.

In India, one notes two characteristics of the "Hinduism" invoked by psychoanalysts from Girindrasekhar Bose onwards: (a) "Hinduism" is assumed to be "Indian" in opposition to Western psychoanalysis; and (b) What is claimed as Hinduism is Brahminism.

Bhargavi Davar made both these points in an early work,[103] arguing that the "Indian assimilation of psychoanalysis in its early colonial history is underlined by patriarchal and Hinduistic interests. In its formation, psychoanalysis facilitated the representation of upper-caste Hindu ideas like no other theory or practice."[104] The intimate connection between psychoanalysis and upper-caste Hinduism derived from two sources, she says. First, the public health discourse in India that came via colonialism, which fitted comfortably into caste and gender discourses of purity and pollution. Second, there was "a profound affinity shared between the two in terms of the hierarchical structures, especially of patriarchy, that each encapsulated."[105]

Davar points out other affinities. During the colonial period, Hinduism was produced as text-based and highly verbal, and it is this version of "Hinduism"—or more accurately what I have called Brahminism—that related to the equally text-based and verbal psychoanalysis. Just as mantras and ritual *sloka*s were performative and affected human agency, so did the talking cure. Then there was the evolutionism of psychoanalysis which Hinduism/Brahminism related to in its *varnasrama* theory. Finally, while the racism of Western psychology did not appeal to Indian practitioners, "psychoanalysis and Hinduism together were analytically useful in differentiating civilised Indians/Hindus from other barbaric tribes and castes . . . Hindu psychology was said to be 'ancient', not 'primitive'; it was eternal, timeless, and therefore, universal and true, like all good, modern science."[106]

Davar offers an extended critique of Sudhir Kakar who, as she points out, is "synonymous with 'Indian psychoanalysis'," and whose work,

---

[103] Davar 1999.
[104] Ibid.: 175.
[105] Ibid.: 177.
[106] Ibid.: 177–8.

she shows, assumes the upper-caste Hindu self as "Indian." In this sense, Kakar's works demonstrate a continuity with early Hindu psychoanalysis.[107] For instance, Kakar, while seeing himself as dealing "primarily with Hindu India, and with the cultural traditions and psycho-social identity of so-called 'caste' Hindus at that,"[108] nevertheless makes broader statements such as on "the universal beacon of 'higher feeling' (*moksa*) in the lives of most Hindus, cutting across class and caste boundaries."[109]

A more recent critique of Kakar has been made on similar grounds by Zehra Mehdi when writing about the politics of secular psychoanalysis in India through the lens of Sudhir Kakar's work. She argues that "in rendering a psychoanalytic explanation of Indian identity, the writing of Sudhir Kakar not only excludes Muslims but also unwittingly identifies Islam as a religion which is incompatible with the secular Indian identity."[110] Kakar invokes an overarching Indic, "primarily Hindu" civilisation that constitutes "the cultural gene pool of India's people."[111] Mehdi's project is to "uncover the unconscious mechanism of power relations that govern the way Hindus and Muslims organise each other as well as themselves . . . Indian identity defines the constituents of Hindu identity but also hides it in the argument of secularism. This secular Indian identity, primarily Hindu, exerts a power of domination which produces religion. This religion becomes Islam."[112]

How "Hinduism"-as-culture functions in Kakar's work is an instance of the misdirection of secularism that I explore in different fields throughout this book. That is, the majoritarian claim of "Hinduism" occupies the space of secularism, itself appearing as neutral, unmarked, leaving "other" faiths and practices to be identified as "religion"—as Mehdi notes in this instance.

[107] Ibid.: 182.
[108] Ibid.: 8.
[109] Kakar 1981: 30, cited in Davar 1999: 178.
[110] Mehdi 2018: 49.
[111] Ibid.: 49–50.
[112] Ibid.: 58.

There are other instances: for example, an essay titled "Indian Perspectives on Cognition" by R. C. Mishra counterposes to "Western" conceptualisations of cognition the "philosophical and religious thought of the ancient sages,"[113] citing the authority of the Vedas, the Upanishads, "the theory of yoga," and drawing exclusively on Sanskrit terms and categories. This is presented as "Indian" quite unproblematically. Nor is this an unusual conflation, as we have seen.

Given that psychoanalysis in India was always drenched, so to speak, in a Brahminical Hindu understanding, Davar contests Kakar's claim about the "rejection" of psychoanalysis, especially of Freud, by the Indian intellectual milieu as a result of tension between Hindu metaphysics and science.[114] Davar says, "what we find is rather an amicable and active assimilation of psychoanalysis through Hindu metaphysics." She suggests that Kakar's own "Hindu psychoanalysis, which is systematically integrative" follows this tradition.[115]

Secularism as Standardisation

The reader unfamiliar with psychoanalysis is likely to be struck by two levels of standardisation that take place over time, and which may proceed on parallel tracks. One is the standardisation of local, indigenous notions of the self with reference to the universal, secular, modern self normalised by psychoanalysis. The second, where indigeneity is asserted, is the standardisation of subaltern notions of the self with reference to whatever the dominant indigenous framework happens to be in that location.

In Mexico, according to Rolando Diaz Loving, the scholar Ezekiel A. Chavez had argued in 1901 that "character" varies across ethnic groups, and therefore institutions and the law must not be geared to the abstract; rather, "it is indispensable that they concretely adapt to the special conditions of the people they were created for."[116]

[113] Mishra 2006: 265.
[114] Davar 1999: 180.
[115] Ibid.
[116] Loving 2006: 315.

Chavez's recognition was lost in the following decades, and in the 1930s Samuel Ramos, greatly influenced by Adler's theory of the development of personality—in which autonomy and independence are higher stages—conducted interviews with indigenous people to arrive at a model of the Mexican sense of self. He found that, overwhelmingly, depictions focused on the importance of community and family, and on "the cardinal place that others have in the definition of the individual self."[117] Ramos arrived at the conclusion that the Mexican self was "covered by an inferiority complex."[118] Loving says that this became the "self-fulfilling prophecy" for other writers and philosophers for decades. But from the 1970s scholars such as Diaz Guerrero, and in the 1990s La Rosa and Loving himself, had attempted to understand the Mexican self on its own terms, not in critical comparison to "the instrumental, individual, autonomous and independent self so prevalent in Western psychological depictions."[119] Not surprisingly, they found the sense of self among Mexicans rooted in social ties and interdependence, and gave this a positive valence.

In Morocco Pandolfo sees a shift in the midst of the "Islamic Revival" from "'traditional' cures associated with spirit possession and the cult of saints and debased by colonial and postcolonial health institutions" to what she calls "reformed Islamic cures known as *ilaj shar'i*"—cures according to the shari'a or "lawful cures"—drawing legitimacy from "a renewed investment of the spiritual medical tradition of prophetic medicine and an integral understanding of human life and subjectivity in relation to God."[120] The argument of her book therefore is that "a conversation is possible between the ethics of psychoanalysis and ethics in the Islamic tradition."[121] But this conversation appears to be set on the terms of shari'a or lawful cures as opposed to pre-Islamic belief systems.

[117] Ibid.: 316.
[118] Ibid.: 317.
[119] Ibid.: 320.
[120] Pandolfo 2018: 25.
[121] Ibid.: 27.

However, the standardising move is constantly challenged too. The continuing engagement between psychiatry and traditional forms of healing leads to a continuous reshaping of both fields. Anna Vlnea, outlining the debates around jinn possession/mental disorder in Egypt, for instance, says that psychiatrists, some Islamic scholars, and secular intellectuals argue that jinn possession is unsupported by both science and religion, while Quranic healers insist there are religious texts that prove jinn possession. In the space produced by this debate, a new disease category has emerged—"*wahm*, the affliction of experiencing real possession symptoms while being unconsciously, but falsely, convinced one is possessed. This novel malady has emerged as a third way that tries to overcome the jinn possession/mental disorder binary while keeping the reality of jinn possession intact."[122] Vlnea suggests that the prominent debates in Egypt around the jinn possession/mental disorders pair reveal a "vibrant therapeutic landscape that cannot be frozen in a secular/religious divide but remains haunted and partially shaped by it."[123]

The other level of standardisation is seen with reference to alternative, equally "secular" (non-religious) models of healing centred on communities. In Morocco, for instance, the Hopital ar-Razi was established in 1963 as a model psychiatric institution to replace the French-style asylum. Located at the site of a shrine, Sidi Ghazi, the hospital is named after a tenth-century physician and polymath, Zakariyya al-Razi. Pandolfo says that patients call the hospital Sidi Razi "in a willing confusion of the two names, the mystic's and the physician's." In the 1970s–80s, the hospital worked with the medieval Muslim and Arabic therapeutic form—*bimaristan*—"a space of communal life where lunatics were treated with music and song," nurses participated in decision-making, families came to spend the day with patients, and artists were invited to share their work at the hospital. But by the 1980s, under new leadership and in response to

---

[122] Vlnea 2021.
[123] Ibid.

the shift from the psychological to the biological model in American psychiatry, the hospital began to attempt to meet these new "scientific" standards amidst much internal debate and challenge.[124] Thus, one can see two levels of standardising processes at work in what Pandolfo describes—local Islamic and Arabic practices standardised with reference to secular, scientific, international psychiatry on the one hand, and "pre-Islamic" faith healing practices standardised with reference to shari'a and Islam on the other. The latter lays claim to being able to converse with psychoanalysis on its own terms, and therefore to a secular status vis-à-vis superstition.

Secular Psychotherapy, Religious Faith, and Healing the Self

A fascinating instance of different levels of standardisation at work is offered by Sabah Siddiqui in her study of faith-healing practices in India in the first decade of the twenty-first century. Siddiqui begins by placing a question mark over the terminology itself which produces an implicit hierarchy: "Why invoke faith (and not science) and why invoke healing (and not cure)?"[125] And, "Are there some forms of healing that do not require the adherent to have faith in them?"[126]

This hierarchy between psychiatry as science versus faith healing as exploitation of superstitious beliefs about mental illness has resulted in different kinds of state intervention. An ordinance was passed in 2013 by the state of Maharashtra against "evil and sinister practices . . . propagated in the name of supernatural or magical powers or evil spirits," the fruit of decades of work by Dr Narendra Dabholkar and his rationalist movement, against the Hindu right wing and what they saw as its mobilisation of superstition to promote the politics of Hindu nationalism. Dabholkar was assassinated in broad daylight by, it is widely believed, Hindu right-wing groups. Since the passing of the

---

[124] Pandolfo 2018: 79–81.
[125] Siddiqui 2016: 2.
[126] Ibid.: 88.

ordinance, several arrests have been made for ritual beheadings and other such practices. Siddiqui notes that these actions could as well have been covered by ordinary criminal law against murder and fraud; she is critical of the rationalist movement's blindness towards how science and secularism can function in ideological ways, "being deployed (or not) for the establishment of the Indian state."[127]

She offers instances of state intervention in faith healing at the instance of professional psychiatrists. In 2001, following a fire at a *dargah* in Ervadi in the state of Tamil Nadu, in which over twenty-five people died, civil society groups working on mental health petitioned the Supreme Court to ensure that all mentally ill people in India receive proper care and treatment. The conditions of asylums and hospitals in India offering such services are often abysmal, but these were not the target of the petition. The target was the condition of patients at the *dargah* of Syed Ibrahim at Ervadi (who died in the fire because they were chained) and the Supreme Court directed the government to conduct a survey of "registered and unregistered asylums." Siddiqui notes how, through this directive, the *dargah* was no longer a shrine at which people of all communities came to be freed of magical maladies, a shrine the very soil of which was supposed to have the soil from Madinah mixed into it. It became instead an "unregistered asylum" and thus brought under the purview of psychiatry, science, and the law—or what Siddiqui terms the Science–State complex.[128]

In 2009, in another instance, an inspection was carried out by an "expert committee" of psychiatrists, of the *dargah* of Syed Shah Meeran in Hyderabad. The committee found "human rights violations" and petitioned the Supreme Court to direct the *dargah* to turn over all mentally ill patients to their families or to state-run asylums. The caretakers of the *dargah* framed their response in an entirely different language, emphasising the belief and faith that voluntarily brought people there for the "consolation" offered by the saint. They stated that the *dargah* was not a mental hospital and the devotees (both Hindus and Muslims) were not patients.

[127] Ibid.: 9.
[128] Ibid.: 4.

A third instance of the Science–State complex intervening in *dargah*s is the *dava-dua* programme of the government of Gujarat—an intervention by the Science–State complex intended to weed out the non-rational aspects of faith-based treatment. *Dava* (medicine) is dispensed by psychiatrists working alongside *dua* (blessings) offered by traditional healers. This project emerged from the Supreme Court directives after the fire at Ervadi and was directly influenced by the rationalist anti-superstition movement of Maharashtra. Siddiqui notes that psychiatry was welcomed by rationalists as an agent of science, being more neurologically and chemically oriented. Siddiqui is not celebrating non-science traditions of engaging with the psyche as more authentic. Rather she is concerned with the way in which the State–Science complex assumes an unquestioned superiority, despite the many flaws in psychiatric practice and in state-run institutions, and its insistence on translating non-science-driven traditional practices into its own terms.

Siddiqui raises a question about why the *dava-dua* programme was implemented only in *dargah*s and not in Hindu, Christian, or Dalit sites of faith healing, but it seems that similar projects were in fact implemented in other religious sites too—in Tamil Nadu, for example at Saint Michael Church at Rajavur and the Gunaseelam Temple.[129] At Chottanikkara Temple in Kerala priests advise those coming there to be healed of mental distress "to seek medical advice and to continue medication prescribed to them to improve sleep and enable patients to comply with the rituals of temple-healing. Patients who don't improve within 3 days are also referred for psychiatric care"—as stated in a letter to the *Indian Journal of Psychiatry* in 2020.[130]

The *dava-dua* project is a specific programme of the Gujarat government implemented, it appears, only in a *dargah* in Gujarat, but this collaboration between psychiatry and faith healing appears to be rather common now across religious sites of different denominations. The overall argument made by Siddiqui, thus, regarding the

---

[129] Saglio-Yatzimirskya, et al.: 2014.
[130] Radhakrishnan 2020.

hegemonising drive of the State–Science complex over other forms of healing, is still an important one.

We may consider here the critique of the movement for Global Mental Health (GMH) allied to the WHO, made by China Mills. This movement calls for a scaling up of access to psychiatric treatments (that is, access to medicines), particularly within the global South. Mills argues that these kinds of influences, closely linked to, even driven by, the powerful pharmaceutical lobby, focus on chemical "imbalances" in the brain as the source of distress, rather than recognising the role that social and political environments play.[131] This "psychiatrisation of the majority world," as the title of Mills' book puts it, seems to be the drive behind using spiritual spaces to push medication, because the people of the global South continued to turn to these spaces rather than to psychiatrists.[132] The status that psychiatry has as "Science," and therefore "secular," obscures the profit motive and power of the pharmaceutical industry, and automatically grants psychiatry a higher status among the decision-making elites, and those who can influence them, than traditional faith healers who can only be seen as representing backwardness and superstition.

However, the opposing trend is not to be easily dismissed, that is, the resistance to being hegemonised. For instance, the Ervadi Dargah Committee chief told a journalist that the religious leaders at the Gujarat *dargah* told them that "the medicines had more power since it was

---

[131] Mills 2014. Mills discusses the issue of suicides of Indian farmers and points out that while the farmers see suicides as linked to structural reasons such as capitalist transformations of the agrarian sector and debts, the government tends to respond through an individual and psychiatric framework, medicalising the issue because it is not interested in a change of policy.

[132] This section and the previous one benefited greatly from a presentation to the students and faculty of CSSS, JNU. The questions, comments, and suggestions received there considerably reshaped and filled out my argument. Special thanks to V. Sujatha for the China Mills reference.

being administered within the holy premises of the *dargah*. They said that the medicines would not work outside the *dargah*, and that the holy seer magnifies the power of these medicines."[133] So, while psychiatrists might think of faith as producing a placebo effect in such collaborations, it seems the keepers of shrines and devotees accept medical intervention as just another context—to recall Ramanujan again. For them allopathic medicine becomes something the sacred space of the shrine renders meaningful.

These partnerships between psychiatry and traditional healing practices are now common across the globe, which we can see either as the growing hegemony of the Science–State complex, or conversely as the growing acceptance by modern psychiatry that it cannot function in the global South according to the diktats of the *Diagnostic and Statistical Manual of Mental Disorders*, which determines what "madness" is based on the experience of the global North. In the context of Africa, Dr Frank Njenga, a Consultant Psychiatrist practising in Nairobi, and founding president of the African Association of Psychiatrists and Allied Professionals (AAPAP), says:

> Psychiatrists who have Western-style training are only able to handle a small number of these conditions. So what we have deliberately and consciously done is to develop partnerships—firstly with traditional healers. They are the ones who come face to face with the huge majority of people who suffer from mental disorder. And we try to get them to understand that there are some conditions they treat better than we do, and some conditions we treat better than they do.[134]

While this statement is expressed more in the hegemonising mode of the Science–State complex—even while acknowledging the fact that in some conditions faith healing works better—there are also strongly articulated decolonial critiques from Africa of mainstream, secular psychoanalysis. Lesiba Baloyi and Mogobe Bernard Ramose, for example, hold that since modern psychology and psychotherapy in

[133] Ravishankar 2015.
[134] Cited in Duncan 2012.

Africa are based on the Western epistemological paradigm, they cannot "accurately and authentically represent and reflect indigenous realities, in particular African experiences." They "arbitrarily exclude and alienate other realities, particularly indigenous knowledge systems." As a result, "the legitimacy and meaning of the African construction of knowledge is always determined and measured by concepts, standards and experiences that distort African reality . . . This epistemological injustice is ethically unsustainable, and thus calls for rectification."[135] Baloyi and Ramose then mine indigenous language resources to arrive at African ways of understanding life, good and evil, and other such questions around ontology and eschatology. They propose the term *moya* from the Sotho group of Bantu languages as one of the basic concepts to be considered in the construction of African psychology and psychotherapy. *Moya* has different meanings depending on the context, but can be interpreted as a life force "belonging to the 'ontology of invisible beings'."[136] Baloyi and Ramose carefully build a new vocabulary based on African languages and belief systems, and propose taking seriously the questions that Africans would ask about mental illness—the answers to which could be in terms of spirits, sorcery, and witchcraft. Since theory, Baloyi and Ramose hold, is a reflection of "experiences about the most deeply held values and thinking of the theorist and theorizing community," theory cannot be divorced from the cultural domain.[137] They also foreground the issue of language, arguing that the use of English and French limits and distorts the African experience. African languages use metaphors, *diane* (proverbs), *direto* (praise songs), and idioms as forms of expression, and psychotherapists working within the African context should "take note of these forms of expression, and use them to create an authentic way of connecting to and being with clients."[138] The adoption of *moya* and the teaching of psychology in indigenous languages is therefore an ethical imperative. Once

[135] Baloyi and Ramose 2016: 13.
[136] Ibid.: 15.
[137] Ibid.: 20.
[138] Ibid.: 26.

language is understood in a broader sense, they conclude, going beyond words, spoken or written, then African healing practices such as rituals and artefacts would need to be taken seriously as well, and traditional healers would have to be genuine partners in the process.

Psychoanalysis, as opposed to psychiatry, offers much more scope to enter into such spaces. In the context of women being possessed by the Devi, Sabah Siddiqui and Bhargavi Davar have reflected on how psychoanalysis must react to a phenomenon "irreducible to what is conventionally understood as either religion or science."[139] They point to a whole realm of subaltern practices that cannot be labelled as customary or religious and which fall therefore into something called "superstition."[140] Through a study of two Dalit women of the Matang caste who experienced possession by the goddess Tuljabhavani, they consider the relation of the self of the one possessed with the larger community and "how the experience of possession increases or decreases the social capital of the medium."[141] The very English term "possession" is problematic, as it has in the clinical context been diagnosed as hysteria. The Marathi term used by the *aradhis* (the possessed women) is *angamadhe devaahe* (the deity inhabiting the body).

Siddiqui and Davar argue that when psychoanalysis came to India it confronted something that "does not conform to the canonical versions of religion." The subaltern practice of Devi-possession cannot be fitted into the label of religion; if it is one, then it is

> a religion without a canon or text; the *Aradhi* herself speaks to the community in the voice of the Goddess. In this woman-to-woman relation, Aradhi-Guru-Aai-Devi, the priestly class cannot intervene . . . At once the practice sets up a religion without Religion as it has been understood, as well as a politics of relating that will not become the politics of the University, Science, or the State.[142]

Drawing on Obeyesekere's notion of Buddhist *askesis* or technology of the self—through his development of the idea of it-thinking

[139] Siddiqui and Davar 2018: 20.
[140] Ibid.: 19.
[141] Ibid.: 27–8.
[142] Ibid.: 34.

(discussed earlier) as "the conceptuality of thinking itself"—Siddiqui and Davar suggest that Obeyesekere "displaces the conscious subject of the Enlightenment but also the unconscious subject of psychoanalysis."[143] What psychoanalysis encounters here, therefore, according to them, is subaltern *askesis*, of which Devi-possession is one form.

Aditya Nigam refers to this domain as "the paramodern"—"that which modernity seeks to expunge and expel but which . . . accompanies it . . . as its inseparable shadow. The paramodern, populated by humans, spirits, jinns and demons" constitutes, he says, the biggest challenge for the modernist project of the Enlightenment.[144] The paramodern represents an uncolonised, unsubordinated "outside" that may get reconstituted in its encounter with the modern, but is certainly not to be understood as a product of or produced by the modern. The modern, in trying to expunge it, drives it underground, yet it does constitute a dominant experience of these societies. The vast majority of people in societies of the global South live their everyday in such a paramodern domain simultaneously along with the modern, well into the twenty-first century. Instances abound, as we have seen, in Africa, in the Arab world, and in India.

In February 2022, in a Kerala temple, a performance of *theyyam*—an ancient non-Brahminical dance ritual drawn from tribal beliefs, in which the performer is transformed into Mutthappan (the deity) himself—resulted in a widely circulated video showing the performer focusing on a Muslim woman in a burqa. Initially, she smiles at him, but as he places his hand on her shoulder and refers to her deep sadness, she breaks down as the Mutthappan himself comforts her and promises that her suffering will not last.[145]

Anand Vivek Taneja has written of "jinn-saints," a living presence in North India, and of the hundreds of Muslims and non-Muslims who reach monuments—such as the fourteenth-century fort and palace complex of Firoz Shah Kotla in Delhi—to address their complaints

---

[143] Ibid.: 30–1.
[144] Nigam 2020: 175.
[145] Varma 2022.

and requests (*shikwe*) to them. The stories told about jinns, he says, are "linked to deep time, connecting human figures thousands of years apart . . . In these stories jinns are the figures of the transmission of memory beyond all possibility of human history."[146] Those who arrive at Firoz Shah Kotla are often drawn by dreams of the saint Nanhe Miyan, and their *shikwe* are in the form of letters deposited in niches and corners of the complex. These letters are reminiscent of the medieval *shikwe* addressed to the emperor, often photocopied multiple times and deposited in different parts of the monument complex, "as if addressed to the different departments of a modern bureaucracy." The letters are almost always accompanied by a legible and detailed address and, increasingly, with photographs. At irregular intervals the letters are taken down, swept up into piles by workers of the Archaeological Survey of India, and burnt.[147]

It is this world, in which jinns and the modern nation-state occupy the same space, from which the patient walks into the clinic, a fact increasingly being recognised and addressed by psychoanalysis and psychotherapy from the global South.

The Other in the Analyst's Chair

Most practising analysts tend to be—unsurprisingly—from the dominant group in a society, thus producing familiar issues of power in the analytical space vis-à-vis the non-dominant patient. However, the analyst from a non-dominant group facing patients from the dominant group occupies an even more complex space of negotiation and mutual recognition (and lack of it).

Writing as practising Muslim psychotherapists in India today, Shifa Haq and Saba Siddiqui reflect on how obeying the maxim to preserve the neutrality of the analyst in the eyes of the analysand in effect requires them to appear by default as Hindu, for revealing their Muslim identity is to become non-neutral, to occupy a particular identity.

[146] Taneja 2018: 10.
[147] Ibid.: 11.

Although their names reveal their identity, it seems their patients do not necessarily absorb this information unless faced with it when explicitly articulated. And when confronted with this "difference" from themselves, the patients invariaby respond—negatively or positively. Haq and Siddiqui point to how Brahminical the very idea of neutrality is—the idea of "staying above the muddy waters—the filth of a chaotic interpersonal field."[148] It is as if, they say, "there is something like an analytic religion performing . . . at the unconscious of Indian psychoanalysis, which becomes explicit when Indian Muslim psychotherapists interact with it." They conclude therefore that the principle of neutrality "bars an authentic engagement with the other in psychoanalysis."[149]

Zehra Mehdi too, as a Muslim analyst attempting to explore "how Hindus and Muslims converse with each other, given their historical relation in an analytic setting,"[150] writes of her experience with a Hindu patient who reacts specifically (not necessarily negatively), to her Muslimness: "It appeared as if she had ideas about what being a Muslim meant, while I had none."[151] The analyst being a Muslim "had no place in the psychoanalytical frame," and so "In sessions, I could only speak as the Muslim in her head, which was her reality."[152]

The "analytic religion" at the heart of psychoanalysis that Haq and Siddiqui refer to is also of course *savarna* by default. Meena Sawariya points out that although "the recognition of caste signifies that it is a psychological reality in social life and is further a signifier of power, position, and collective experience," there is nevertheless a lack of reflectivity on caste experiences in the discipline.[153] Sharing her "journey as a Dalit counselling psychologist," Sawariya points to the way in which her caste identity and the inability of the discipline and

---

[148] Haq and Siddiqui 2018: 66.
[149] Ibid.: 68.
[150] Mehdi 2018: 113.
[151] Ibid.: 107.
[152] Ibid.: 111.
[153] Sawariya 2021: 191.

its practitioners to recognise its significance led to her "exile inside the discipline and its practice."[154] Sawariya argues that if "the derivatives of caste" cannot be isolated from "the intrapsychic and interpersonal functioning of a practitioner as a whole," the therapeutic process will be effective only if the psychologist attempts to "understand the psychological and social construct of a client's identity" and "incorporate their experiences in the therapeutic processes and alliance."[155] Considering the somewhat more "rare pairing" of the Dalit psychologist and the non-Dalit client, Sawariya sees this dyad as holding the potential for "the emergence of egalitarian and emancipatory social realities," because when the Dalit is the "expert" it both presents "a sense of dilemma in the client's psyche" as well as opens up the possibility of generating egalitarian values.[156]

The supposedly secular space of psychoanalysis is thus shot through with identity and difference, and the refusal to recognise this essentially leaves the "analytic religion" as invisibly coded with the dominant identity. Secular with reference to the South, then, is "Western"; while inside the South, secular would be normed as the internal dominant identity, in India that would be Hindu and *savarna*; in other places it would be other dominant identities.

Global South as Analyst, not Analysand

A significant development in the field appears to be the claim that the South is not merely different, with its own spatio-temporal and cultural co-ordinates. Rather, the claim is that what is considered the specificity of the South may be universalisable globally, that something presented as a counter to Western notions of the self is not peculiar to that particular culture alone but has more universal valence. Consider the example of the Japanese concept of *amae*, first written about by the

---

[154] Ibid.: 192.
[155] Ibid.: 193.
[156] Ibid.: 195.

Japanese psychiatrist Takeo Doi—whose 1971 book was translated into English in 1973 as *The Anatomy of Dependence* (1973). *Amae* roughly corresponds to "dependency need," or "basking in another's indulgence."[157] In Japan, Takeo noted, babies and young children seek "a sense of oneness" with their mothers through *amae* behaviour, such as acting helpless in a playful way to encourage holding and cuddling. *Amae* also colours adult relationships, such as when a woman or man playfully acts childlike with a romantic partner to invite intimacy.[158] Taketomo (1990) has systematically developed Doi's argument, suggesting that *amae* episodes are characterised by two specific features: (a) the suspension of some normal restraints of expected behaviour; and (b) this being agreed upon by the interactants. The examples he gives are of a 10-year-old boy asking his mother to dress him, or a husband behaving like a child with his wife.[159]

The interesting trend here is that Japanese scholars have been for some time arguing that *amae* is not to be conflated with attachment or dependence, and that "amae episodes are universal rather than unique to Japanese culture."[160] This claim to universality of a particular feature or process from a non-Western location is noteworthy. From India, Anup Dhar reads Girindrasekhar Bose's contribution as more than an argument for cultural relativism—that Indian and European patients are different in psychic disposition. Rather, as he puts it, "in the 'Indian' outline of psychoanalysis, the phallus is not considered the fundamental object or signifier of sexed subjectivity. Here 'India' is not an analysand who offers different case experiences to phallocentric psychoanalysis. Instead, India is an analyst of the European obsession with the phallus (and the Oedipal) as the structuring principle of psychic constitution."[161] Dhar argues that it is time to move to understanding *how* psychoanalysis is done *from* India rather than seeing it as

---

[157] Yamaguchi and Ariizumi 2006: 164.
[158] Bower 2004.
[159] Cited by Yamaguchi and Ariizumi 2006: 164.
[160] Yamaguchi and Ariizumi 2006: 171; Behrens 2004, cited by Bower 2004.
[161] Dhar 2018: 195.

doing Freudian or post-Freudian psychoanalysis *in* India. He is part of a collective institutional project begun in 2009 at Ambedkar University, Delhi, in which psychoanalysis is not about "psychological interiority and the confessional attitude" of classical Freudian psychoanalysis, but about groups and community.[162] As Dhar and Siddiqui put it, "What if the 'individual' does not come alone to the clinic? What if the individual comes as an entangled mass of communal memory traces?"[163] Such a relationship is not just transferential (which is dyadic) but is understood in terms of transversality, a transformational relationship of both self and the social.[164] Honey Oberoi Vahali, a key founder of the initiative at Ambedkar University, Delhi, calls it "psychosocial clinical studies,"[165] attempting to bridge worlds generally seen as divorced from one another—"those focusing on subjective and unconscious processes and those emphasising the study of structural politics and mega discourses of power and injustice."[166] The human subject in this understanding is one in which "dense connections of psyche-body-soma create complex pathways and in whom thinking, memory, feelings and perceptions cohere to create a moment of lively responsiveness." In this "intricate terrain" inner forces

[162] A key contribution to this project has been by thinker-teacher-practitioner Ashok Nagpal, who has "done much to establish a psycho-social clinical, culturally sensitive and associatively rich version of psychoanalysis"—as Honey Oberoi Vahali pointed out to me in a personal communication, to emphasise the importance of non-written/non-published intellectual contributions. In Vahali's words, Nagpal "may be considered, without doubt, as a pioneer and teacher who from the 1980s onwards has established the university as a space where psychoanalysis could thrive in the city of Delhi. His mode of psychoanalytic work is secular as he upholds the position that psychoanalytic practice and thinking are ways of thinking beyond binaries and polarities, that the opposite exists in the self and the self and the anti-self are to be considered in relation to one another. His stress on a nuanced associative way of thinking-feeling-dreaming has become a mode through which psychoanalytic thinking has been passed on to generations of students who are now thinkers and practitioners in their own right."

[163] Dhar and Siddiqui 2013: 510.

[164] Ibid.: 198.

[165] Vahali 2019: 130.

[166] Ibid.: 132.

interact with those of the social, while the psychotherapist becomes a "co-sufferer participant" or a "co-vulnerable expert."[167]

Psychoanalysis *from* the global South seeks to speak to such experiences located elsewhere (than the South) too, experiences which do not fit into mainstream Western psychoanalytic conceptual frameworks.[168]

Historicising "Myth"

Other social science disciplines such as political science, history, and sociology have—at least by the end of the twentieth century (with many earlier instances too)—come to recognise that what are termed the "non-rational" and "irrational" have a key role in politics, society, and history. The role of the unconscious, of repression, faith, and desire, all inexplicable in mainstream social science terms, have led scholars towards psychology and psychoanalysis in their quest to escape the limits set by disciplinary borders. Psychoanalysis has perhaps not made the reverse journey to the extent it could have, especially with regard to myth, and the letting in of history into myth.

Despite over a century of critical scholarship globally on Freud's Oedipus Complex, especially from a feminist perspective, this idea continues to shape much of psychoanalytic thinking. Kosawa, Bose, and Kakar too, as we saw above, continued to accept the central frame of Oedipus by stating a difference "here" as opposed to "there," or between Indian and European patients. Coming from a feminist and anti-Brahminical position, however, Bhargavi Davar offers a more thoroughgoing critique of the Indian/Hindu psychoanalytic explanation of

---

[167] Ibid.: 138, 142.

[168] In contrast to this approach, the essays in an earlier volume edited by Salman Akhtar, *Freud Along the Ganges* (2005), seem to me to read through a classic psychoanalytic lens various aspects of "India"—for instance philosophy (*Bhagavad Gita*, Buddhist theory, Advaita Vedanta), philosophers (Gandhi, Tagore), culture ("Bollywood"), and identities (Hindu–Muslim relations). There is a strong criticism of work that reads Indian styles of self as deficient from the psychoanalytic point of view, but the overall framework both reifies "India" and sees it as translatable into psychoanalytic terms.

Indian women's depression in oedipal terms—whether as being pre-oedipal (privileging the early mother–infant attachment, especially the mother–son dyad); or as oedipal (involving developmental issues about individuation and separation). Davar argues that "treating syndromes like "depression" or "hysteria" in terms of an infantile sexuality, desire for the penis, oedipal aggression, and the associated feelings of guilt is the denial of the often oppressive social realities within which Hindu women function."[169] After a brief discussion of Western feminist critiques of concepts of oedipal theory and penis envy, she goes on to argue that in the Indian context the oedipal story is really about upper-caste Hindus for whom caste purity, ritual authority of men/sons, social hierarchy, and patriarchal control are important, while in the subaltern castes patriarchal controls are less rigid. She points out that the subaltern castes also celebrate the female body, its sexuality and fertility.[170]

It is from here that I would like to move into a consideration of what historicising myth could mean for psychoanalysis, as well as of course for any attempt whatsoever to understand society and politics. As we saw in Chapter 3, in India there has since antiquity been a project to establish Brahminical hegemony over a heterogeneous field of pre- and non-Vedic cultures. The effort has been and continues to be to try connecting the gods and goddesses of this landscape—male, female, black, lower-caste, forest deities, multi-/non-gendered, non-human—to the Vedic pantheon in familial ways, spousifying and infantilising them, or drawing them into Brahminical narratives through stories linked to the heroes of the epics. The Puranas—the earliest of which were composed between the fourth and eighth centuries CE—have been, as noted, one such crucial Brahminical intervention. Thus, the recognition today of wilder notions of divine femininity and powerful female deities among subaltern castes must acknowledge this history of continuous appropriation, as also the refusal of these cultures

[169] Davar 1999: 184.
[170] Ibid.: 186.

to be fully disciplined and accommodated. This heterogeneity has tended to be read as indicating the generosity of an accommodative Hinduism; but I have argued, rather, that the heterogeneity indicates a radical alterity. There are multiple beliefs and practices across communities which cannot be brought under one label. What is called "Hinduism" is only Brahminism, a minority strand of belief and practice among multiple others which continually claims to include all that is not Muslim or Christian. In modern India, as we have seen, this claim has only a legal basis, which is periodically challenged.

What in the Indian context gets read as "Hindu myths," therefore, has to do not with deep untouched archetypes of a "Hindu mind" but indications of the multiple layers that have accumulated over time around sets of beliefs and practices. To assume that all "Hindu" patients would readily access the same myths is extremely problematic. Even more problematic is to term as "Indian" mythology figures from the Hindu epics, for example Hanuman,[171] although the author's project of accessing figures in the cultural landscape of India in the course of psychotherapy is, of course, one that resonates with the argument here.

Let us consider the Ganesha narrative in some detail. Daniel J. Meckel, in "Hinduism and Psychoanalysis," refers to the "abundance of scholarly reflection from within and outside the disciplines of psychoanalysis" on the Ganesha mythology which is "replete with unmistakable oedipal themes such as violent confrontation with the father, competition and conflict with the brother, erotically charged adoration of the mother and yes, castration."[172] He refers to Ganesha's competition with Skanda for the fruit, the story retold by Kakar (discussed earlier); as well as another story of Ganesha guarding his mother's inner chamber, on her orders, from his father Shiva, who beheads him and later revives him by placing an elephant's head on his body. As Meckel puts it, classic psychoanalytic readings "plunge headlong

---

[171] Wig 2004.
[172] Meckel 2009: 213.

into the realms of murderous oedipal hatred, precarious immersion in the mother, and searing unconscious fears of paternal retribution."[173] And yet, he notes (as do we) that Girindrasekhar Bose "revises psychoanalysis to such an extent as to render Oedipus unrecognizable; that is, by non-Indians."[174]

We may note that the Ganesha narrative does not have the same valence in Bengal, Bose's own terrain, but there is a more important point I wish to make here about the elephant-headed god being too easily read in oedipal and Freudian terms. The Puranic stories incorporate Ganesha, a part-human god, and Skanda/Subramanian, a forest god, into the Vedic pantheon as children of Shiva and Parvati (herself a domesticated, "spousified" version of wild female powers worshipped by subaltern castes, as discussed in Chapter 2). These deities are non-Vedic, and carry layers of other meanings that escape the familial formula so essential to an oedipal reading. It is revealing that the Brahminical assimilative project produces narratives that need to justify or explain why Ganesha has an elephant's head. We discussed one story above, but there is another one too, involving no violence, only a deeply erotic charge between the parents. As one Shaivite myth has it, Shiva and Parvati, watching a pair of elephants in sexual intercourse, are aroused themselves and transform themselves into elephants to experience sexual play like them. Ganesha is born of this particular act of sex.[175]

What is important to note is that an elephant-headed deity could well have preceded the Vedic male pantheon. Balaji Mundkur, tracing the history of Vainayaki, an elephant-headed female deity, presents a rich palimpsest of associations between elephants and divinity going back to Vedic times. The earliest invocation of Ganesha is in the *Sama Veda*, but there it is a name for Rudra-Shiva himself. While accepted scholarship backed by archaeological evidence holds that the full-fledged cult of an elephant-headed Ganesha cannot be traced back

---

[173] Ibid.
[174] Ibid.: 214.
[175] Mundkur 1975: 301.

earlier than the fifth century CE, Mundkur does not consider it impossible that "an anthropomorphic, elephant-headed deity, male or female" existed in pre-Aryan India.[176] Elephant worshippers existed among Buddhists in 400 BCE, but the earliest known representation of an elephant-headed human figure can be traced to a plaque in Rajasthan from about the first century BCE to the first century CE, which is considered to represent a goddess. Crucially, there are no symbols which could associate this figurine with Shiva or other gods. But that the name Vainayaki "has aboriginal connotations is apparent from the suffix yaki (jakkhi, jakkhini), the Prakrit for yaks or yaksii—the feminine generic term for any chthonic [underground] semi-divinity. The etymology of the prefix is less certain. It may be traced to 'vana', forest."[177] An elephant-headed female deity could also have been a Tantric goddess of the seventh to twelfth centuries CE.[178]

In short, there is no foundational or unitary Ganesha narrative in "Hinduism" on the basis of which a Freudian reading can be made. It is possible that a patient might relate to Ganesha, but they might more readily relate to other myths, narratives, and divinities, the meanings of which cannot be determined in advance through an oedipal reading.

Freud famously said about Oedipus, "It is the fate of all of us, perhaps, to direct our first sexual impulse towards our mother and our first hatred and our first murderous wish against our father."[179] One wonders about the cross-cultural applicability of that confident "all of us" thus burdened with parricidal desire. In this part of the world, the living myths with contemporary resonance are very different. For instance, we have Yayati's son Puru and Shantanu's son Devavrata, both of whom attained full masculine subjectivity through *sacrificing* for their fathers their own youth and sexual desire. Puru took on the untimely old age that was cursed upon his father, and in turn ascended the throne, though he was the youngest son. It was his lineage that produced the

[176] Ibid.: 292.
[177] Ibid.: 296.
[178] Ibid.: 298.
[179] Freud 1965: 296.

dynasty of the Pandavas and Kauravas, protagonists of the Mahabharata. Devavrata took an oath of lifelong celibacy so that his father's
desire for the beautiful Satyavati could be fulfilled, for she would not
marry him unless he promised that *her* son would be king after him.
Devavrata thus not only gave up the right to the throne himself, he
promised he would never beget progeny at all, obviating the possibility
of rivals for the throne. This vow of lifelong celibacy made the gods
shower flowers on Devavrata, proclaiming him Bhishma—he of the
terrible oath—and his father granted him the boon of *Svechha Mrityu*
(control over his own death). Bhishma went on to become the revered
patriarch of the Mahabharata.

Interestingly, the absence of Oedipus tales and therefore of an
Oedipus Complex can also be seen as a lack, preventing the emergence
of Indians into full maturity and modernity—as Ramanujan points
out. And so he embarks on the project of finding "Oedipus-like pat-
terns" in Indian myth and folklore, keeping Sophocles' *Oedipus Rex* as
the model.[180]

Interestingly, Freud's Oedipus Complex is assumed as so universal
that all myths and ancient lore connected with incest are read through
this template. Incest, both its possibility and its interdiction, have accompanied human society from its inception. Every myth about incest
seems to have simultaneously built into it the theme of its rejection
and punishment—for example, the *Rig Veda*, 3500 years ago, has
Dyaus the sky god who has sex with or rapes his daughter Ushas and is
cast out as punishment. The Greek myth of Oedipus, from which Freud
draws out his own version of a universal human conflict, is dated to
about a thousand years after the *Rig Veda*.

Michael Carroll reminds us that Freud himself did not identify the
Oedipus story as a myth, but rather that he read Oedipus through the
story as told specifically in a literary text, Sophocles' *Oedipus Rex*. Carroll holds it to be problematic that distinctions between literary texts,
myths, dreams, folk tales, and clinical narratives are routinely blurred

[180] Ramanujan 1995: 236.

by modern commentators who discuss the psychoanalytic study of myth.[181] In Carroll's reading Freud, from *The Interpretation of Dreams* (1900) to *Totem and Taboo* (1913), developed his theory of the two unconscious wishes of the child. In the former through literary texts he outlined the young child's sexual desire for the mother and the resulting hostility towards the father. In the latter he posited his belief that the incest taboo arose from the guilt experienced by the primal band of brothers who killed their father to have sexual access to their mothers and sisters, the unconscious memory of which was passed from generation to generation and shaped religious ritual and belief.[182] The universality of this primal parricide and guilt is assumed to such an extent that Oedipus can be sought (and found) everywhere. Consider a volume embarking upon a search for Oedipus in global folklore which indeed finds "Oedipus" everywhere in the early to late twentieth century.[183] A lullaby among Albanian tribes in which the child is addressed as "my son, brother of my husband" is one instance.[184] Another is a gypsy version from Hungary in which a woman dreams she married her son, so to prevent this abandons him at birth; but they meet, become lovers, and when discovering who each is the man goes away, locking himself into a room from which he is led out after many years by priests. He forgives his mother and is made Pope—the first Pope after St Peter.[185] In another gypsy myth the father is the incestuous husband of his sister, and while on an expiatory pilgrimage to Jerusalem he dies. The son, on discovering his wife is his mother, retreats in penance to a cave from where he, Gregorius, is freed to become Pope.[186] From Papua the tale in this volume is of a father sodomising his thin and sickly son to make him grow through the power of his semen; after his transformation the son and his mother become lovers because she

[181] Carrol 2009:163.
[182] Ibid.: 164.
[183] Edmunds and Dundes 1995.
[184] Hasluck 1995: 5.
[185] Karpati 1995: 23–4.
[186] Ibid.: 25.

desires him, and it is the father who kills the son. This story is titled "Oedipus in Papuan folklore" despite not being an Oedipus-type story at all.[187]

Ramanujan finds eight "variants" in India. In one, a folk tale in North Karnataka, a woman born cursed to marry her own son retreats to a forest and eats only fruit, forswearing male company. But she happens to eat a fruit from a tree under which a passing king has urinated; the mango impregnates her, she abandons the son, but they meet when he is grown up and they bear a child together. When she discovers the truth she hangs herself after singing a lullaby to her son: "Sleep, oh son, oh grandson, oh brother to my husband . . ." Which is almost exactly the lullaby sung in Albania.

In none of the variants Ramanujan finds does the woman get pregnant through sexual intercourse. Many of the tales of incest are told as illustrations of the sinfulness of all worldly relations, or as conundrums or guessing games, "not as deeply tragic tales." In all the variants the protagonist is the woman—"the men are pawns in the story of women's fate."[188] In many of the stories that this volume tells, the father is entirely absent or already dead, or the father kills the son and thus parricide is not a theme at all.

So, *Oedipus Rex* by Sophocles is merely one version of this preoccupation of human societies with incest, and in it one could see other themes featured—for instance, the key theme of the gradual delegitimisation of matrilineal societies and their replacement by patriliny (such replacement would not have been without violence). Also, we could focus on the emergence of the incest taboo almost from the moment that incest is confronted as such, the taboo coming into being for reasons of wider alliances and the avoidance of familial conflict. But when read through the Freudian Oedipus template, all these complex narratives about incest that suggest historical changes and shifts are understood simply as reversals, or as different versions of the "original"

[187] Williams 1995.
[188] Ramanujan 1995: 241.

Sophocles telling, although many, being oral tellings, may in fact be older.

Ramanujan's essay in this volume recounts and participates in the oedipal interpretation by scholars such as Goldman of conflicts between Brahmin sages and Kshatriya rulers in the epics and in temple legends. The Brahmin is read as the father and the Kshatriya as the son in such interpretations, with the son losing the battles for supremacy.[189] But to impute a transhistorical, primal, familial frame to a historical process in which one social group is establishing control over others through violence, alliance building, and hegemonising narratives is the equivalent of understanding the capitalist transformation in England in terms of oedipal conflict. Even though Ramanujan asks whether the Oedipus Complex is universal, he struggles to accommodate all difference in the Indian context in terms of Oedipus—"negative" Oedipus; "reverse" Oedipus; the absence of parricide stories indicating an even greater repression, and so on.[190]

In a classically oriented psychoanalytic response to Ramanujan on Oedipus, Nilofer Kaul draws attention to matricide in Indian myth, showing a connection between the presence of matricide and the absence of patricide. She suggests that the figure of Putana, the "demoness" who breastfeeds Krishna with poison and is killed by his sucking the life out of her, "harks back to a pre-oedipal psychic structure where splitting and projection rather than repression appear to be psychically more consonant."[191] Letting history into this myth, as we did in Chapter 3, would remind us that the figures of Asuras (demons) are the non-Aryan people—the Dalit Bahujan of today—who are both violently defeated in battle by the Devas (gods) and also redeemed in different ways in order to secure willing compliance to Brahminical hegemony. Putana, therefore, after being killed by the infant Krishna, is cut into many pieces and burnt outside Gokul. While her body is burning, the fragrance of *agar* fills the air. Because the Lord himself has fed on her milk, she is redeemed. But other texts, such as the *Garga*

---

[189] Ibid.: 246.
[190] Ibid.: 254.
[191] Kaul 2018: 59.

Samhita and the *Brahma Vaivarta Purana*, reveal her to have been the daughter of Mahabali in a previous birth, seeking revenge for the treacherous murder of her father by Vishnu, of whom Krishna is an avatar.[192] Thus Putana is offered a justification for her murderous act, but is simultaneously brought under the protective and forgiving umbrella of the Brahminical god.

Referring to fierce and destructive aspects of the feminine in different Puranas, Kaul suggests that this "lurking presence" is a reminder of "the dark, uncanny force that resides in the woman and must be placed far away from the 'good' mother." And "the hushing of plurality and the dominance of the ur-text is not only to uphold the authority of the omnipotent father over the unruly sons, but also to exorcise the disquieting, unruly aspects of the mother, feared and fantasised by the infant."[193] But plurality is never entirely hushed outside of the Puranas, and dark, fierce "outcaste goddesses" continue to be worshipped by non-Brahminical castes millennia later, well into the twenty-first century.[194] They are in fact living presences, as we saw in Chapter 2. Here it is particularly apt to recollect Priyadarshini Vijaisri's study of a rare Dalit Purana, the *Jambava Purana*, on the basis of which there is a "vibrant and effervescent ritual tradition" centred on the outcaste clan goddess Matangi of the Madiga community across villages in Andhra Pradesh.[195] In that "tumultuous ritual space," outcaste ritual specialists are "awe-inspiring, feared, and at the same time revered as representatives of the goddess."[196] The Madigas worship Matangi in "her unblushing fierce and erotic form."[197] While Brahminical mythology spousifies Matangi as Renuka,[198] the outcaste mother goddess tradition recognises "the virility of the goddess."[199]

---

[192] Herbert 1996.
[193] Kaul 2018: 61.
[194] Vijaisri 2015: xiii.
[195] Discussed in detail in chap. 3.
[196] Ibid.
[197] Ibid.: 64.
[198] See chap. 3.
[199] Ibid.: 83.

Putana thus is not an enduring archetype of the bad mother but a figure representing the history of the military and cultural conquest of non-Aryan peoples, and while one Brahminical Purana tells the story of her evil, others give her a backstory to redeem her and assimilate the descendants of the "Asuras." If Putana is a figure in anybody's field of consciousness, a *savarna* analyst or patient would relate to her actions and death in one way, while non-*savarna* analysts and patients would relate in completely different ways. And, of course, the figure behind this attempt on Krishna's life, his maternal uncle Kamsa, represents— as does the other evil maternal uncle of the Mahabharata, Shakuni— the systematic delegitimation of matrilineal kinship ties. And yet, despite this demonisation, till today, even in societies with no matrilineal history, the mother's brother continues to be seen as a warm protective figure. The Brahminical project, as we have seen again and again, remains incomplete.

Kosawa's Ajase Complex draws on the version of the Ajase story appearing in the *Kanmuryojukyo*, a Buddhist scripture centring on the salvation of the mother. This myth has no sexual relationship at all between mother and son. The son Ajase is angered when he learns the secret of his birth—that his mother killed a hermit who was to be reborn as her son in order to hasten the event, for she feared her husband Bimbisara's loss of interest in her in her infertile condition. But she is fearful of her unborn son, who will seek revenge for his death in his previous birth, and so she attempts to kill him at birth by dropping him from a great height off her womb. He survives the fall and is later reminded of his origins during a period of depression by an enemy of the Buddha. Enraged, he attempts to kill his mother Idaike (Vaidehi in Sanskrit), but is overcome by such feelings of guilt that he falls seriously ill and is only nursed back to health by his mother. Idaike's charitable act resolves her own conflicts over her son, who recovers to become a wise king.[200] In his essay Kosawa renders the guilt of the child from this story in the following way: "The child asks the mother for for-

---

[200] Blowers and Chi: 119.

giveness—and receives it. The mother takes the child's fearful and rebellious guilt and alchemises it into a 'reparative guilt': an overwhelming response to total, unconditional forgiveness. This latter reaction was, for Kosawa, a truly 'religious state of mind' and he saw it as the core of his own Shin tradition."[201]

As with Oedipus, of which *Oedipus Rex* is only one version, there are other versions of the birth of Ajatshatru in Buddhist and Jain traditions. As contemporaries of the Buddha and Mahavira, Ajatshatru and his father Bimbisara—whom he executed to ascend the throne—are historical figures from the first Magadhan dynasty to leave verifiable historical evidence.[202] But the mythical accounts of Ajatshatru's birth and parentage in the Buddhist *Tripitaka* and Jain *Nirayavalika Sutra* differ significantly from Kosawa's Ajase narrative. The mother (Vaidehi in both traditions) desires during her pregnancy to eat part of the body of the king, and he obligingly offers it to her. Later she repents of this demonic desire and casts out her baby, fearing he will bring destruction on the family, but the baby is rescued by the father.[203] Thus these versions offer a central restorative role to the father, who heals the son abandoned by the mother, while historically, as we noted, Bimbisara was executed by Ajatshatru to ascend the throne.

In his response to an essay which tries to complicate psychoanalytic reading of myths, Balaji Mundkur challenges the author, Eichinger Ferro-Luzzi, for continued reliance on certain ideas—such as water as a predominantly female symbol, the serpent as associated with the male, and the snakebite as suggestive of the perils of sex. Mundkur draws on "labyrinthine Hindu iconography" as well as on the mythology and iconography of the Shuswap Indians of British Columbia, Shinto beliefs, the Semitic deity Ishtar, and Egyptian images to demonstrate that symbols—in this case of sexuality and male/female identity—are ambivalent even within a single culture. He shows that they are not universally translatable across cultures and time, nor amenable to systematic

[201] Harding 2018.
[202] Singh 2021.
[203] Jain 1974.

explanation and generalisation. This casts doubt, therefore—in his understanding—on "the usefulness of conjectures about symbolism that are beholden to the psychoanalytic precepts of the Freudian, Jungian, Adlerian, or similar schools."[204] I would read Mundkur not as dismissing psychoanalysis but as offering the possibility of fluid readings of myth, inflected by location.[205]

The practice of psychoanalysis in the global South has shown what stepping out of the secular can look like. While the more conventional mode of translating the self into terms recognisable to established psychoanalytic frameworks is very much in place, we see across languages and cultures the two other modes of engagement as well. That is, the translation of psychoanalysis into location-specific contexts; and the internal tensions between hegemonic and counter-hegemonic traditions. By adding to the cultural dimension the idea of letting history into myth, I hope to suggest a continuing dynamism and heterogeneity in the way that various sections of society access different myths, folk stories, and other cultural resources—depending on the histories of domination, resistance, and identity formation in their societies and their own position within these. My contention is that a secular framework does not permit any serious engagement with this aspect without assimilating or translating these elements of self-making into terms legible to itself.

---

[204] Mundkur 1980: 60.

[205] Alf Hiltebeitel's *Freud's Mahabharata* makes a creative and fascinating argument, but its project is to read the Mahabharata through Freudian concepts such as the "uncanny"; to offer "post-Freudian" readings of scenes, themes, and episodes. Hiltebeitel pursues Freud's argument that religions should be studied in terms of their unconscious past and repressed trauma. He reads the Mahabharata, therefore, as expressing a "polytheistic Vedic past"—it is in short the "recovered memory" of a Vedic past (Hiltebeitel 2018). The book is an unputdownable read, but, as chap. 3 has indicated, the project of the epics and the Puranas can be read in an entirely different way. To assume that the polytheistic past is entirely Vedic, or entirely in the past, is to evacuate myth of all history and to treat the Mahabharata as a fixed and homogeneous text. In addition, in terms of its argument, *Freud's Mahabharata* is precisely what Mundkur indicates is a deeply problematic way of reading heterogeneous cultures.

5

Capitalism as Secular Science

WE COME NOW to another element obscured by the grid of secularism—capitalism and its operations.

Capitalist transformation both dispossesses communities from their land and resources as well as brings the world ever closer to ecological catastrophe. However, both these processes appear in the guise of progress, modernity, and technological advance, devoid of politics, devoid of identities, devoid of emotions. One of the most striking instances of this is to be found in Dolly Kikon's account of the militarised landscape of the states of Assam and Nagaland in northeast India, in which the Indian nation-state ruthlessly enforces a securitised "carbon citizenship regime" based on the extraction of hydrocarbon resources, oil in particular; "where knowledge, procedures and legal rights of its subjects are drawn from the extractive resource regime."[1] Through extra-constitutional regulations like the Armed Forces Special Powers Act (1958) and the Disturbed Areas Act (1955), which have been in force across the North-East for decades, the Indian security forces protect the processes of oil drilling and gas exploration from identity-based insurgent movements seeking autonomy, or at least the local control of resources. This carbon citizenship regime involves surveillance of the population at large, indiscriminate arrests, brutal torture, and large-scale profiling of people as "reliable good citizens"—as opposed to potential insurgents.[2] In this landscape, frequently drenched in

[1] Kikon 2019: 135.
[2] Ibid.: 146–7.

violence and bloodshed, Kikon found that the geologists and engineers of the Indian government-owned Oil and Natural Gas Corporation (ONGC)—an organisation slated to be privatised and sold to private international bidders—go about their work in an aura of technical purity, addressing hydrocarbon exploration as a depoliticised, scientific, and therefore secular enterprise.[3]

It has been evident from the beginning of the enterprise of capitalist transformation that the project cannot succeed without the massive backing of the modern state with all its coercive resources. And yet the state is even now not all-pervasive. There are innumerable ways of living and working that escape the gaze of the state. All over the world indigenous peoples, in particular, represent the limits to state power in different ways and at different levels, even though most of them, especially in North America and Australia, have been decimated and thoroughly contained. James Scott reminds us that only the modern state since the eighteenth century in Europe, and in its colonial and post-colonial avatars in the rest of the world, has had the resources to attempt to bring all non-state spaces and people under its control. He calls this "the last great enclosure," referring to the process of enclosures in England that began in the sixteenth century and "swallowed half of England's common arable land in favour of large-scale, private, commercial production." The modern state attempts to "integrate and monetize the people, lands and resources of the periphery" in order to make them "auditable contributors to the gross national product and to foreign exchange."[4] Scott also points out that despite this massive endeavour, for much of history living outside the state or in an intermediate zone was a real option for many kinds of groups and communities. I begin by mapping how the misdirection of secularism works in this instance, and then go on to consider two specific instances that illustrate the larger argument being made here: the controversy over the construction of a shipping canal by the Indian state; and the recognition of individual land rights for women as a capitalist agenda.

[3] The ONGC has been frequently reported as up for privatisation—see PTI 2021—but remains as of now an Indian government undertaking.
[4] Scott 2009: 4–5.

The Construction of Nature

The emergence of the category of nature as separate from humans—and its desacralisation—is a key intellectual development in modernity, making nature commodifiable. This reconceptualising of nature is central to the normalisation of capitalism. The power of the idea colours all modern ideologies, including Marxism. Bruno Latour sees the separation of the world into the natural and the social-political as the founding mythology of modern thought. His formative idea is that the natural and social orders are "co-produced," i.e. produced together. He uses the word "collective" to describe the association of humans and non-humans, and the word "society" (implying humans) to designate "one part only of our collectives, the divide invented by the social sciences."[5]

In a parallel move, Walter Mignolo says that in decolonial thinking "nature" is already a colonial term, desacralised and separated from the human world, the latter assumed to be superior in both Christian theology and secular thinking. But the indigenous peoples of the global South see themselves as inside nature, not apart from it—in this context Mignolo refers to the concept of Pachamama of the Aymaras and Quechuas as one instance. In colonial thinking, nature "became a repository of objectified, neutralised and largely inert materiality" that existed for the fulfilment of economic goals.[6] In the theo-politics of knowledge, Secularism displaced God. However, the key idea in Mignolo's thinking on the decolonial is that when the first world order or *nomos* (polycentric and non-capitalist) was replaced by the second *nomos* (monocentric, interconnected by capitalism) over five or six centuries, the earlier forms of intellection, thought, and life were not destroyed and relegated to the past as remnants of past history—as colonial thinking assumes.[7] It is because they survived that they are able to emerge again in the twenty-first century in the form of assertions of religious and ancestral identities, and in the reassertion by Indigenous peoples of nature as having agency.

[5] Latour 1993: 4.
[6] Mignolo 2011: 12.
[7] Ibid.: 28–9.

Mignolo understands spirituality as going beyond organised religion and finds "reinscriptions" of spirituality in "the desire to find ways of life beyond capitalism."[8] Drawing on Native American philosophy, he links to the spiritualities rooted in their lands the struggles of these Indigenous inhabitants against American settler colonialism—the latter an embodiment of the capitalism within which land is only a commodity.

Tribal people in India too have asserted their traditional spiritual beliefs while resisting state takeover of their lands, whether for "public purpose" or, since the 1990s, by being handed over to corporate capital for exploitation of their resources. The Pathalgadi movement in Central India links tribal traditions of collective ownership, the protection of land, and tribal self-government with the modern Constitution in creative and powerful ways.[9] The Dongria Kondh tribe of the Niyamgiri Hills of Odisha has waged a successful struggle against a powerful mining company backed by the government. This it has done by drawing on its spiritual and sacred relationship to the hills, in which it lives a sustainable life based on forest produce.[10] In 2022 the Sarnas of Jharkhand launched a struggle to be recognised as a separate religious community, neither Hindu nor Christian, based on their own beliefs—whereby the forest is worshipped and protected. Their demands include their own religious code and the strict implementation of the Schedule V provisions of the Constitution which protect tribal self-government.[11] In short, Indigenous people, for so long globally consigned to "the past" of "our" present, are claiming the present as theirs too.

There is a long history of feminist critiques of the invisibility of ecology as a concern for both capitalism and Marxism, and a recognition of the parallels between nature and women in the masculinism that

---

[8] Ibid.: 62.

[9] The Pathalgadi movement is examined in greater detail in chap. 6.

[10] George 2014. The Dongria Kondhs were able to successfully use the Forest Rights Act passed in 2006 by the Congress-led UPA government, under pressure from social movements. This Act is discussed later in the chapter.

[11] Sinha 2022.

characterises modernity. In a classic statement, Ariel Salleh points out the congruence between the global push "for resource management" and "to appropriate women's reproductive processes"—as if, she says, women are "*terra nullius.*"[12] Ecofeminist perspectives have noted the masculinist mode of instrumental rationality that drives capitalist transformation, a mode that matches secular modernity perfectly. Vandana Shiva, for instance, argues that two opposing worldviews clash when it comes to forests. On the one hand is the life-destroying and masculinist perspective of the commercial forestry system, which treats forests as a resource to be exploited and which sets up private property in forest wealth. This perspective has the backing of the state and has colonised, "cognitively, economically and politically," the local men. On the other hand she sees the feminine and life-conserving principle embodied in viewing the forest as divine, and as a diverse and self-reproducing system shared as a commons by a diversity of social groups.[13] This view came under criticism for what appeared in the 1990s—when Hindutva was on the rise—to be Brahminical vis-à-vis Dalits, and a Hinduisation of Adivasi worldviews. However, in the twenty-first century, in the face of non-Hindu spiritual assertion by Adivasis facing the destruction of their *jal, jangal,* and *jameen* (water, forests, land), as well as Dalit environmentalism, Shiva's views appear to have found their place in ecological thinking.

The socialist-feminist Gabriele Dietrich—a practising Christian in the liberation theology tradition—and influenced by Simone Weil, whom Dietrich describes as "too secular to enter the Church but religious enough to be a mystic"—has spoken of having "spontaneous access to Hindu symbols and contents" through the poor among whom she works.[14] Her access has been equally to the struggles of Dalits who want to confront Hinduism as a whole, and to Muslims who do not reject Islam but want to "dismantle their cultural oppression."[15] Dietrich sees religious/spiritual beliefs as central to ecologically sustainable

[12] Salleh 1997: 53.
[13] Shiva 1988.
[14] Dietrich 1992: vii.
[15] Ibid.

lives—as evident from the lives of the poor among whom she works. She sees as "simplified and reductionist" the views of many Indian feminists whose secularism involves rejecting religion, not just for themselves but for the movement as a whole.[16] She speaks of cultural and religious practices that link women and nature—for instance, a dance (*karagattam*) by Dalit women in Tamil Nadu who place pots of water on their heads, explicitly linking this with the power of the goddess Mariamman to bring rain. This dance, Dietrich says, has become commercialised and is now a mere tourist attraction. Can such practices instead be revitalised—refreshed with their spiritual roots is the implication—to become part of a counter-culture?[17] She is explicitly critical of the oppressiveness of organised religion and of communalism but is insistent that "religions have given inner spaces to women and ecological spaces to larger communities." And therefore secularism has to go beyond its "narrow bourgeois" limits of seeing religion as only a "private affair."[18]

Dietrich is critical of what was "actually existing socialism in eastern Europe" for falling into a "growth oriented paradigm of industrialism," treating nature merely as a resource to be exploited.[19] She points out that in the 1970s there were debates on the Left about whether the ecological question could be solved within capitalism, suggesting a lacuna in theorising that delinked capitalism and industrialisation. It was the alliance of peace and environmental movements and the women's movement that addressed this conceptual shortcoming. For Dietrich, then, Marxism needs to be transformed from its heart outwards to accommodate the ecological question; and it needs to retune its modernist obsession with science and technology to recognise that these are not neutral forms of knowledge but violent and destructive of nature. This is an argument she draws from anti-modernity critics such as Shiv Visvanathan and Vandana

---

[16] Ibid. 1992: 14.
[17] Ibid.: 113.
[18] Ibid.
[19] Dietrich 2003: 4549.

Shiva, while being sceptical of the implication of their arguments that patriarchy is a newly minted product of the Enlightenment.[20]

In India, however, Dietrich sees the women's movement—to the extent that it consists of NGOs—as co-opted by the state into the "ideology of empowerment" and argues that this has made it difficult to think of alternatives. Her own socialist feminism is part of a strand in India, like that of Chhaya Datar and Maria Mies, which is influenced by a reading of Rosa Luxemburg—seeing capitalism as producing several internal colonies, of which women are the "last colony."[21] She does feel that Mies too attributes patriarchy's origins to modernity, and is critical of this aspect. But she draws on Mies to argue that a socialist-feminist vision must bring women, "the last colony," into alliances with other "internal colonies" like Dalits, Adivasis, unorganised-sector workers, and minorities. Ecological concerns are at the centre of her socialist feminism—"the deepening ecological crisis is the deepest contradiction in the 'total market' policies of global capitalism."[22]

The Secular Reason of State

In India, agrarian colonialism, or—as Neeladri Bhattacharya calls it—"the great agrarian conquest" was a "deep conquest." It developed a "new and enabling imaginary" whereby the rural universe was "revisualised, reordered, reworked." It refigured "terms used for describing social relations and the ties that bound communities together. It altered perceptions of time and space, of the legal and the permissible, the ideal and the normal."[23] It was the process that demystified land and the magical processes of nature, making them legible to the law and bureaucratic processes.

As Ashis Nandy points out, the modern state was assumed to be the main instrument of social change, which in the European

[20] Ibid.: 4551.
[21] Mies, et al. 1988.
[22] Dietrich 2003: 4549.

context meant helping to create and protect modern institutions associated with industrial capitalism, these being carried over into the understanding of the postcolonial nation-state. In addition, the modern state represented the principle of scientific rationality and was considered to be a means of secularising society.[24] After Indian independence secularism was intimately linked to a notion of "development" predicated on the large-scale appropriation of collective tribal resources and individual peasant lands—all supposedly in the greater interest of the "Indian citizen." The citizen to which the term refers is exclusively, in Partha Chatterjee's terms, the denizen of civil society.[25] We cannot re-imagine secularism today without coming to terms with the violent histories of subordination and repression that have produced the secular citizen. Consider the massive displacements by secular high-modernist states of populations across the globe—for example in the interests of irrigation, power, and defence projects—in the style that James Scott has termed *Seeing Like a State*.[26] In India, as has been extensively documented, this "development" has benefited specific sections of society and specific regions of the country.[27] The highly centralised, capital-intensive, and high-technology-based development model adopted by the Indian elites requires the homogeneous subject constructed by the discourse of citizenship.

[23] Bhattacharya 2018: 1.

[24] Nandy 2003.

[25] The reference here is to the distinction that Partha Chatterjee makes between civil society and political society in postcolonial democracies (Chatterjee 1997, 2001, 2008). "Civil society," according to Chatterjee, is constituted by the institutions of modern associational life, and is marked by *modernity*, while "political society" is a domain of mediating institutions between civil society and state and is the sphere of *democracy*. He sees a contradiction between "modernity" and "democracy"—what characterises non-Western modernity (that which marks postcolonial societies) is precisely the hiatus between the two. That is, between civil society, composed of a small section of "citizens," and political society, composed of the "population."

[26] Scott 1998.

[27] Menon and Nigam 2014.

It is from the point of view of "civil society"—the rights-bearing urban middle classes—that it seems necessary and progressive to dislocate communities for development projects. A striking illustration is the report of the Dhebar Commission on Scheduled Areas and Scheduled Tribes set up in 1960, on the basis of which successive governments in Kerala formulated policies on tribals. A. Damodaran argues that three strands of thinking underlie the report: that the tribes of India need to be weaned away from their traditional habitats towards alternative life-support systems, that they need to be trained in non-conventional vocations, and that they should be rapidly "acculturised" and "modernised."[28] This perspective on tribal ways of life continues unchanged into the twenty-first century. An article on the website of Niti Aayog, the government "policy think-tank" that replaced the Planning Commission in 2015, notes that "tribals being cut off from the civilized world . . . are unable to adapt to modernization," and therefore struggle to meet their minimum needs.[29] The logic makes sense only in a framework that assumes capitalism to be inevitable and desirable, for if they are not "modernised" surely their "minimum needs" are also low? That it is the savage depredations of capitalist transformation itself that have impoverished them is of course not under consideration—nor that what they need is not integration into the capitalist system but disconnection from it.

In a recent instance—in April 2020, during the Covid lockdown—of such an understanding of Adivasi lifeworlds, the Supreme Court reversed a government order in the state of Andhra Pradesh which had mandated that only Adivasi schoolteachers would be appointed in publicly funded schools in Adivasi homelands (protected under Schedule 5 of the Constitution). Rolling back special protections, the Court observed that they were put in place for tribes in the first instance because "their language and their primitive way of life makes them unfit to put up with the mainstream and to be governed by the

[28] Damodaran 2003.
[29] Muniraju and Sirisha: no date.

ordinary laws."[30] The implication of course is that the Adivasis have now fully entered the non-primitive mainstream and no longer require such protection.

It is the faithful application of such policies that has resulted in the marginalisation of these communities, who are not deemed fit to exist except as "insignificant cogs of a monolithic state."[31] The militant Adivasi rights movement in Kerala has grown out of resistance to this marginalisation, resulting in protests such as the supposedly illegal occupation of the Muthanga forest in 2003, which was met with police firing. This has been the largest Adivasi uprising in Kerala. From the point of view of the leader of the Adivasi Gothra Mahasabha (AGM), C. K. Janu, the occupation of the forest was an attempt to simply take back land stolen from them by the government and the land mafia: "We are raising the simplest of demands: right to live and die in the lands where we were born." During the forty days of their occupation, they attempted recreating an autonomous village life and began to take steps for the rejuvenation of the forest, which had been made barren by industrial forestry. Janu said in an interview when she was released from prison on bail: "Adivasi and environment are one and the same. These two cannot be separated. It is not that Adivasis use nature for their own benefits as the mainstream society imagines. Our people are not exploiting nature, we are being a part of it. And similarly, nature is there within each Adivasi too."[32]

Paradoxically, many communities are also dislocated from their traditional ways of life in order to mitigate the long-term ecological consequences of unbridled capitalist development elsewhere. For

[30] Cited in Kannabiran 2021: 238.

[31] Damodaran 2003.

[32] Janu 2003. The agitation has carried on in different forms, militant confrontations with the state as well as attempted political alliances with different parties, including the BJP. All of these have failed to achieve any of the AGM's objectives. Close to twenty years after the Muthanga occupation, the situation of the Adivasis of Kerala remains unchanged, and the struggle continues: Ameerudheen 2021.

instance, the creation of National Parks for the protection of forests and wildlife treats forest communities living there for centuries as responsible for the destruction of the forest cover, rather than blaming the depredations of wood contractors and the encroachments of urbanisation. The boundaries of these parks, administered by government, therefore treat forest dwellers as trespassers, dispossessing them of their lives and livelihoods.[33] Similarly, the continuous process of dispossessing the urban poor in order to build the modern city is impeccably couched in the secular language of rights and has increasingly, since the 1990s in India, been initiated by the courts. The spate of judgments by the "Green Bench" of the Supreme Court through the 1990s, ordering the closure of "polluting" industries, simply threw out of work with no rehabilitation thousands of workers, some of whom had been in secure employment for over three decades. In the face of mass protests by the workers over its orders, the Supreme Court justified its decision by asserting that "health is more important than livelihoods."[34] Clearly, the health of the workers was not an issue, nor the need to compensate them for working for years in hazardous and polluted conditions. "Health" here referred to health in civil society and to the health of civil society, regardless of the mere livelihoods and health of those that comprise "political society."

Capitalism versus Religious Sectarianism

This false dichotomy is reflected most famously in India by Nehru's claim that big dams are the temples of modern India, suggesting that the modern secular development brought by big dams will replace premodern religious ties and hatreds. Needless to say, what is suppressed or invisibilised is how massively big dams dispossess hundreds of thousands globally and pose irreversible threats to the environment—as they did in Nehru's India too. Then there is the equally famous

---

[33] Rangarajan and Saberwal 2003.
[34] Delhi Janwadi Adhikar Manch, February/March 1997.

"McDonald's Peace Theory" offered by Thomas Friedman, that no two countries which have McDonald's will ever fight a war, the assumption being that capitalist integration will end sectarian conflicts.[35] This claim too has fallen to the dust.

Caught up as we are globally when facing majoritarian violence, both material and ideological, we turn to secularism as the opposite and fail to notice the trick that secularism performs as we cling to it: the secular/communal/majoritarian framework obscures the violence of capitalist transformation that is carrying on undisturbed. Secularism performs a flamboyant misdirection, placing capitalism alongside values such as science, modernity, and progress, while relegating "identity politics" and ecological concerns to non-science, superstition, and religious sectarianism. The project of secular modernity, as is well established, emerged alongside capitalist transformation in the West, and colonialism carried this project to the global South.

But the argument here is not that capitalism is incompatible with religion, or that capitalist development will end religious sectarianism. Even today, a large part of philanthropic expense by wealthy businessmen all over the world goes towards religious establishments and ceremonies. Indeed, both Weber and Marx noted the connection between Christianity and capitalism. Weber argued that the values of individualism and the ethic of hard work and thrift, fostered by Calvinist Protestantism, enabled early capital accumulation and the growth of capitalism.[36] Marx too has been read as indicating the affinity between capitalism and Christianity, especially in assertions such as that the bourgeois state is the full dialectical realisation of the "Christian state."[37] With reference to Islam, Maxime Rodinson has argued that nothing in Islamic belief militates against capitalism,[38] and for later scholars the question then becomes why "the largely commercial, premodern or medieval form of capitalism" in West Asia

[35] Friedman 1999.
[36] Weber 1905/1930.
[37] Boer 2018; Forte 2008.
[38] Rodinson 1966/2007.

did not evolve into a modern capitalist economy.[39] When it comes to Hinduism, too, there are deep historical connections between merchant communities in India and various religious sects, temples, and pilgrimage centres. However, the heterogeneity of the label that has been discussed at length in this book requires us to distinguish between the modern Brahminised "Hinduism" that came to be formulated in the nineteenth century, and the multiple beliefs and practices both within and outside Brahminism that continue to deify nature.

So, two issues need to be highlighted. First, the argument here is that the manner in which modernity and secularism desacralise nature and evacuate it of meaning renders it inert and enables its characterisation as merely a resource for capitalist production. Thus, modernised and organised religions that do not sacralise nature are entirely compatible with capitalism. However, spiritualities that continue to see nature as densely populated with meaning and sacrality are confronted as regressive and backward-looking by secular, capitalist world-views. And secular political parties across the board are unsympathetic to any obstacles in the way of "development."

Capitalist transformation and neoliberal restructuring has been carried on in India by successive secular governments. The first major structural adjustments were in fact carried out by a Congress government in the 1990s. Secular communist (CPI[M]) governments in Bengal and Kerala have, in alliance with large corporations, followed exactly the same processes of forcible land acquisition and ecologically destructive projects that ruin livelihoods. Singur and Nandigram in Bengal and Vizhinjam in Kerala are landmarks in this process. Massive popular protests have mostly been countered by state repression.[40]

The second issue has to do with Hindutva, where we find that it adopts a "secular" stance towards non-Brahminical spiritualities, while Brahminically inflected sacrality attributed to nature is respected and promoted. The former aspect is evident in the dispossession of indig-

---

[39] Banaji 2020.
[40] Menon and Nigam 2014; Devika 2022.

enous and tribal people from their lands, while the latter is illustrated by the Sethusamudram Project (discussed at length below). And, as we saw in Chapter 2, there are explicitly articulated arguments for the freeing of Hindu temples from government control and permitting the market to generate sufficient profits enabling "the freedom for creative use of funds that could benefit Hindu society at large."[41] Therefore, Hindutva politics is perfectly compatible with capitalism too, although a key difference between the Congress-led UPA and the BJP-led NDA is that the UPA was constrained to some extent by pressure from social movements, while the NDA has been unfettered by democratic pressures of any kind. This compatibility is not surprising because the BJP is equally enamoured with what Ashis Nandy terms the "romance of the state."[42] The enemies of this national-security-development state project are "anti-national" too, just as much as the Muslim is perpetually labelled as being. Hence the mythology of the "Urban Maoist-Jihadi network"—a deranged script, concocted in the RSS headquarters,[43] which blends the twin enemies of Hindu supremacism ("jihadi") and predatory capital ("urban Maoist") to effectively silence opponents of these projects. Within the multitude of politically motivated arrests in the last few years are those of journalists, academics, and artists accused of being urban Maoists.

The capitalist policies of the Hindu Rashtra also maintain the anti-Muslim thrust of Hindutva ideology. For instance, the RSS and the BJP have quite smoothly marginalised Muslim small businesses,[44] as well as Muslim fisherpeople,[45] partly formally, and partly through Hindutva organisations that call for and enforce a social boycott of Muslim businesses. The BJP's government in India since 2014 has accelerated the processes of dispossessing Indigenous people from their lands, restructuring the economy along a neoliberal worldview, and

---

[41] Shastry and Ananthkumar 2022.
[42] Nandy 2003.
[43] Organiser Web Desk 2020.
[44] Express News Service 2022.
[45] Kshatriya 2022.

selling the country's public assets to corporates. In Kashmir, within seventy-five days of the abrogation of Article 370, 125 projects were cleared in just three meetings; they involved diverting forest land for "development" projects, the details of which were not divulged to journalists.[46]

Also, within a week of the Covid-linked lockdown being declared, the government issued a Gazette Notification changing the domicile rules for Jammu & Kashmir to redefine as resident anybody who had lived for fifteen years in the former state, or studied there for seven years—permitting them to apply for jobs and own immovable property.[47] This essentially meant opening up Kashmir for settlement by non-Muslim non-Kashmiris—an old RSS dream. The decision fulfils the agenda of both Hindu supremacism and predatory capitalism because land can now be bought by outsiders for any purpose, including commercial. In November 2022 the Union Ministry of Environment, Forest and Climate Change approved Stage 1 clearance for the diversion of 130.75 sq. km of forest in Great Nicobar Island, which is nearly a quarter of all the forest land diverted in the past three years across the country. The trees to be felled are primary evergreen tropical forests. Indigenous tribes that inhabit these forests will be fatally displaced, and hundreds of rare species of fauna and coral cover are to be destroyed.[48]

Here are a few more examples of the compatibility of Hindu Rashtra with predatory capitalism.

In 2014 the waters of the Narmada Dam were directed to Coca-Cola's new bottling plant, though for decades farmers protesting against dispossession had been castigated for selfishly denying water for drinking and irrigation to others.[49] Since 2014 a one-time capacity expansion of 25 percent given to coal mines in 2012 has been extended twice without taking into account the impact on the

---

[46] SabrangIndia 2019.
[47] Scroll Staff 2020.
[48] Sekhsaria 2022.
[49] Menon 2014.

environment, and now a new draft policy plans to make such expansions the norm.[50] In the state of Odisha mining companies are supreme, with fraudulent permissions from village committees being used to legitimise the open loot of Adivasi resources and the destruction of their forests for mining.[51]

In the field of education the National Education Policy of 2020 formalises the ongoing process of making public universities self-financing and encouraging private capital in education, while simultaneously establishing government control over research and content of education in a manner compatible with the ideal of a Hindu Rashtra.[52] The public sector in infrastructure is simultaneously being rapidly dismantled.[53]

G. Sampath recognises "the emerging contours of a distinctive political project" in some of the features of current policies in India:

> The Jan-Dhan Yojana set out to make every Indian accessible to global finance. The Aadhaar card set out to make every Indian identifiable and enumerable as data—the currency of global tech. The high mobile penetration has connected every Indian to the global digital network. An element that was missing was consumer behaviour, which the recent demonetisation sought to address, by force-feeding "cashless" to a cash-dependent population.[54]

---

[50] Datta 2019.

[51] Choudhury 2016; Kukreti 2022.

[52] Menon 2020.

[53] Hemalata 2017.

[54] Sampath 2017. The Jan-Dhan Yojana set up in 2014 is a "financial inclusion" scheme under which 15 million bank accounts were opened with no minimum balance to provide "universal and clear access to banking facilities." The Aadhar Card or UID is a Unique Identification biometric system which is de facto necessary to access government benefits. In 2016 the government announced demonetisation of all banknotes of Rs 500 and Rs 1000, supposedly to eliminate "black money," but achieved one more goal for corporations. We now know that over thirty-five Indian and international organisations—largely IT and payment service providers—partnered with the Ministry of Finance and USAID, profiting from digital payments and associated data generated on users: Haering 2017.

Thus, while the neoliberal agenda is not necessarily linked to the Hindu Rashtra, instances of when they are indeed working in tandem show that the impact of the combination is even more devastating.

Coronacapitalism in India

And now a quick look at capitalism in India as inflected through the pandemic-linked lockdown under a Hindu supremacist regime that showed a "secular" lack of compassion towards all workers, regardless of religious affiliation. The "low end" of coronacapitalism is forced labour and the "high end" is data capitalism.

The gut-wrenching picture of migrant workers who managed to reach their home states being sprayed with disinfectant provoked such widespread outrage in India and negative publicity in the foreign media that the health ministry issued a hasty statement saying it should not be done.[55] The brutality and callousness towards workers and the poor emanated from the top of this particular regime, as is routine in authoritarian regimes. The disparity between the treatment offered to civil society and political society became clear during the lockdown: thousands of workers walked long distances home because all transport facilities had been suspended to prevent them leaving the states in which they were stranded; at the same time, many state governments organised buses to bring students studying elsewhere back to their home states; and special flights and hospital beds were prepared by the central and state governments to bring home Indians stranded abroad.

When news emerged of a brewing economic crisis for capital because of labour shortages, the Ministry of Home Affairs issued an order on 19 April 2020—an extraordinary document described as a Standard Operating System for the movement of stranded labour which established:

(i) an outright prohibition on migrant labour, even those tested and found "asymptomatic," from moving out of the state in which they were

[55] PTI 2020b.

currently trapped, and on going back to their home states; and (ii) the recruitment of "asymptomatic" workers in "industrial, manufacturing, construction, farming and MNREGA works" *only in the state in which they are currently located* (stranded), for which they must be "registered with the local authority concerned . . ."[56]

This amounts, quite straightforwardly, to establishing forced labour. After testing for Covid-19, asymptomatic workers would be forced to remain within the states they were located, or be transported to where their labour was needed.

There was an uproar, the order was not implemented, and eventually we heard no more about it. However, attempts by industry in collaboration with the government to force labour to stay where it was needed continued, and in some cases were thwarted by public pressure.[57] However, the opposite also happened—based on complaints by employers of migrant labour, those who tried to help them reach home faced punishment from the government. Government officials who organised buses for labour to go home were suspended.[58] Political activists were arrested for providing train tickets to workers.[59]

In retrospect it appears that the declaration of a harsh and punitive lockdown with only four hours' notice was not inefficiency, it may have been deliberately intended to stop labour from leaving cities.

Data Capitalism and the Aarogya Setu App

At the "high end" of the spectrum of coronacapitalism there was huge pressure from the government to download Aarogya Setu, a contact-tracing mobile application launched by the union health ministry, which would supposedly help users identify if they were at risk of a Covid-19 infection. The ministry asked social media platforms to promote installation of the app among their users, giving these platforms a target of minimum downloads amounting to millions.[60] Some

[56] GoI Order 2020.
[57] Philip 2020.
[58] India News 2020.
[59] Pereira 2020.
[60] Variyar 2020.

departments of government made the app mandatory for employees, as did some food-delivery companies for their delivery partners.[61] Microsoft's Bill Gates wrote a letter to the Indian prime minister congratulating him for Aarogya Setu.[62] The reason for Gates' delight in an app that collects data from potentially the entire mobile phone-owning population of India does not require much speculation. The Gates Foundation has made at least one attempt, in the USA, to collect massive amounts of unspecified data via school test scores;[63] this project was thwarted by parents and school administrations who challenged it over privacy and security issues.[64]

The Aarogya Setu app has been shown to be deeply problematic. A thorough report by the Internet Freedom Foundation (IFF) says the app is "a privacy minefield and it does not adhere to principles of minimisation, strict purpose limitation, transparency and accountability."[65]

State surveillance is not exclusively a capitalist project, but surveillance is not the only issue here. What is relevant is the emergence of *data capitalism* globally since the mid-1990s as a well-entrenched phenomenon. In data capitalism, data is the source of monetisation. It's a closed system in which for-profit entities have successfully managed to extract, transform, and capitalise on the data—our data. The relentless push by the Indian government for downloading the app, the data generated on which can be used, shared, and stored in ways about which we know nothing, and over which we have no control, is high-end coronacapitalism.

The Sethusamudram Ship Canal Project (SSCP)

Some interesting and revealing aspects of Hindutva politics vis-à- vis capitalism and the environment emerge from the Sethusamudram

[61] PTI 2020b.
[62] HT Correspondent 2020.
[63] Rugh 2013.
[64] Singer 2014.
[65] IFF 2020.

Project. The BJP government dismisses indigenous practices of worship of natural formations, forests, and other kinds of sacrality that indigenous people ascribe to their lands, and thereby assists their takeover by corporates. Hindutva's opposition to non-Brahminical practices of worship, its drive to establish Brahminism as Hinduism in every domain, is the corollary of what Anustup Basu has termed "Hindu political monotheism"—the modern project of inducting "the privileged and the pariah into a universal, congregational plane of Hindu identity."[66] This project requires that what refuses to be inducted, and will not be assimilated, must be annihilated.

At the same time, when it comes to Brahminical deities Hindutva politics stands firmly in the way of capitalist projects. One example of this is the SSCP, which aims to reduce the shipping distance from the southern tip of the east coast of India to the northern parts of the coast by constructing a route through the Gulf of Mannar to the Bay of Bengal. Ships will then be able to go northwards directly through the narrow and shallow Palk Strait between the east coast of India and the west coast of Sri Lanka, rather than having to swing around Sri Lanka, as at present. There has been a long history of hesitation about the project—it was conceived in the nineteenth century by a colonial official—and eventually it was the Congress-led UPA government that inaugurated the project in 2005, despite the report of the Sethu Samudram Project Committee (1955) which had recommended an overland passage. It is claimed that this project will save time and money for shipping companies and is expected to radically increase the volume of traffic in the region.

In order to build the canal, an underwater bridge connecting India and Sri Lanka along the Palk Strait would have to be destroyed. Depending on your point of view, this bridge is either a natural millennia-old formation of limestone shoals which linked Sri Lanka to the Asian continent in the last Ice Age, or was built by Hanuman's army to cross over to Sri Lanka to rescue Sita—in which case you will see it as Ram

[66] Basu 2020: 2.

Sethu/Setu, known locally in Tamil as Ramar Sethu. The reef is also called Adam's Bridge, a nomenclature to which we will return later.

This project has got caught up in a debate that counterposes Hindutva opposition to destroying the bridge—on the grounds that the limestone formation was built by the BJP's preferred Hindu deity, Rama of the Ramayana—to modernist and secular arguments that it is a natural formation, that "myths" cannot stand in the way of development, and therefore it may be legitimately destroyed. A third position, the secular environmentalist one, although vocal and informed, has rarely emerged in the public domain because the media has not considered it worthy of notice.

What is intriguing is that the limestone formation is also known as Adam's Bridge, which suggests a Christian sacred geography around the reef. Arup K. Chatterjee traces nineteenth-century colonial history writing which indicated a Portuguese belief—that after Adam's expulsion from Paradise he set foot on southern Sri Lanka's Adam's Peak. So the first colonial narratives are about supposed native beliefs that Ceylon was the Paradise from which Adam was expelled, or the place where he first set foot after his Fall. By the late nineteenth century colonial historians started referring to the Ramayana and local beliefs that the reef was the bridge built by Rama to cross to Lanka.[67] So, how strongly were these local beliefs held, if the sources we have are colonial narratives? Why is Ramar Sethu given greater credence than Adam's Bridge, and by whom?

Three petitions filed in the Madras High Court by the Hindu Munnani were transferred to the Supreme Court in 2007. The Court stayed dredging operations by its interim order in August 2007. The petitions argued against the Sethusamudram Project because the planned route would damage the Ram Sethu; they demanded that an alternative route be adopted. There was also a demand to declare Ram Sethu a national archaeological monument.[68] In response, the government filed

[67] Chatterjee 2022: 99.
[68] Singh 2007.

an affidavit from the Archaeological Survey of India (ASI) stating that the so-called Ram Sethu was in fact a natural formation. This affidavit argued that the ASI is a "science and technology department," and that while "due deference may be given to the feelings of the petitioners" the issue had to be approached in "a scientific manner."[69] Therefore, mythological texts could not form the basis for government policy. "The Valmiki Ramayana, the Ramcharitmanas by Tulsidas and other mythological texts, which admittedly form an ancient part of Indian literature, cannot be said to be historical records to incontrovertibly prove the existence of the characters or the occurrence of the events depicted therein."[70]

Because of the uproar created by Hindutva formations, including the BJP opposition in parliament, two officials of the ASI were suspended and the controversial passage withdrawn from the affidavit. The government went into overdrive to limit the damage. The law minister, H. R. Bhardwaj, said "Ram is an integral part of our history and culture. *Ram ki vajah se saari duniya* exist *karti hai.* [The entire world exists because of Ram.] It is an article of faith and cannot be made a matter of litigation."[71]

Natural or Man-made? Secularism versus Hindutva

The entry of secularists in this debate was inevitable, given the framing of the question in terms of the religious faith of Hindus. A well-known environmentalist, Praful Bidwai, titled one of his first writings on the issue with crystal clarity: "Spineless secular government retreats when fundamentalists invoke mythology." Defending the withdrawn statement in the affidavit, Bidwai said it was crucial to refute the contention that the *Ramcharitmanas* provides clinching evidence that the Ram Sethu is man-made. Or else it means "giving in to the idea that faith must always trump history, archaeology, even geology—

[69] Sinha 2007.
[70] TNN 2007.
[71] Nagi 2007.

which explains the existence of natural formations like Adam's Bridge—and accepting that the project must be scrapped because of myths and scriptures, not fact."[72]

Thus, the initial secular argument justifying the destruction of the limestone formation was that the bridge is not "man-made" but natural. As Bidwai noted approvingly, the ASI affidavit quotes studies by the Space Applications Centre, Ahmedabad, which "conclusively show that the Sethu formation is purely natural." Claims by Hindutva politicians and activists that the imagery collected by the US National Aeronautics and Space Administration (NASA) proves that the structure is "man-made" were refuted by the ASI, backed by a statement from NASA with the argument that remote visual images are not sufficient to establish the origin of the structure. A study conducted by the Geological Survey of India around Adam's Bridge was cited by the "secular" side, which, based on drilling holes into submerged rocks, found no evidence of man-made structures. It revealed, rather, that the reef consists of three cycles of sedimentation of clay, limestone, and sandstone—a natural phenomenon that occurred thousands of years before humans settled in peninsular India.[73]

The discourse of science was thus effectively mobilised by the "secular" camp to establish the true "history" of the formation as natural and not made by "men"; this sought to contradict the "myth" that a real living Rama, and real living beings, made it with their own hands. The conflict here is quite straightforward: Scientific History (in the service of capitalism) versus Religious Myth.

The contestation continued with the tabling in parliament in December 2008 of a government publication. *Images India*, a book published by the National Remote Sensing Agency (NRSA), an outfit under the Department of Space, says satellite images have revealed an "ancient bridge between India and Sri Lanka in Palk Strait . . . Its structure suggests that it may be man-made . . . This has an echo in the ancient

---

[72] Bidwai 2007.
[73] Ibid.

Indian mythological epic, the Ramayana . . . Studies are still on but the bridge is seen as an example of ancient history linked to the Indian mythology."[74] The revelations in the book, with a foreword by the Indian Space Research Organisation's chairman G. Madhavan Nair, contradicted the government stand. The BJP was jubilant: "Finally, science has prevailed upon the politics of Congress. Now they have to accept the scientific evidence and . . . must accept not only Lord Ram but also Ram Sethu," a party spokesman, Prakash Javadekar, told a news agency.[75] On the website of the Hindu Janajagruti Samiti, three kinds of arguments are given for why the Ram Sethu should not be damaged:

"spiritual"—the divine origin of the bridge;

"physical"—(a) the reef acted as a barrier to the tsunami [of 2004 around Sri Lanka] and (b) according to naval officers, the canal will not be deep enough for large vessels;

"social"—(a) trampling on Hindu sentiments and (b) it is the oldest man-made structure in the world, older than the Pyramids of Egypt and the Great Wall of China.[76]

In this narrative, the divine origin of the bridge is not seen as contradicting the physical and social aspects, which emphasise ecological factors and the "man-made" character of the reef.

What was at stake for the secularists in insisting that the project be permitted to continue? Their claim is that the canal will increase shipping traffic through the Palk Strait and save ships time and money moving from the west coast of India to the east. Why should a commitment to secularism entail a commitment to this goal? We must seek an answer to this question in the link between science, the modern nation-state, and its agenda of development as noted by Ashis Nandy, Shiv Visvanathan, and other scholars over three decades ago.

Nandy traced the idea of science as a reason of state to a speech made by John F. Kennedy in 1962 which declared one of America's

[74] IANS 2007.
[75] Ibid.
[76] Hindu Janajagruti Samiti, no date.

national goals to be the scientific feat of putting a man on the moon. A state, for the first time, thus sought "to outrival another state not in the political or military arena, nor in sports, but in science redefined as dramatic technology."[77] The Indian state, too, in the early years after Independence, and the political elites it represented, chose to see science as a responsibility of the state and ensured that "the scientific estate had a direct privileged access to the state."[78] Modern science has since then established a secure relationship, says Nandy, with the "philosophy and practice of development in India" and development is the goal of the secular state.[79] According to Shiv Visvanathan, "It is not accidental that when the first protests against the Narmada dam took place, the protesters were arrested under the Defence of India rules. The dam became a reason of state."[80]

As I have been arguing here, "secularism" in India went much further than the state–religious community relationship. It has been the term which stands in for the entire modernising project of the Indian elites. As Gyan Prakash points out, this project was based on Science— planning having been seen by Nehru as the *scientific* instrument of social change, in which nature was a resource to be utilised.[81]

These unexamined linkages underlying the triad of Science-Development-Secularism are responsible for the initial implication, even by a writer as sensitive to ecological issues as Bidwai, that if a structure is *merely* natural and built up over millennia, it bolsters the "secular" claim that it can legitimately be destroyed.[82] It is clear that once the political grid of "secularism" descends on a contested field, certain fixed equations come into play—Secularism implies Science and Development; Myth and Faith can only be Communalism.

[77] Nandy 1988: 3.
[78] Ibid.: 4–5.
[79] Ibid.: 9.
[80] Visvanathan 1997: 11.
[81] Prakash 1999: 234.
[82] Very soon after, his signature was on a statement by civil society organisations protesting the project on ecological grounds, which I discuss below.

But what is striking in this case is that while the Indian state, invoking secularism, continually counterposed "religious belief" to "scientific facts," the Hindu Right, as we have seen, far from invoking faith and belief, was in fact insistent that the structure is "man-made" and therefore amenable to historical proof, precisely *not mythical*; that it is *not* natural. Thus, both secularists and Hindutva ideologues claimed science would determine whose version of history was true.

Natural or Man-made?
Environment versus Development

While science has been invoked by both sides—the competing interpretations of the data produced by NASA, for example—another voice from within the field of science was initially marginalised and ignored. For example, in a national daily—on the same day as a series of stories were published titled "Ramayana no basis for Ram Sethu: ASI," "Faith versus necessity," "Lord Ram is back on BJP agenda," and "Nervous government chants Ram Naam"—there was also one titled "Recipe for Disaster: Scientists."[83] This last story quoted tsunami experts warning that the destruction of the millennia-old limestone shoals would be disastrous for the ecology of the coast. Adam's Bridge is held to have deflected the fury of the tsunami in 2004, forcing it back into the open ocean. This story stands independently and none of the other stories, each about the interrelation of religion and politics, refers to it. This perspective did not come up before the Supreme Court till much later.

Thus, significant alternative voices from within the field of science now tell us that the Sethusamudram Project will be an unmitigated ecological disaster. More importantly, this alternative reading of the history of the reef as a natural formation gives the reef *greater* value, not less.

An instance of a position like this was a website which is no longer accessible.[84] It was at *sethusamudram.info* and had as its tag "No

[83] *Hindustan Times* 2007.
[84] This site was last accessed in 2014.

Ram—no Ram Sethu—let's save our environment." The site said it was "dedicated to bring out an unbiased version of information related to Sethusamudram shipping canal project (SSCP). It is not about Religious Sentiments or Economic projections. It is the Ground Reality, Environmental aspects and Livelihood of thousands of Fishermen and the Benefit of the People of Tamil Nadu that should drive the Project." The website took a clear stand on myth, as distinct from history, deplored the caving in of politicians to the communal BJP, offered Tamil versions of the Ramayana in which Ravana is the hero, and was firmly opposed to the SSCP. Apart from privileging local interests (Tamil Nadu) over the national, the site highlighted another neglected aspect: the concerns of Sri Lanka. It posted a piece by Hemantha Withanage who, in addition to general ecological questions, expressed concern over the fact that 35 percent to 70 percent of the fish stock for the Sri Lankan side comes from these reefs.[85] Thus this site represented a coalition of voices that invoked science to put environment-with-people first—as opposed to bourgeois environmentalism, in which something called "environment" refers only to "nature" devoid of people. It refused national borders and rejected the nexus of statecraft, the nation-state, and development.

Arising from this position, a statement by civil society groups, people's movements, human rights organisations, and concerned individuals put out a statement in September 2007 which said:

> The Sethusamudram Project was introduced by the BJP while they were in power at the centre without considering the ecological and human problems. The Sethusamudram Project will endanger a rich biosphere reserve with 400 endangered species, including sea turtles, dolphins, dugongs and whales. The project will destroy the livelihood of 15 lakh people who depend on fishing and allied areas in the waters where the canal will be dug. Several fisher people's organisations and human rights groups had protested against the project for a long time without getting any recognition from the mainstream political parties.[86]

[85] Separately available at Withanage 2008.
[86] Statement 2007.

In an open letter to the president, prime minister, and Sonia Gandhi, retired Major-General S. G. Vombatkere, formerly with the Corps of Engineers of the Indian Army and an activist on environmental issues, wrote:

> It is piquant that those who now oppose the Sethusamudram Project on religious grounds have gained media attention and those who have from the outset been opposing it on grounds of human displacement, ecological reasons and even on economic viability grounds have been side-lined and forgotten. The displacement of thousands of fisherfolk and their loss of livelihood and the undoubted environmental damage that will occur due to dredging the channel to create a canal do not need elaboration, except to say that if these costs are taken into consideration, the project may actually prove economically unviable.

He pointed out that no economic feasibility report was submitted to the public domain and outlined a number of factors because of which the project is unlikely to be economically viable.[87] Others too have argued that claims about the economic benefits of the SSCP are exaggerated.[88]

Religious Belief and Science on Trial

Despite the strong views expressed against the project in Sri Lanka and India on the grounds outlined, over the decades, and with greater urgency over the past few years, all that has been permitted to be visible in the public discourse is the debate over belief in the existence of Lord Rama, in which science was mobilised on both sides.

As far as the courts were concerned, both in the Madras High Court and in the Supreme Court, the only question being considered was religious belief. In April 2008 the question being pondered in the Supreme Court was about whether the Ram Sethu is actually a place of worship, as claimed by the petitioners—"Who does puja in the middle

[87] Vombatkere 2007.
[88] John 2007.

of the sea?," the Bench at that point remarked sceptically.[89] In May 2008 a report of proceedings in the Supreme Court paraphrased the submission of the lawyer Soli J. Sorabjee, appearing for the Hindu Munnani, as follows:

> The issue before the Court is not whether this belief [in Rama] can be historically and scientifically established. The Court cannot sit in judgment over that belief. The Court's role is to determine whether the aforesaid belief is genuinely or conscientiously held over a period of time by Hindus and if that be so it falls within the ambit of the freedom of religion guaranteed by Article 25. The right to worship and make offerings and perform rites at Ram Sethu is in pursuance of the integral belief of the adherents of Hindu religion; therefore, any State action which results in impairment or even partial destruction of Ram Sethu and leads to extinction or diminution of the right to worship at Ram Sethu as at present is per se violative of the guarantee of freedom of religion . . .[90]

In other words, the debate in the Supreme Court was still being framed in terms of religious faith and whether faith can be scientifically established. After these submissions the Court, before adjourning the hearing of the Sethusamudram case to July 2008, asked the Centre to consider an alternative alignment for the proposed canal that would not damage the Ram Sethu, and to consider whether an archaeological study could be conducted to declare the Ram Sethu a "national monument"—not, it may be noted, a protected ecologically diverse area like a forest. In other words, religious belief was all that the Court asked the government to take into account while implementing development policies, and to alter the proposed project accordingly. It also seems very likely, given the history of court decisions over the 1990s to the early 2000s, that had the appeal against the project been made on environmental grounds, it would have been denied. The trend has been for the Supreme Court to take distinctly different stands on two kinds of Public Interest Litigations, with Environment trumping

[89] Mahapatra 2008.
[90] Venkatesan 2008.

People, but Development trumping Environment.[91] Meanwhile the Sethusamudram matter has remained pending with the Supreme Court as of 2020, and the project has looked poised to be wound up in the face of petitions by VHP-led groups and individuals.[92]

Thus, in the controversial SSCP we see science and secularism performing different roles in three completely different narratives. In the *secular developmentalist* one, science comes to the aid of history by establishing the reef as "natural," thus debunking myth and enabling the endorsement of "development" over "religious belief." In the second, the *Hindutva* narrative, science is claimed to "prove" that the structure is "man-made," not a natural formation, and this fact is taken to strengthen the claim of religious belief with the added legitimacy of history—the claim in this narrative being that Lord Rama is a historical figure. In the third, the *environmentalist* narrative, science is mobilised to use the "natural" status of the reef to reject both the others—endorsing ecology and sustainable livelihoods over development (with regard to the first) and denying religious belief/myth (with regard to the second).

It would be a mistake to read these contradictory narratives as the misuse of science by some parties as opposed to its correct utilisation by others. Rather, what we see here is science's ability to establish something as "nature," counterposing it to "created by humans" in order to produce specific political effects. In one kind of scientific discourse the demarcation of something as "nature" opens it up to human intervention as passive, inert material whose sole purpose is the furthering of human good. In another kind of scientific discourse the marking of something as "natural" protects it from human intervention in the long-term interests of human survival. However, if viewed solely through the grid of secularism, this issue looks like a victory for Hindutva *alone*. It is of course a victory for Hindutva *too*, and for its project of recognising only Brahminism as Hinduism, which is worthy of respect, even as the BJP government shows little compunction when it comes to

[91] Menon 2019.
[92] Bhaskar 2021.

the destruction of sacred landscapes and the forests of tribal people in the interests of extractive capitalism.

Arup K. Chatterjee suggests that the Ram Sethu should be seen as an "aquapelago," a term coined by Philip Hayward to mean "an assemblage of the marine and land spaces of a group of islands and their adjacent waters" essential to a social group's "habitation of land and their senses of identity and belonging."[93] While Hayward's own argument begins from archipelagic nation-states like Indonesia and Japan, it shifts to the idea of an aquapelago as indicating a "land-oceanic continuum," which effectively displaces the idea of nation-states. Thus, if the Ram Sethu is to be conceived of as an aquapelago—a productive theoretical move with which I am in agreement—then two factors need to be taken into account. If it is an aquapelago, the reef becomes something that is fluid between two nation-states (India and Sri Lanka), in one of which a particular community worships Rama while the other does not have such a tradition. In fact, as we know, Ravana, the ruler defeated by Rama in the Ramayana, was the king of Lanka. Second, by taking seriously "senses of identity and belonging" what is clear is that local relationships to both the deity and the waters are quite different from what Hindu nationalist politics projects—prominent Dravidian voices either simply disparaged Rama as an Aryan who attacked a just Dravidian king, or chose to reject the project on environmentalist grounds.[94] Local fishing communities, both Christian and Hindu, worship another set of deities altogether—for example, the Sufi saint Shahul Hameed whom the fishing community calls "Nagore Andavar"; the goddess Ellaiamman; Velankanni Matha (a Tamil form of the Virgin Mary, probably pre-dating Christianity); and Murugan (also known as Subramanian and in Sri Lanka as Katargamar).[95] Rama does not figure in the sacred geography of the aquapelago for local communities who live there and draw their identity from it. Rama has a role

[93] Chatterjee 2022; Hayward 2012: 5.

[94] Chatterjee 2022: 109–10. The salience of counternarratives to hegemonic dominant narratives was discussed in chap. 3 above.

[95] Selvam 2022.

only in the non-local Hindu nationalist imaginary, which becomes evident from the fact that petitions in court citing religious belief are filed by national-level Hindutva organisations, not local communities. This, as discussed, reinforces my argument about the longstanding and still unsuccessful project to claim India as Hindu and to establish Brahminism as "Hinduism," as well as the continuing resistance to this project.[96]

Land Rights for Women as a Capitalist Agenda

Bringing women into the ambit of individual property rights has long been one of the key issues in feminist practice and scholarship. Women being denied rights to land has been seen in terms of the constitutional, secular right to equality wielded against the traditional patriarchies of religious and tribal communities. But what happens to the feminist understanding of land rights for women in the face of large-scale land acquisitions for corporate globalisation? The only real challenge to capitalist ambitions is posed by collective ownership of land and strong assertions of the commons. What does this recognition mean for feminist campaigns in favour of individual land rights for women?[97] At this moment in time, several kinds of political movements and several strands of scholarship have, since the end of the twentieth century, been coming together to alert us to a need for a shift in feminist perspective on land rights for women.

[96] In an interesting development in 2022, a BJP minister stated in the Rajya Sabha that "we have certain limitations in discovering Ram Setu because the history dates back to more than 18,000 years and the bridge was about 56 kilometres long." This was in response to a question by another BJP minister as to whether any efforts were being made for scientific assessment of India's Vedic past, referring to the Ram Setu in particular (Ghosh 2022). It is possible that the economic benefits to corporate capital from dredging the canal may overtake "Hindu beliefs" now that the BJP is firmly entrenched.

[97] I am setting aside for the moment as undisputed from a feminist perspective the rights of women to non-landed property in natal and matrimonial families and to the matrimonial home.

Land Struggles in India

Let's begin with what we learn from struggles against accelerated and large-scale land acquisitions by the state for use by private corporations. Activists in these movements and scholars engaged in understanding land relations are increasingly coming to see that the Indian state is now very amenable to joint *patta*s (title deeds), which has been the main demand of the women's movements for decades—that is, joint title deeds for husband and wife to family land. However, as Smita Gupta argues, while joint *patta*s are important, sole preoccupation with them is a problem thrust upon us by international agencies with a neoliberal agenda. The women's movement must, says Gupta, focus far more on dispossession, land-use change, lack of access to commons, and the depletion and degradation of the commons. Small individual plots in a context of rising and widespread agrarian distress will, in fact, increase women's drudgery. Gupta believes that collective farming with state support is the way forward.[98] Individual land rights, whether for men only or also for women, restrict farmers to family plots by giving them formal title deeds, even joint *patta*s, while the state takes control of common and public lands. Enclosures, evictions, and land-use policies are all state strategies for taking over common and public lands, and of course title deeds are no magic potion against land acquisition. Rather, individual title deeds facilitate land acquisitions by the state. Anthony D'Costa and Achin Chakraborty argue that land acquisition and dispossession dilute or deny both individual and communal property rights since the state mediates coercively in the process of transferring land cheaply to capitalists. The losers are marginal and small farmers, poor tenants, and agricultural workers who lose livelihood options along with land.[99] Furthermore, it has long been understood in the context of land reforms that "joint *patta*"

[98] Gupta 2018.

[99] The volume edited by D'Costa and Chakraborty is an excellent collection of theoretical essays and case studies on the land question, and the state's role in capitalist transition in India: D'Costa and Chakraborty 2017.

in effect sidelines the question of land redistribution and, in that sense, is not a radical agenda. As Mercia Andrews, a land-rights activist from South Africa, puts it, no effective land struggle is possible without breaking up the nuclear family.[100]

Roma, an activist with the All India Union of Forest Working People, is opposed to the *patta* as such, which she sees as looking at land use and ownership exclusively through the prism of the family. In her experience, only collective ownership can fracture patriarchy, and her organisation works with movements that collectively cultivate land. This would be a movement of the landless, not of the middle and upper peasantry. There is thus, in this understanding, a contradiction between the interests of upper-caste peasants who own land and the interests of the landless, largely Dalits, who use common lands. In her understanding, then, an alliance of marginal farmers and landless needs to be built, and this would have to address the caste divide as well.[101]

Common lands that embody historical layers of customary-use rights are the biggest challenge to market relations, and prime among such lands are forests. It is in this context that land-occupation movements by castes and tribes traditionally excluded from agriculture must be viewed and understood—the occupation of the Muthanga Forest lands in Kerala by Adivasis, mentioned earlier, evacuated by the police in 2003. C. K. Janu, chairperson of the Adivasi Gothra Mahasabha which spearheaded this struggle, said in an interview, "Adivasis are the real owners of land . . . [Our main slogan is] the right to live in the land where we are born till death."[102]

This "occupation" of lands by the poor is in fact a *reoccupation* of common lands which were turned into state-owned land overnight through colonial legislations such as the Indian Forest Acts of 1878 and 1927, subsequently equally fiercely enforced by the post-

[100] Presentation at workshop on women and land rights, "Theory & Experiences from the Field: Fostering Rural Women's Access & Ownership to Land and Collectives," 14–15 May, Jawaharlal Nehru University, New Delhi.

[101] Ibid.

[102] Gatade 2005.

Independence Indian state. Globally, the trend is towards the legitimisation by states and World Bank institutions of property titles for the poor and women, even as these states engage in large-scale land acquisition in the interests of extractive capital. We will see that this is not a contradiction, and how the first works in the interests of the second. Is there, then, a disjuncture between on the one hand women's individual rights to land, and on the other struggles against land acquisition to protect or create a commons? It seems that something counterintuitive with regard to feminist common sense is being articulated in these contexts.

Land Rights Through Custom and Tradition in India

There are three kinds of access to land rights in India—through religious personal laws to agricultural land, through forest acts to forests, and through customary laws to agricultural and forest lands occupied by tribal people.

It is important to keep in mind that neither personal laws nor customary laws exist in any pure sense, traditional or indigenous. A large body of scholarship has shown that even up to the eighteenth century there was across India a considerable range of authorities offering different types of justice, and a multiplicity of scriptural and customary sources of right. The colonial state's efforts to consolidate a body of Hindu and Islamic law to vindicate its claim to be ruling on the basis of the laws and customs of the people in fact resulted in a body of jurisprudence that modified both "scriptures" and "custom" in keeping with official objectives wherever necessary.[103] Similarly, regarding the customary laws of tribal people of the North-East and Central India, while the British claimed to leave them to be governed by their customary practices, in fact traditional communities were reshaped as viable revenue-generating areas, and colonial village heads

[103] For instance, see Derrett 1968; Nair 1996; Anderson and Guha 1998; Singha 1998; Kugle 2001.

such as *gaonburha* were established in parallel with traditional chieftains.[104] Colonial control of the North-East was important for strategic reasons, and Central India was rich in minerals. It is impossible today, therefore, to excavate any practice that is purely indigenous. It is also important to note the continuity of tribal policy between the colonial and post-Independence Indian states. The next three subsections look at women's land rights under the three kinds of laws listed above.

Women's Rights to Land in Personal Laws

Personal laws are based on religious community identity and any attempt to change them automatically enters the space of our debate on secularism. It is also assumed that the "reform" of personal laws is necessarily fulfilling the agenda of modernity and progress. Feminist scholars like Bina Agarwal have long argued for women's "independent rights in land" on grounds of welfare, efficiency, equality, and empowerment.[105] Agarwal has pointed out that it has been easier to push the welfare and efficiency arguments with state planners than equality and the empowerment of women. The former are more easily understood within a poverty-alleviation framework, she suggests, while the latter kind of arguments run counter to "deep-rooted notions of appropriate gender relations shared by many men who make and implement policy," for whom more equal gender relations appear as "threatening to existing family and kinship structures."[106]

Certainly, nothing leads us to think that these attitudes have changed; on the contrary, policy-makers continue to express the most appallingly sexist and misogynist opinions quite freely. And yet, in 2005, the amendment to the Hindu Succession Act (HSA) of 1956, giving women rights to ancestral property, was declared "passed unanimously" in both houses of the Indian parliament, first in the upper

[104] Kurup 2008.
[105] Agarwal 1994: 27.
[106] Ibid.: 45.

house, the Rajya Sabha, and then the same year in the lower, the Lok Sabha. Several states had already passed such legislation between 1986 and 1994—Andhra Pradesh, Tamil Nadu, Karnataka, and Maharashtra, while Kerala abolished the joint family altogether in 1975.

What did the HSA Amendment Act of 2005 accomplish? Bina Agarwal calls it a landmark because it established gender equality on agricultural land and in coparcenary joint family property.[107] The debate on the HSA Amendment Bill in the Lok Sabha is intriguing, partly because of the enthusiastic support from many MPs who had clearly not read the proposed amendments with any care, and sometimes made mistaken claims and demands, but even more so because in fact several MPs had very negative responses to the Bill.[108] Despite such views expressed across party lines, the Bill passed unanimously in the Lok Sabha. Earlier, when it was discussed in the Rajya Sabha, "Only one male member (the rest were women) participated in the discussion that came at the fag end of the day. Some of the members pointed to the low attendance in the House during the debate."[109] But there too the Bill passed unanimously and the Minister for Law, H. R. Bhardwaj, "expressed happiness at the unequivocal support given to the Bill by the BJP-led opposition National Democratic Alliance."[110]

As regards Muslims, the Shariat Act of 1937 which governs Muslims permits agricultural land rights to be governed by custom, as a result of which in many states Muslim women are excluded from ownership of land. There has been an ongoing campaign to end this discrimination along the lines of the 2005 amendment of the law.[111] Christians and Parsis are governed now by the Indian Succession Act which permits ownership rights to ancestral property to women.

But our concern here goes beyond asking whether women have

[107] Agarwal 2005.
[108] Lok Sabha Debates 2005.
[109] Special Correspondent 2005.
[110] Ibid.
[111] Agarwal 2005.

equal rights to land: the question to ask is *why* women's individual rights to land are so centrally on the agenda of the Indian state, and what the transformation is that is being brought about in the name of equal rights for women. Let us go back about a century to seek some answers before we return to 2005.

Some interesting historical work started emerging in the first decade of the twenty-first century on Hindu law reform and codification in late colonial India, a process that has hitherto been debated in feminist scholarship exclusively in terms of the enhancement or the curtailing of women's rights to property. This work—that of Ritu Birla and Eleanor Newbigin, for instance,[112] is enabling a reframing of this codification as "the making of capitalist subjects."[113]

The focus on Hindu law here is largely because, through law reforms in the 1860s, colonial officials both created and formalised (or codified) "personal laws," the effect of which, as Newbigin demonstrates, was different on Muslim and Hindu personal law. Quranic shari'a law, the "outcome of the hybrid Company legal system,"[114] was presented as "traditional"' as well as clear-cut and easily applied, under which "Muslim families were considered to comprise of property-owning individuals, whereas the natural condition of a Hindu family was assumed to be 'joint'."[115] Contrary to later discourses about Muslim law being backward, then, at that point it was Hindu laws that were considered as requiring reform to bring them into the modern world of individual property rights.

The impetus towards reform came, argues Newbigin, from conflicts between Hindu professional and mercantile elites on the one hand, and agrarian elites on the other, putting pressure on the Mitakshara coparcenary and "its system of joint, intergenerational property ownership" through which agrarian elites maintained their authority; while for Indian merchants competing with European capital this focus on joint rights and its effect of locking away capital in land was

---

[112] Birla 2009; Newbigin 2009.
[113] Birla 2009: 199.
[114] Newbigin 2009: 87.
[115] Ibid.

problematic. Of course, both groups were found in the same families, and younger men gradually opposed joint-family living and collective property ownership in the emerging Anglo-Hindu law.[116] The movement towards the legal abolition of matriliny in Kerala must be seen as part of the same process. The last vestiges of Nair matriliny, which had gradually been delegitimised, were finally removed with the Hindu Succession Act of 1956 giving men equal rights to matrilineal ancestral property. The historian Pravina Kodoth has pointed out that the abolition of matriliny was produced within a narrative of Historical Progress and the newly emerging discourse of individual rights. That is, the end of Nair women's exclusive rights to natal property under matriliny was conducted impeccably in the language of rights—pitting the rights of "the wife" against those of "the sister" of the Nair man; the subject of rights was never of course assumed to be the Nair woman herself.[117]

These developments cannot be seen independently of the longer process of turning land into a commodity, which began with the Permanent Settlement of 1793 and culminated in the Land Acquisition Act of 1894. By this process "a rule of property" was sought to be established over heterogeneous practices of land use and land relations,[118] thus creating "a precise and definitive location of saleable property right."[119] We should also note, however, that this process was far from successfully completed by the end of colonial rule, for, as Ranajit Guha argues, the grafting of a capitalist vision of land rights on to the Indian agrarian system without an understanding of the traditions on which it was based resulted in continuing forms of feudal land relations at Independence.[120]

The independent Indian state thus still needed to address the land question. Let us turn to the debate on the First Amendment to the Constitution in 1951, in which the right to agrarian property was

[116] Ibid.: 88.
[117] Kodoth 2001.
[118] Guha 1963 [1996].
[119] Sarkar 2014: 89.
[120] Guha 1963 [1996].

significantly limited by an amendment to Article 31 through which the individual's right to property was made subject to the state's right to acquire property to resolve what Nehru termed "the land problem."[121] Government acquisition of land could no longer be challenged on grounds of inadequate compensation and a "Ninth Schedule" was created in the Constitution within which land reform legislation was placed, protecting it from judicial review. This amendment shows the nation-state in the process of establishing a capitalist economy through a "passive revolution."[122]

Revealingly, the fact that these reforms were not meant to weaken property rights as such, but only landed property in feudal estates, was spelt out by Finance Minister T. T. Krishnamachari in a letter to Nehru during discussions on the Fourth Amendment in 1954: "We have to move to the left on agricultural land, but moving left in industry will prevent expansion."[123] It is significant that no voice in parliament explicitly opposed the abolition of *zamindari* (large land-holdings). The debate was over whether compensation should be "just" and "adequate." Here was the fledgling bourgeois state putting in place notions of legitimate and illegitimate property.

Soon, through the Hindu Marriage Act of 1955 and the Hindu Succession Act of 1956, far-reaching changes were brought about. These were presented as the reform of Hindu laws to give women equal rights to property, rights to divorce, and so on. However, as discussed in Chapter 1, it has been convincingly demonstrated by Flavia Agnes

[121] Lok Sabha Debates 1951.

[122] I refer here to Sudipta Kaviraj's development of the Gramscian notion to explain the pattern of development adopted by the Indian state: for a thoroughgoing bourgeois revolution to be effected, for industrialisation to take place, a domestic market must be built up by reducing poverty in the countryside. This can only be done by effective land reforms—which have been legislated but never effectively implemented because of the influence of landed interests in the coalition of ruling classes. The entire planning process until the 1980s has therefore been an exercise in trying to promote industrialisation without the radical transformation of agriculture: Kaviraj 1988.

[123] Cited in Austin 1999: 104.

and Madhu Kishwar that what in fact these legislations achieved was a codification of the vast and heterogeneous practices of communities that were not Muslim/Parsi/Christian, bringing them into conformity with what was assumed to be the "Indian" and "Hindu" norm—that is, North Indian, upper-caste practices.[124] This process obliterated many customs that had been advantageous to women in other communities, while giving North Indian upper-caste women some limited rights they did not have before.

Forests and Community Rights

Through the Forest Acts of 1865 and 1878, the Forest Department came to control one-fifth of British India's land area and, overnight, communities that had lived for generations in forests became "encroachers" on newly enclosed forest lands; their everyday subsistence activities became crimes—cattle grazing, cutting low-hanging branches, gathering leaves, and so on. Other key legislations are the National Forest Policy of 1894, which regulated rights further and restricted privileges of "users" in forest areas for the "public good"; the Land Acquisition Act of 1894, which permits compulsory acquisition of land for a "public purpose"; and the Indian Forest Act of 1927, which remains the main legal basis for depriving forest dwellers of their user rights to forest resources.

There were two main purposes behind these moves—developing forests for the modern timber industry through "scientific forestry"; and expanding arable farming "at the cost of nomadic communities of pastoralists and hunter-foragers" for "reasons of extraction of land revenue and enhancing of export surplus in foodgrains and cash crops."[125] This process has carried on apace in independent India, with the National Forest Policy of 1952 focusing on protecting forest resources while commercially exploiting minor forest produce; and the Forest Conservation Act of 1980 placing all forests under the control of the

[124] Agnes 199; Kishwar 1994.
[125] Sarkar 2014: 88.

Central government. The post-Independence state also continued utilising other colonial land acquisition laws for the "public good" in the name of development.

The Supreme Court has now integrated into Indian environmental jurisprudence the idea of "the state as trustee of all natural resources."[126] Essentially, this marks a shift in state policy from the colonial objective of encouraging sedentarisation to dispossessing forest dwellers so that forests can be handed over to private interests for a more efficient extraction of forest produce.

During the UPA regime the movements by forest peoples, supported by Left parties in parliament, were able to get passed the Scheduled Tribes (Recognition of Forest Rights) Act 2006.[127] Since the advent of colonial rule, the usufructuary rights to land of millions of tribals and forest dwellers has remained disputed or unacknowledged because of a lack of records on land rights. A Supreme Court judgment in 2001 put the final seal on the extinguishing of such rights when the Court issued a stay on the regularisation of tribal villages in forest areas. So the movement for FRA 2006 was a militant campaign for the recognition and formal codification of these rights. Interestingly, though, since the FRA 2006 came out of a campaign driven by forest people, the rights that are sought to be recorded are not only *individual* rights to "cultivated land in forested landscapes" but also *collective* rights to control, manage, and use forests and their resources as common property. The FRA 2006 also stipulates the conditions for relocation of forest dwellers from "critical wildlife habitations" solely with their "free informed consent" and their rehabilitation in alternative land.[128] It is clear that, through the involvement of forest peoples' movements, it is not "traditional" rights that are being asserted through the FRA 2006 but new forms of collective rights and claims that are being fashioned. These movements represent the powerful presence of thousands affected by the "brutal violence of the forest bureaucracy."[129]

[126] Rajamani 2007: 294.
[127] FRA 2006.
[128] Samarthan 2012.
[129] Ramdas 2009: 65.

Collective rights are, of course, not desirable from the point of view of either the Forest Department, which has set up patronage networks through bribery and which gives selective permissions to tribal people to use forest produce; nor for supporters of corporate investment-based development.[130] The provision in FRA 2006 making it mandatory to take "prior informed consent" of the Gram Sabha (village council) for any diversion of forest land is also an obstacle to the corporate exploitation of forests. But within a hundred days of the first BJP government of Narendra Modi, the Ministry of Environment and Forests passed 240 of 325 projects that had been held up for lack of environmental clearance. It emerged in the media that the government was planning to bypass FRA 2006 by using the provisions of the Environment Protection Act 1986, which only requires a public hearing before giving permission to any project, not the informed consent of Gram Sabhas. This would not only undermine the Gram Sabha but establish the dominance of bureaucrats, experts, and politicians on decisions in relation to the diversion of forest land.[131]

The FRA 2006, which emerged out of movements and has enormous potential for rejuvenating forests and the collective livelihoods of forest people, can be a threat to expanded regimes of individual property rights amenable to capital, and, not surprisingly, is itself threatened under corporate-friendly regimes.

Customary Laws and Women

"Customary laws" is a term used to refer to the bodies of unwritten usages that govern the lives of communities called tribes, in North-East and Central India. Tribes consider these laws intrinsic to their identity, culture, and tradition, but of course they have not remained unchanged through time. As noted earlier, although the colonial government did not formally intervene in customary practices, informally it intervened extensively. Two legislations of 1838 and 1886 facilitated

---

[130] Choubey 2014.
[131] Ibid.

land acquisition by the colonial state and these formed the basis for post-1947 laws that enabled the state takeover of tribal lands.

The land tenure system is not uniform over tribal lands, there being different systems in place within both Central and North-East India. A survey of scholarship on the North-East shows great diversity. Some tribes have complete community-based ownership with no notion of individual ownership till recently, others combine individual with clan ownership. Some tribes practise shifting cultivation and so their villages do not have a fixed boundary or name, and communal ownership has been the norm among them. Others allot land to each family in return for free labour for about a third of the year. Practices of community ownership were basic to intra- and inter-generational equity as well as the relatively high status of women, because even individually owned land was treated as a community resource inherited from ancestors that people could use to meet their needs but which they had to preserve for posterity in line with ecological imperatives.[132]

The argument is not that tribal societies were free of gender hierarchy, but that if resources like land, forests, and waterbodies are community-owned women have more of a say in their management. However, the relatively high status it confers on them is based on their role as economic assets in the family, not in society. Most tribal traditions kept a clear separation between the family and society. Women were in charge of the family production and economy while men controlled social power.[133] Thus, the argument is that while gender hierarchy did operate, the economic power women had in practice mitigated the higher social status attributed to men.

A study of five tribes that are at different stages of the interface between customary law and the modern legal system notes that land relations are being modified by several factors—immigration and encroachment but, most crucially, changes introduced by the modern legal system. When modern land laws enter such societies through the process of codification, it is found that the result is class formation

[132] Fernandes and Bharali 2002.
[133] Ibid.

and a stronger patriarchal ethos. The intervention of individual own-ership-based laws first turn land without an individual title into state property, but this prepares the ground for transferring power from the community to a few elite men who take control of all decision-making and interpret the customary law to their own benefit, thus deepening and entrenching gender and class inequality.[134] State policies further strengthen these processes, for example by giving loans and subsidies for commercial crops only to individual landowning family heads—interpreted as men. Community property-oriented tribes are thus forced to change over to individual title deeds or *pattas*. For example, among the matrilineal Garo of Meghalaya, the state encour-aged rubber plantations and gave subsidies and loans to individual owners, thus forcing them to get *pattas*. The administration treated men as family heads and consulted them alone in decisions concern-ing land use and transfer. Today women continue to inherit land but men wield more political and social power than in the past.[135] Women's organisations in the North-East—for example, the Aruna-chal Pradesh Women's Welfare Society and the Naga Mothers' As-sociation—while pushing for land rights for women and equality in representative institutions, simultaneously defend the protection af-forded by customary laws from land acquisition by the state and private corporations. Perhaps this is why reservation for women in local bod-ies, in accordance with the Indian Constitution, is being so strongly opposed by the tribal male elite—activists from the women's organi-sations that oppose land acquisition for ecologically harmful and cap-italist purposes argue that while male elites are open to transgressing customary laws in order to sell community lands to private corporate interests, they invoke customary laws only to prevent women from having a say in these matters.[136]

Codification and individual rights to land for women are seen as

[134] Fernandes, Pereira, and Khatso 2008.

[135] Marak 1997: 60–9, cited in Fernandes, et al. 2008.

[136] Jarjum Ete of the Arunachal Pradesh Women's Welfare Society and Rosemary Dzuvichu of the Naga Mothers' Association have publicly stated this at workshops of women's organisations at which I was present.

progressive and some tribes are bringing about inheritance rights for women. For instance, in 2004 the Paite Tribal Council introduced provisions in favour of daughters, widows, and illegitimate or adopted and other disinherited sons.[137] Matrilineal Meghalaya has begun the process of giving equal land rights to all children, including sons.[138] However, two decades ago the legal scholar and activist Nandita Haksar wrote critically of an initiative by Madhu Kishwar to press for individual over community rights to property for Ho tribal women. She saw the initiative as uncomprehending about the complex community practices that make up a tribal understanding of property and its ownership, and urged, rather, the need for a struggle within tribal communities to evolve new customs that are more egalitarian, rather than forcibly introducing individual rights to property from above.[139]

Haksar's argument is all the more relevant today in the context of accelerated land acquisition by the state over the last few years, now not only for a "public purpose" but for private capital. The "progressive" changes in customary laws that tend towards individual rights and now property rights for women must also be seen in the same background discussed at length in the context of "reforms" in Hindu Personal Law.

Let us now return to the present moment.

Property Titling for Capitalist Transformation

In June 2010 a news report noted that the Peruvian economist Hernando de Soto, hailed as the "poor man's capitalist," had arrived in India to help the UPA-led government to "merge the informal economy in the slums of the country with the formal or mainstream one."[140] De

---

[137] Kamkhenthang 2005, cited in Fernandes, et al. 2008: 4.
[138] Karmakar 2021.
[139] Haksar 1999
[140] Chatterji 2010.

Soto said in this news report that he was invited by the Federation of Indian Chambers of Commerce and Industry (FICCI—the tag line on its website is "Industry's Voice for Policy Change"). Among the people in government he met was Prime Minister Manmohan Singh, who later presented to the union minister for Housing and Urban Poverty Alleviation two books written by de Soto "for a better understanding of issues relating to urban poverty and slum development."[141] A government official said to a journalist: "The group led by de Soto will be providing us a methodology for changing the face of the informal economy through routes like property titles and landownerships." Another official added: "de Soto's approach is essentially based on capitalist economic principles. Our government will try to meld them into our socialist objectives." The news report said de Soto's Institute for Liberty and Democracy (ILD), a Lima-based non-profit organisation, "has advised governments in many countries to vest slumdwellers with property rights to maximise the economic use of assets in slums, create organisational forms to increase the productivity of enterprises and *provide identity devices to allow entrepreneurs to operate in expanded markets*."[142] The de Soto agenda has long been recognised by some scholars as a project of attempting to bring about capitalism globally through sustained state intervention. Timothy Mitchell points out that de Soto's two books, *The Other Path* (1989) and *The Mystery of Capital* (2000), became "the most widely cited studies of non-Western economic development in a generation," and that the Institute for Liberty and Democracy in Peru, which carried out the research presented in these books, has been called the second most influential think tank in the world.[143] In Mitchell's rendering de Soto's argument, based on findings from research in five countries, is that a large amount of wealth lies outside the formal economy, trapped in forms that cannot enter the market, and therefore cannot be invested to create further wealth. Described as "dead capital," this wealth

[141] Ibid.
[142] Ibid.; emphasis added.
[143] Mitchell 2007.

consists principally of land and housing, to which most people in non-Western countries have no formal title registered with the state. Live capital, according to de Soto, is created by transforming the value of material assets "into abstract forms, which can live an 'invisible, parallel life' alongside their physical existence."[144] This abstract form is credit and capital.

Mitchell points out—using the example of Egypt, one of the countries studied by de Soto—that the prevalence of "informal property arrangements" is not because of ignorance of notions of private property or because the West did not try to "export its property system abroad." On the contrary, in the nineteenth century the Ottoman and European rulers in Cairo launched a series of attempts to transform property arrangements into systems based on an absolute right of private ownership. But Egyptian farmers were able to prevent the complete destruction of livelihoods that absolute property rights entailed because "Egypt controlled no overseas colonies or Indian territories to which to ship a dispossessed rural population, so could not afford the rates of dispossession that private ownership produced." Mitchell argues that the position of ordinary Egyptians "outside" the mechanisms of private property ownership was "the outcome of a long, often violent, but ultimately relatively successful objection to undergoing the dispossession inflicted on the rural populations of Europe or the complete marginalisation or elimination of native populations in parts of the world where settler colonialism was carried through."[145] Mitchell is referring to the process of the dispossession of peasantry that has accompanied the regime of private property rights inaugurated by capitalist transformation in Europe since the sixteenth century. There, governments were able to mitigate the effects of this kind of devastating uprooting by sending the newly dispossessed to overseas colonial territories. Because Egypt did not have recourse to this strategy, the resistance posed by Egyptians to being dispossessed was relatively successful until the mid-twentieth century.

[144] Mitchell 2007: 248–9.
[145] Ibid.: 253.

However, once de Soto's programme was adopted from the late 1970s as part of neoliberal reforms in Egypt, the situation changed drastically. ILD-drafted legislation was pushed through in the early 2000s to bring about a mortgage law, a property titling programme, and new rules for licensing small businesses. The government and the courts began to alter laws protecting commercial and residential tenants, freeing property developers from the constraint of rent controls. The share of manufacturing in the economy declined, non-oil exports fell, and no significant efforts were made to increase large-scale employment.[146] Addressing de Soto's programme, scholarship on other parts of Africa comes to the conclusion that formal and privatised systems of property rights are not fully implementable, even if desirable. One reason is that people prefer to go through locally recognised institutions of exchange.[147] This preference may be explained by Sindiso Mnisi's argument that there is a disjuncture between what is termed customary law in South Africa, for example, which is merely "official customary law" applied in civil courts, and the "law that is lived in rural communities of South Africa."[148] She uses the term "living customary law" to refer to "an array of varying, localised systems of law observed by numerous communities," as opposed to official customary law.[149] She makes a general argument not directly related to property titling – but the accommodation of living customary law alongside the state system, she suggests, would certainly challenge the idea that universal individual rights to land are inevitable and desirable.

More significantly, rather than promoting security of tenure, titling efforts lead to higher levels of conflict over land. When it comes to women, because they are not customarily entitled to own land autonomously, formal titling deprives them of even use rights recognised by the community. It is therefore being suggested that joint ownership for women should be instituted before formal titling takes place.[150]

[146] Ibid.: 263.
[147] Joireman 2008: 1237.
[148] Mnisi 2007: 241.
[149] Ibid.: 241–2.
[150] Joireman 2008; Sjaastad and Cousins 2008.

As Sjaastad and Cousins put it, "massive, nation-wide formalisation programmes can be seen as risky social experiments that gamble with the livelihoods of the poor."[151]

A study based on extensive scholarship from the countries of Latin America and Africa found that land-titling programmes have not achieved the benefits claimed by their proponents. There has been no increase of investment in land and housing, or in access to formal credit, and municipal revenues have not increased noticeably more than under other tenure regimes, including those that allow many unauthorised settlements. There is no significant evidence of poverty levels being reduced. Not only does titling not provide increased tenure security, but many alternative forms of tenure, including those in many informal settlements, also provide high levels of security. In addition, in many countries land titles do not necessarily protect people from eviction and expropriation of their land.[152]

All the evidence from India, Africa, and Latin America thus goes to show that the demand for individual rights to land is a strategy that achieves nothing more than opening up land for capitalist transformation, often via the state. De Soto's programme was promoted powerfully by bodies like the UNDP High Level Commission on Legal Empowerment of the Poor, and in fact India's introduction to de Soto was not in 2010, with his first visit. This High Level Commission, cochaired by former US Secretary of State Madeleine Albright and Hernando de Soto, with India as one of the founding members, was set up in September 2005—around the same time as the amendments to the Hindu Succession Act were being passed with such a puzzling lack of enthusiasm, but nevertheless unanimously, in the Indian parliament.

Individual Rights to Land and Land Acquisition

It has been argued by Aditya Nigam that the widespread *continuation* of "pre-capitalist" forms of production both in agriculture and in

[151] Sjaastad and Cousins 2008.
[152] Payne, et al. 2009.

non-agricultural sectors is what "confronts capital's onward march." Nigam argues that these are actually non-capitalist rather than pre-capitalist forms and they "represent the recalcitrant other of capital and capitalism—that which capitalism must attempt to seize, discipline, control and subsume within its own domain but which constantly escape its logic." The transformation to bourgeois private property therefore involves and has always involved, he says, "a violent decimation of all forms of common property and even non-capitalist private property."[153]

This is evident from the story of land-acquisition legislation in contemporary India. In 2013 the Right to Fair Compensation and Transparency in Land Acquisition, Rehabilitation and Resettlement Act (LARRA) was passed, replacing the 1894 Act. Key provisions of this new legislation re-enshrined the state's power to dispossess land for private profit, but ensured farmers a share of the profits that would accrue to capital in the form of higher prices for land and rehabilitation and resettlement benefits. Michael Levien sees this as an attempt to substitute one-time payouts for development. LARRA thus represents the contradiction between the land requirements of neoliberal capitalism and the pressures on the state on account of electoral democracy. More importantly, this policy concretises a significant shift. From the state dispossessing people of their land for public sector infrastructure, mining, and heavy industry, the state in effect becoms a land broker for private capital.[154]

However, this 2013 law can also be seen as an advance on the 1894 law because it gave people a say in land acquisition and made the process participative. It promised to put an end to forcible acquisitions and enhance compensation to landowners to resettle and rehabilitate families displaced by land acquisition, and it gave the Gram Sabha decision-making powers in land acquisition.

These features were not acceptable to corporate interests and they were critical of what they called the general "policy paralysis" of the

---

[153] Nigam 2014.
[154] Levien 2018.

UPA (which was constrained in its neoliberal ambitions because of the backing of social movements). Soon after it was enacted on 1 January 2014, the newly elected NDA government diluted many of its provisions through an ordinance by which the government could acquire land for any private entity without obtaining the consent of affected people and do so without the precondition of Social Impact Assessments. In addition, even the filing of complaints regarding the state's failure to follow due process now needs the prior consent of the state itself. The ordinance has formally lapsed, but several states have bypassed the law and implemented their own Acts by replicating the ordinance, even as the Amendment Bill is still under consideration by a Joint Committee of Parliament.[155]

Alongside this is the big push towards enshrining individual rights to land, replacing community rights where they existed. We have noted the enthusiasm with which women's rights to land are being promoted by the Indian state. Community rights are also being gradually replaced by individual rights. In March 2018 the Arunachal Pradesh Land Settlement and Records Amendment Act was passed, giving ownership rights to indigenous people of the state of Arunachal Pradesh—people who had earlier held lands jointly as a community. The state government said in a statement, echoing de Soto, that with this legislation "huge investments are expected, which will augment the economy of the state," and that with ownership rights, tribal people will be able to lease out their land, and use it as collateral to get loans from banks.[156] As we saw above, none of these benefits have actually accrued in places all over the world where individual land titling has taken place. We also know that individual titles to land make land acquisitions for any purpose easier for the state, and their only purpose is the commodification of land.

Michael Levien has starkly defined dispossession as "state-sponsored redistribution of land from the poor to the wealthy."[157] It seems that

[155] Sonak 2018.
[156] Chandran 2018.
[157] Levien 2015.

"land rights for women" and "property titles for the poor" are the banners that fly before this process of dispossession, leading towards an economy driven by capitalist imperatives.

The discourse of women's rights arose at the historical moment of the rise of capitalism, and hence the focus on individual rights, but today that language must be radically rethought. This is the moment of the search for a new commons, a new language, and a grammar of transformative justice.

It is becoming increasingly clear that women's rights to land are an integral part of the agenda of forcibly constructing capitalism through the agency of the state. From the perspective that this chapter offers, all three—the state, the traditional religious community, and the customary community—are equally problematic from the point of view of equitable access to land for women as well as other excluded castes and groups. A truly radical agenda would thus have to challenge all three simultaneously—state-led capitalist enclosures of commons, which is part of what Veltmeyer and Petras call the "new extractivism";[158] private individual landownership; and gender- and caste-based forms of exclusion from land use. This struggle will have to be waged in a context of the accelerated decline of agriculture in an era of rampant dispossession: but this is also an era of widespread and militant peasant mobilisation for land reclamation all over the world, as we will see in the final chapter.

What I have attempted to demonstrate in this chapter is that the discourse of secularism and the debate around its presence or absence swallows up the possibility of addressing the fact that "secularism" is not just compatible with capitalism but essential for it to succeed. The status of capitalism as indicating progress, modernity, and technological advance is closely linked to secularism, which enables the desacralisation of nature, making nature commodifiable. This reconceptualisation of nature is central to the normalisation of capitalism. In addition, secularism uses the modern language of individual rights to

[158] Veltmeyer and Petras 2014.

prepare conditions for breaking up collectivities and community rights which have acted as a barrier to capitalist transformation. Since collective and community rights are often linked to "tradition" and "religion," the push to end these presents itself as the historically progressive, secular move. By stepping out of the secular, the operation of capitalism is made visible in all its dimensions.

6

Insurgent Constitutionalism and Radical Frames of Citizenship

THIS CHAPTER AND the next open up to the ways in which stepping out of the secular enables new visions of constitutionalism, citizenship, and anti-capitalist modes of existence, many of which we see articulated in the twenty-first century. What implications these have for other imaginable worlds is of course the key question to reflect upon. The task is not so much to reinvent or reject secularism, as to "step out" from the field stabilised and made visible by the concept—to accept that secularism is not a value in itself but only a strategy of governance.

I have earlier distinguished between Secularism (with a capital "s") as a strategy of rule, and secularism (with a small "s") as the lived experience of coexistence among multiple communities.[1] However, this distinction, made in a last desperate attempt to as it were salvage something out of "secularism," is not really sustainable. What appeared as the peaceful and mutual coexistence of heterogeneous communities turns out to have been largely marked by the violence of the powerful, by the hegemonising assimilationist moves of the dominant, and by the silencing of heterogeneous voices. Of course, there was also mutual coexistence, made possible by fuzzy boundaries between identities and mutual toleration, not necessarily out of respect or love but by maintaining strict limits to interaction.[2] However, through the arguments

[1] Menon 2007b.

[2] In the context of Kerala, for example, James Chiriyankandath has argued that "the pragmatic politics of communal rivalry and accommodation" form "an

315

in this book, which take into account knowledges from the broader global South as well as Dalit Bahujan scholarship, it seems to me the process of stepping out of secularism requires us to now identify the actual values that we consider meaningful, and seriously consider practices across the globe that try to bring any of these into being.

The three values that would best capture ideas discussed in this book are these:

First, democracy—as locally inflected and permanently heterogeneous. It should be clear that democracy here does not refer to the particular electoral procedure by which a government is put in place in a nation-state, this being only a recent phenomenon in human history. Democracy refers to something more fundamental, to the ways in which people seek autonomy to shape their lives and worlds, whether as individuals or as communities. Such struggles are "postnational"—in the sense that they represent ideas that are counter-hegemonic, regardless of whether that hegemony refers to capitalism, sexuality, community-based majoritarianism, casteism, racism or any other. But, equally importantly, the "postnational" can be manifested in one of two dimensions—first, "over" the nation, across national borders; and second, "under" the nation, resisting inclusion into the larger national identity, insisting on space/time trajectories that are independent of and that do not mesh with progressivist dominant narratives of nation and history.[3]

Second, social justice—with class, caste, race, gender, and multiple other dimensions.

And *third*, ecological justice—considering the human as merely one part of a vaster nature.

---

essential part of the political milieu of contemporary Kerala": Chiriyankandath 1993. Ashis Nandy, too, drawing on scholarship such as this, has suggested that the "communal harmony" found in Kochi is based not on feelings of brotherly love but mutual dislike and minimum interaction: Nandy 2014.

[3] I have developed this particular idea of the postnational, marking its difference from Habermasian frameworks, along with a group of scholars from India, Pakistan, and Sri Lanka. See De Alwis, et al. 2009.

These three values stand in an uneasy relationship with secularism/secularisation. Secularism per se does not guarantee democracy because it is perfectly compatible with majoritarianism. Secularism has certainly been historically very dismissive of non-economic claims to justice, especially of caste and race. And, finally, secularism has at best been blind to, and at worst has rejected, the idea of ecological justice because secularism is rooted in a modernist and progressivist frame and is unable to recognise as paramount those claims that counter the values proposed by modernity.

The present chapter considers the kind of strategies to bring about these values that are most located within existing systems; the next moves towards strategies and understandings that are most outlying, focusing on anti-capitalist frames. To follow this trajectory, I will consider two themes here: constitutionalism as a radically transformative framework, and an expansion of the idea of citizenship.

Insurgent Constitutionalism— Chile and India

Can a Constitution be insurgent? Insurgency implies rising up against established authority, not necessarily with arms. To be insurgent is to resist an established order. How then can a Constitution, as a set of principles which establishes an order, be insurgent, as many Left-oriented movements seem to produce it? By using the term "insurgent" alongside "Constitution" I am reformulating an argument I have made earlier regarding a dilemma that arises at the interface of radical political practice and the logic of constitutionalism.[4] By "constitutionalism" I refer to a specific method adopted by modern democracies for safeguarding the autonomy of the individual self. It is now generally recognised, however, that this objective is achieved by a process of enforcing universal norms that marginalise, render obsolete, and delegitimise contesting worldviews and value systems. This particular method

---

[4] Menon 2004.

of organising democracies has a specific history and arose in a particular geopolitical location—that is, in Europe in the seventeenth century. By historicising this method we remind ourselves, to use Upendra Baxi's words, that "much of the business of 'modern' constitutionalism was transacted during the early halcyon days of colonialism/imperialism. That historical timespace marks a combined and uneven development of the world in the processes of early modernity . . . [C]onstitutionalism inherits the propensity for violent social exclusion from the 'modern'."[5] The drive of constitutionality, then, is towards the erasure of any kind of normative ethic which differs from its own unitary central ethic.

The dilemma that faces radical politics is what I called the "paradox of constitutionalism"—that is, the tension in which the need to assert various and differing moral visions comes up against the universalising drive of constitutionality and the language of universal rights.

A Constitution is usually seen as a legal document that embodies a new dispensation or structure of power and which becomes a crucial reference point in the resolution of disputes between groups. Marxists, for instance, speak of bourgeois or socialist Constitutions—and there certainly is an element of truth in the characterisation of many modern Constitutions as bourgeois insofar as they protect property rights and civil rights, not economic democracy. However, that does not exhaust what Constitutions do. The hope inspired by the idea of a Constitution as the basis of a democratic state is as vibrant in the twenty-first century as it was in the mid-twentieth, when the first wave of decolonisation took place across the global South.

A comparison of Chile's draft Constitution of 2022 and India's enacted in 1950 yields some productive insights. As I will argue here, unlike the Constitutions of the West—which in a sense marked a closure of and an end to political ferment—the postcolonial moment inaugurated in the mid-twentieth century is very different. This difference lies in the fact that, rather than closing down possibilities and freezing

---

[5] Baxi 2004: 1184–5.

power structures, the more modern Constitutions tend to be documents about open futures based on both democracy and social justice. They are also more likely to maintain the tension between competing interests rather than dissolve them in one direction or the other. This may not be true of all postcolonial Constitutions—a subject in need of a whole other book—but the two instances I consider below do embody such a perspective.

Chile

In Chile there were mass protests against the government in 2019–20. Caused by growing inequality, in these protests feminists, environmentalists, Indigenous groups, and anti-neoliberal activists wanting progressive socio-economic change came together. Chileans soon elected a left-wing president, Gabriel Boric, by an overwhelming majority. A widespread and inclusive public debate followed regarding the best way forward, and in October 2020 voters approved the creation of a constituent assembly to draft a new Constitution, replacing the Constitution of the dictator Pinochet. The constituent assembly that came into being was based on reserved seats for Indigenous candidates and gender parity. The largest bloc of the 155 members of the constituent assembly were independents, largely left-wing in their politics. The person elected to oversee the process was an Indigenous left-wing academic, Eliza Loncón. The document that emerged envisaged a range of political and social reforms guaranteeing social rights—including housing, social security, health, work, and access to food. Environmental reforms were part of the Constitution, so that fighting climate change and protecting biodiversity, native species, and natural spaces became a state duty. Political reforms included an element of direct democracy, gender parity, indigenous rights, and a restructuring of the bicameral parliamentary system to give the Chamber of Deputies (the lower house) more power at the expense of the Senate.[6] A visionary document

---

[6] Miranda 2022.

that represented the spirit of the mass social movement that brought Boric to power, it was put to a plebiscite in September 2022, at which it was decisively defeated by 62 percent of the popular vote. Boric was forced into a cabinet reshuffle, removing key left-wing ministers and bringing in some figures from Chile's traditional, conservative political class. How did this defeat come about, and what should we learn from it?

Conservative think tanks and media celebrated the defeat of this "populist" Constitution as "a flawed vision of Utopia,"[7] and as indicative of "democratic maturity."[8] Evidently the possibility of a Constitution such as the one that was expected to emerge was considered a dangerous threat to a presumably "democratically mature" neoliberal order, and a massive campaign of disinformation was carried out leading up to the plebiscite. An early 2022 survey found that 58 percent of Chileans had been exposed to some form of misinformation. Ciper, an investigative media outlet, found that most of those who voted against the new Constitution did so because of false information:

> Ciper surveyed 120 people across 12 districts of Santiago and found that the main reasons for rejecting the new constitution were people's fear of having their property expropriated, scare campaigns about unrestricted abortions and the spectre of indigenous people having more rights than the rest of the nation. None of these are accurate reflections of the proposed reforms.[9]

The Chilean-American writer Ariel Dorfman, however, holds that rejection of the Constitution cannot be ascribed entirely to the massively well-funded disinformation campaign. He believes it must be equally attributed to the uneasiness within a large majority about "the emphasis on the autonomy of Indigenous peoples, and the insistence on 'plurinationalism' in a land that prides itself on its unity." Dorfman suggests that plurinationalism—the attempt to bring Indigenous

---

[7] Stott 2022.
[8] Stuenkel 2022.
[9] Bell 2022.

nations and their languages, customs, and culture out of invisibility—threatens an identity innumerable Chileans felt to be their deepest—that is, their European heritage.[10]

What we learn from this is that the "European" heritage cannot accommodate the rejection of secular-nationalism by Indigenous peoples—both through their non-secular beliefs and practices, as well as through the challenge to the idea of one nation founded on the dominant values of that society.

Nevertheless, Dorfman does not see the plebiscite as the end of the road, but as "one more faltering step in the search for justice": after all, 80 percent of the electorate voted to end the existing Constitution instituted under the authoritarian Pinochet regime. This indicates "the desire for significant reforms—for a different, participatory, vision of our future, for a nation that protects nature and cares for its most vulnerable people, that expects women to be protagonists and diversity to be tolerated."[11] We cannot therefore see Chile's rejection of the new Constitution as a simple victory for conservatism. Any truly democratic road reflects heterogeneity and differences, and the fact that the people of Chile participated assertively in this process, sending the draft back to be reconsidered, indicates confidence among them that their voices matter. The very process of drafting a radical Constitution is linked to the battle for transforming common sense. Any new Constitution that emerges will represent a great deal of compromise, to be sure, but I suggest that such a Constitution can be insurgent too, provided that, rather than erasing internal tension between polar opposite political positions, that tension is maintained.

The Indian experience with a 72-year-old Constitution is an important illustration of this claim.

India

In April 2019, on the eve of the general elections that would bring the Hindu supremacist BJP into power for a second term, the performance

[10] Dorfman 2022.
[11] Ibid.

artist Maya Rao staged an event at a Women's March. Ceremoniously, she stripped herself of her sari, and then slowly dressed herself afresh with cloth on which were inscribed the values of the Preamble to the Constitution—Equality, Liberty, Justice, Fraternity. Her perform- ance invoked the scene from the Mahabharata of the stripping of Draupadi in the royal court, and of her being saved from shame by the god Krishna, who miraculously lengthens her strip of cloth in- finitely. Rao draws on the wellspring of Hindu culture to subvert it, and to indicate that today the protection of the powerless will ema- nate from the Constitution.

As noted, by the end of the first term of the BJP, the Hindutva proj- ect of establishing a Hindu Rashtra was well in place. Minorities and Dalits, as well as dissident voices even from within the Hindu commu- nity, were ruthlessly subjugated. Legal and mob-implemented diktats on whom to love and what to eat, targeted lynchings, and assassinations had already, via approval indicated by state silence, become the norm. A parallel project of the present dispensation has been the acceleration of predatory capitalism, with the state acting as an agent for crony capitalists. Through all of this there has been a growing sense that as- serting the values of the Constitution is a powerful tool of resistance.

The term "constitutional morality" has taken on a new life. B. R. Ambedkar used this phrase in his speech "The Draft Constitution," de- livered on 4 November 1948. Analysing the phrase as he used it, Pratap Bhanu Mehta identified three strands to Ambedkar's understand- ing of constitutional morality—freedom and self-restraint; recogni- tion of plurality; suspicion of any claims to singularly and to uniquely represent the will of the people.[12] These are, one could argue, the es- sential conditions of a democracy—mutual respect for one another's rights; acceptance and protection of a plurality that is not closed (that is, more and newer pluralities can emerge); and third, that no single movement or party or government can claim to fully represent the will of (all) people.

[12] Mehta 2010.

In 2009, when Justice Shah's court decriminalised sex between con-
senting adults of the same sex, the judgment invoked constitutional
morality again. This reading added another dimension to it, contrast-
ing it to popular morality. Popular morality is shifting, subjective, and
changes with time, the judgment said. But constitutional morality
in this view, represents the fundamental values of the constitution.[13]
These values have come to be understood, in the mass movements of
twenty-first-century India, as the values embodied in the Preamble—
justice, equality, liberty, and fraternity (which we can understand
more generally as mutual solidarity).

Jignesh Mevani, a charismatic young Dalit leader and now a member of the Gujarat state legislature, said before the 2019 elections that
he would place before the prime minister the Constitution and the
Manusmriti—the ancient text venerated by the RSS which sets out
the hierarchical caste system—and ask him to choose between them.[14]
Mevani was referring to the police complaints against himself and other
activists, and their potential arrest for attending a massive assembly
of Dalits. This dramatic counterposition of the Constitution to the
caste order has a long history going back to B. R. Ambedkar and
highlights the insurgent possibilities in the Constitution.

Similarly, the passing of the Constitutional Amendment Act (CAA)
in December 2019, by which (as noted in Chapter 2) only Muslims
in neighbouring countries were excluded from seeking refugee status
in India, and which the BJP home minister indicated was the first
step towards disenfranchising India's Muslim citizens,[15] evoked massive countrywide protests, led by Muslims, but including people from
virtually all other communities. These protests, beginning at the end
of 2019, and continuing with vigour until Covid restrictions began
to be implemented with severity in March 2020, were remarkable for

[13] *Naz Foundation v Union of India*, 2-7-2009 WP(C), no. 7455/2001 at para
79.

[14] Mevani 2018.

[15] Link to a video of the speech of 2019 connecting the CAA and the NRC:
https://www.youtube.com/watch?v=Z__6E5hPbHg.

performances around the Preamble to the Constitution guaranteeing equal rights to all citizens. The 24-hour sit-ins occupied public spaces for months in numerous parts of the country, the sites growing into festivals celebrating the Constitution through music, dance, speeches, wall art, and periodic recitations of the Preamble. Public readings of the Preamble were organised at multiple sites, with hundreds showing up just to read out the Preamble in local languages and English. Overwhelmingly, it was women who led these protests.[16] The best-known of the protest sites was Shaheen Bagh, a Muslim neighbourhood in Delhi which has consequently acquired iconic and legendary status.[17]

Chandrashekhar Azad, founder of the Bhim Army (invoking B. R. Ambedkar's first name), a mass social movement advocating dignity for Dalits, has been arrested more than once. At his meetings, attended by thousands of Dalit youth, he routinely holds up a Hindi copy of the Constitution.[18] His face on an iconic poster widely publicised by the Bhim Army sports a proud moustache and stylish dark glasses, a direct performative challenge to the vicious caste system in which Dalit men have been physically attacked for daring to grow moustaches— and for that matter riding a horse to their own weddings as the upper castes do, or dressing well.

These are just a few instances of the manner in which the Constitution has been owned, reiterated, and performed as the source of political legitimacy by different kinds of movements challenging contemporary injustice. What we have seen is that the Constitution no longer lives the singular life that liberal constitutionalism laid out for it, but has become for very many a call to radical transformation as well. The document has broken out of the confines of the liberal imagination that attempts to keep it in the safe custody of constitutional experts.

There are two reasons for this. First, the Indian Constitution is

[16] This Wikipedia entry is the best collation of the protests around CAA. https://en.wikipedia.org/wiki/Citizenship_Amendment_Act_protests.

[17] Mustafa, ed. 2020; Us Salam and Ausaf 2020; Khalid 2021.

[18] *Hindustan Times* 2020.

not merely a liberal document in any sense. The debates in the Constitutent Assembly show that it emerged out of a variety of political opinions from Left to Right. Also, emerging as it did from a mass anti-imperialist struggle, it tried to balance individual and community, formal equality and special provisions for historically disadvantaged groups, the drive towards industrialisation and the rights of the peasantry. This mid-twentieth-century moment is very different from that which produced the Constitutions of the West, which in a sense marked a closure of and an end to political ferment. The Indian Constitution contrasts with those by being widely seen as the *beginning* of a journey towards what its Preamble promises.[19]

The second reason why the Constitution is emerging as the banner of revolt for some struggles is the nature of Indian democracy, which has rarely remained confined to participation in elections. Of course, many movements have never accepted the Indian Constitution as a basis of legitimacy, but my focus here is only on movements that express their anger at their government by reasserting a vision of the Constitution. The explosion of mass movements across the country over the past decades, and especially against the BJP since 2014, is an indication that continuous democratic participation in decision-making has come to be taken for granted by most Indians. There is thus a growing divide between the people and the ruling elites, including all political parties, with the Constitution seen as standing by the people even as ruling elites deploy the state machinery and the law to subvert it.

Faisal Devji terms the Indian Constitution a "document of conquest,"[20] similar to the Euro-American Constitutions of the seventeenth–eighteenth centuries. While his analysis rightly tracks the heterogeneous competing visions that come together around the Indian Constitution, Devji then translates them through the lens of "American" and "French" constitutional experience, hence losing the specificity of time and place that should be central to all theorising. I

[19] Menon 2008.
[20] Devji 2021.

am also puzzled by his characterisation of French constitutionalism as involving the acceptance of positive discrimination—in my view it embodies the quintessential Enlightenment perspective demanding elimination of all difference. As I have been arguing, it seems that at this moment in history a certain static understanding of *secularism*— as referring to the interrelationship of settled religion-based communities—has acted as a "misdirection," drawing our attention away from the dynamism of a dense undergrowth of other relations, identities, and power structures that remain out of sight, ungrasped, untheorised.

What we see in the contemporary moment is a revitalisation and reclamation of an over seven-decade-old Constitution which does not express a singular will or a singular ruling order. As suggested earlier, it would be a mistake to think of the Constitution as limited by elite discussions within a homogeneous body based on restricted franchise— although scholarship along these lines is to be taken seriously too.[21] My argument is that we must equally seriously reconsider this view when the Constitution is being reimagined in such radically transformative ways by mass movements.

Recent scholarship shows, moreover, that in the making of the Constitution hundreds of individuals and civic organisations were involved. They wrote to the Constituent Assembly with requests for "representation of their group, religion, caste, tribe, or profession in the assembly's advisory committee, or with demands to be recognised as minorities in the constitution." Their engagement with the drafting of the Constitution continued throughout the three years of its process.[22] Within months of its enactment, many groups, including those socially marginalised, claimed in court proceedings the Constitution for legitimation of their rights to their practices and livelihoods.[23] Gautam Bhatia terms it a "transformative constitution" which, first, transformed the subjects of a colonial regime into the citizens of a re-

[21] For an argument of this kind that surveys other scholarship along similar lines, see Singh 2015.

[22] Shani 2022.

[23] De 2018.

public, and second, sought to transform society itself. This second goal is linked to the recognition that citizens needed protection not only from a despotic state but from traditional and feudal authorities.[24]

There are several important and productive tensions in the Constitution, of which I will mention just two: one arises from its push to end *zamindari* by bringing about a modern, individualist, capitalist regime of property, as opposed to the Fifth Schedule which protects collective ownership of tribal lands. As we shall see, the Fifth Schedule has been reanimated in the twenty-first century by the Pathalgadi movement of tribals, who invoke it to resist state takeover of their lands for handover to corporates. For their invocation of the Constitution, the Pathalgadi leaders are arrested on charges of sedition.

Another such tension is within the Fundamental Rights clauses of the Constitution which establish both individual and community rights. This dilemma has often played out in courts as the rights of individuals versus the rights of communities to "their culture"—which can discriminate against, for instance, certain castes and women. The rights of communities are nevertheless protected in order to ensure safeguards against majoritarianism—the tension is not resolved but can be productive.

In other words, the Indian Constitution is not a document that has managed to establish any kind of single or unitary order. If it was meant to legitimise the Brahminical, patriarchal, class society that India is, it certainly failed, for it ended up reflecting the heterogeneity of impulses of the anti-imperialist moment. It ended up, therefore, being a porous document with one foot in the future. While I do not suggest that the Constitution exhausts all possibilities for radical politics, it certainly seems to offer some kinds of movements the resources to think in radically transformative terms.

Here I consider one movement of many that have invoked the Indian Constitution against state power in India in the twenty-first century— Pathalgadi. Many others have also invoked the Constitution in the last two decades—for example the successful appeal to the Supreme Court

[24] Bhatia 2019.

against the criminalising of queer sexualities, and earlier the campaign for the Right to Information Act.[25] But from the point of view of the argument about stepping out of secularism, the best illustration is Pathalgadi.

Pathalgadi

Sweeping across the tribal belt of the states of Jharkhand, Chhattisgarh, and Odisha since early 2018 is a political movement of tribal people which has reworked a tradition of putting up stone slabs across their lands. These areas are also the heartland of armed Maoist activity against the Indian state and the state response has included setting up counterinsurgency groups among local Adivasis.[26] Some of these have been set up by the local police under the guise of splinter groups from within the Maoist organisation, but in fact they have acted for the Indian state and local police. The Pathalgadi movement finds its place in this complex and deceptive political landscape.

Traditionally, *pathalgadi* is a generic name for a ritual performed by many tribes of this region for several purposes: during the last rites of a person who has died; to perpetuate the existence of ancestors; to demarcate a village boundary; to show the existence of generations in claims to land. Thus there are many kinds of *pathalgadi* and they have different names; for example, the burial ritual is called *sasandiri*, and the stones that make a public declaration of customary rights are called *hukumdiri*.

The contemporary political performance of *pathalgadi* involves the erecting of giant green-painted stone slabs with lettering on them asserting tribal sovereignty over lands, and prohibiting the entry of government officials and other "outsiders." Some of these slabs list the

[25] I have discussed the legal campaign against Section 377 in "Performing the Constitution" (Menon 2023) and the insurgent constitutionalism of the RTI Act in Menon 2022.

[26] Adivasi is the general word used for the indigenous tribal and ethnic groups of East, Central, West, and South India. It is a politically assertive term, like Dalit. Tribal and Indigenous people of the North-East refer to themselves as "Tribes," not as Adivasis. The Indian Constitution refers to all such groups as Scheduled Tribes.

names of those martyred in the cause of tribal autonomy. The Pathalgadi revolution is capturing the imagination of village after village, and the movement declares that where these slabs stand indicates the limit of authority of the Indian government. The erecting of such slabs is a ceremonial process involving the whole village.[27] The current movement draws on a practice initiated after the Panchayat (Extension to Scheduled Area) Act (PESA) was passed in 1996, which explicitly gave tribal people rights over their lands. This legislation was the outcome of a long struggle and negotiations with the government. Two eminent former bureaucrats who have worked with the tribal people for decades, and who have acted as conduits to the government in getting PESA passed, B. D. Sharma and Bandi Oraon, suggested using the *pathalgadi* tradition—putting up stone slabs inscribed with rules and provisions of the PESA in villages—to raise awareness about this legislation. It was during this time that the word *pathalgadi* gained popularity, eventually replacing the more commonly used traditional word for burial rituals, *sasandiri*. Now the word *pathalgadi* is used for burial rituals as well.[28] Interestingly, contemporary political practice has seeped back to an earlier time and renamed the older tradition.

Inscribed on most of the stone slabs are these words taken from PESA 1996:

> Every village shall have a gram sabha (village council) . . . and every gram sabha shall be competent to safeguard and preserve the traditions and customs of the people, their cultural identity, community resources, and the customary mode of dispute resolution.

"Customary mode of dispute resolution" refers to the traditional institutions of tribal communities which exercise social, moral, religious, economic, and political authority over them, most of which have preserved their own distinct cultural identities through their unwritten code of conduct, and traditional mechanisms to enforce the odes. The customary laws of the tribes and jurisdiction of the traditional council were marginalised by the introduction of statutory

[27] Louis 2021: 39–41.
[28] Kiro 2018.

Panchayati Raj Institutions (PRI, that is, state-mandated village councils) all over the country, including the tribal areas, in 1992.[29] The PES Amendment of 1996 is seen as having restored these rights to tribal communities, but the PRI continue to hold sway and the assertion of PESA is part of what the Pathalgadi movement is about. Of course, customary tribal councils are often patriarchal and entrench the rights of local traditional elites, but on the other hand the PRI often act as agents of the Indian state in dispossessing tribal communities; and since central legislation too has consistently eroded the community rights of tribals to their lands, the struggle is at many levels.[30]

Many of the stones directly invoke the Constitution, since by its Fifth Schedule and other specific Articles it protects the collective ownership of tribal lands. British colonial rule began the process of dispossessing tribal people of their land, forests, and water (*jal, jangal, jameen*, as the Adivasis call them) in the interests of capitalist expansion, and the independent Indian state continued this process. Tribal people make up less than 10 percent of India's 1.3 billion population, but account for 40 percent of people who were uprooted from 1951 to 1990 by dams, mines, industrial development, and wildlife parks.[31] The history of the militant struggle by tribal people against this dispossession also started in the nineteenth century and continues into the present.

These regions have been in ferment for decades, but the immediate trigger for the current militant phase of the Pathalgadi movement can be traced to 2016, when amendments were proposed by the BJP government of Jharkhand to two key legislations that protect tribal rights to their land. The legislation was passed but aroused such widespread opposition that it had to be withdrawn. Subsequently, in 2017, the BJP government at the Centre passed amendments to another legislation, the Land Acquisition Act, 2013. The amendments enable the acquisition of tribal land for "development," reduce the scope

[29] Rao, no date.
[30] Chandran 2020.
[31] Ibid.

for social impact assessment, and reduce the powers of the Gram Sabha to merely giving "advice." This legislation received the assent of the state's governor in 2018. All of this has aroused enormous anger across the area, the expression of this anger being through the performative assertion of supremacy of the Indian Constitution, and against the government in power which has, in letter and spirit, eroded its provisions.

The inhabitants of the village of Ghagra told a journalist:

> We wanted to do the Pathalgadi programme peacefully, without confrontation or fighting with anyone. We wanted to erect a stone on the basis of our Adivasi parampara (custom). Our aim is simply to inform people, to educate them about Adivasi customs. Why does the state have a problem with that? Pathalgadi is our culture . . . We want to tell them that this is how our law is. The law for Adivasis is completely different from that for others. And everything should work according to law.[32]

Several leaders of the movement—who include former senior bureaucrats—have been arrested under charges of sedition. The movement faces the full might of state repression. However, a second rung of leadership has emerged and the movement appears to be gaining strength, discussing the setting up of an Adivasi Educational Board, an Adivasi bank, and other such institutions through public meetings held under trees.[33] In 2021, after a lull because of Covid, there has been a resurgence of the movement.[34]

It is telling that the performative act of erecting traditional tombstones to invoke the Constitution and legal provisions as a way of declaring tribal sovereignty over their own lands is declared sedition by the government. Sedition is a colonial-era provision—Section 124A of the Indian Penal Code (1860)—and applies when anybody "by words, either spoken or written, or by signs, or by visible representation, or otherwise, brings or attempts to bring into hatred or contempt, or excites or attempts to excite disaffection towards, the

[32] Iqbal 2018.
[33] Sundar 2018; Tewary 2018.
[34] Saran 2021.

Government established by law."[35] In India, it appears that the current government places its own authority over the authority of the Constitution. So, Pathalgadi is doing more than simply translating local demands into terms the bureaucracy and state can understand. The very enshrining of rights of tribal communities to autonomy in Schedule V of the Constitution is revealing of the tension between on the one hand modern bourgeois individual rights protected by Fundamental Rights and the sovereignty of the Indian state, and on the other community rights based on local beliefs that pre-date colonialism and modernity. As noted earlier, the tension reflects the complex discussions in the Constituent Assembly and the fraught negotiations of that time. Equally significant is the fact that the meaning of the Constitution for Pathalgadi is not that it is secular and modern but that it affirms tribal traditions, culture, and ancestral beliefs and claims.

To reiterate, the Indian Constitution turns out not to be a simple seal of legitimacy on ruling dispensations of caste, class, and gender. As a document that emerged from the anti-colonial struggle *outside*, and from debates *inside* the Constituent Assembly, its vision was never singular. Rather, it became something of a manifesto of a future state of affairs in which an ethos of egalitarianism could be invoked. The invocation of the Constitution in the twenty-first century, then, is not necessarily simply a demand for legal changes but can indicate, rather, alternative visions of democracy in practice that go beyond obeying a government elected every five years.

Constitution-as-Commons versus Populism

The phrase constitution-as-commons comes from a legal scholar, Kalpana Kannabiran.[36] We may productively counterpose it to the label "populist," with which the new (rejected draft) Constitution of Chile

[35] India Code https://www.indiacode.nic.in/show-data?actid=AC_CEN_5_23_00037_186045_1523266765688&orderno=133#:~:text=%2D%2DWhoever%20by%20words%2C%20either,%5Bimprisonment%20for%20life%5D%2C%20to.

[36] Kannabiran 2021.

has been criticised by neoliberal commentators. This could help us understand how and why the constitutionalist path to social transformation appears as a radical one even today. But first, a discussion of the term populism.

It is useful to remember the specific context of the global South. In the North, it was the breakdown of community ties and the normalising of the disengaged, autonomy-seeking, rational subject that led to the rise of the resisting subject—the masses. This divide is not inherent in the global South, where, as Aditya Nigam points out, there is no pejorative charge to populism, or "the people." Most Indian languages use words for "the people" in a positive way. Nigam traces this to the fact that the "widespread breakdown of community and the emergence of the atomised 'mass man' does not constitute the dominant experience in these parts of the world." He suggests that because of the context of nationalist mobilisation under colonial rule, "a different relationship was carved out between the nationalist elites and the common folk, given that the lot of the former was thrown together with that of the latter."[37]

Is the Chilean Constitution reflective of what Chantal Mouffe calls left populism—a "populist moment" arising whenever, due to various kinds of transformations, "the dominant hegemony is being destabilized by the multiplication of unsatisfied demands."[38] She argues that we face such a populist moment globally when we see a variety of resistances to the neoliberal transformations of the last decades; she calls for a "left populism" to grow out of these.[39] Mouffe outlines the modern political regime that is called liberal/constitutional/pluralist democracy as the articulation of *two different traditions*. First, that of *political liberalism*, exemplified by the rule of law, separation of powers, and defence of individual freedom. She does not explicitly note that freedom in this tradition necessarily includes the defence of individual private property. The other, the *democratic* tradition, where the central ideas are equality and popular sovereignty. There is no necessary relationship

[37] Nigam, forthcoming.
[38] Mouffe 2018: 11.
[39] Ibid.: 12.

between the two, Mouffe argues, only a contingent historical articulation.[40]

Nevertheless, she conceives the articulation of these two ultimately irreconcilable traditions positively—as the "locus of a tension" in which the democratic element keeps in check liberalism's "tendency to abstract universalism," while liberalism enables democracy to challenge the "forms of exclusion inherent in the political practices of determining the people that will govern."[41] Mouffe conceives of liberalism as enabling inclusion, and to that extent acting as a check on exclusionary kinds of mass upsurges. However, moving beyond Mouffe, we must remember that the core idea of *liberalism* is the possessive individual in a market society,[42] and it is this core idea that *democracy* addresses and challenges.

This brings us to the assumed distinction between democracy and populism. It seems to me that "democracy" is the term used by the Left, as well as by neoliberal thought, for populations properly disciplined by the institutions of parliamentary democracy, while "populism" refers to the mass public presence of people outside such institutions, sometimes clearly right or left wing; sometimes not clearly identifiable with any one particular political ideology, but coming together around an empty signifier like corruption or economic inequality.

From this launching point I want to ask a question: What is the value of the term populism? Does it not simply indicate the assertion of an uncontrolled *democracy* against *liberalism*? What we have seen globally over the late twentieth century onwards is a hijacking of institutions of liberal democracy by economic, social, and political elites to subvert both the possibility of redistribution and the protection of older collective rights. Indeed, neoliberal regimes have ensured a redistribution of wealth from the poor to the wealthy.[43]

[40] Ibid.: 14.

[41] Ibid.: 15.

[42] This is of course the formative conceptualisation developed by C. B. Macpherson (1962, 1973, 1977, 1985).

[43] Roychoudhuri 2020; Chancel and Piketty 2021.

Mass movements of this century, for which the term populist has been widely used—the Arab Spring, Indignados, Syriza, India Against Corruption, and so on—were all in one way or the other manifestations of a popular pushback against this elite hijack. Given the composition of these movements, they all had the potential both for democratisation as well as a rightward shift. Neither trend was inevitable; and which trend emerged triumphant, depended precisely on the kind of democratic politics that proved decisive.

If we recognise that the pejorative charge of the term "populism" is intended to recover "democracy" as civilised by liberal institutions, we might need to be more suspicious of its usage. The insurgent constitutionalism that I have discussed here may be a way of doing democracy from the Left that challenges, redefines, and questions the assumed link between liberalism and democracy.

This is where we can take seriously, instead, the notion of constitution-as-commons in Kannabiran's phrasing. The supposedly objective analyses by think tanks of the rejection of Chile's first Constitution, drafted through a process of popular participation, claim that "the elected drafting body lacked expertise and political acumen," consisting as it did of "inexperienced independents and leftists."[44] It has been suggested that the next attempt at a draft should include more experienced "experts," and political parties rather than independents. The necessity for a new Constitution not to "undermine the country's reputation among international investors" is seen as an important prerequisite.[45] In other words, everything that has been rejected globally by movements pushing for forms of direct democracy in this century—political parties, experts, the neoliberal order—are to be brought back for any Constitution to "work."

What we are seeing since the first decades of this century is recognition of the failure of representative democracy to in fact represent anything but the ruling elites. However, there is no clear universal

---

[44] Polga-Hecimovich 2022.
[45] Ibid.

alternative yet of the forms that direct democracy can look like. That such forms cannot be "national" or "universal" but would have to take the shape of highly localised and connected networks is one direction that our thinking should take.

In this context, constitution-as-commons is a fruitful direction. Kannabiran outlines the idea as "an insurgency to wrest citizenship from the jaws of enclosure." In her words, "The Indian constitution-as-commons resurrects the moral economy of the constitution and its ethical foundations immersed in empathy ("fraternity"), most evident in the work of B. R. Ambedkar." In a situation of extreme repression and the near-total capitulation of constitutional courts, Kannabiran points out, "The resurgence of collective action in hitherto unknown ways, and the crafting of social capital around the radical public reading of the Constitution (notably the preamble) defines constitutional communities in deeply insurgent ways." This way in which the Constitution enters the streets and universities, which I characterised above as escaping the safe custody of constitutional experts, is noted by Kannabiran too, as the "shift in legitimacy from the formal holders of constitutional power to the multitudes that deliberate on the Constitution (on streets and campuses) and explore/interpret its meanings."[46] The rejection of the draft constitution by the people of Chile is as much an indication of people's claim to ownership of the process of constitutionalism, as is the performance and claim to the Indian Constitution by diverse groups and communities. Unlike the liberal idea that a Constitution is about establishing a minimum framework for engagement with difference, which implies a consensus, the most productive outcome is for a Constitution to retain tensions that reflect the fault lines in a society. A consensus would involve a closure that can render invisible the operation of power, conflict, and heterogeneity in a society. On the other hand, a retaining of tension would enable democratic politics to dance along those fault lines, such that hitherto unimagined futures may be seen gleaming in the distance.

[46] Kannabiran 2021: 233–4.

Citizenship

When the idea of citizenship is wielded like a deadly weapon to deprive people of basic rights rather than to empower them, it's time to think about the basis of justice differently. The people of a land precede the creation of "citizens"—what are the implications of recognising this? The idea of citizenship emerges with modernity and secular-nationalism, claiming to be an empowering move away from feudal, premodern structures of power that marked certain categories of people as undeserving of human dignity through gradations of caste, class, race, and religious identity. The new secular and unmarked identity was supposed to establish equality for every individual. But, as we know, modernity only established new hierarchies and gradations, or justified older inequalities through new forms of knowledge—for instance, racism and sexism have been justified by the use of science rather than religion.[47]

Michael Mann has pointed out that murderous ethnic cleansing is quintessentially modern: it is "the dark side of democracy." Democracy means rule by the people, but in modern times "people" has come to mean not just the masses but also the nation, or a particular ethnic group, or a people that share "a common heritage and culture." What happens, Mann asks, when "people" is defined in ethnic terms, outweighing the diversity that is central to democracy? "If such a people is to rule (in its own nation state), what is to happen to those of a different ethnicity?" Answers to this question, he adds, "have often been unpleasant."[48]

Within this framing, we can reconsider citizenship, generally presented in emancipatory terms, through four questions:

First, are citizenship and citizenship rights unambiguously empowering?

Second, why is citizenship a feminist issue?

---

[47] This scholarship is too well known to be reiterated here. Some of it is discussed in Menon 2004.

[48] Mann 2005: 3.

Third, should citizenship rights be cast within the frame of place of work rather than place of birth?

Fourth, does citizenship have to be devoid of other identities?

Are Citizenship and Citizenship Rights Unambiguously Empowering?

On the contrary, the very idea of "citizen" produces simultaneously, as its shadow, the "non-citizen" in the form of the refugee and the migrant.

The shadow cast by the idea of citizenship has been long recognised. This darkness arises from the location of citizenship rights in the nation-state. As Ranabir Samaddar points out, a nation-state is made up of citizens, but it is the nation-state which defines who its citizens can be. Not everyone who is willing to be a citizen, not all those willing to participate in nationhood, can do so. The rights of citizenship are powerful precisely because they are available only to the community delimited by the discursive practices of the nation-state.[49] The point is that, however inclusivist they may be, citizenship rights within nation-states are necessarily exclusionary. The resources of the nation, it is assumed, should be used for the benefit of citizens, thus creating a zone of privilege for them. As Samaddar points out, the nation-state always has two subjects, the Citizen and the non-Citizen—the latter in the forms of the migrant and the refugee.

The refugee, according to Hannah Arendt, is the paradigm of a new historical consciousness: "Refugees expelled from one country to the next represent the avant-garde of their people."[50] Giorgio Agamben, in an intense reflection on Arendt's essay fifty years later, notes that the appearance of refugees as a mass phenomenon comes into being with the emergence of the modern nation-state system which began to be put into place after World War I. Only a world of sovereign states that had categories of people called "citizens," and that were intent on

[49] Samaddar 1999.
[50] Arendt 1943: 274.

regulating population flows across/s "borders," could produce the legal category of "refugees." The collapse of multi-national, multi-ethnic empires—the Russian, Austro-Hungarian, and Ottoman—and the creation of new ethnically defined states forced minorities to flee, but with few places to go to because of new, increasingly restrictive immigration laws. It was in response to this development that the High Commission of Refugees was formed in 1921, to deal with the enormous problem without impinging on the sovereignty of nation-states. After World War II this became a permanent international institution in the form of the UNHCR.

The UNHCR was clearly limited in the way in which "refugee" was defined by the 1951 Convention Relating to the Status of Refugees: only displaced people on the other side of the territorial border were to be considered refugees, not internally displaced people, and only those who could prove "persecution" by national governments—not those fleeing their countries because of economic hardship, ecological disaster, or famine. The refugee law was also very clearly worded in order not to recognise Palestinians—Israel having been formed in 1948—as refugees. "In the best of cases," writes Agamben, "the status of the refugee is always considered a temporary condition that should lead either to naturalisation or repatriation. A permanent status of man in himself is inconceivable for the law of the nation-state."[51]

If the refugee is a modern phenomenon produced by the emergence of the nation-state system, the migrant represents an age-old phenomenon of movement of populations that has been widespread and common over the globe for several hundreds of years. This movement has been both voluntary—seafaring traders, pastoral nomads, invading armies that end up settling in the lands they conquer; as well as forced—slave trade, indentured labour to run plantations. Thus, what is called "migration" is actually a continuation of natural human flows through the centuries, suddenly rendered illegal by new national borders. Samaddar says that what now need to be called new rights—

[51] Agamben 1995: 117.

such as the right to move across national borders for trade, work, or for grazing animals, for example—are not new privileges but simply the re-legitimation of old practices.[52]

However, once the nation-state system was put firmly in place, such movements themselves came under scrutiny from the new "homelands." From this point onwards, in approximately the early twentieth century, migration began to be closely linked to the issue of the security of nation-states. Migration became no longer simply an issue of demography or labour economics, it was now perceived as an issue concerning a nation's very survival.

The other side of this is that not all immigrants *want* to become citizens in the country where they work. With reference to Bangladeshi workers in India, for example, Samaddar says that "in their own minds they are only temporary shelter seekers since they are still Bangladeshis to their own selves."[53] Migration, thus, is often accompanied by a sense of desolation, loss, and nostalgia.

Across India, Adivasi migrant labourers, for example, travel because they have been driven by the violent appropriation of their *jal*, *jangal*, and *jameen*. Nirmala Putul, an Adivasi poet, writes to "Maya," an Adivasi woman she invokes, who has migrated to Delhi:

दिल्ली	Delhi
नहीं है हम जैसे लोगों के लिए	Is not for us folks.
क्या तुम्हें ऐसा नहीं लगता माया	Don't you sometimes feel Maya
कि वह ऐसा शमशान है जहाँ	That it's the kind of cemetery
जिंदा दफ़न होने के लिए भी लोग लाईन में खड़े है?	Where people line up even to be buried alive?
झारखण्ड की धरती संताल परगना की माटी दुमका के पहाड़ और काठीकुंड के उजड़ते जंगल पुकार रहे हैं तुम्हें	The earth of Jharkhand The mud of Santhal Pargana The hills of Dumka And the ravaged jungles of

---

[52] Samaddar 1999: 40.
[53] Ibid.: 107.

तुम जहाँ भी हो लौट आओ माया!   Kathikund call out to you.
लौट आओ!!   Wherever you are, come
                                 back, Maya! Come back!!

All of this should lead us to question the nation as the space of liberation and emancipation, the natural home of the citizen. Challenging this assumption requires us to recognise that nation-states were formed by and continue through the unceasing, relentless drive to erase heterogeneity. Take Europe, where the birth of nation-states took place. Etienne Balibar points out that the construction of European nations involved the constitution of a "fictive ethnicity" through the nationalisation of cultures, languages, and genealogies with different histories, leading to "permanent rivalry" from the inside.[54] Similarly, Crispin Bates points out that the English believe their own history to be continuous, but the so-called English culture is a mélange of Celtic, Pict, Angle, Saxon, Viking, Norman, Asian, Caribbean, Polish, Italian, Huguenot, French, East European, and of course American cultures. By selecting from this mélange a set of ideas is upheld that somehow enshrines a single "English" identity.[55]

The Indian project of "nation-building" has been similarly beleaguered, whether we consider flashpoints like the North-East and Kashmir, or day-to-day politics among the state units of India's federal polity, which in instances like river-sharing and linguistic reorganisation take on the language of exclusive nationalism vis-à-vis one another. We have no option but to recognise such instances as illustrating the historical impossibility of attaining one kind of final nationhood.[56] The "homelandist imagination" is ever-limiting, and its ties to notions of shared historical culture can only be disempowering for those defined as the Other.[57] For example, in the Indian North-East,

---

[54] Balibar 2004: 8. An analogous historical argument for India has been made in detail by Dalmia 1997 [2010].

[55] Bates 2001: 22.

[56] Menon and Nigam 2014.

[57] Baruah 2005 for the phrase "homelandist imagination."

within struggles for self-determination vis-à-vis the Indian state are present also internecine violence and rival claims to territory between different tribal and religious groups—between Bodos and Muslims, between Manipuris and Nagas.

Another illustration of how nation-state boundaries and citizenship can be disempowering is the story of the enclaves of "Indians" inside Bangladesh and of "Bangladeshis" (formerly East Pakistanis) within India who lived their lives in these enclaves for generations after the partition of the subcontinent in 1947. The enclaves existed because the people living in them were not accommodated by the new maps drawn up at Partition. The states within which they were located turned a blind eye, seeing the enclaves as foreign territory. The people in them lived as virtually illegal entities—registering their school-going children under false certificates because the enclaves themselves had no infrastructure, and because the infrastructure outside their enclaves belonged to the "other" state and its citizens.[58] In 2015 a treaty was signed between India and Bangladesh which enabled the exchange of territory and people, but this generated "split-citizenship" which was expressed, says Anupama Roy, "through idioms of loss and betrayal."[59] Bangladeshi citizens in territory transferred to India were given the option of Indian citizenship. They were considered "new citizens," while those who "returned" to India from Indian enclaves in Bangladesh were considered "returnees." Returnees lost the land they had lived in for generations and struggled to meet the requirements of the new legal requirements to establish claims. The new lives of all of these as "proper citizens" did not turn out to be the romance of "homecoming" that we might imagine.[60]

And now we turn to the next question, arising from the fact that migration as human flows pre-dates nation-states. Given this, we recognise yet another aspect of migration—migration as empowering. This aspect of migration leads us to our second question.

[58] Banerjee, Chaudhury, and Guha 2017.
[59] Roy 2022: 30.
[60] Singh 2020.

Why Is Citizenship a Feminist Issue?

The answer: because citizenship is primarily based on proof of birth in a heterosexual patriarchal family, an institution that structurally undergirds caste, class, and gender injustice.[61]

The structure and ideology of the patriarchal family is best illustrated by the reactions to the growing feminisation of migration flows, both internal and external, and increasing flows of "single" women migrating abroad as independent labourers in search of better lives for themselves and their families.

One response has been to frame such movement in terms of "trafficking." But an intensely destabilising perspective on citizenship and migration is provided by feminist critiques of anti-trafficking initiatives. The notion of "trafficking in persons" has become closely linked to the abolitionist position on sex-work. It has acquired great clout and visibility internationally, with feminists from the first world leading anti-trafficking campaigns. In their definition, trafficking is linked to migration, and understood as "forced migration." Many feminists, on the other hand, are critical of anti-trafficking initiatives, particularly of the US Anti-Trafficking Act 2000. They show how these initiatives collapse the distinction between (voluntary) sex-work and (coerced) trafficking, treating all cross-border movements of women as coerced, thus excluding these women from legal recognition and casting their families as criminals. There is also militant opposition from sex-workers themselves to anti-trafficking policies being promoted by Western and South Asian countries, and some feminists and human rights groups.[62]

The feminist legal scholar and activist Flavia Agnes has suggested a conceptual move away from the notion of a *vulnerable subject* to that of the *risk-taking subject*. She argues that migrants, including those in sex-work, exercise agency and demonstrate decision-making abilities which seek to maximise their own survival as well as the survival of their families. For example, many women negotiate the terms of

[61] Menon 2000a.
[62] Kapur 2005.

their own movement and utilise technological networks to plan their migration and keep in touch with others in their country of origin. Women's perceptions of themselves and of their "exploiters" provide a further challenge to the traditional and stereotypical images of victim and perpetrator. For example, while the dominant image of women in the sex industry is that of subjugated, dominated, objectified, and abused persons who are preyed upon by conniving men, studies of women in the sex-tourism industry in various countries reveal that women view it as an arena of negotiation to improve their own economic situation.

In addition, Agnes points out (as do many other feminists) that the trafficking agenda has come to be increasingly influenced by a conservative sexual morality which casts "good" women as modest, chaste, and innocent. Challenges to this understanding are seen as posing a dual threat—to women themselves and to the security of society. This produces a "protectionist agenda" within which no distinction is drawn between willed and coerced movement. All movement of women is seen as coerced, thus reinforcing assumptions of third world women as infantile victims incapable of decision-making.[63] From this feminist perspective we can see migration not just as loss, but also as empowering, as producing new subjectivities.

But there is yet another layer here—when we consider the phenomenon of migration from the point of view of the transformations within these relocated communities. For instance, Naila Kabeer points to the apparent paradox that while women garment workers in Dhaka enter garment factories and work unveiled, Bangladeshi women in the garment industry in London were almost entirely confined to homeworking.[64] One of Kabeer's main explanations for this is that women in Dhaka came from diverse geographical backgrounds into a relatively anonymous urban setting, while the women in London came mostly from one province, Sylhet, where society is extremely conservative—even by Bangladeshi standards. In London they tended

[63] Agnes 2007.
[64] Kabeer 2001.

to settle in one part of East London because of community networks drawing new migrants into that area of Bangladeshi concentration. This concentration and regrouping of the community is, of course, set within a context of growing racist hostility, leading to the familiar phenomenon of minority communities drawing "their" women "inside." Men, then, work in the factories and the women at home—with the additional labelling of women's labour as unskilled and men's as skilled. Kabeer argues that, by contrast, in Dhaka the processes of globalisation by which garment factory sweatshops get located in countries like Bangladesh empower women who, despite exploitative conditions of work, find their options have increased. She presents a paradoxical picture in which the agency of women can be enhanced by the effects of globalisation in the South, but not necessarily in the North.[65]

Many scholars and activists have suggested that we need a political practice that questions the very legitimacy of the sealed national borders which we have come to take for granted over the last century. National border regimes must be opened up as well as labour markets organised through them. There must be an end to discrimination based on one's nationality: these are the demands of the growing group of *No Borders* activists across the world. A radical political practice is called for—"struggles for a decolonized commons" that challenges the barbed-wire borders of nation-states.[66]

We need to question citizenship by birth also from the perspective of the biological, familial foundation of citizenship outlined at the beginning of this section. This foundation remains unthought and unquestioned in progressivist narratives of citizenship. Compulsory heterosexuality undergirds most forms of identity—caste, race, and community identity are produced through birth. But what we fail to note and criticise adequately is that birth in a particular kind of family also determines the quintessentially modern identity of citizenship. The purity of these identities, of these social formations, and of the

[65] Ibid.
[66] Sharma 2020.

existing regime of property relations is protected by the strict policing and controlling of sexuality, and by the institutions of compulsory heterosexuality. Thus, the family as it exists, the only form in which it is allowed to exist—the heterosexual patriarchal family based on marriage and the sexual division of labour—is key to maintaining nation, state, and community. The imperative need is to restructure institutional and public spaces in a manner that will enable the breaking down of this division of labour as well as the normativity of this particular form of the family.

What then would be the basis of citizenship if the naturalised notion of "birth" is deconstructed in this way? We would be forced to think of alternative sources of citizenship rights—through claims to family ties by heterogeneous and fluid forms of intimacy that refuse to be legible to the state, and, equally importantly, as located in place of labour, not birth.

And this brings us to our third question.

Should We Not Cast Citizenship Rights Within the Frame of Place of Work, Not Place of Birth?

Asking this question brings us up against a possible irreconcilable disagreement between a radical anti-capitalist politics of indigeneity and a politics that values migration of populations. Mahmood Mamdani argues, in the context of Africa, that the notion of citizens' rights as attached to place of birth has increasingly anti-democratic consequences because of the history of large-scale migration on the continent, which means that at any given time hundreds of thousands of people are not living in the land of their birth.[67] They thus have no citizens' rights for the large part of their lifetime. Mamdani rejects the postcolonial assumption that cultural and political boundaries should coincide, and that the natural boundaries of a state are those of a common cultural community. This assumption makes indigeneity the

[67] Mamdani 1992.

litmus test for rights under the postcolonial state. He argues, contrary to nationalist wisdom, that cultural communities rooted in a common past do not necessarily have a common future. Political communities are to be defined, rather, not by a common past but by the resolve to forge a common future "under a single political roof." He believes therefore that citizens' rights should be attached to place of labour, not place of birth.[68]

Consider the overseas supporters of Hindutva politics in India—that is, people of Indian origin who live and work in the USA and UK, and who take advantage of citizenship rights there that protect immigrants and minorities. They publicly celebrate the prime minister of their erstwhile country, publicly observe Hindu festivals, and build Hindu temples. They even try to direct the foreign policy of political parties in the countries in which they live and work: for instance, in 2019, under pressure from the Overseas Friends of the BJP, the UK's Labour Party backtracked on its Kashmir resolution criticising the Indian clampdown on the state of Jammu & Kashmir.[69] Such diasporic Indians demand full citizenship rights for themselves in their country of residence while financially supporting the policies of Hindutva in India—an ideology dedicated to disenfranchising minorities and immigrants in India.

The Indian poet Rahat Indori's famous words in Urdu—*sabhi ka khoon shaamil hai is mitti mein* (the blood of each one of us is mingled in this soil)—indicate, in my reading, not just the shared blood of birth and martyrdom. We can derive a different sense of ownership of "India" from Indori's stirring words. I read *khoon* as used in the common term *khoon pasina*—meaning the blood and sweat of toil. If our blood and sweat is fused with this soil, it far exceeds the mere accident of birth. In other words, we must take seriously the implications of the fact that the Preamble of the Indian Constitution is in the name of *Hum bharat ke log*—We, the people of India, not *Hum bharat ke nagrik*—We the citizens of India. Or, as the South African

---

[68] Ibid.
[69] Wintour 2019.

Constitution puts it, "South Africa belongs to all who live in it, united in our diversity."

How will everyone be looked after if we take this sense of belonging seriously? The resources are not lacking—their distribution is the problem. In Kerala, for instance, the children of immigrants from Bihar and UP get free education and everything else that residents of Kerala get, not just those born in Kerala or those who bear a "Malayali" identity.[70] We have recently learnt that the total income of sixty-three individual Indian citizens was greater than India's annual budget for 2018–19.[71] Where did that income come from? We are made to take it for granted that subsidies for the poor mean vote-bank politics, while subsidies for the rich mean development.

What was the cost of conducting the National Register of Citizens (NRC) in Assam—eventually rejected for being incomplete and faulty by the groups and organisations that had demanded it? The answer is Rs 12.2 billion.[72] A massive and complete waste of public money, especially as the whole operation will now be repeated.[73] In December 2019 the union cabinet sanctioned for the National Population Register Rs 40 billion,[74] an exercise that overlaps with the census and is therefore redundant, but which has the only feature the census does not have—the category "doubtful citizen" which throws the fate of hundreds of thousands into uncertainty.[75] Clearly there is no shortage of resources even in India to ensure state funding for basic human rights for all residents—healthcare, education, food.

But how does a democratic politics of expanded citizenship reconcile the politics of indigeneity with the politics of migration? In India, for example, the protests against the CAA in the North-East are not cast in the Hindu versus non-Hindu frame at all, but in the frame of insider/outsider in ethnic terms. The complex histories of the

[70] Peter, et al. 2020.
[71] Roychoudhuri 2020.
[72] Zahan 2019.
[73] Kalita 2022.
[74] Mohan 2019.
[75] Mohanty 2019.

states of that region come into play here. Evidently citizenship by birth, based on ethnic identity and protection of that identity, is the primary concern there. There are legitimate fears that implementation of the CAA will lead to the local population being overrun by an influx of outsiders—whether the outsiders are Hindu or Muslim is not the issue.[76] Similarly, as discussed earlier, the opening up of Kashmir to non-Kashmiri entrepreneurs has both demographic as well as ecological implications.

New kinds of conversations are possible between those who oppose authoritarian states but are divided on whether access to resources should be based on residence and labour, or else on birth-based identity. Also between those who believe in a borderless world— within which no human being is illegal—and those who want to protect indigenous cultures from outsiders. There will be no single universally applicable framework, only many separate conversations.

Citizenship and "Non-Secular" Identities

My fourth question has to do with religious and ethnic identities in a national space. Dorfman says in the context of Chile that unity and assimilation were the values Chile espoused, and that the assertion of indigenous identities is seen as disruptive to this national ambition. Essentially this means, he says, an "unwillingness to deal with the atrocities of history, and the dispossession of those native Chileans."[77]

We face a similar situation in India. When the attack of Hindutva is directly against non-Hindus, but against Muslims in particular, then Muslims will speak up *as* Muslims—whether Muslims by birth; Muslims by faith; born Muslim but practising atheists; identifying as non-religious but branded as Muslims anyway; or identifying as believing, practising Muslims. Muslims of India are now speaking up as Muslims, as well as citizens, and Indian secularism has reached a new phase. The old Leftist mantra of "leave your identities behind

[76] Gohain 2019.
[77] Dorfman 2022.

when you enter the realm of secular class politics" is worn out, but also expressive of the power of patriarchy, caste privilege, and *savarna* Hindu domination.

After Islamic outfits in Kerala fielded burqa-clad women as the face of the state's protest against the CAA, the CPI(M) warned that "using religious symbols and organising people on a religious basis would only serve to further the agenda of the Sangh Parivar."[78] But Indian secularism has to learn that within its space multiple religious and other identities will now reside and stake a claim. This realisation holds for societies globally. If religious identities are prohibited from entering the public domain, that excludes only practising minorities from being publicly political. The dominant religious identity normalises its own functioning. In secular India, for decades, we have had *bhumi puja* (a Brahminical ritual of worship of the soil) to inaugurate the construction of public buildings, coconuts broken at the start of public functions, and recitations of Sanskrit *shloka*s to Hindu gods in public institutions. We see a similar normalisation of Christianity in European states that call themselves secular. In the face of this we see claims to democratic aspirations and social justice expressed in terms not recognisable to secular modernity, and we need to learn new ways of thinking about them.

This chapter has attempted to show through two kinds of assertions—one that reanimates constitutionalism, and another that fills abstract citizenship with difference—that the framework of secularism has directed our attention elsewhere. Our attention has been drawn away from both older and newer expressions of democracy; from internal contestations, and from claims to justice that remained illegible and illegitimate. Lifting that framework enables a fresh vision which can be critical of both majoritarianism and capitalism—to which we will turn in the last chapter.

[78] Philip 2019. "Sangh Parivar" is the collective noun for the "family of organisations" headed by the RSS and its Hindutva affiliates, including the BJP.

7

Reshaping Worlds—Beyond the
Capitalist Horizon

THIS FINAL CHAPTER continues the task started in the previous one by focusing on the substantive values revealed once
we are no longer distracted by the misdirection performed
by secularism. As argued in this book, and in the previous chapter in
particular, secularism per se is not a value. For secularism is compatible
with democracy, authoritarianism, and majoritarianism; with capitalism and socialism. It is merely a strategy of rule.

This chapter considers different levels of politics around capitalism,
ranging from state policies to handle the ongoing crisis of capitalism,
to state-led and non-state collective ecological strategies—the chapter
moves, that is, from the more practical to the most utopian. Remaining
within the framework of secularism renders invisible the injustice and
violence perpetrated by capitalism because secular regimes and policies,
both socialist and non-socialist, are unproblematically geared to building capitalism as a historically progressive stage.

However, all over the globe the pandemic has sparked some extraordinary reflections—on the future of capitalism and anti-capitalism,
on ecology, democracy, representative government, and collective
action. Many of these point the way to radically different modes of
thought and activism, modes that refuse to recognise "common sense,"
"practicality," and other such sage notions that restrict our imagination. How are we to combine, come together, connect to other stories, find our way to other lanes? How will we find and inhabit those

fissures and chinks in which green things can grow—solidarities, compassion, and hope?

Before discussing ideas that can spark our imagination in these directions, let us critically consider a strategy that has caught on globally, especially during the pandemic lockdown—namely, cash transfers. These range from transfers only to the poor and more vulnerable, to others that conceive of cash transfers to all citizens—the proposition of a Universal Basic Income (UBI).

The Universal Basic Income Debates

For some time now, the argument for cash-income grants has been made by two opposing political tendencies—broadly, Left-wing and neo-liberal economists. But whether from the Left or the Right, both proposals for UBI, as well as critiques of it and of cash-income grants more generally, remain within a horizon in which capitalism appears omnipresent and inescapable. To anticipate my argument here, UBI is necessary and works best in a landscape where the destruction of small-scale artisanal production—and of all links between people and land is complete. UBI intends to draw the entire population into the gaze of the capitalist state. As discussed in Chapter 5, this destruction of links to land is high on the agenda of secular modernity and involves the commodification and desacralisation of land, freeing it from community linkages and rendering it available for capitalist development.

First, let us consider the long history of conservative and libertarian arguments supporting guaranteed—or universal basic—income, arising from the idea that it reduces government interventions in social-welfare schemes. Milton Friedman, in *Capitalism and Freedom* (1962), proposed a guaranteed income which he termed a "negative income tax," and argued for these benefits—reduction of government bureaucracy; the efficiency of free markets in which people vote with cash, as it were; and enabling people to do work that cannot bring in a living wage within a market economy—such as charity and volunteer work.

Friedrich Hayek, the libertarian philosopher, had earlier supported the idea that the state should ensure a minimum income for everyone in a society where state interference would be minimal and the twin pillars of free market and private property would be protected. In the US such a policy, though never implemented, was advocated by political figures as opposed in their ideology as Martin Luther King and Richard Nixon.

The next set of arguments supporting UBI comes from the other side of the political spectrum. Guy Standing, a labour economist and author of *The Precariat: The New Dangerous Class* (2011), is one of the key proponents of UBI from the Left. Standing's conception of the "precariat" includes large sections of the global population—the millions who have simply fallen out of the net of the corporate global capital that has rendered them superfluous to its needs. The precariat, in his understanding, is "a growing mass of people—potentially all of us outside the elite, anchored in their wealth and detachment from society—in situations that can only be described as alienated, anomic, anxious and prone to anger."[1] UBI, in his opinion, redistributes *security*, not *income*.[2]

In India the economist Reetika Khera, who has been active along with Jean Drèze in the Right to Food Campaign, agrees with Guy Standing that UBI grants are desirable, but not at the cost of existing social benefits. Khera argues for a phased implant of UBI, "a sensible way of making UBI affordable. Two existing schemes and entitlements—pensions for the elderly, widows and disabled persons and universal maternity entitlements—can be thought of as a universal basic income for these demographic groups." These two policies "combine universality with targeting: they reach *all* individuals in the most vulnerable population group." Khera points out that "scaling up pensions and maternity entitlements will not displace any existing form of social support." Thus, "Universalising pensions and maternity entitlements

[1] Standing 2011: 24.
[2] Ibid.: 173.

is a rare case of consensus among three otherwise-at-loggerheads constituencies. We have a government that wants to scale up 'direct benefit transfers', economists who favour UBI and civil society groups clamouring for universalising these two forms of cash transfers."[3]

Jean Drèze is strongly in favour of UBI as a policy: "In countries (like Finland) that can afford a generous UBI and also have first-rate public services, it has two attractive features. First, UBI is a foolproof way of safeguarding the right to dignified living. Second, it gives people the option to live without working (or rather, without doing paid work) if they are willing to settle for a simple life. And why not?"[4] But he is suspicious of the pro-UBI propaganda in the business media, seeing "a real danger of UBI becoming a Trojan horse for the dismantling of hard-won entitlements of the underprivileged."[5] He sees the apparent consensus on UBI on the Right and Left as masking deep differences:

> For the left, UBI is part of a comprehensive social security system that would also include universal health care, free education, good public services, some transfers in kind (e.g. school meals) and other forms of social support. For the right, especially in India, UBI is an adjunct of deep cuts in other social programmes such as the Public Distribution System and the National Rural Employment Guarantee Act (NREGA). Some UBI advocates have already made an explicit case for dismantling both.[6]

The third perspective to consider is a Left critique of UBI. Thomas Piketty has strongly argued against UBI and Basic Income Grants—an idea that has achieved consensus across Right and Left in France— saying it "expresses a concept of social justice on the cheap." He argues that a fair and just society must have more ambitious objectives that address "the distribution of income and wealth in its entirety" which would affect "the distribution of access to power and opportunities." The ambition should be to achieve "a fair return to labour, in other words, a fair wage and not simply a basic income."

[3] Khera 2016.
[4] Drèze 2017.
[5] Ibid.
[6] Ibid.

He argues that a progressive property and income tax, greater say for workers in companies, fair wages, and an education system that is less biased against the poor is what we should be fighting for.[7]

However, Pranab Bardhan who strongly supports basic income grants from a "moderate Left" perspective, argues that what may be relevant for France is not necessarily relevant for India. Bardhan supports UBI from the pragmatic point of view that targeted programmes are leaky and inefficient, while UBI can cut through such impediments.[8] The availability of a basic cash income would increase the bargaining power of the poor against traders, middlemen, and landlords. Bardhan is also clear that UBI should not be at the cost of dismantling social security schemes such as the Public Distribution System (PDS) and NREGA.

In effect, Bardhan's response to Piketty is that his arguments against UBI may be relevant for an advanced capitalist country with strong trade union and social democratic traditions, but they do not suit India's specific conditions.

This reduces Piketty's critique of UBI to a question of pure policy choice for different capitalist societies, when the critique in fact gestures towards a realm of alternative politics. Piketty is reasserting, in the face of UBI, a social democratic, trade union politics involving redistribution of wealth (not just income). If Piketty is to be seriously addressed, the response would have to be mounted from a radically different perspective.

A similar Left critique of UBI has been made by the Socialist Party of Great Britain, which believes that UBI would result in an across-the-board decrease in wages, because employers would use it to justify lower wages, and governments to justify cuts in social benefits. The only kind of political struggle envisaged in these Left critiques is trade union bargaining within a familiar capitalist order.[9]

---

[7] Piketty 2016.
[8] Bardhan 2016.
[9] Buick 2008.

Universal Basic Income—
An Anti-Capitalist Critique

It is my argument that Left or Right, support for UBI or critique of the policy, all the arguments so far discussed stay within a framework that assumes both the omnipresence and inescapability of capitalism.

Let us discuss in more detail Guy Standing's argument for UBI, which is the best illustration of this "inescapability" position. Based on the understanding that a large proportion of the world's population has become dispensable for capital, "more decent jobs" is simply not the answer. The precariat is a class-in-the-making, but unless it becomes a class-for-itself with effective agency, the anger and anxiety that lie at its heart could lead to "a politics of inferno."[10] Standing traces the first stirrings of the global precariat to May Day 2001 in Europe, where hundreds of thousands of mostly young people marched to demand free migration and a universal basic income, demands that had little to do with traditional unionism. So Piketty's solution, from Standing's perspective, is simply reiterating a model that has failed.

The UBI is meant to give people the basic security which would take them away from this dangerous direction, make them "work harder and more productively, not less." It will not solve all social ills; but what it will do is provide basic (not total) security and reduce income inequality "while promoting that most precious of objectives, republican freedom, the freedom to be undominated by bureaucrats or figures of autocratic authority."[11] Standing's rationale for the UBI, thus, is predicated on changed requirements of capital that render globally redundant large sections of population. But it is also justified on the grounds that without such security the precariat is dangerous, prone to be drawn to "irrational" right-wing mobilisation. In other words, neoliberalism needs to redistribute some of its super-profits if this precariat is to work "more productively," and not push society towards

---

[10] Standing 2011: vii.
[11] Standing 2015.

"a politics of inferno."[12] Capitalism is thus assumed to be inescapable and omnipresent.

Another well-known proponent of UBI is Kathi Weeks who, in *The Problem with Work* (2011), ties in the idea of UBI with a critique of work itself, which she argues has been culturally overvalued. In a later interview she explains that this ethic of work has undergirded an economic system of wealth for a few who work very little, and "poorly paid and all-consuming waged work for the rest." According to Weeks, "Where a strong work ethic is a key element of productivity, our willingness to call these values and modes of being into question is a potentially effective mode of rebellion."[13] Drawing on Marxist feminist literature on social reproduction, Weeks develops the idea of social reproduction as referring to "all the social, cultural and subjective infrastructures on which the more narrowly conceived structure of production (that is, work covered by the wage) depends, just as a smaller parasite lives by drawing sustenance from the body of a stronger host."[14] Thus, maintaining the two separate spheres of waged work and social reproduction becomes conceptually impossible. Both "work" and "family" have failed as inclusive and sustainable social forms. As Weeks conceives of it, "the political movement for a basic income can be advanced as a way to open conversations about what counts as work, about the value of different kinds of work, and also about what else besides work we might want to do with our time, what other models of care, creativity and cooperation we might want to build."[15]

James Ferguson, another proponent of cash-income grants, studies Basic Income Grants (BIG) programmes in Africa, showing how the focus shifts away from production, so that practices of sharing and dependence are brought into a politics of distribution. In Ferguson's words, BIG payments "can be conceived as rightful shares . . . there is no expectation of a return, no debt, and no shame. *No one is giving anyone*

---

[12] Standing 2011: vii.
[13] Weeks 2016.
[14] Ibid.
[15] Ibid.

anything. One is simply receiving one's own share of one's own property."[16] He thus sees cash-income payments by the state as something citizens are entitled to, not a loan to be repaid or largesse.

While Standing, Weeks, and Ferguson all believe that new forms of solidarities and political utopias will emerge from the guarantee of a basic income, they do not address the fact that the very provision of this income would require capitalism to carry on its (ecologically devastating) business as usual, and all income receivers would become fully legible to the state. That is, receiving a regular income from the government requires one to be inserted fully into the banking system, and for one's financial activities to be fully under the surveillance of the state. Indeed, it has been argued by some on the Left that BIG would help to solve the crisis of falling demand in the capitalist economy, a crisis that can no longer be dealt with by the three methods of stimulating demand that history has seen—war, rise in wages, and high levels of private debt. And as technological progress enables growth in production alongside vanishing jobs, only BIG can ensure that the global economy keeps ticking: "By giving every citizen a monthly cheque, a Basic Income Guarantee will be as fiscally stimulative as World War II without requiring the murder of millions."[17]

Towards Escaping a Capitalist Horizon

With this last critique we move towards an entirely different set of problems with UBI, which can be articulated from a point of view that does not assume capitalism to be inevitable in the way that proponents and opponents of capitalism have both tended to believe. Rather, it is worth reiterating what was stated earlier—that capitalism has to be built painfully with heavy state intervention. This fact was recognised by one of the most articulate and powerful contemporary proponents of capitalism, Hernando de Soto. As noted earlier, de Soto made it his life's mission to understand "why capitalism triumphs in the west and

[16] Ferguson 2015.
[17] Streithorst 2015.

fails everywhere else," and to redress the situation by getting states "everywhere else" to adopt policies that would enable capitalism to triumph.[18]

The thrust of policies such as land rights for women, UBI, and demonetisation in India tie in together as part of larger projects to universalise capitalism.[19] The purpose of all such policies is essentially to transform all forms of collective wealth into individual property; to render all forms of wealth alienable; to convert wealth into a monetary form; and to ensure that all this alienated and monetised wealth is fully visible to, and available to, the state so that it may be mobilised for capitalist investment.

Recovering the subversive potential which lies beyond UBI in the work of Standing, Weeks, and Ferguson would, I suggest, require re-conceptualising the notion of "work" and a rejection of the capitalist horizon altogether. Here we can draw on J. K. Gibson-Graham's insight that capitalism does not encompass all of society, that it is not a complete, closed structure, but that there is an outside to it—multiple non-capitalist practices exist alongside or outside it. Gibson-Graham argues for the need to destabilise the hegemony of "capitalocentrism" that produces the idea that capitalism is inescapable and omnipresent.[20]

Weeks, Ferguson, and Standing all consider "work" as alienated wage labour, hence the attempts to devalorise it. However, I suggest we need a conception of "work" as activity that can be performed by all human and non-humans and retain the term "labour" for waged or unwaged work involving exploitation and alienation. Everything is work that humans and non-humans do, from singing to swimming to grazing to working on a construction site, to thinking. It is "alienated labour" if it does not contain elements of self-creation and involves exploitation. Developing the idea of alienation away from its humanist form in Marx's *Economic and Philosophical Manuscripts of 1844*,

[18] de Soto 2000.
[19] Demonetisation was discussed in chap. 5.
[20] Graham-Gibson 1996.

we could imagine elements of alienation in unwaged labour and moments of non-alienation in otherwise exploitative labour—that is after all how humans survive—the music of slaves, of migrant labour, the creativity involved in cooking, often a compulsory activity for women. Or in teaching, or studying.

The goal would not be to escape *work*, then, but to escape (alienated) *labour*, to encourage and be in solidarity with all the ways in which people's activities escape capitalism, or are invisible to it. The goal would be to be in solidarity with struggles of people to build and protect non-capitalist ways of life, collective rights to land and property of different sorts. All over the global South can be found such communities and pockets, either actively resisting incorporation into the capitalist order or escaping it.

Moving away from UBI as the most system-embedded strategy of change in this chapter, let us consider some other counter-capitalist strategies that are more wilful and strange.

Rewilding

Rewilding is a specific ecological strategy, but I want to use the term also as a metaphor for a conscious political retreat from "civilisation," which is usually counterposed to "wildness." We will return to rewilding as a metaphor in conclusion.

What is rewilding? "Rewilding wants the earth to become self-willed," as Anna Souter puts it in a thoughtful review of Daisy Hildyard's book *The Second Body*.[21] Then she reflects:

> But to *rewild* a place in order for it to become *self-willed* is a strange contradiction in terms. One half of the sentence linguistically contains the dualistic subject–object relationship between human and nonhuman that lies behind the current ecological crisis. The second half of the sentence wants the nonhuman to become the active subject. Are both possible? Perhaps there is a sense of temporality at play here, a feeling that rewilding is an action that unfolds over time, where agency is passed over from human

[21] Souter 2020.

to nonhuman and where the timescale and completeness of that hand-over depends on the specificities of the people and places involved.[22]

At the heart of rewilding is the idea that all life is just—simply—life. Souter quotes Daisy Hildyard: "To be an animal is to be in the possession of a physical body, a body which can eat, drink and sleep; it is also to be integrated within a local ecosystem which overlaps with ecosystems which are larger and further away. To be a living thing is to exist in two bodies."[23] According to the True Nature Foundation, rewilding can be of three kinds:

> *Pleistocene rewilding* entails reintroducing species or descendants of megafauna species from the Pleistocene era, more commonly known as the Ice Age. Rather than the reintroduction of a species that recently disappeared from the area, Pleistocene rewilding potentially involves introducing a completely foreign species to an ecosystem.
> *Passive rewilding* aims to reduce human intervention in ecosystems, giving human cultivated land back to nature, with the goal of restoring natural ecosystem processes and reducing human influence on landscapes.
> *Translocation rewilding* is a more active approach, also involving the reintroduction of species, but the species it focuses on reintroducing are of more recent origin. It seeks to restore missing or dysfunctional processes and ecosystem functions by reintroducing current descendants of lost species.[24]

Serious debates swirl around these ideas that constitute rewilding, but what is clear is that rewilding is not conservation—it is anti-conservation, anti-preservation. However, negotiating in the world as it is requires those who try to rewild, at least at this stage, to build networks with conservation and preservation strategies too. To remind ourselves about the way Souter puts it, "rewilding is an action that unfolds through time."

[22] Ibid.
[23] Hildyard 2017, cited in Souter 2020.
[24] True Nature Foundation, no date.

Pradip Krishen is someone who practises rewilding in India, "a form of small-scale ecological restoration," as he puts it in an article contesting the idea of "compensatory afforestation."[25] "An old forest is a whole lot more than the sum of its trees. How do you recreate a community of plants, fungi, microbes, insects and animals that are all part of a living jungle ecosystem? How many decades might it take? And how do you call into being a soil teeming with micro-organisms and mycorrhiza that inhabit the humus that has taken 30,000 years to build up?"[26] Rewilding initiatives are happening in various parts of India, some initiated by middle-class people with an ecological vision, the cultural capital to embody it, and the capacity to attract funding, but these facts do not necessarily delegitimise what they are achieving.[27] Most such initiatives do involve local communities in the process, people who do not otherwise find a voice or the space to act.

However, the stress laid by the Indian state on introducing individual species rather than rebuilding ecosystems has been criticised as misconceived. One such well-discussed and thoroughly criticised move is the introduction of African cheetahs to Madhya Pradesh in 2022. The wildlife biologist and Director of the Centre for Wildlife Studies, Ullas Karanth, for example, says "rewilding is not about unthinkingly dumping wild (caught or captive bred) animals in an ad hoc manner. Species go extinct because of impacts and threats. These could be social [human and livestock density], cultural [hunting practices], and ecological [size and quality of available habitat]. If these threats have not been addressed, rewilding is unlikely to work."[28]

Alongside these, though, we must take on board living Adivasi and global indigenous people's practices that preserve the biodiversity threatened, and often destroyed, by predatory capital in partnership with the state. An eighteen-part series by various authors on Adivasis and the Indian state in *Firstpost* discusses the multiple aspects of the

---

[25] Krishen 2018.
[26] Ibid.
[27] Cotta, et al. 2022; Adlakha 2021.
[28] Adlakha 2021.

crisis for Adivasi lives, beliefs, and practices from rampant industri-alisation. Many of them reiterate the norms of collective living that characterised these communities, and their passion to protect *jal, jangal, aur jameen,* and show how both capitalist incursion and bour-geois environmentalism have dispossessed Adivasis of resources they have protected for millennia.[29] Of course there is resistance too, and the Pathalgadi movement which claims sanction from the Consti-tution is but one example of Adivasi militancy to protect their com-mon lands and collective ways of functioning.[30]

Conflict Between Dalit and Ecological Concerns?

As consistently shown throughout this book, heterogeneity is central to any democratic imagination, and we must consider seriously the fissures between different visions of justice that could be allies.

At one level there is an immediate conflict between Dalit and eco-logical concerns, which arises from valorising pre-industrial forms of social organisation—and which can for Dalits only mean the violence of a brutal caste system that has confined them to the most humiliating and filthy work. "Traditional livelihoods" for Dalits does not mean what it means for Adivasis, or for caste-Hindu landowning castes. Brahminical discourse has thus been central to the way envi-ronmental discourse has come to be structured in India.

One kind of response, therefore, has been by proponents of Dalit capitalism and Dalit entrepreneurship, such as Chandrabhan Prasad.[31] He is among the contemporary heirs of an earlier moment of B. R. Ambedkar's thought on machinery and technology. Ambedkar's 1945 text *Gandhism* reflects the understanding of the European Enlighten-ment that "the distinctively human function is reason, the purpose of which is to enable man to observe, meditate, cogitate, study and

---

[29] *Firstpost* 2019.
[30] The Pathalgadi movement is discussed in chap. 6.
[31] Prasad 2018.

discover the beauties of the universe . . . and control the animal elements in his life." Ambedkar goes on to add, "Man thus occupies the highest place in the scheme of animate existence," and says, *contra* Gandhi, that "the slogan of a democratic society must be machinery, and more machinery."[32] Gandhi's celebration of manual labour (voluntary for *savarnas*), cannot of course be shared by Ambedkar who knows what coerced manual labour means for his people.

However, there appears to be a radical shift in Ambedkar's thought from this high-modernist and anthropocentric instrumentalising of nature, especially after his conversion to Buddhism. According to V. M. Ravi Kumar, Ambedkar offers us in his last text, *The Buddha and His Dhamma* (1957), an "egalitarian environmentalism." For Ambedkar, says Kumar, "a biotic world does not have any superior and inferior qualities"; he quotes Ambedkar—"all individual things are analogues to one another and therefore, no one can be regarded as the final sources to any other." Ravi Kumar draws a direct link between Ambedkarian Buddhism (or Neo-Buddhism) and a perspective of ecological justice, for Neo-Buddhism proposes an organic relationship with all living forms. Ambedkar, says Ravi Kumar, invoked the Buddha to reflect upon this aspect: "Love is not enough; what is required is Maitri. It is wider than love. It means fellowship not merely with human beings but with all living beings." Thus, Ambedkar proposes what Ravi Kumar calls "a self emphatic and reflexive ethical code for human beings while engaging with other species, meaning he was not satisfied with the dominant anthropocentric conception of the world but prefers an inclusive bio-ecological centric world wherein all species have equal rights for their existence."[33]

This later development in Ambedkar's thought suggests that his views on technology and its relationship to nature were reshaped by a Buddhist perception of the interrelatedness of all things in the universe, even as he retained a socialist/Marxist critique of the deeply

[32] Ambedkar 1945.
[33] Kumar 2014.

iniquitous Brahminical caste order. The contours of the conflict between ecological consciousness and Dalit claims to justice are outlined by Mukul Sharma, who concludes his study of the struggles, myths, and memories of various Dalit communities by arguing that a Dalit environmentalism alive to caste oppression is very possible and in fact exists.[34]

Life Itself—The Virus and the Human

What the Covid pandemic has taught us is that we can no longer continue to think of life as "human" life alone, counterposing it hierarchically to all other forms of life as being (mere) "nature." Human life is a part of nature, and conversely the virus is life too.

One of the most informative and insightful essays on the roots and ramifications of the pandemic emerged in China by the Chuang Collective.[35] In this argument, because capitalist production relates to the non-human world "at a more fundamental level" two things follow:

(a)   the "natural world," including its microbiological substrata, cannot be understood without reference to how society organises production, because the two are not separate.

(b)   the only communism worth the name is one that includes the potential of a fully politicised naturalism.

The first point leads to the assertion that "the basic logic of capital helps to take previously isolated or harmless viral strains and place them in hyper-competitive environments that favor the specific traits which cause epidemics," such as "rapid viral lifecycles, the capacity for zoonotic jumping between carrier species, and the capacity to quickly evolve new transmission vectors." Analysing different kinds of virus

[34] Sharma 2017.

[35] Chuang Collective 2020. Chuang is "a collective of communists who consider the 'China question' to be of central relevance to the contradictions of the world's economic system and the potentials for its overcoming": https://chuangcn.org/journal/one/a-thousand-li/.

behaviour, the essay points out that any virus developing more virulent strains could have the effect of a rapid extinction of itself, since killing the host sooner provides less time for the virus to spread. Consider the virus that causes the common cold, which by generally maintaining low levels of intensity facilitates its own widespread distribution through the population. But in certain environments, goes the essay, the opposite logic makes more sense: "when a virus has numerous hosts of the same species in close proximity, and especially when these hosts may already have shortened life cycles, increased virulence becomes an evolutionary advantage."[36]

I read this analysis of different kinds of virus action as a reminder that viruses have "agency" (drawing on the work of Bruno Latour) and the will to survive—just as much as humans have. For the virus, then, the human is but a means to an end, just as for capitalism nature is but a means to an end.

However, the second point—about communism requiring a "fully politicised naturalism"—seems to be limited by an orthodox Marxist frame. The essay uses the term just that once and does not explain it further. So, one is left to interpret it in the way in which that term is usually used. Naturalism is generally understood to mean a philosophy that sees nature as explicable by science, thus rejecting supernatural or spiritual explanations for natural phenomena. So it seems the Chuang Collective understands nature as fully comprehensible in the terms set by science, and "politicised naturalism" would then be a rejection of capitalism on a secular and scientific basis. But this would require a rejection of all knowledge systems that do not conform to "Science"—including the "supernatural" and the "spiritual."

Perhaps at this point in the history of the earth these distinctions and hierarchies cannot and should not be sustained? After all, we are coming to understand how the earth and its biodiversity have been protected for millennia by practices and beliefs that cannot be contained within the framework of secularism and science. This book has attempted to bring together scholarship that asks such questions;

---

[36] Chuang Collective 2020.

and there are of course many important works relevant to the discussions in the present book.[37]

I would, however, like to pick up on the first idea, which I have chosen to read, inspired by Bruno Latour, as the "agency" of the virus. Latour has argued that the nature/culture divide is the founding mythology of modern thought. Latour and Michel Callon, who have collaborated extensively, are noted for their development of Actor Network Theory, in which they suggest that scientific theory emerges out of complex actor-networks in which the human and the non-human participate equally—the latter including everything from laboratory equipment to the object of study. This last aspect of their understanding is often misunderstood. "Agency," as I understand them to be implying here, suggests that humanity is not the only force in the universe that functions with purpose.[38]

In an essay in the context of the pandemic, Latour reiterates this understanding. He says we have been forced to come to "the sudden and painful realisation that the classical definition of society—humans among themselves—makes no sense." He restates his well-known argument that the state of society "depends at every moment on the associations between many actors, most of whom do not have human forms." There are, for example, microbes, but also associations of other non-human actors—the internet, the law, the organisation of hospitals, the logistics of the state, and the climate. In the "state of war" against the virus, Latour reminds us, the virus "is only one link in a chain where the management of stocks of masks or tests, the regulation of property rights, civic habits, gestures of solidarity, count . . . [equally] in defining the degree of virulence of the infectious agent." Thus, once the entire network, of which the virus is only one link, is taken into account, the same virus "does not act in the same way in Taiwan, Singapore, New York, or Paris." The pandemic is no more a

[37] To offer three examples: a volume on indigenous belief systems and practices— Venkateswar and Hughes 2011; an essay on eco-religion in Jharkhand—Borde 2017; and an essay on how Indigenous peoples, though themselves endangered, protect the earth's biodiversity—Raygorodetsky 2018.

[38] Callon and Latour 1992.

"natural" phenomenon than the famines of the past or the current climate crisis. Society, says Latour, "has long since moved beyond the narrow confines of the social sphere."[39]

However, Latour does not explicitly take into account hierarchies of power. Humans are not a homogeneous mass. There are those who run the world, and then there are those who evade, resist, or go with the flow of how the world is run. The language of war and counterinsurgency that permeates the discourse of states around the virus is testimony to the fact that nothing has been learnt by those in power. What is missing in Latour's analysis is an identification of the precise tendency that has led us to this pass. Joshua Clover points out that "Ecological despoliation is a consequence not of *humans*, as the name 'Anthropocene' and Latour's essay suggest, but of industrial production and its handmaidens . . ." He insists that capital, with its "inescapable drive to reproduce itself," is not merely one actor in a network, equivalent to other actors, but in a sense the director and producer of this script: "The compulsion to produce, and to produce at a lower cost than competitors, in turn compels the burning of cheap and dirty fuels to drive the factories, to move the container ships, even to draw forth from the ground the material components of green energy sources."[40]

The Problems with "Green Energy"

This last point Clover makes about the "material components of green energy" has been at the centre of a huge controversy among Left ecologists. A 2019 film by Jeff Gibbs, produced by Michael Moore, *Planet of the Humans*, claims that green energy (wind, solar power, biomass) cannot solve the problem of climate change because

(a) the components required for these (for example, for solar panels), are materials like quartz that have to be mined in the same ecologically damaging ways, thus creating new mining threats for biodiversity.[41] Biomass energy requires deforestation (and

[39] Latour 2020.
[40] Clover 2020.

turning of food-crop farming into crops that can be used to produce energy).

(b) that since sunshine and wind are intermittent, these forms of energy require fossil fuel backup, and so green energy is not in fact replacing fossil fuels.

(c) that green forms of transport like electric cars still tap into conventional electricity grids run by fossil fuels.

The film also argues that capitalism has taken on green-energy production as its latest profit-making enterprise. Although the film has been severely attacked for this claim (among others), this argument is not a new or startling one. In India, green energy is the domain of powerful industry players like Tata and Adani.[42] It is also fast becoming a "hotspot for renewable energy investors" from around the world.[43] This is in fact true everywhere. Barbara Harris-White and Elinor Harris have argued in the context of the UK that "the politics of renewable energy is enmeshed in the interests of capital."[44]

The film, having torn down green-energy claims to controlling climate change, offers no alternatives but concludes with a Malthusian pronouncement about the urgent need for population control. It has come under tremendous attack from climate-change activists for feeding oil and gas company claims against renewable energy. The film is charged by climate change activists with presenting old data to bolster its argument, saying that clean technology has made huge advances in the decade the film took to be completed, but the filmmaker denies his data is dated.[45]

Amidst this controversy, the film was taken down by YouTube on a copyright violation claim by a photographer whose clip was used in the film, and who is severely critical of the film. This looks like censorship by other means because the clip has been duly credited. The photographer claims violation of fair use only because he

[41] Also see Sonter, et al. 2020.
[42] ETEnergyworld 2019.
[43] Sinha 2020.
[44] Harris-White and Harris 2007.
[45] Gibbs 2020.

does not agree with the use of his clip in the context of the argument of the film, which he rejects.[46]

Without getting into the details of the controversy, or the quality of the film qua film, I would like to address what I see as the key question it raises. We can set aside the population control argument as specious because it is not the poor masses that consume energy but the "top 10 percent of the global income spectrum that consumes 20 times as much final energy as the bottom 10 per cent."[47] Which is not to ignore the fact that over the past 200 years across the globe, both life expectancy and population numbers in general have increased, and even a marginal increase in energy consumption by the bottom 20 or 30 percent will mean a further heavy toll on the environment. But "population control" appears to want to address the consumption of the rich by controlling the population of the poor.

The troubling and important question the film raises really is this – is green energy simply becoming part of the discourse of "sustainable development" which, as Thomas Lemke has pointed out, is central to "the government of new domains of regulation and intervention"? Nature in this understanding is the "environment" of the capitalist system, and needs to be protected for that reason: "In an age of 'sustainable development', previously untapped areas are being opened in the interests of capitalisation and chances for commercial exploitation. Nature and life itself are being drawn into the economic discourse of efficient 'resource management'."[48] Or, as Arturo Escobar puts it, "the key to the survival of the rainforest is seen as lying in the genes of the species, the usefulness of which could be released for profit through genetic engineering and biotechnology in the production of commercially valuable products, such as pharmaceuticals. Capital thus develops a conservationist tendency, significantly different from its usual reckless, destructive form."[49]

---

[46] Whitlock 2020.
[47] Roberts 2020.
[48] Lemke 2002: 55.
[49] Cited in ibid.: 56.

The key idea here is "regulation"—the environment is to be regulated in the interests of long-term extraction. Within this perspective, even renewable sources of energy are envisaged as being the means to ensure endless production and consumption. A characteristic statement illustrating this perspective is Barack Obama's Inaugural Address after his first election, in which he declared poetically, "We will harness the sun and the winds and the soil." To what end? "To fuel our cars and run our factories."[50] These words convey no sense of the fact that assumptions about consumption, urbanisation, and endless growth have to be urgently and drastically rethought.

Bolivia's *Law of Mother Earth and Integral Development for Living Well* (2010),[51] which establishes eleven "rights" of Mother Earth – including the right to life, biodiversity, pure water, clean air, and freedom from genetic modification and contamination—is potentially revolutionary. Who is to protect these rights, though? If local communities were the guarantors of these rights, that would mean a significant break from the nation-state paradigm. However, this law too appears to be designed to enable the state to facilitate resource extraction and industrial development while keeping "Mother Earth" viable. Vice-President Alvaro Garcia Linera stated at the law's promulgation ceremony: "If we have to extract some mineral, we have to extract it, but finding equilibrium between the satisfaction of needs and protecting Mother Earth." Critics say that the law may essentially help to legitimise the government's neo-extractivist economic model.[52]

Adrienne Buller, author of *The Value of a Whale: On the Illusions of Green Capitalism* (2022), suggests that as outright climate-science denial has become untenable within a private-sector strategy, "green capitalism" has come to the rescue. Increasingly, climate change is "being recognised as a branding opportunity by oil majors and financial firms, and to address it as such is proving a much smarter strategy than to

[50] Obama 2009.
[51] Bolivia 2010.
[52] Achtenberg 2012.

deny or outright ignore it."[53] What's worse, green capitalism continues to promote "renewable" energy that actually requires large inputs of non-renewable resources, as Jeff Gibbs' film claims. Let us consider two more illustrations of this before moving on.

Across Central Europe, ancient forests are being cut down, ground to sawdust and formed into pellets to be shipped across Western Europe, thus helping the region's countries reach their renewable-power commitments. This process is completely legal and encouraged by green-energy government subsidies. Pellets were initially meant to be made out of waste sawdust and wood chips. Because of the subsidies, wood pellets are now Europe's largest renewable energy source, far ahead of wind and solar. But as demand has soared, and Russia's war against Ukraine has created an energy crunch, entire forests are being cut down to make these pellets.[54]

In a study of solar energy in India, Nandita Badami points out some disturbing features of the construction of solar-energy parks, features that are worth considering for an understanding of how green capitalism—aided by the state, of course—works:

(a) They involve land acquisition on a massive scale, often by classifying agricultural land as "waste land," "unproductive land," or "fallow land," terms that are merely listed in policy documents with no further description or explanation in order for them to be "ostensibly returned to productivity/modern regimes of value."[55] This classification, taken from zone notification documents, says Badami, "betrays a peculiar vision of solar technologies as deployed not in environments, but on surfaces that do not qualify as environments."[56]

(b) Solar Zones are granted the "most glaring of exemptions" within Environmental Impact Assessments, this being in the name of "efficiency and easing the flow of investment." Badami

[53] Buller 2022.
[54] Hurtes and Cai 2022.
[55] Badami 2021: 126.
[56] Ibid.: 143.

points out that the assumption in several policy documents in relation to solar energy seems to be that solar technologies, being "environmental" technologies, have no environmental impact.[57]

(c) Referring to a particular solar-energy project in Pavagada, Karnataka, Badami points out that the area has experienced extreme droughts, which was in fact a major factor in the decision to set up solar farms there. The same reasoning lies behind "the logic of picking sites for 94% of the currently installed solar capacity in India."[58] However, the operation of solar technologies requires large quantities of water to clean the surfaces of panels from "dust, bird shit and other kinds of particulate matter that serve to block sunlight and reduce the efficiency of energy production." Panels spread across nearly 10,000 acres of land demand huge amounts of water. Badami cites reports saying each megawatt worth of panels requires anywhere between 7000 and 20,000 litres of water per wash.[59] Pavagada currently produces 2050 megawatts of electricity. This means it needs anywhere between 14,354,000 and 41,000,000 litres of water each time it is washed. Optimal plant operations require at least two if not more full washes a year. As Badami points out, "for an area that is already killing livestock from a lack of access to water, this is an unthinkable quantity to be extracting from bore wells."[60]

Decentralising solar energy is a more sustainable way to go—that is, instead of facilitating capitalist profits from massive centralised grids, with all the problems outlined above, it would be better to facilitate solar energy at the household level, with government subsidies if necessary. This alternative would still require non-renewable resources like water, but in much reduced quantities and at a much

[57] Ibid.: 142–3.
[58] Gaddam 2015, cited in Badami 2021: 145.
[59] Ibid.
[60] Ibid.: 146.

smaller and decentralised level. This is the direction in which a movement espousing "Degrowth" would take us.

The much-talked-about Green New Deal, espoused by Left-of-Centre forces in the global North, calls for a reduction of dependence of their economies on fossil fuels, and the curbing of greenhouse gas emissions. It also aims to guarantee new high-paying jobs in clean energy industries.[61] But is this too simply a way of keeping capitalist production alive and well? "Degrowth" argues it is. Green Energy without a rejection of the capitalist imperative of perpetual economic growth is meaningless.

Degrowth, the Pandemic, and Radical Change

Degrowth philosophy rejects GDP as an indicator of economic well-being and proposes a framework for transformation to a lower and sustainable level of production and consumption, "a shrinking of the economic system to leave more space for human co-operation and ecosystems." Degrowth calls for

shrinking the economy

downscaling production and consumption in a way that increases human well-being and enhances ecological conditions and equity on the planet

focus on sufficiency not efficiency

innovation not just to take technology to higher levels (I-Phone Level n!) but to build new social and technical arrangements that will enable us to live convivially and frugally.

Degrowth calls for a future where societies live within their ecological means, with "open, localised economies and resources more equally distributed through new forms of democratic institutions."[62]

In the context of the pandemic, the Degrowth movement has made it clear that moving towards a low-energy society remains the

[61] Sierra Club: no date.
[62] Degrowth: no date.

only way to avoid climate catastrophe. Thus, its advocates are in conversation with Green Energy proponents, but they insist that while wind and solar power, depending on where they are sited, can be among the "lowest-impact" and "lowest-carbon" forms of energy, Green Energy cannot be a substitute for Degrowth:

> "lowest-impact" is far from "low impact," and lower carbon is nowhere near "zero carbon." Nor, as we have seen, is it realistic to expect such forms of energy to replace current fossil fuel use, and certainly not in the time necessary to prevent the most disastrous effects of climate change. Moving towards a low-energy society remains the only path for avoiding a climate catastrophe.[63]

In the specific context of the pandemic, Degrowth proponents make a distinction between the slowdown of economic activity due to the pandemic and the "societal transformation" Degrowth is struggling for: "the crisis shows the failure of the current political-economic system and its inadequacies in dealing with such crises in a humane and just way." Degrowth by contrast offers "a more resilient, just, and sustainable alternative way of organising society." Overall, though, the movement is hopeful that the pandemic crisis has highlighted the potential for a Degrowth transformation: "States are planning, regulating and being challenged, communities are creating mutual support networks, and individuals are radically adjusting their way of living."[64]

Food and Land Sovereignty

Any attempt to deal with the ecological crisis only in centralised ways at the level of nation-states is bound to fail. Equally important are the secessions into decentralised but interconnected local ways of life, a replenishing of the commons, and absolute rejection of the idea of growth. Such a retreat might require state facilitation, at least for a start. That would not be a passive apolitical act but rather a deeply

[63] Ernsting 2015.
[64] Hepp, et al. 2020.

political blowback against the continuing violence of corporate capital and the state systems that sustain it.

The two ideas of food sovereignty and land sovereignty, connect with rewilding and Degrowth to create a tapestry of linked practices that could escape, even triumph over, capitalism's dreary concrete, like the pipal tree which secures its roots in high-rise building walls, threatening to split them open as it pushes deeper; or like the weeds that spring up in the cracks of grey pavements.

Food sovereignty is a radical alternative to "food security," which refers only to the availability of food. Food sovereignty, on the other hand, as defined by the Nyeleni Declaration of 2007, is "the right of peoples to healthy and culturally appropriate food produced through ecologically sound and sustainable methods, and their right to define their own food and agriculture systems. It puts the aspirations and needs of those who produce, distribute and consume food at the heart of food systems and policies rather than the demands of markets and corporations."[65] Food sovereignty includes subsistence farming but is not limited to it, for everyone cannot grow their own food. In addition therefore, it is based on

- sharing sustainable and organic food production methods;
- organising to sell food collectively for fair prices;
- protecting biodiversity and genetic resources within ecosystems;
- lowering costs while improving the quality and quantity of yields;
- educating their governments to put smallholder farmers' interests before those of multinational corporations.

La Via Campesina, made up of 200 million family farmers, peasants, landless people, rural workers, indigenous people, rural youth, and rural women is a food-sovereignty network with a significant presence in Latin America, South Asia, South East Asia, Africa, Europe, and North America.[66] South Africa, too, has a strong food-

[65] Nyeleni Declaration 2007.
[66] La Via Campesina: no date.

sovereignty campaign.[67] In the University of Witswatersrand in Johannesburg a fledgling food-sovereignty initiative by faculty and students has started planting vegetables and fruit trees on campus, the idea being that, gradually, the campus can become self-sufficient in food and prevent hunger on the campus.[68] India too has a growing food-sovereignty movement which began in 2013.[69]

J. Devika has made some concrete suggestions for food sovereignty in the context of Kerala, albeit she conceives of it (in this particular essay) as state-led.[70] The state government should encourage farming through measures such as

- Offering migrant workers small patches of land, to farm vegetables and tubers for their own consumption, leased out by the government, with any excess production reaching the market
- Addressing the environmental concerns of the fisherfolk, and their demand for a ban on middlemen in selling the catch
- Urban and semi-urban homes should be made to have a mandatory food patch of vegetables that require little space and tending, and those that don't have land should be helped with terrace gardening
- All urban buildings and houses should be made to plant a minimum number of fruit trees including a coconut tree around them
- There should be a total ban on the felling of all fruit trees—from the larger ones such as the jackfruit and mango, to the smaller ones such as the guava and bird cherry
- All tourist resorts, hotels, and other such institutions where food is prepared and served should be required to devote a certain portion of their land to farming their own food.

These are all key moves towards food sovereignty in which Devika envisages the state as a facilitator.

[67] SAFSC: no date.
[68] Satgar and Cherry 2019.
[69] Food Sovereignty Alliance India, no date.
[70] Devika 2020.

However, the idea of food sovereignty is intimately linked to land sovereignty that goes beyond "land reforms"—the limitations of which we saw in Chapter 5—and partnership with the state. Land sovereignty involves democratic control of land and the (re)occupation of lands that have been removed from the commons and relocated in the speculative market. Massive peasant movements of land reclamation have been going on across Africa, Asia, and South America since the late 1990s.[71] We may recollect in this context the (re)occupation of the Muthanga Forest in Kerala by Adivasis.

Commoning

A related idea is "commoning." As David Bollier and Silke Helfrich put it, commoning is not a utopian fantasy—"Commoning is everywhere but widely misunderstood." In their words:

> Our capacity to self-organize to address needs, independent of the state or market, can be seen in community forests, co-operatively run farms and fisheries, open source design and manufacturing communities with global reach . . . The elemental human impulse . . . to help others, to improve existing practices, ripens into a stable social form with countless variations: a commons.
>
> The impulse to common plays out in the most varied circumstances—impoverished urban neighbourhoods, landscapes hit by natural disasters, subsistence farms in the heart of Africa, social networks that come together in cyberspace.[72]

The commons is about more than just sharing, say Bollier and Helfrich. "It is about sharing *and* bringing into being durable social systems for producing shareable things and activities."[73] For example, as universities are increasingly privatised and inaccessible—especially with the accelerated thrust towards online education post-Covid—we could think of how to bring about durable social systems for a knowledge commons free of both state and the market. We did see across

---

[71] Moyo and Yeros 2005.
[72] Bollier and Helfrich 2019: 15.
[73] Ibid.

India, in the face of the terrible state-created tragedy of millions of migrant workers stranded far from their homes, the spontaneous emergence of non-state, non-market networks of a kind of commons of resources, food, and solidarity.

Pirate Care

One recognition from the Covid-19 lockdown globally is the value of care-work and the enormous burden it places on women. Morse and Anderson have termed it "the shadow pandemic, which is rapidly unraveling the limited, but precious, progress that the world has made toward gender equality in the past few decades."[74] Degrowth feminists have issued a statement calling for a recognition of care-work as work, and "an end to the subalternisation of reproduction in service to the realm of production." The social organisation of labour and care-work needs to be democratically rebuilt. The realm of public welfare "that has been so depleted by decades of neoliberalism, austerity, structural adjustment, and the privatisation of education and healthcare" needs to be reconstructed. Above all, our economies that are in the grip of "the growth paradigm founded in heteropatriarchal capitalist principles" must be led towards emancipation.[75]

The feminist Degrowth response is one within an efflorescence of thinking around this core feminist idea of the value and marginalisation of care-work.[76]

Let us now consider a rather subversive take on care-work, "Pirate Care." This is a conceptual intervention that tries to map activism "at the intersection of care and piracy," in a world in which

> downloading scientific articles faces 35 years in jail; where people risk charges for bringing contraceptives to those who otherwise couldn't get them. Folks are getting in trouble for giving food to the poor, medicine to the sick, water to the thirsty, shelter to the homeless . . . These practices

[74] Morse and Anderson 2020.
[75] Feminist Degrowth: no date.
[76] Patel and Goelnitz 2020; Tuckey 2020; Toynbee 2020; Lewis 2020.

are experimenting with self-organisation, alternative approaches to social reproduction and the commoning of tools, technologies and knowledges. Often they act disobediently in expressed non-compliance with laws, regulations and executive orders that criminalise the duty of care by imposing exclusions along the lines of class, gender, race or territory.[77]

This is an initiative drawing on the experience in Europe, but in India too, during the crisis created by the pandemic lockdown for migrant labour, those who tried to help them reach home—thus putting capital into crisis—faced punishment of different kinds from the government.[78]

Care-work, in civil disobedience of oppressive laws, is Pirate Care, which, along with Rewilding, can be understood as a withdrawal from civilisations built by and for capitalism.

Escaping the Rulers

James Scott points out two inconvenient facts about the emancipatory and empowering narrative about states-and-citizens. Historically, most of the populations in the early states had to be coerced into being in them, they were subjects under duress. Second, "it was very common for state subjects to run away. Living within the state meant . . . taxes, conscription, corvée labour, and for most, a condition of servitude; these conditions were at the core of the state's strategic and military advantages."[79] In light of the narrative I have offered here, I conclude that it is a mistake to see *all* forms of political activity as "making demands on the state" or as an assertion of the rights of citizenship. Radical political activity also lies in evading and escaping the state, as well as imposed order, offers of largesse, and the codification inherent in citizenship.

It might be productive to see some ways of doing politics as *escaping governmentality* rather than being *objects of governmentality*

---

[77] Pirate Care Syllabus 2020; Pirate Care Project, no date.
[78] This crisis is discussed in detail in chap. 5.
[79] Scott 2010: 7.

(through making demands of the state). And not necessarily only through conscious political acts, but also simply through myriad everyday practices—from "public" and visible acts such as squatting on public land, to "private" and invisible acts such as same-sex love that do not seek to be recognised by the state—continuously, unself-consciously, embodying breached boundaries and unrespected limits.

For instance, in Japan young people are quietly dropping off the consumerist map—not buying cars, not consuming alcohol, voluntarily living simple lives. Norihiro Kato says it's a "new sort of maturity." Japan does not have to be No. 1 or 2, "we're okay with small," they seem to be saying. Japan, he says, is at "the vanguard of a new downsizing movement," remembering what it is to "be old, to be quiet, to turn inward."[80]

In China, the "lying flat youth" movement threatens the state's programme of unrestricted growth—young people opting out of the rat race, doing the bare minimum, not working hard to earn money to spend on consumer goods, refusing to put in the long hours and hard work that gives them only a pittance in any case. The movement is inspired by an internet post (now removed by China's censors), called "lying flat is justice," in which a user called Kind-Hearted Traveller refers to Greek philosophers while celebrating "not working" for two years, living on a basic income, and two meals a day. "Since there has never really been a trend of thought that exalts human subjectivity in this land, I can create it for myself. Lying down is my wise man movement," the person wrote.

In a survey by the Chinese microblogging site Weibo, conducted between 28 May and 3 June 2021, 61 percent of the 241,000 participants said they want to embrace the lying flat (*tang ping*) attitude. So great is the threat from the movement to China's growth economy and the labour it requires that state authorities are anxious. President Xi Jinping himself has condemned it, and state-run media have launched campaigns against the movement. Social media chat groups

---

[80] Kato 2010.

which discuss how to participate have been blocked. Lying flat is both a form of protest by young people against exploitation of their labour as well as an alternative vision of how to live a good life.[81]

I differentiate this kind of everyday insurgence from the massive popular upsurges in the first decade of the twenty-first century—which happened from the Arab world to Africa and South Asia to Iran and Wall Street—over issues ranging from corruption to sexual violence to secularism to patriarchal controls to financial probity; all seeking not to "capture" political power but rather to make it accountable and answerable to "the people." In one sense these upsurges are varying assertions of citizenship, but they are producing a very subversive understanding of democracy and citizenship and are no longer participating in the old twentieth-century model of democracy.

The features of this twentieth-century model are concisely captured by Timothy Mitchell as involving first, the organising of mass democracy by the separation of "professional politicians, authorized and regulated through political parties" from ordinary citizens who delegated to the former their role in decision-making. Second, from the mid-twentieth century, democratic politics has been further regulated by the interventions of "techno-scientific experts," specialists in the fields of science, technology, management, law, and economic planning.[82] Mass upsurges across the globe in the first decades of the twenty-first century reveal that "the people" have had enough of representative democracy and the "expertise" of "specialists." People's representatives (politicians) and political parties are utterly delegitimised, with their hijack of institutions noted; simultaneously, the opinions of technical experts are frontally challenged by many movements, for example in the resistance to nuclear-energy plants.[83] These mass protests and movements stake a claim to directly determine state policy,

[81] AP News 2021; Siqi, et al. 2021.

[82] Mitchell 2011: 240–1.

[83] Fossil fuels are accepted as being "dirty," but nuclear energy is claimed to be "clean, safe and cheap." These claims have been contested strongly by the anti-nuclear energy movement (Leman 2022) and at the beginning of the twenty-first century,

laws, and so on, and it is in this sense that they are no longer participating in the twentieth-century understanding of democracy and citizenship.

This is the context in which I suggest we need to note three simultaneous developments in these first decades of the current century. Two of them are well known—first, that states and supra-state corporations continue to spin the fine webbing of governmentality wider and deeper; second, more and more assertively, challenges are being posed to states in new and unrecognisable languages of politics.

But perhaps we need to be alert also to a third phenomenon, that is, the powerful pull by different groups of people and individuals *away* from states—from their largesse and their surveillance. Some instances of this deliberate "pulling away" have been discussed all through this book. Such pulling away can happen within states or at borderlands. To use Samaddar's words, it is always a struggle for the state and its institutions to produce pure citizens out of recalcitrant people.[84] A radical political agenda must recognise which side to take in this struggle. This is the tendency of pulling away from being "seen" by the state.[85] It is a self-marginalising move away from citizenship as well as a valuable act of self-construction by individuals and groups.

From the perspective that this book offers, the state and the traditional community are both equally problematic from the point of view of the values listed at the beginning of the previous chapter—

---

been proved to be false. See Urvashi Sarkar for a quick recap of the state of the global nuclear power industry today, eleven years after the Fukushima disaster (Sarkar 2023). Protests over nuclear-energy plants continue throughout the world. In India, the protests against a nuclear plant at Kudankulam in Tamil Nadu (2011 onwards), raising concerns of the local people about harmful effluents, suspected radiation, and the storage of nuclear waste, as well as the effect of the plant on marine life and fisher people's livelihood, have been met with massive repression by the Indian state (Chandrababu 2022). A new nuclear plant is planned at Jaitapur in Maharashtra with French collaboration and assistance, with claims to being the world's most powerful nuclear power plant. Protests against it are building up.

[84] Samaddar 1999: 107.

[85] Scott 1999.

democracy, ecological justice, and social justice. New forms of collectives have to emerge—and have emerged globally—that resist both and are alert to hierarchies of gender, class, ethnicity, caste, race. We have discussed some instances in this book, all of which are non-violent even as they are militant; but we cannot conclude without a quick reference to the valiant autonomous zones of the Zapatistas and Rojava, both of which have military and armed aspects as well as radical democratic politics that respects heterogeneity. These legendary, long-lived experiments have been much written about and therefore I merely refer to them here.

Utopia, the "Outside," and Solidarity

In conclusion, then, if our struggle is to recover knowledges buried by history, to subvert existing knowledge formations, and to generate new knowledges out of local histories and practices, we cannot be training ourselves merely to enter existing fields of settled knowledge that have emerged from the history and location of the global North. Here it is instructive to consider critically a text generally accepted to be an illustration of radical pedagogy, *The Ignorant Schoolmaster* (1987) by the French philosopher Jacques Rancière, which from the perspective of the global South seems curiously innocent about the drive of assimilative power. In what follows I compare it to Paulo Freire's model of subversive pedagogy which sees knowledge as dynamic and unsettled.

In his text Rancière writes about Joseph Jacotot, a schoolteacher driven into exile during the period of monarchical restoration in France in the early nineteenth century. Jacotot developed a method of showing illiterate parents how they themselves could teach their children to read. Landing up with a job in a Flemish-speaking part of Belgium, he had to teach children who spoke no French, while he spoke no Flemish. He tried an experiment with a recently published bilingual (French and Flemish) edition of Homer: he asked his students, through an interpreter, to learn on their own the French text with the help of the

Flemish translation. After a time he asked them to write about the text in French and was astonished to find they could do so as well as French students would have done. He had not taught them the elements of French, neither spelling nor grammar. The students had looked for the French words that corresponded to words they knew in Flemish and figured out the grammar by themselves.

Jacotot's experience shows us, says Rancière, that the pedagogical problem is "to reveal an intelligence to itself."[86] Anything can be used— a song, a prayer that the student knows by heart, a calendar—there is always something the student knows that can be used as a point of comparison. The teacher's two fundamental tasks, then, are *interrogation*—he demands speech, the manifestation of an intelligence that was not aware of itself; and *verification*, that the work is done with attention.[87] Anyone is capable of grasping the most difficult of ideas since the same intelligence is at work in all human endeavour.

Now, while this is the kind of radical pedagogy in which we can immediately see the progressive potential, it seems to me that it addresses only one kind of knowledge and one kind of learning. That is, its radicalism lies in using one's own intelligence rather than that of a teacher to enter into an existing body of knowledge, with its own established rules, "to learn how to do x." But what if one thinks of knowledges as having to be subverted, of existing knowledges as embodying dominant discourses of power, of knowledges as constituting the subjects of governmentality in Foucauldian terms? Then the point would not be to learn the rules well, but also to subvert them, to constitute new bodies of knowledge and counter-selves.

For instance, Rancière does not consider the politics of the gradual marginalisation of Flemish by the French nation-state in the making, so that it would always be Flemish speakers having to learn French rather than vice versa. He does not consider the ways in which modernity in general introduced standardised forms of organising time and space (maps, calendars) that did considerable violence to the

[86] Rancière 1991: 28.
[87] Ibid.: 29.

peasant knowledges it was still replacing in Jacotot's time. Thus, Rancière says that the locksmith who does not know the alphabet can look at a calendar—"Doesn't he know the order of the months and can't he thus figure out January, February, March . . . He knows that February has only 28 days. He sees that one column is shorter than the others and he will recognize '28'."[88] However, the Gregorian calendar that Rancière takes for granted has nothing to do with the natural cycles by which peasants live, and illiterate people have to learn to read the calendar as much as they have to learn the alphabet; it is not a knowledge that is inborn or naturally imbibed in all worlds and contexts even in the twenty-first century.

This way of learning appears, then, to be about learning to enter and negotiate existing formations of knowledge. From the perspective of the global South, such education would amount to learning to negotiate worlds of already produced knowledge emanating from the powerful parts of the world. It would amount to learning how to do x, where x remains uninterrogated and its status as knowledge unquestioned.

The reason Jacotot's method requires no teacher, or the "ignorant teacher," is that education is seen as learning to do in a new language what you already know in another. You don't see beyond or question the world you are given, you learn to negotiate it. The calendar can teach you numbers and the alphabet only if you are already immersed in a world marked by these things. Rancière thus fails to question how some knowledges attain the status of *knowledge*, while other knowledges are discarded.

The scholar-activist Paolo Freire, in *Pedagogy of the Oppressed* (1972), offers a different view of knowledge and learning. In "problem-posing education," as he calls it, no one teaches anyone else, but nor is anyone self-taught. Through dialogue, the teacher-of-students and students-of-the-teacher cease to exist and the teacher-student and students-teachers emerge—they become jointly responsible for a

---

[88] Ibid.: 28.

process in which they all grow.[89] Thus this model gives up on the idea of the all-knowing teacher, but not on the idea of a teacher altogether. It seems to me that the "teacher" in this understanding is the entry of *the outside* into one's world, destabilising its codes of meaning, common sense, and order. In this sense, the students are the outside of the teacher's world, and she of theirs. The teacher knows ten things her students do not know, but they know ten things she doesn't—as Freire finds when he plays a game with the peasant group he is visiting, in which they ask him ten questions (What's soil liming? What's green fertilizer?) and he asks them ten (What's an intransitive verb? What's epistemology?).[90] In problem-posing education everybody is a student-teacher, people are in the process of *becoming*, "unfinished beings in and with a likewise unfinished reality," thus necessitating that education be an ongoing activity, an activity that asks us to "consider reality critically."[91]

This idea of the "outside" is inspired both by J. K. Graham-Gibson's work which rejects capitalocentric frameworks that refuse to see there is a lived outside to capitalism; and by the idea of "border thinking" first used by Gloria Anzaldúa and subsequently developed by decolonial thinkers, most prominently Walter Mignolo. The term indicates already existing theories that are located at the very borders of the colonial matrix of power—as their outside. As Mignolo puts it, "border thinking implies dwelling in the border, not crossing borders." He sees border thinking as much in the American philosopher W. E. B. Du Bois and his idea of "double consciousness" as in Fanon and his double relationship to the colour of his skin (not realising from within that he is Black, but being recognised as Black from outside). Decolonial border thinking, says Mignolo, involves "epistemic disobedience" towards normative, Eurocentric frameworks of knowledge.[92] I would

[89] Freire 1972: 80.

[90] Freire 1994: 46–7.

[91] Freire 1972: 56–7. I am aware of readings of Freire's pedagogy as being paternalist, but I find them unconvincing.

[92] Mignolo 2017.

use the idea of the outside to indicate multiple and shifting borders even inside decolonial thinking. This is the heterogeneity that democracy needs to value.

If we were to own up to seeking Utopia, as the Chilean Constitution did, that Utopia would simultaneously embody a promise and negate it. We can but hope for moments of Utopia—those moments that dismantle settled knowledge and set up unprecedented conversations; conversations which permit the outside to enter and transform them, and which enter the outside to transform it.

And finally—solidarity. In light of all of the above, we are faced with a fresh set of questions on solidarity. What kind of creative thought is possible, what kind of transformative action—globally, locally; as individuals, as communities, as collectives? How will we deal with the fractures amongst ourselves that have since emerged, in constructive ways that do not further empower authoritarian states, and in India the projects of Hindu supremacy and predatory capitalism? How do we foreground and reject privilege, how do we talk to one another while building solidarity? How do we respect difference of opinion among ourselves, both substantively on understanding of issues and on political strategy (when to escalate, when not to do so), recognising that mistakes can be made, and that positions can change?

I have ended with questions that will I hope begin new chapters.

Bibliography

Achtenberg, Emily. 2012. "Earth First? Bolivia's Mother Earth Law Meets the Neo-Extractivist Economy," *NACLA*, 16 November, https://nacla.org/blog/2012/11/16/earth-first-bolivia%25E2%2580%2599s-mother-earth-law-meets-neo-extractivist-economy.

Adlakha, Nidhi. 2021. "Rewilding India," *The Hindu*, 4 June, https://www.thehindu.com/sci-tech/energy-and-environment/rewilding-indias-landscapes-and-cities/article34725675.ece.

Agamben, Giorgio. 1995. "We Refugees," *Symposium*, no. 49 (2), 117.

Agarwal, Bina. 1994. *A Field of One's Own: Gender and Land Rights in South Asia*, Cambridge: Cambridge University Press.

Agarwal, Bina. 2005. "Landmark Step to Gender Equality," *The Hindu*, 25 September, http://www.thehindu.com/thehindu/mag/2005/09/25/stories/2005092500050100.htm.

Agarwal, Poonam. 2022. "More Transparency Needed on Malfunctioning EVMs," *Deccan Herald*, 1 July, https://www.deccanherald.com/opinion/more-transparency-needed-on-malfunctioning-evms-1122973.html.

Agnes, Flavia. 1999. *Law and Gender Equality. The Politics of Women's Rights in India*, Delhi: Oxford University Press.

Agnes, Flavia. 2007. "The Bar Dancer and the Trafficked Migrant Globalisation and Subaltern Existence," *Refugee Watch*, 30 December, issue no. 30.

Agnes, Flavia. 2016. "The Debate on Triple Talaq and Muslim Women's Rights is Missing Out on Some Crucial Facts," *Scroll*, 25 May, https://scroll.in/article/808588/the-debate-on-triple-talaq-and-muslim-womens-rights-is-missing-out-on-some-crucial-facts.

Agnihotri, Aradhya. 2016. "Madhya Pradesh Towns Where Ravana is Worshipped and His Death is Mourned," *Times of India*, 9 October.

Ahmed, Hilal. 2013. "Secularising the 'Secular': Monumentalisation of the Taj Mahal in Postcolonial India," *Economic & Political Weekly*, 14 December, vol. 48, no. 50.

Ahsan, Sofi. 2021. "Don't Send Notices to Parents of Couples Under Special Marriage Act: Delhi Government," *Indian Express*, 16 December, https://indianexpress.com/article/cities/delhi/no-notices-parents-cou ples-special-marriage-act-delhi-7675184/.

AIR. 1995. 2089, https://main.sci.gov.in/jonew/judis/10725.pdf.

Akhtar, Salman, ed. 2005. *Freud Along the Ganges*, New York: Other Press.

Al Jazeera News. 2019. "Pools in France Close After Women Defy Burkini Ban," *Al Jazeera*, 27 June, https://www.aljazeera.com/news/2019/6/27/ pools-in-france-close-after-women-defy-burkini-ban#:~:text=Ban ning%20burkinis&text=France%20%E2%80%93%20the%20coun try%20with%20Europe%27s,in%20public%20spaces%20in%20 2011.&text=The%20European%20Court%20of%20Human,face%20 veils%20breached%20religious%20freedom.

Alam, Muzaffar. 2004. "Shari'a, Akhlaq and Governance," in *The Languages of Political Islam in India, c.1200–1800*, Delhi: Permanent Black.

Alcoff, Linda Martin, and John D. Caputo. 2011. *Feminism, Sexuality and the Return of Religion*, Bloomington: Indiana University Press.

Alone, Y. S. 2022. "Shiva: Not a God of the Subaltern Communities," *Outlook*, 22 October, https://www.outlookindia.com/national/ shiva-not-a-god-of-the-subaltern-communities-magazine-231239.

Alouane, Rim-Sarah. 2019. "Islam, Made in France? Debating the Reform of Muslim Organizations and Foreign Funding for Religion," *Brookings*, 1 May, https://www.brookings.edu/blog/order-from-chaos/2019/ 05/01/islam-made-in-france-debating-the-reform-of-muslim-organi zations-and-foreign-funding-for-religion/.

Aluri, Ramachandra. 2017 "The Cow is Not Our Mother, Hindutva Means Nothing to Us: A Devout and 'Proud' Malayali Hindu," *Sabrang*, 7 April, https://www.sabrangindia.in/content-authors/ramachandra-al uri.

Alvarez, Sonia E. 2014. "Introduction to the Project and the Volume/Enacting a Translocal Feminist Politics of Translation," in Sonia E. Alvarez, Claudia de Lima Costa, Vernoica Feliu, Rebecca Hester, Norma Klahn, and Millie Thayer, eds., *Translocalities/Translocalidades: Feminist Politics of Translation in the Latin/a Américas,* Durham: Duke University Press, 1–18.

Ambedkar, B. R. 1936. *The Annihilation of Caste*, https://ccnmtl.columbia .edu/projects/mmt/ambedkar/web/readings/aoc_print_2004.pdf.

Ambedkar, B. R. 1945. "Gandhism," https://www.roundtableindia.co.in/ gandhism-the-doom-for-untouchables/.

Ambedkar, B. R. 1946. *The Riddle of the Shudras*, https://www.ambed karitetoday.com/2019/10/who-were-shudras-the-riddle-of-shudras .html.

Ambedkar, B. R. 1987. *Revolution and Counter Revolution in Ancient India*, http://drambedkar.co.in/wp-content/uploads/books/category1/6revo lutionandcounterrevolution.pdf

Ameerudheen, T. A. 2018. "In Sabarimala Temple's Shadow, a Kerala Mosque Stands Witness to a Long History of Communal Amity," https://scroll .in/article/899503/in-sabarimala-temples-shadow-a-kerala-mosque-stands-witness-to-a-long-history-of-communal-amity.

Ameerudheen, T. A. 2019. "Gender Justice Activist and a Devout Hindu: Meet the Women Who Made History by Entering Sabarimala," *Scroll*, 2 January, https://scroll.in/article/907934/gender-justice-activist-and-a-devout-hindu-meet-the-women-who-made-history-by-entering-sabarimala.

Ameerudheen, T. A. 2021. "Land Agitation, Gothra Maha Sabha & C. K. Janu's Party: What's in Store for Adivasi Politics in Kerala," *On Manorama*, 3 March, https://www.onmanorama.com/news/kerala/2021/03/02/ adivasi-politics-gothra-mahasabha-ck-janu-kk-surendran-interview .html.

Anderson, Michael, and Sumit Guha, eds. 1998. *Changing Concepts of Rights and Justice in South Asia*, Delhi: Oxford University Press.

Anshuman, Kumar. 2022. "States Free to Legislate on Uniform Civil Code: Law Minister Kiren Rijiju," *The Economic Times*, 23 July, https://eco nomictimes.indiatimes.com/news/india/no-decision-taken-as-of-now-on-implementing-uniform-civil-code-as-matter-is-sub-judice-govt-in-lok-sabha/articleshow/93059966.cms.

AP News. 2021. "Why China's Youth are 'Lying Flat' in Protest of Their Bleak Economic Prospects," 9 June, https://apnews.com/article/china-business-health-coronavirus-pandemic-09d95bf3d7ae4db394103c7be517cfb8.

Arendt, Hannah. 1943. "We Refugees," in idem, *The Jewish Writings*, ed. Jerome Kohn and Ron H. Feldman, New York: Schocken, 2007.

Arnold, David, and Stuart Blackburn. 2004. *Telling Lives in India: Biography, Autobiography, and Life History*, Delhi: Permanent Black.

Asad, Talal. 1993. *Genealogies of Religion: Discipline and Reasons of Power in Christianity and Islam*, Baltimore: Johns Hopkins University Press.

Asad, Talal. 2003. *Formations of the Secular: Christianity, Islam, Modernity*, Stanford, CA: Stanford University Press.

Aswal, Abhay. 2016. "Duryodhana Temple: A Revered Deity or a Cruel Villain?" https://www.euttarakhand.com/duryodhana-temple#respond.

Ataman, Joseph, and Tara Subramaniam. 2022. "French Court Confirms Ban on 'Burkinis' in City's Swimming Pools," *CNN*, 21 June, https://edition.cnn.com/2022/06/21/europe/grenoble-france-burkini-ban-pools-upheld-intl/index.html.

Austin, Granville. 1999. *Working a Democratic Constitution. The Indian Experience*, Delhi: Oxford University Press.

Awaya, Toshie, and Kazuo Tomozawa, eds. 2022. *Inclusive Development in South Asia*, London: Routledge.

Badami, Nandita. 2021. "Shadows for Sunlight: Epistemic Experiments with Solar Energy in India," unpublished Ph.D thesis, University of California Irvine, https://escholarship.org/uc/item/9pb3d8d5.

Balibar, Étienne. 2004. *We the People of Europe?* Princeton: Princeton University Press.

Baloyi, Lesiba, and Mogobe Bernard Ramose. 2016. "Psychology and Psychotherapy Redefined from the Viewpoint of the African Experience," *Alternation*, Special Edition, vol. 18, 12–35.

Banaji, J. 2020. "Appendix: Islam and Capitalism," in *A Brief History of Commercial Capitalism*, Chicago: Haymarket Books.

Banerjee, Abhishek. 2021. "How the 'Dismantling Global Hindutva' Conference in the US Dehumanises Hindus Everywhere," *News18*, August 23. https://www.news18.com/news/opinion/how-the-dismantling-global-hindutva-conference-in-the-us-dehumanises-hindus-everywhere-4116956.html.

Banerjee, Sriparna, Anasua Basu Ray Chaudhury, and Ambalika Guha. 2017. "The 2015 India-Bangladesh Land Boundary Agreement: Identifying Constraints and Exploring Possibilities in Cooch Behar," *Observer Research Foundation*, 13 July, https://www.orfonline.org/research/the-2015-india-bangladesh-land-boundary-agreement-identifying-constraints-and-exploring-possibilities-in-cooch-behar/#_edn59.

Bardhan, Pranab. 2016. "On Piketty's Arguments Against Basic Income: How Applicable Are They to India?" *The Wire*, 17 December, https://thewire.in/87605/piketty-bardhan-basic-income-india/.

Barnwal, Amrita. 2019. "Know 10 Different Ways of Celebrating Dussehra in Various Indian States," 29 August 29, https://www.easemytrip.com/blog/unique-dussehra-celebration-in-various-indian-states.

Baruah, Sanjib. 2005. "Nations Within Nation-states," *Hindustan Times*, 13 October.

Basu, A., N. Sarkar-Roy, and P. P. Majumder. 2016. "Genomic Reconstruction of the History of Extant Populations of India Reveals Five Distinct Ancestral Components and a Complex Structure," *Proceedings of the National Academy of Sciences of the United States of America*, February, vol. 113 (6), 1594–9.

Basu, Anustup. 2020. *Hindutva as Political Monotheism*, Durham: Duke University Press.

Bates, Crispin. 2001. "Introduction: Community and Identity among South Asians in Diaspora," in idem, ed., *Community, Empire and Migration South Asians in Diaspora*, London: Palgrave.

Bauman, Chad M. 2008. "Postcolonial Anxiety and Anti-Conversion Sentiment in the Report of the Christian Missionary Activities Enquiry Committee," *International Journal of Hindu Studies*, vol. 12.2, 181–213, https://digitalcommons.butler.edu/cgi/viewcontent.cgi?article=1108& context=facsch_papers.

Baxi, Upendra. 1995. "Emancipation as Justice," in Upendra Baxi and Bhikhu Parikh, eds., *Crisis and Change in Contemporary India*, Delhi: Sage Publications.

Baxi, Upendra. 2000. "Constitutionalism as a Site of State Formative Practices," *Cardozo Law Review*, February, vol. 21, no. 4.

Beckwith, Christopher I. 2009. *Empires of the Silk Road: A History of Central Eurasia from the Bronze Age to the Present*, Princeton: Princeton University Press.

Behrens, K. Y. 2004. "A Multifaceted View of the Concept of Amae: Reconsidering the Indigenous Japanese Concept of Relatedness," *Human Development*, January–February, vol. 4, 1–27.

Bell, Carole Concha. 2022. "Chile's Progressive New Constitution Rejected by Voters After Campaign Marred by Misinformation," *The Conversation*, 13 September, https://theconversation.com/chiles-pro gressive-new-constitution-rejected-by-voters-after-campaign-marred-by-misinformation-190371.

Benslama, Fethi. 2006. "Islam and Psychoanalysis: A Tale of Mutual Ignorance," *Qantara*, https://en.qantara.de/content/islam-and-psychoanal ysis-a-tale-of-mutual-ignorance.

Bernal, Martin. 1987. *Black Athena: The Afroasiatic Roots of Classical Civilization*, vol. 1, New Brunswick: Rutgers University Press.

Bernal, Martin. 2005. *Black Athena Writes Back: Martin Bernal Responds to His Critics*, ed. David Chioni Moore, Durham: Duke University Press.

Berreman, Gerald Duane. 1963. *Hindus of the Himalayas*, Berkeley: University of California Press.

Berruz, Stephanie Rivera. 2018. "Latin American Feminism," *Stanford Encyclopedia of Philosophy*, https://plato.stanford.edu/entries/feminism-latin-america/#PoliTranLoca.

Betros, Gemma. 2010. "The French Revolution and the Catholic Church," *History Review*, December, issue 68, https://web.archive.org/web/20160413110005/http://www.historytoday.com/gemma-betros/french-revolution-and-catholic-church.

Bhagat, Ram B. 2003. "Cencus [*sic*] and the Construction of Communalism in India," *Economic and Political Weekly*, 24–30 November, vol. 36, no. 46/47, 4352–6.

Bhargava, Rajeev. 1998. "What is Secularism For?," in idem, ed., *Secularism and Its Critics*, Delhi: Oxford University Press.

Bharti, Kanwal. 2016. "'Holi: Ek Mithakiya Adhyayan" (Hindi), *Streekal*, 25 March, https://streekaal.com/2016/03/festivals-holi-mythology/.

Bharucha, Rustom. 1993. *The Question of Faith*, Delhi: Orient Longman.

Bharucha, Rustom. 1998. *In the Name of the Secular. Contemporary Cultural Activism in India*, Delhi: Oxford University Press.

Bhaskar, Utpal. 2021. "SPV for Sethusamudram Project to be Wound Up," *Mint*, 16 March, https://www.livemint.com/news/india/spv-for-sethusamudram-project-to-be-wound-up-11615834213074.html.

Bhatia, Gautam. 2015. "'Essential Religious Practices' and the Rajasthan High Court's Santhara Judgment: Tracking the History of a Phrase," *Indian Constitutional Law and Philosophy*, 19 August, https://indconlawphil.wordpress.com/2015/08/19/essential-religious-practices-and-the-rajasthan-high-courts-santhara-judgment-tracking-the-history-of-a-phrase/.

Bhatia, Gautam. 2019. *The Transformative Constitution. A Radical Biography in Nine Acts*, Delhi: HarperCollins Publishers.

Bhatia, Gautam. 2022a. "The Essential Religious Practices Test and the Inversion of Agency: Notes from the Hijab Hearing," *Indian Constitutional Law and Philosophy*, 9 February, https://indconlawphil.wordpress.com/2022/02/09/the-essential-religious-practices-test-and-the-inversion-of-agency-notes-from-the-hijab-hearing/.

Bhatia, Gautam. 2022b. "Discipline or Freedom: The Supreme Court's Split Verdict in the Hijab Case," *Indian Constitutional Law and Philosophy*, 13 October, https://indconlawphil.wordpress.com/2022/10/13/discipline-or-freedom-the-supreme-courts-split-verdict-in-the-hijab-case/.

Bhattacharya, Abhik. 2022. "Conversion to Buddhism: Rejection of Hinduism Was Ambedkar's Choice, Nothing Less But Much More," *Outlook*, 18 October, https://www.outlookindia.com/national/conversion-to-buddhism-rejection-of-hinduism-was-ambedkar-choice-nothing-less-but-much-more-news-230394.

Bhattacharyya, Krishna Chandra. 1931/1954. "Swaraj in Ideas," *Visvabharati Quarterly*, vol. 20, 103–14, https://multiversityindia.org/wp-content/uploads/2009/12/Swaraj-in-Ideas.pdf.

Bhattacharya, Neeladri. 2018. *The Great Agrarian Conquest. The Colonial Reshaping of a Rural World*, Ranikhet: Permanent Black.

Bhavishya Purana. No Date. http://hinduonline.co/Scriptures/Puranas/BhavishyaPurana.html.

Bhushan, Nalini, and Jay L. Garfield, eds. 2011. *Indian Philosophy in English. From Renaissance to Independence*, Delhi: Oxford University Press.

Bhushan, Prashant. 2019. "Current Threats to the Constitution," *The Wire*, https://thewire.in/law/current-threats-to-the-constitution-prashant-bhushan.

Bidwai, Praful. 2007. "Spineless Secular Government Retreats When Fundamentalists Invoke Mythology," *The News International*, 22 September.

Birla, Ritu. 2009. *Stages of Capital: Law, Culture, and Market Governance in Late Colonial India*, Durham: Duke University Press.

Biswas, Atreyi. 1971. *The Political History of the Hū]nas in India*, Delhi: Munshiram Manoharlal Publishers.

Blowers, Geoffrey H. 2004. "Bingham Dai, Adolf Storfer, and the Tentative Beginnings of Psychoanalytic Culture in China: 1935–1941," *Psychoanalysis and History*, vol. 6 (1), 93–105.

Blowers, Geoffrey H., and Serena Yang Hsueh Chi. 1997. "Freud's Deshi: The Coming of Psychoanalysis to Japan," *Journal of the History of the Behavioral Sciences*, Spring, vol. 33 (2), 115–26.

Boehmer, Elleke. 2005. *Stories of Women: Gender and Narrative in the Postcolonial Nation*, Manchester: Manchester University Press.

Boer, Roland. 2018. "Religion and Capitalism," *Culture Matters*, 19 February 19, https://www.culturematters.org.uk/index.php/culture/religion/item/2738-religion-and-capitalism.

Bolivia. 2010. "The Mother Earth Law and Integral Development to Live Well, Law No. 300," https://www.climate-laws.org/geographies/bolivia/laws/the-mother-earth-law-and-integral-development-to-live-well-law-no-300#:~:text=The%20Mother%20Earth%20Law%20is,the%20country's%20majority%20indigenous%20population.

Bollier, David, and Silke Helfrich. 2019. *Free, Fair and Alive: The Insurgent Power of the Commons*, Gabriola Island, Canada: New Society Publishers.

Borde, Radhika. 2017. "The Sarna Movement in Jharkhand," in Sajal Nag, ed., *Force of Nature: Essays on History and Politics of Environment*, Delhi: Routledge.

Bower, Bruce. 2004. "The Japanese Social Concept of Amae Goes Global," https://dornsife.usc.edu/assets/sites/782/docs/beg_your_indulgence_science_news_online__june_26__2004.pdf.

Braidotti, Rosi. 2008. "In Spite of the Times. The Postsecular Turn in Feminism," *Theory, Culture and Society*, vol. 25, no. 6, 1–24.

Brar, Kamaldeep Singh. 2019. "RSS and Sikhs: Defining a Religion, and How Their relationship Has Evolved," *The Indian Express*, 18 October, https://indianexpress.com/article/explained/rss-and-sikhs-defining-a-religion-and-how-their-relationship-has-evolved-6075272/.

Brass, Paul R. 2003. *The Production of Hindu–Muslim Violence in Contemporary India*, New Delhi: Oxford University Press.

Brennan Center for Justice. 2022. "Roe v. Wade and Supreme Court Abortion Cases," 28 September, https://www.brennancenter.org/our-work/research-reports/roe-v-wade-and-supreme-court-abortion-cases#:~:text=In%20Roe%20v.,on%20the%20stage%20of%20pregnancy.

Bronkhorst, Johannes. 2016. *How the Brahmins Won. From Alexander to the Guptas*, Leiden, Boston: Brill.

Buick, Adam. 2008. "Basic Income: A Dangerous Reform," http://www.worldsocialism.org/spgb/socialist-standard/2000s/2008/no-1243-march-2008/basic-income-dangerous-reform.

Buller, Adrienne. 2022. "Green Capitalism is a Scam: A Conversation with Adrienne Buller," Interview with Cal Turner, Sara Van Horn, *Los Angeles Review of Books*, 27 October, https://lareviewofbooks.org/article/green-capitalism-is-a-scam-a-conversation-with-adrienne-buller/.

Callon, Michel, and Bruno Latour. 1992. "Don't Throw the Baby Out With the Bath School! A Reply to Collins and Yearley," in A. Pickering, ed. *Science as Practice and Culture*, Chicago: University of Chicago Press.

Campanella, Emanuela. 2016. "People Share Photos of Nuns on the Beach in Response to Burkini Ban in France," *Global News*, 25 August, https://globalnews.ca/news/2903036/people-share-photos-of-nuns-on-the-beach-in-response-to-burkini-ban-in-france/.

Carroll, Michael. 2009. "The Psychoanalytic Study of Myth Since Freud," in Jacob A. Belzen, ed., *Changing the Scientific Study of Religion: Beyond Freud?* Berlin and Heidelberg: Springer Media.

Casanova, Jose. 2006. "Rethinking Secularization. A Global Comparative Perspective," *The Hedgehog Review*, vol. 8, nos 1–2.

Casolari, Marzia. 2000. "Hindutva's Foreign Tie-up in the 1930s—Archival Evidence," *Economic & Political Weekly*, 22 January.

Chakravarti, Ankita. 2020. "Explosive Report Reveals Caste Discrimination in Silicon Valley, 30 Dalit Engineers Call Out Indian Bosses," *India Today*, 28 October, https://www.indiatoday.in/technology/news/story/explosive-report-reveals-caste-discrimination-in-silicon-valley-30-dalit-engineers-call-out-indian-bosses-1735792-2020-10-28.

Chakravarti, Uma. 1983. "The Development of the Sita Myth: A Case Study of Women in Myth and Literature," *Samya Shakti*, vol. 1, July.

Chancel, Lucas, and Thomas Piketty. 2021. "Global Income Inequality, 1820–2020," *Journal of the European Economic Association*, vol. 19 (6), 3025–62.

Chandra, Bipan. 1984. *Communalism in Modern India*, Delhi: Vikas.

Chandra, T., and A. Kumaraswamy. No Date. "Agitation for Upper Cloth in Kanyakumari District," *Research Journal of Indian Studies*, https://www.rjisacjournal.com/agitation-for-upper-cloth-in-kanyakumari-district/.

Chandrababu, Divya. 2022. "A Decade On, Kudankulam Nuclear Plant Protesters Say Still Face Ordeal," *Hindustan Times*, 6 June, https://www.hindustantimes.com/india-news/a-decade-on-kudankulam-nuclear-plant-protesters-say-still-face-ordeal-101654455406226.html.

Chandrachud, Abhinav. 2020. *Republic of Religion. The Rise and Fall of Colonial Secularism in India*, Delhi: Penguin Random House.

Chandran, Rina. 2018. "Individual Land Rights to India's Indigenous People Could Be 'Disastrous', Expert Says," *Reuters*, 15 March, https://in.reuters.com/article/india-landrights-lawmaking/individual-land-rights-to-india-indigenous-people-could-be-disastrous-expert-says-idINKCN1GR1U8.

Chandran, Rina. 2020. "Reform of Customary Laws Urged to Protect India's Indigenous Land," https://www.reuters.com/article/us-india-landrights-lawmaking-trfn-idUSKBN1ZY0MK.

Chatterjee, Arup C. 2022. "Lord Ram's Own Sethu: Adam's Bridge Envisaged as an Aquapelago," *Shima: The International Journal of Research Into Island Cultures*, vol. 16 (1), 94–114.

Chatterjee, Partha. 2010. "A Response to Taylor's 'Modes of Civil Society'," in idem, *Empire and Nation. Essential Writings 1985–2005*, chap. 16, Rani-khet: Permanent Black.

Chatterjee, Partha. 1997. "Beyond the Nation? Or Within," in idem, *Empire and Nation. Essential Writings 1985–2005*, chap. 10, Ranikhet: Permanent Black.

Chatterjee, Partha. 1998. "Secularism and Tolerance," in Rajeev Bhargava, ed., *Secularism and Its Critics*, Delhi: Oxford University Press.

Chatterjee, Partha. 2001. "Democracy and the Violence of the State: A Political Negotiation of Death," in idem, *Empire and Nation. Essential Writings 1985–2005*, chap. 11, Ranikhet: Permanent Black.

Chatterjee, Partha. 2008. "Democracy and Economic Transformation in India," *Economic and Political Weekly*, 19 April, vol. XLII, no. 16.

Chatterjee, Ramkrishna. 1986. "Christian Missionaries and Labour Migration to Assam Tea Gardens in Colonial Times," CSSSC Occasional Paper No. 80, Calcutta: Centre for Studies in Social Sciences.

Chatterji, Angana P., Mihir Desai, Harsh Mander, and Abdul Kalam Azad. 2021. "Detention, Criminalisation, Statelessness: The Aftermath of Assam's NRC," *The Wire*, 9 September, https://thewire.in/rights/detention-criminalisation-statelessness-the-aftermath-of-assams-nrc.

Chatterji, Saubhadro. 2010. "UPA to Try 'de Soto Model' for Slum Development," *Business Standard*, 29 June.

Chaturvedi, Vinayak. 2022. *Hindutva and Violence: V. D. Savarkar and the Politics of History*, Ranikhet: Permanent Black.

Chen, Kuan-Hsing. 2010. *Asia as Method: Toward Deimperialization*, Durham: Duke University Press.

Chenal, Leonce. 2021. "How to Wear a Scarf Like a French Woman," 1 February, https://leoncechenal.com/french-scarf/.

Chiriyankandath, James. 1993. "'Communities at the Polls': Electoral Politics and the Mobilization of Communal Groups in Travancore," *Modern Asian Studies*, July, vol. 27, no. 3, 643–5.

Choubey, Kamal Nayan. 2014. "'Red Carpet' in Forests," *Kafila*, https://kafila.online/2014/09/28/red-carpet-in-forests-kamal-nayan-choubey/.

Choudhury, Chitrangada. 2016. "Mining at Any Cost: The Odisha Government's Continued Dismissal of Adivasi Rights," *The Wire*, 16 May, https://thewire.in/rights/mining-at-any-cost-the-odisha-governments-continued-dismissal-of-adivasi-rights.

Chuang Collective. 2020. "Social Contagion. Microbiological Class Warfare in China," https://chuangcn.org/2020/02/social-contagion/.

Clarke, Sathianathan. 1998. "Paraiyars Ellaiamman as an Iconic Symbol of Collective Resistance and Emancipatory Mythography," in Gnana Robinson, ed., *Religions of the Marginalised: Towards a Phenomenology and the Methodology of Study*, Bangalore: UTC, and Delhi: ISPCK.

Clover, Joshua. 2020. "The Rise and Fall of Biopolitics: A Response to Bruno Latour," *Critical Inquiry*, 29 March, https://critinq.wordpress.com/2020/03/29/the-rise-and-fall-of-biopolitics-a-response-to-bruno-latour/.

Connolly, William E. 2011. "Some Theses on Secularism," *Cultural Anthropology*, vol. 26, 648–56.

Coperahewa, Sandagomi. 2019. "The Politics of Language in Sri Lanka," Interview by Uvin Dissanayake, *Daily News*, 20 August.

Cotta, Francesca, Sejal Wohra, Nirmal Kulkarni, Ahmed Chamanwala, and Aditya Dicky Singh. 2022. "Rewilding India, One Parcel Of Land At A Time," *Sanctuary Nature Foundation* https://www.sanctuarynaturefoundation.org/article/rewilding-india%2C-one-parcel-of-land-at-a-time.

Coulthard, Glen. 2007. "Subjects of Empire: Indigenous Peoples and the 'Politics of Recognition' in Canada," *Contemporary Political Theory*, vol. 6 (4), 437–60.

Coulthard, Glen. 2014. *Red Skins, White Masks: Rejecting the Colonial Politics of Recognition*, Minneapolis: University of Minnesota Press.

Coyle, Marcia. 2021. "The Supreme Court's Religion Conundrum," *Constitution Daily*, 8 February, https://constitutioncenter.org/blog/the-supreme-courts-religion-conundrum.

Dalal, John. 2016. "The Closure of Forward Press Print Edition is a Backward Step for Journalism," https://scroll.in/article/804865/the-closure-of-forward-press-print-edition-is-a-backward-step-for-journalism.

Dalmia, Vasudha. 1997 [2010]. *The Nationalization of Hindu Traditions*, rpntd Delhi: Permanent Black.

Damodaran, A. 2003. "The Wayanad Imbroglio. Result of Skewed Development?" *The Hindu Magazine*, Sunday, 27 April, 4.

Dani, Ahmad Hasan. 1999. *History of Civilizations of Central Asia: The Crossroads of Civilizations: A.D. 250 to 750*, Delhi: Motilal Banarsidass.

Daniyal, Shoaib. 2016. "History Lesson: How 'Bharat Mata' Became the Code Word for a Theocratic Hindu State," *Scroll*, 17 May, https://scroll.in/article/805247/history-lessons-how-bharat-mata-became-the-code-word-for-a-theocratic-hindu-state.

Das, Veena. 2006. "Secularism and the Argument from Nature," in David Scott and Charles Hirschkind, eds., *Powers of the Secular Modern: Talal Asad and His Interlocutors*, Stanford: Stanford University Press, 93–112.

Datta, Aesha. 2019. "Magic! How the Government Stretched a 'One-time' Measure to Bypass Environment Checks for Coal Mines," *The Economic Times*, https://economictimes.indiatimes.com/prime/environment/magic-how-the-government-stretched-a-one-time-measure-to-bypass-

environment-checks-for-coal-mines/primearticleshow/69780902
.cms?from=mdr.

Datta, P. K. 1999. *Carving Blocs. Communal Identity in Early Twentieth Century Bengal*, Delhi: Oxford University Press.

Davar, Bhargavi. 1999. "Indian Psychoanalysis, Patriarchy and Hinduism," *Anthropology and Medicine*, vol. 6 (2), 177–93.

D'Costa, Anthony P., and Achin Chakraborty. 2017. *The Land Question in India. State, Dispossession and Capitalist Transition*, Delhi: Oxford University Press.

De Alwis, Malathi, and Sharni Jayawardene. No Date. *Invoking the Goddess*, http://invokingthegoddess.lk/.

De Alwis, Malathi, Satish Deshpande, Pradeep Jeganathan, Mary John, Nivedita Menon, M. S. S. Pandian, Aditya Nigam, and S. Akbar Zaidi. 2009. "The Postnational Condition," Special Issue of *Economic and Political Weekly*, vol. 44, issue no. 10, 7 March.

De Soto, Hernando. 1989. *The Other Path: The Invisible Revolution in the Third World*, New York: Harper and Row.

De Soto, Hernando. 2000. *The Mystery of Capital. Why Capitalism Triumphs in the West and Fails Everywhere Else*, New York: Basic Books.

De, Rohit. 2018. *A People's Constitution. The Everyday Life of Law in the Indian Republic*, Princeton: Princeton University Press.

Deccan Herald. 2022. 24 February, https://www.deccanherald.com/state/top-karnataka-stories/hc-interim-order-not-applicable-on-turban-wearing-students-bc-nagesh-1084863.html.

Degrowth. No Date. "Definition," *Research and Degrowth*, https://degrowth.org/definition-2/.

Dehejia, Vidya. 1999. "Encountering Devi," in Vidya Dehejia, ed., *Devi: The Great Goddess. Female Divinity in South Asian Art*, Ahmedabad: Mapin Publishing, and Munich: Presten Verlag.

Delhi Janwadi Adhikar Manch. 1997. *The Order that Felled a City. A Citizens' Report on the Politics of Pollution and the Mass Displacement of Workers in Delhi*. February–March.

Dermendzhiyska, Elitsa. 2021. "Feeling, in situ," *Aeon*, 8 October, https://aeon.co/essays/what-if-emotions-arent-universal-but-specific-to-each-culture.

Derrett, J. D. M. 1968, *Religion, Law and the State in India*, London: Faber and Faber.

Devadevan, Manu V. 2016. *A Prehistory of Hinduism*, Warsaw/Berlin: De Gruyter Open Ltd.

Devika, J. 2020. "The Limits of Public Health Management: Time to Rethink Development in Kerala," *Kafila*, 26 April, https://kafila.on line/2020/04/26/the-limits-of-public-health-management-time-to-re think-development-in-kerala/.

Devika, J. 2022. "Who Are These Hindus? The Tragedy of Vizhinjham and the Despicable Cruelty of the Majority," *Kafila*, 1 December, https:// kafila.online/2022/12/01/who-are-these-hindus-the-tragedy-of-vizhin jham-and-the-despicable-cruelty-of-the-majority/.

Devji, Faisal. 2021. "An Impossible Founding." *Global Intellectual History*, 25 October, https://www.tandfonline.com/doi/full/10.1080/238018 83.2021.1962584.

Devy, G. N. 2009. "Tradition and Amnesia," in idem, *After Amnesia (The GN Devy Reader)*, Hyderabad: Orient Blackswan.

Dhar, Anup. 2018. "Genealogies of Aboriginalization," in Manasi Kumar, Anup Dhar, and Anurag Mishra, eds., *Psychoanalysis from the Indian Terroir. Emerging Themes in Culture, Family and Childhood*, New York: Lexington Books.

Dhar, Anup, and Sabah Siddiqui. 2013. "At the Edge of (Critical) Psychology," *Annual Review of Critical Psychology*, vol. 10, 506–48.

Dhar, Parul Pandya. 2022. "The Past is a Familiar, Composite Structure," *The Economic Times*, 19 June, https://m.economictimes.com/opinion/ et-commentary/the-past-is-a-familiar-composite-structure/article show/92306055.cms.

Dietrich, Gabriele. 1992. *Reflections on the Women's Movement in India: Religion, Ecology, Development*, Delhi: Horizon India.

Dietrich, Gabriele. 2003. "Loss of Socialist Vision and Options Before the Women's Movement," *Economic and Political Weekly*, 25 October.

DNA. 2015. "Govt-funded Mosque Revives Church–State Debate in France," 24 September, https://www.dnaindia.com/world/report-govt-funded-mosque-revives-church-state-debate-in-france-7925.

DNA. 2021. "Karnataka Anti-conversion Bill Approved by Governor, Know What the New Law States," https://www.dnaindia.com/india/ report-karnataka-anti-conversion-bill-approved-by-governor-know-what-the-law-states-2953852.

Dorfman, Ariel. 2022. "Chileans Rejected the New Constitution, But They Still Want Progressive Reforms," *The Guardian*, 6 September, https:// www.theguardian.com/commentisfree/2022/sep/06/chile-new-consti tution-reject-pinochet.

Drèze, Jean. 2017. "Universal Basic Income for India Suddenly Trendy. Look Out," *NDTV*, 16 January, http://www.ndtv.com/opinion/decoding-universal-basic-income-for-india-1649293.

Duncan, Jonathan. 2012. "Rethinking Mental Illness," *Africa is a Country*, https://africasacountry.com/2012/12/the-delusions-in-decontextualising-mental-illness.

Eco, Umberto. 2003. *Mouse or Rat? Translation as Negotiation*, London: Phoenix.

Edmunds, Lowell, and Alan Dundes, eds. 1995. *Oedipus. A Folklore Casebook*, Madison: University of Wisconsin Press.

El Shakry, Omnia. 2017. *The Arabic Freud: Psychoanalysis and Islam in Modern Egypt*, Princeton: Princeton University Press.

Ernsting, Almuth. 2015. "Renewables Cannot Sustain the Globalized Growth-economy," *Degrowth*, 24 February, https://degrowth.info/blog/renewables-cannot-sustain-the-globalized-growth-economy.

ETEnergyWorld. 2019. "India's Largest Renewable Energy Companies: Acme, Adani and Greenko Top the List," *The Economic Times*, 29 July, https://energy.economictimes.indiatimes.com/news/renewable/indias-largest-renewable-energy-companies-acme-adani-and-greenko-top-the-list/70429534.

Express News Service. 2022. "Muslims Need Not Do Business Near Temples: RSS Leader Kalladka Prabhakar Bhat," *The New Indian Express*, 30 March, https://www.newindianexpress.com/states/karnataka/2022/mar/30/muslims-need-not-do-business-near-temples-rss-leader-kalladka-prabhakar-bhat-2435713.html.

Fanon, Frantz. 1965. "Algeria Unveiled," in idem, *A Dying Colonialism*, New York: Grove Press.

Fanon, Frantz. 2009. "The Fact of Blackness," in Les Back and John Solomos, eds., *Theories of Race and Racism. A Reader*, London: Routledge, 257–66.

Feminist Degrowth. No Date. "Collaborative Feminist Degrowth: Pandemic as an Opening for a Care-full Radical Transformation," https://degrowth.info/en/collaborative-feminist-degrowth-pandemic-as-an-opening-for-a-care-full-radical-transformation.

Ferguson, James. 2015. *Give a Man a Fish. Reflections on a New Politics of Distribution*, Durham: Duke University Press.

Fernandes, Walter, and Gita Bharali. 2002. "Customary Law–Formal Law Interface: Impact on Tribal Culture," in T. N. Subba, Joseph Puthenpurackal, and Shaji Joseph Puykunnel, eds., *Christianity and Change in Northeast India*, New Delhi: Concept Publishing Company.

Fernandes, Walter, Melville Pereira, and Vizalenu Khatso. 2008. *Tribal Customary Laws in Northeast India: Gender and Class Implications*, Guwahati: North Eastern Social Research Centre, http://www.nesrc.org/Mono graphs/Customary-Laws.pdf.

Firstpost. 2019. *Adivasis and the Indian State* (18 part series), https://www .firstpost.com/tag/adivasis-and-the-indian-state.

Food Sovereignty Alliance India. No Date. https://leisaindia.org/seeds-of-re sistance-for-food-sovereignty/.

Forte, Juan Manuel. 2008. "Religion and Capitalism. Weber, Marx and the Materialist Controversy," *Philosophy & Social Criticism*, vol. 34 (4), 427–48.

François, Myriam. 2021. "'I Felt Violated by the Demand to Undress': Three Muslim Women on France's Hostility to the Hijab," *The Guardian*, 27 July, https://www.theguardian.com/world/2021/jul/27/i-felt-violated-by-the-demand-to-undress-three-muslim-women-on-frances-hostility-to-the-hijab.

Freedom Forum Institute. No Date. "Has the U. S. Supreme Court Defined 'Religion'?," https://www.freedomforuminstitute.org/about/faq/has-the-u-s-supreme-court-defined-religion/.

Freud, Sigmund. 1965. *The Interpretation of Dreams*, New York: Avon Books.

Friedman, Milton. 1962. *Capitalism and Freedom*. Chicago: University of Chicago Press.

Friedman, Thomas. 1999. *The Lexus and the Olive Tree. Understanding Globalization*, New York: Farrar, Straus and Giroux.

Frykenberg, Robert. 2003. "Introduction: Dealing with Contested Definitions and Controversial Perspectives," in idem, ed., *Christians and Missionaries in India: Cross-Cultural Communication Since 1500*, Grand Rapids: William B. Erdmans.

Fuchs, Martin. 2001. "A Religion for Civil Society? Ambedkar's Buddhism, the Dalit Issue and the Imagination of Emergent Possibilities," in Vasudha Dalmia, Angelika Malinar, and Martin Christof, eds., *Charisma and Canon. Essays on the Religious History of the Indian Subcontinent*, Delhi: Oxford University Press.

Gaddam, Aditi. 2015. "India's Solar Dream: Does the Country Have Enough Water?," *The Third Pole* (blog), 5 March, https://www.theth irdpole.net/en/energy/indias-solar-dream-does-the-country-have-enough-water/.

Ganeri, Jonardon. 2007. *The Concealed Art of the Soul*, Oxford: Oxford University Press.

Gatade, Subhash. 2005. "Interview with M. C. K. Janu, Leader of Tribals in Kerala," *South Asia Citizens' Web*, 18 March, http://www.sacw.net/Nation/gatade18032005.html.

Gatade, Subhash. 2019. *Modinama. Issues that Did Not Matter*. Delhi: Left Word Books.

Gatwood, Lynn E. 1985. *Devi and the Spouse Goddess: Women, Sexuality and Marriages in India*, New Delhi: Manohar.

Ge, Freya, and David Ownby. 2020. "Liu Xinting, 'Contemporary Youth'," *Reading the China Dream*, https://www.readingthechinadream.com/liu-xinting-contemporary-youth.html.

Geetha, V., and S. V. Rajadurai. 2008. *Towards a Non-Brahmin Millennium. From Iyothee Thass to Periyar*, Kolkata: Samya.

George, Anjali. 2014. "Claiming Niyamgiri: The Dongria Kondh's Struggle against Vedanta," *Ritimo*, 18 December, https://www.ritimo.org/Claiming-Niyamgiri-the-Dongria-Kondh-s-Struggle-against-Vedanta.

Ghosh, Poulomi. 2022a. "'Difficult to Pinpoint Ram Setu': Govt's Statement in Parliament Triggers BJP vs Congress," *Hindustan Times*, 23 December, https://www.hindustantimes.com/india-news/difficult-to-pinpoint-ram-setu-govt-s-statement-in-parliament-triggers-bjp-vs-congress-101671815904084.html.

Ghosh, Poulomi. 2022b. "Shashi Tharoor, Accused of Politicising Karnataka Hijab Row, Says This," *Hindustan Times*, 4 February, https://www.hindustantimes.com/india-news/shashi-tharoor-accused-of-politicising-karnataka-hijab-row-says-this-101643943022564.html.

Gibbs, Jeff. 2020. "'Old Data' Is a Lie," *Planet of the Humans*, 18 May, https://planetofthehumans.com/2020/05/18/old-data-is-a-lie/.

Glauser, Benno. 2011. "Being Indigenous: The Concept of Indigeneity: A Conversation with Two Ayoreo Leaders," in Sita Venkateswar and Emma Hughes, eds., *The Politics of Indigeneity. Dialogues and Reflections on Indigenous Activism*, London: Zed Books.

Gnanambal, K. 1969. *Festivals of India*, vol. 19, Delhi, Government of India: Anthropological Survey of India.

Gohain, Hiren. 2019. "It is Important to Contextualise the NRC," *The Hindu*, 5 September, https://www.thehindu.com/opinion/op-ed/it-is-important-to-contextualise-the-nrc/article29334764.ece.

GoI Order. 2020. Order no. 40-3/2020-DM-I (A), https://www.mha.gov.in/sites/default/files/MHA%20Order%20Dt.%2019.4.2020%20with%20SOP%20for%20movement%20of%20stranded%20labour%20within%20the%20State%20and%20UT.pdf.

Goitein, Shelomo Dov. 2010. *Studies in Islamic History and Institutions*, Leiden: Brill.

Golwalkar, M. S. 1939. *We, or Our Nationhood Defined*, Nagpur: Bharat Publications.

Gordon, Lewis. 2015. *What Fanon Said. A Philosophical Introduction to His Life and Thought*, Johannesburg: Wits University Press.

Govind, Rahul. 2022. "The Hindu Deity as Juristic Person—A Dangerous Path, Yet Again," *Kafila*, 1 June, https://kafila.online/2022/06/01/the-hindu-deity-as-juristic-person-a-dangerous-path-yet-again-rahul-govind/.

Govindrajan, Radhika. 2018. *Animal Intimacies. Interspecies Relatedness in India's Central Himalayas*, Chicago: University of Chicago Press.

Graeber, David, and David Wengrow. 2021. *The Dawn of Everything: A New History of Humanity*. New York: Farrar, Straus and Giroux.

Graham-Gibson, J. K. 1996. *The End of Capitalism (As We Knew It). A Feminist Critique of Political Economy*, Minneapolis: University of Minnesota Press.

Grewal, Amanpreet. 2022. "Hindutva Groups Are Organizing in Canada and Our Politicians Need to Be Vigilant," *Baaz*, 7 January, https://www.baaznews.org/p/vhp-canada-international-student-event-vigilant.

Grovogui, Siba. 2013. "Siba Grovogui on IR Theory as Theology, Reading Kant Badly, and the Incapacity of Western Ideas to Travel Very Far in Non-western Contexts," Interview with B. Creutzfeldt, *Theory Talks*, https://www.files.ethz.ch/isn/168715/Theory%20Talk57_Grovogui.pdf.

Guardian, The. 2001. https://www.theguardian.com/books/2001/nov/24/books.guardianreview2.

Guha, Ranajit. 1963/1996. *A Rule of Property for Bengal: An Essay on the Idea of Permanent Settlement*, Durham: Duke University Press.

Guha-Thakurta, Tapati. 2022. "Can a Festival of a Goddess Be Secular?," in Tapati Guha-Thakurta and Vazira Zamindar, eds., *How Secular is Art: On the Politics of Art, History and Religion in South Asia*, New Delhi: Cambridge University Press.

Gupta, Charu. 2001. "The Icon of Mother in Late Colonial North India: 'Bharat Mata', 'Matri Bhasha' and 'Gau Mata'," *Economic and Political Weekly*, 10–16 November, vol. 36, no. 45, 4291–9.

Gupta, Smita. 2018. "Women and Land Rights in India: Towards a Democratic and Gendered Formulation of the Land Question," in Praveen

Jha, Avinash Kumar, and Yamini Mishra, eds., *Labouring Women: Issues and Challenges in Contemporary India*, Hyderabad: Orient Blackswan.

Gutierrez, Gustavo. 1988. *A Theology of Liberation*, New York: Orbis Books.

Habermas, Jürgen. 2008. "Notes on a Post-secular Society," *Sign and Sight*, 18 June, http://www.signandsight.com/features/1714.html.

Haering, Norbert. 2017. "A Well-kept Open Secret: Washington is Behind India's Brutal Demonetization Project," *Global Research*, 1 January, http://www.globalresearch.ca/a-well-kept-open-secret-washing ton-is-behind-indias-brutal-demonetization-project/5566167.

Haksar, Nandita. 1999. "Human Rights Layering: A Feminist Perspective," in Amita Dhanda and Archana Parasher, eds., *Engendering Law. Essays in Honour of Lotika Sarkar*, Lucknow: Eastern Book Company.

Handa, Devendra. 1981. "Coins of Vidisagupta and Other Huna Rulers," *Proceedings of the Indian History Congress*, vol. 42, 669–74.

Hans, Namit. 2017. "Muslim-born Salabeg, the Jagannath Devotee Who Brought the Lord to the Masses," https://indianexpress.com/article/research/salabeg-the-jagannath-devotee-who-brought-the-lord-to-the-masses-4590411/.

Haq, Shifa, and Sabah Siddiqui. 2018. "Between Neutrality and Disavowal—Being Muslim Therapists in India," in I. Parker and S. Siddiqui, eds., *Islamic Psychoanalysis and Psychoanalytic Islam—Cultural and Clinical Dialogues*, London: Routledge, 60–9.

Harad, Tejas. 2022. "Conversion to Buddhism Row: BJP Cannot Deny People Their Fundamental Rights," *The Quint*, 8 October, https://www.thequint.com/voices/opinion/conversion-to-buddhism-row-bjp-can not-deny-people-their-fundamental-rights#read-more#read-more.

Harding, Christopher. 2009. "Sigmund's Asian Fan-Club? The Freud Franchise and Independence of Mind in India and Japan," in R. Clarke, ed., *Celebrity Colonialism: Fame, Power and Representation in Postcolonial Cultures*, Cambridge: Scholars Press, 73–87.

Harding, Christopher. 2018. "Couched in Kindness. How Psychoanalysis Came to Japan and Was Turned on Its Head," https://aeon.co/essays/how-psychoanalysis-came-to-japan-and-was-turned-on-its-head.

Harikrishnan, Charmy, Vasudha Venugopal, and S. Sanandakumar. 2016. "Amit Shah's Vamana Jayanti Tweet Sparks a Row on Onam Eve," https://economictimes.indiatimes.com/news/politics-and-nation/amit-shahs-vamana-jayanti-tweet-sparks-a-row-on-onam-eve/article show/54319937.cms?utm_source=contentofinterest&utm_medium=text&utm_campaign=cppst.

Harris-White, Barbara, and Elinor Harris. 2007. "Unsustainable Capitalism: The Politics of Renewable Energy in the UK," in Leo Panitch and Colin Leys, ed., *Socialist Register 2007: Coming to Terms with Nature*, vol. 43, New York: Monthly Review Press.

Hart, George L. 1979. 'The Nature of Tamil Devotion," in Madhav M. Deshpande and Peter E. Hook, eds., *Aryan and Non-Aryan in India*, Wisconsin: Centre for South and Southeast Asain Studies, University of Michigan.

Hartnack, Christiane. 1990. "Vishnu on Freud's Desk: Psychoanalysis in Colonial India," *Social Research: An International Quarterly*, vol. 57, 921–50.

Hasluck, Margaret. 1984. "Oedipus Rex in Albania," in Lowell Edmunds and Alan Dundes, eds., *Oedipus. A Folklore Casebook*, Madison: University of Wisconsin Press.

Hattangadi, Shekhar. 2015. "Santhara in the Eyes of the Law," *The Hindu*, 15 August, https://www.thehindu.com/opinion/op-ed/Santhara-in-the-eyes-of-the-law/article62117263.ece.

Hawley, John Stratton. 2015. *A Storm of Songs: India and the Idea of the Bhakti Movement*, Boston: Harvard University Press.

Hayek, Friedrich. 1981. *Law, Legislation and Liberty, Volume 3: The Political Order of a Free People*, Chicago: University of Chicago Press.

Haygunde, Chandan. 2018. "Bhim Army Objects to urning Ravan's Effigy, Demands Violators Be Booked Under SC/ST Act," https://indianexpress.com/article/india/bhim-army-objects-to-burning-ravans-effigy-demands-violators-be-booked-under-sc-st-act-5403775/.

Hayward, Philip. 2012. "Aquapelagos and 'Aquapelagic' Assemblages. Towards an Integrated Study of Island Societies and Marine Environments," *Shima: The International Journal of Research into Island Cultures*, vol. 6, no. 1.

Haywood, John. 2002. *Historical Atlas of the Classical World 500 BC–600 AD*, New York: Barnes & Noble.

Hazra, R. C. 1940. *Studies in the Puranic Records on Hindu Rites and Customs*, Calcutta: Abinas Press, online https://archive.org/details/PuranicRecordsOnHinduRitesAndCustoms/page/n1/mode/2up?view=theater.

Hemalata, K. 2017. "3 Years of Modi Government: Country for Sale," *News Click*, 18 May, https://www.newsclick.in/3-years-modi-government-country-sale.

Hepp, Constanza, Joëlle Saey-Volckrick, Joe Herbert, Nathan Barlow, Nick von Andrian, Andro Rilović, and Jacob Smessaert. 2020. "A Degrowth

Perspective on the Coronavirus Crisis," 23 November, https://degrowth
.info/blog/a-degrowth-perspective-on-the-coronavirus-crisis.

Herbert, J. 1996. "Sakata and Putana," in Shyam Singh Shashi, ed., *Ency-clopaedia Indica: Purā]nas*, Delhi: Anmol Publications.

Hildyard, Daisy. 2017. *The Second Body*, London: Fitzcarraldo Editions.

Hiltebeitel, Alf. 1999. *Rethinking India's Oral and Classical Epics*, Chicago: University of Chicago Press.

Hiltebeitel, Alf. 2018. *Freud's Mahabharata*, Delhi: Oxford University Press.

Hindu Janjagruti Samiti. No Date. "Save Shri Ram Setu Campaign," https:// www.hindujagruti.org/hindu-issues/save-ram-setu.

Hindus for Human Rights. No Date. https://www.hindusforhumanrights .org/en/our-vision.

Hindustan Times. 2007. "Recipe for Disaster: Scientists," 13 September.

Hindustan Times. 2016. "Greater Noida: Ravana Idol in Bisrakh Temple Vandalised," https://www.hindustantimes.com/noida/greater-noida-ra vana-idol-in-bisrakh-temple-vandalised/story-zv43F6estPWtjDl37f bJQM.html.

Hindustan Times. 2020. "Constitution in Hand, Bhim Army Chief Azad Returns to Jama Masjid in Delhi," 27 August, https://www.hindustantimes.com/ india-news/constitution-in-hand-bhim-army-chief-chandrashekhar-azad-returns-to-jama-masjid/story-HnxbbUUs3Gj5fHCDG6wMDN.html.

Hirsch, Helen, ed. 2013. *Spirit Eaters*, Vienna: Verlag Fur Moderne Kunst.

Hofmeyr, Isabel. 2012. "The Complicating Sea: The Indian Ocean as Method," *Comparative Studies of South Asia, Africa and the Middle East*, vol. 32, no. 3, 584–90.

Honig, Bonnie. 1999. "My Culture Made Me Do It," in Joshua Cohen, Matthew Howard, and Martha C. Nussbaum, eds., *Is Multiculturalism Bad for Women?* Princeton: Princeton University Press.

Hoskote, Ranjit, and Ilija Trojanow. 2012. *Confluences. Forgotten Histories from East and West*, Delhi: Yoda Books.

HT Correspondent. 2020. "Bill Gates Lauds India's Covid-19 Tracker Aarogya Setu," *Hindustan Times*, 23 April, https://tech.hindustantimes.com/ tech/news/bill-gates-lauds-india-s-covid-19-tracker-aarogya-setu-here-s-how-you-use-the-app-story-3CC54mLz4x0RAzDxPTjMzI.html.

Huang, Hsuan-Ying, and Douglas Kirsner. 2020. "The History of Psychoanalysis in China," *Psychoanalytic Inquiry*, vol. 40, no. 1, 3–15.

Human Rights Watch. 2022. "India: Media Freedom Under Threat," 3 May, https://www.hrw.org/news/2022/05/03/india-media-freedom-un der-threat.

Huntington, Samuel P. 1993. "The Clash of Civilizations," *Foreign Affairs*, vol. 72 (3), 22–50.

Hurtes, Sarah, and Weiyi Cai. 2022. "Europe is Sacrificing Its Ancient Forests for Energy," *The New York Times*, 7 September.

IANS (Indo Asian News Service). 2007. "Ram Setu 'Man-made', Says Government Publication," 8 December.

IANS. 2019. "Clean Chit to PM: Lavasa Opts Out of EC Meetings," *Business Standard*, 18 May, https://www.business-standard.com/article/news-ians/clean-chit-to-pm-lavasa-opts-out-of-ec-meetings-119051800163_1.html.

IFF. 2020. "Is Aarogya Setu Privacy-first?," https://internetfreedom.in/is-aarogya-setu-privacy-first-nope-but-it-could-be-if-the-government-wanted/.

Ilaiah, Kancha. 2001. *Why I Am Not a Hindu: A Sudra Critique of Hindutva Philosophy, Culture & Political Economy*, Kolkata: Bhatkal and Sen.

Images Staff. 2022. "When Vogue France Says 'Yes to the Headscarf,' It Doesn't Mean All Headscarves," *Images*, 2 February, https://images.dawn.com/news/1189398.

India News. 2020. "2 IAS Officers Suspended for Delhi Lockdown Violations, 2 Other Officials Face Action," *The Hindustan Times*, 30 March, https://www.hindustantimes.com/india-news/coronavirus-update-4-senior-delhi-government-officials-face-action-for-lockdown-violations-2-suspended/story-AyIeYCwjazhhnREp26CjtO.html.

India Today Web Desk. 2018. "Centre Rejects Minority Religious Tag to Lingayat and Veerashaiva Communities: Who Are They?," 12 December, https://www.indiatoday.in/education-today/gk-current-affairs/story/centre-rejects-minority-religious-tag-to-lingayat-and-veerashaiva-communities-who-are-they-1407740-2018-12-12.

Iqbal, Javed. 2018. "Jharkhand Gang Rape Survivor's Account Upends Narrative of Pathalgadi Role," *The Wire*, 26 July, https://thewire.in/rights/jharkhand-pathalgadi-movement-gang-rape-police-firing.

Iqtidar, Humeira. 2011. "The Difference Between Secularism and Secularisation," *The Guardian*, 29 June.

Iqtidar, Humeira. 2021. "Representative Democracy and Religious Thought in South Asia. Abul A'la Maududi and Vinayak Damodar Savarkar," in Karen Barkey, Sudipta Kaviraj, and Vatsal Naresh, eds., *Negotiating Democracy and Religious Pluralism. India, Pakistan, and Turkey*, New York: Oxford University Press.

Jadaliyya. 2022. "In Her Name: Women Rise, State Violence, and the Future of Iran," 28 September, https://www.facebook.com/watch/live/?ref= watch_permalink&v=889770585335771.

Jaffrelot, Christophe. 2021. *Modi's India: Hindu Nationalism and the Rise of Ethnic Democracy*, Princeton: Princeton University Press.

Jain, Kailash Chand. 1974. *Lord Mahāvīra and His Times*, Delhi: Motilal Banarsidass.

Jaini, Padmanabh S. 1993. "A Puranic Counter Tradition," in Wendy Doniger, ed., *Puranas Perennis*, New York: SUNY Press.

Jaleel, Bilal. 2019. "'Was Terrorised': Doctor Forced to Chant 'Jai Shri Ram' in Delhi," *The Quint*, 30 May, https://www.thequint.com/news/india/ doctor-forced-to-chant-jai-shri-ram-connaught-place-delhi-goons.

Jamison, S. W., and M. Witzel. 1992. *Vedic Hinduism*, Boston: Harvard University Press.

Jangam, Chinnaiah. 2017. *Dalits and the Making of Modern India*, Delhi: Oxford University Press.

Janu, C. K. 2003. "Tribal Leaders Are Mere Pawns in Politics," Interview in *Down to Earth*, 30 July, http://www.indiaenvironmentportal.org.in/ content/22192/tribal-leaders-are-mere-pawns-in-politics/.

Jha, D. N. 2018 *Against the Grain: Notes on Identity, Intolerance and History*, Delhi: Manohar Publishers.

Jha, Dhirendra. 2021. "Guruji's Lie. The RSS and MS Golwalkar's Undeniable Links to Nazism," *The Caravan*, 1 August, https://caravanmagazine .in/history/rss-golwalkar-links-nazism.

Jiang, Tao. 2013. "Xuanzang and Freud: A Buddhist-Freudian Engagement on the Subliminal Mind," in Tao Jiang and Philip J. Ivanhoe, eds., *The Reception and Rendition of Freud in China. China's Freudian Slip*, London: Routledge.

Jiang, Tao, and Philip J. Ivanhoe, eds., 2013. *The Reception and Rendition of Freud in China. China's Freudian Slip*, London: Routledge.

Jitheesh, P. M. 2018. "Appropriation of Ayyappa Cult: The History and Hinduisation of Sabarimala Temple," https://thewire.in/history/appropriation- of-ayyappa-cult-the-history-and-hinduisation-of-sabarimala-temple.

JKR Staff. 2017. "Gujarat's Rs 20,000 Crore Gas cam and Malfunctioning EVMs: Are They Connected?" *Janta Ka Reporter*, 12 Dec., https://www .jantakareporter.com/india/rs-20000-crore-gas-scam-and-evms/164079/.

John, Jacob. 2007. "Sethusamudram Canal: An Expensive Voyage?," *Economic and Political Weekly*, 21 July.

Johri, Rachana. 2010. "Mothering from the Margins: Mothering Daughters in a Culture of Son Preference," in Phyllis Erdman, Sue Metzger, and

Kok-Mun Ng, eds., *Attachment: Expanding the Cultural Connections*, London: Routledge, Taylor and Francis.

Joireman, S. F. 2008. "The Mystery of Capital Formation in Sub-Saharan Africa: Women, Property Rights and Customary Law," *World Development*, vol. 36, no. 7, 1233–46.

Jones, Kenneth W. 1973. "Ham Hindu Nahin: Arya–Sikh Relations, 1877–1905," *Journal of Asian Studies*, May.

Joseph, Tony. 2017. "How Genetics is Settling the Aryan Migration Debate," https://www.thehindu.com/sci-tech/science/how-genetics-is-settling-the-aryan-migration-debate/article19090301.ece.

J. V. Pawar Interview. 2022. "The Name Dalit Panthers Was Synonymous With Justice for the Poor," Interview by Gautam Bhatia, *The Wire*, 5 June, https://thewire.in/caste/dalit-panthers-jv-pawar-interview.

Kabeer, Naila. 2001. *The Power to Choose: Bangladeshi Women and Labour Market Decisions in London and Dhaka*, Delhi: Sage Publications.

Kaggere, Niranjan. 2022. "HC Interim Order Not Applicable on Turban-wearing Students: BC Nagesh," *Deccan Herald*, 25 February, https://www.deccanherald.com/state/top-karnataka-stories/hc-interim-order-not-applicable-on-turban-wearing-students-bc-nagesh-1084863.html.

Kakar, Sudhir. 1981. *The Inner World: A Psycho-analytic Study of Childhood and Society in India*, 2nd ed. New Delhi: Oxford University Press.

Kakar, Sudhir. 1990. *Intimate Relations. Exploring Indian Sexuality*, Delhi: Penguin Books.

Kakar, Sudhir. 1997. *Culture and Psyche. Selected Essays*, Delhi: Oxford University Press.

Kakar, Sudhir. 2007. *Indians: Portrait of a People*, Delhi: Penguin Books.

Kalidasan, Vinod Kottayil. 2015. "A King Lost and Found: Revisiting the Popular and Tribal Myths of Mahabali from Kerala," *Studies in South Asian Film ad Media*, vol. 7 nos 1 and 2.

Kalita, Kangkan. 2022. "Want Fresh NRC Exercise: Assam CM Himanta Biswa Sarma," *The Times of India*, 28 March, https://timesofindia.indiatimes.com/india/want-fresh-nrc-exercise-assam-cm-himanta-biswa sarma/articleshow/90481352.cms.

Kannabiran, Kalpana. 2021. "Constitution-As-Commons: Notes on Decolonizing Citizenship in India," *The South Atlantic Quarterly*, vol. 120:1, January.

Kapur, Ratna. 2005. *Erotic Justice: Law and the New Politics of Postcolonialism*, Delhi: Permanent Black.

Karmakar, Rahul. 2021. "Matrilineal Meghalaya to Give Land Rights to Men," *The Hindu*, 26 October, https://www.thehindu.com/news/national/other-states/matrilineal-meghalaya-to-give-land-rights-to-men/article37175110.ece.

Karpati, Mirella. 1995. "An Oedipus Myth in Gypsy Tradition," in Lowell Edmunds and Alan Dundes, eds., *Oedipus. A Folklore Casebook*, Madison: University of Wisconsin Press.

Karve, Irawati. 1967. *Yuganta* (Marathi). English translation at Internet Archive, https://archive.org/stream/Yuganta-TheEndOfAnEpoch-IrawatiKarve/yuganta_djvu.txt.

Kato, Norihiro. 2010. "Japan and the Ancient Art of Shrugging," *The Indian Express*, 26 August.

Kaufman, Cynthia. 2002. "Review of Joshua Cohen, Matthew Howard, and Martha C. Nussbaum, eds., *Is Multiculturalism Bad for Women?*," *Hypatia*, Autumn, vol. 17, no. 4, 228–32.

Kaul, Nilofer. 2018. "Myth, Misogyny, Matricide," in Manasi Kumar, Anup Dhar, and Anurag Mishra, eds., *Psychoanalysis from the Indian Terroir. Emerging Themes in Culture, Family and Childhood*, New York, London: Lexington Books.

Kaviraj, Sudipta. 1988. "A Critique of the Passive Revolution," *Economic and Political Weekly*, Annual Number.

Kaviraj, Sudipta. 2005. "An Outline of a Revisionist Theory of Modernity," *European Journal of Sociology*, vol. 46, no. 3.

Kennedy, David. 2001. "The International Human Rights Movement: Part of the Problem?," *European Human Rights Law Review*, vol. 3, 245–67.

Khalid, Umar. 2021. "Ita Mehrotra's Book Portrays the Shaheen Bagh Protest for the Multitude of Things It Was," *The Caravan*, 13 September.

Khamkhenthang, H., et al., eds., 1986. *In Search of Identity*, Imphal: Kuki-Chin Baptist Union.

Khera, Reetika. 2016. "A Phased Approach Will Make a 'Basic Income' Affordable for India," *The Wire*, 20 December, https://thewire.in/88350/basic-income-phased-approach/.

Khoj. 2012. https://khojstudios.org/project/spirit-eaters/.

Kidwai, Nehal. 2022. "Amid Hijab vs Saffron Scarves, Karnataka Bans Clothes That Disturb Law," *NDTV*, 5 February, https://www.ndtv.com/karnataka-news/amid-hijabs-vs-saffron-scarves-karnataka-bans-clothes-that-disturb-law-2751408.

Kikon, Dolly. 2019. *Living with Oil and Coal. Resource Politics and Militarizatin in Northeast India*, Seattle: University of Washington Press.

King, Martin Luther, Jr. 1949/50. "The Influence of the Mystery Religions on Christianity," https://kinginstitute.stanford.edu/king-papers/documents/influence-mystery-religions-christianity.

Kiro, Santosh K. 2018. "The State's Violent Response to Tribal Discontent is Fuelling the Pathalgadi Movement," *The Wire*, 29 June, https://thewire.in/rights/jharkhand-pathalgadi-movement-abduction-violence.

Kishwar, Madhu. 1994. "Codified Hindu Law. Myth and Reality," *Economic and Political Weekly*, 13 August.

Kodoth, Praveena. 2001. "Courting Legitimacy or Delegitimizing Custom? Sexuality, Sambandham and Marriage Reform in Late-Nineteenth-century Malabar," *Modern Asian Studies*, vol. 35, no. 2.

Koobak, Redi, Madina Tlostanova, and Suruchi Thapar-Björkert. 2021. *Postcolonial and Postsocialist Dialogues. Intersections, Opacities, Challenges in Feminist Theorizing and Practice*, London: Routledge.

Kosambi, D. D. 1962. *Myth and History*, Bombay: Popular Prakashan.

Kothari, Rita. 2020. "Secular, Secularism and Non-translations," *Economic and Political Weekly*, 19 September, vol. iv, no. 38.

Krishen, Pradip. 2018. "India: No Tree for a Tree," *The Indian Express*, 3 July, https://indianexpress.com/article/opinion/columns/delhi-tree-cutting-forest-cover-pollution-ngt-5243047/.

Kshatriya, Dilip Singh. 2022. "Gujarat's Muslim Fishermen Seek Mass Euthanasia," *The New Indian Express*, 7 May, https://www.newindianexpress.com/nation/2022/may/07/gujarats-muslim-fishermen-seek-mass-euthanasia-2450733.html.

Kugle, Scott Alan. 2001. "Framed, Blamed and Renamed: The Recasting of Islamic Jurisprudence in Colonial South Asia," *Modern Asian Studies*, May, vol. 35, no. 2, 257–313.

Kukreti, Ishan. 2022. "How to Cheat Forest Dwellers of Their Rights (and Enable Mining)," *Scroll*, 4 May, https://scroll.in/article/1023166/how-to-cheat-forest-dwellers-of-their-rights-and-enable-mining.

Kumar, Ashish. 2021. "The Huns ('Hūnas') in India: A Review," *Studies in People's History*, 16 November, vol. 8, no. 2.

Kumar, Ravi V. M. 2014. "Green Democracy: Relevance of Ambedkar's Ideas for Indian Environmentalism," *Indian Journal of Dalit and Tribal Studies and Action*, June, vol. 2, issue 1, no. 2, 24–34.

Kumar, Udaya. 2016. *Writing the First Person: Literature, History, and Autobiography in Modern Kerala*, Ranikhet: Permanent Black.

Kurup, Apoorv. 2008. "Tribal Law in India: How Decentralized Administration Is Extinguishing Tribal Rights and Why Autonomous Tribal Governments Are Better," *Indigenous Law Journal*, vol. 7, issue 1.

La Via Campesina. No Date. https://viacampesina.org/en/.

Lægaard, Sune. 2017. "Multiculturalism and Secularism: Theoretical Understandings and Possible Conflicts," *Ethnicities*, April, vol. 17, no. 2, 154–71.

Lal, Ratan. 2022. *The Janta Live*, 20 May, https://www.youtube.com/watch?v=uF0TjqcdUGg.

Lankesh, Gauri. 2017. "Making Sense of the Lingayat vs Veerashaiva Debate," *The Wire*, 8 August.

Latour, Bruno. 1993. *We Have Never Been Modern*, trans. Catherine Porter, Cambridge: Harvard University Press.

Latour, Bruno. 2020. "Is This a Dress Rehearsal?," *Critical Inquiry*, 26 March, https://critinq.wordpress.com/2020/03/26/is-this-a-dress-rehearsal/.

Law Library. 2018. "State Anti-conversion Laws in India," *The Law Library of Congress*, October, https://tile.loc.gov/storage-services/service/ll/llglrd/2018298841/2018298841.pdf.

Leman, Mehdi. 2022. "6 Reasons Why Nuclear Energy is Not the Way to a Green and Peaceful World," *Greenpeace*, 18 March, https://www.greenpeace.org/international/story/52758/reasons-why-nuclear-energy-not-way-green-and-peaceful-world/.

Lemke, Thomas. 2002. "Foucault, Governmentality, and Critique," *Rethinking Marxism. A Journal of Economics, Culture & Society*, vol. 14, issue 3.

Levien, Michael. 2015. " Dispossession, Development and Democracy," *The Hindu*, 4 February.

Levien, Michael. 2018. *Dispossession without Development: Land Grabs in Neoliberal India*, Delhi: Oxford University Press.

Lewis, Helen. 2020. "The Coronavirus Is a Disaster for Feminism," *The Atlantic*, 19 March, https://www.theatlantic.com/international/archive/2020/03/feminism-womens-rights-coronavirus-covid19/608302/.

Loewenberg, Peter. 2020. "Chinese Culture and Psychoanalysis," *Psychoanalysis and Psychotherapy in China*, vol. 3, 22–9.

Lok Sabha Debates. 1951. Pt. II, vol. XII.

Lok Sabha Debates. 2005. "Motion for Consideration of the Hindu Succession (Amendment) Bill, 29 August 2005, https://indiankanoon.org/doc/842089/.

Louis, Prakash. 2021. *Fr Stan Swamy. A Maoist or a Martyr?*, Delhi: Media House, and Kottayam: Sahitya Pravarthaka Cooperative Society.

Loving, Rolando Diaz. 2006. "An Historic-Psycho-Socio-Cultural Look at the Self in Mexico," in Uichol Kim, Kuo-Shu Yang, and Kwang-Kuo Hwang, eds., *Indigenous and Cultural Psychology. Understanding People in Context*, Berlin: Springer, 315–26.

Lubotsky, Alexander. 2020. "What Language Was Spoken by the People of the Bactria-Margiana Archaeological Complex?," in Paul W. Kroll and Jonathan A. Silk, eds., *'At the Shores of the Sky': Asian Studies for Albert Hoffstädt*, Leiden/Boston: Brill.

M Siddiq v Suresh Das. 2019. https://www.sci.gov.in/pdf/JUD_2.pdf.

Macpherson, C. B. 1962. *The Political Theory of Possessive Individualism: From Hobbes to Locke*, Oxford: Oxford University Press.

Macpherson, C. B. 1973. *Democratic Theory: Essays in Retrieval*, Oxford: Clarendon Press.

Macpherson, C. B. 1977. *The Life and Times of Liberal Democracy*, Oxford: Oxford Paperbacks.

Macpherson, C. B. 1985. *The Rise and Fall of Economic Justice*, Oxford: Paperbacks.

Madan, T. N. 1998. "Secularism in Its Place," in Rajeev Bhargava, ed., *Secularism and Its Critics*, Delhi: Oxford University Press.

Madhavan, N. S. 2018. "How Long Has the Ban on Women Entering Sabarimala Existed? Debate Ensues," *The News Minute*, 1 October, https://www.thenewsminute.com/article/how-long-has-ban-women-entering-sabarimala-existed-debate-ensues-89279.

Mahapatra, Dhananjay. 2008. "SC: Is Sethu a Place of Worship?," *Times of India*, 16 April.

Mahmood, Saba. 2005. *Politics of Piety: The Islamic Revival and the Feminist Subject*, Princeton: Princeton University Press.

Mahmudabad, Ali Khan. 2020. "Manufacturing Conflict: Indian Muslims and the Shift from Marginalisation to Exclusion," *Observer Research Foundation*, 22 August, https://www.orfonline.org/expert-speak/manufacturing-conflict/.

Maldonaldo-Torres, Nelson. 2022. "Is Decolonial Theory Secular? Lessons from Frantz Fanon," *Contending Modernities*, 27 January, https://contendingmodernities.nd.edu/decoloniality/decolonial-secular-fanon/#_ftn9.

Mamdani, Mahmood. 1992. "Africa: Democratic Theory and Democratic Struggles," *Economic and Political Weekly*, 10 October, vol. xxvii, no. 41.

Mamdani, Mahmood. 2010. "Beware Bigotry—Free Speech and the Zapiro Cartoons," *Kafila*, 31 May, https://kafila.online/2010/05/31/beware-bigotry-free-speech-and-the-zapiro-cartoons-mahmood/.

Mamdani, Mahmood. 2012. "Reading Ibn Khaldun in Kampala," *Makerere Institute of Social Research*, https://misr.mak.ac.ug/publication/working-paper-no-10-reading-ibn-khaldun-in-kampala.

Mani, Lata. 2009. *SacredSecular. Contemplative Cultural Critique*, New Delhi and London: Routledge.

Mann, Michael. 2005. *The Dark Side of Democracy: Explaining Ethnic Cleansing*, Cambridge: Cambridge University Press.

Manoj, M. B. 2012. "Another Onam. M. B. Manoj on Dalits, Onam and Malayali Identity," *Kafila*, 28 August, https://kafila.online/2012/08/28/another-onam-mb-manoj-on-dalits-onam-and-malayali-identity/.

Marak, Caroline. 1997. "Status of Women in Garo Culture," in Soumen Sen, ed., *Women in Meghalaya*, New Delhi: Omsons Publications.

Matchett, Freda. 2003. "The Puranas," in Gavin Flood, ed., *The Blackwell Companion to Hinduism*, Oxford: Blackwell Publishing.

Mathrubhumi. 2022. https://youtu.be/dRYN7RDjllk, 25 March.

Mathur, Aneesha. 2020. "Anti-conversion Laws in India: How States Deal with Religious Conversion," *India Today*, 23 December, https://www.indiatoday.in/news-analysis/story/anti-conversion-laws-in-india-states-religious-conversion-1752402-2020-12-23.

Mayaram, Shail. 1997. *Resisting Regimes: Myth, Memory, and the Shaping of a Muslim Identity,* Delhi: Oxford University Press.

Mbembe, Achille. 2022. Interview with Joseph Confavreux, "Decolonial Anxieties in a Postcolonial World," *Postcolonial Studies*, vol. 25, no. 1, 128–35.

Meckel, Daniel J. 2009. "Hinduism and Psychoanalysis," in Jacob A. Belzen, ed., *Changing the Scientific Study of Religion: Beyond Freud?* Berlin: Springer Media.

Meghwanshi, Bhanwar. 2020. *I Could Not Be Hindu: The Story of a Dalit in the RSS*, Delhi: Navayana.

Mehdi, Zehra. 2018a. "Only Hindu, Also the Patient; Only Muslim, Also the Therapist: Recovering the Historical Other," in Manasi Kumar, Anup Dhar, and Anurag Mishra, eds., *Psychoanalysis from the Indian Terroir. Emerging Themes in Culture, Family and Childhood*, New York, London: Lexington Books.

Mehdi, Zehra. 2018b. "Politics of Secular Psychoanalysis in India: Hindu-Muslim as Religious and Political Identities in Sudhir Kakar's Writing," in Ian Parker and Sabah Siddiqui, eds., *Islamic Psychoanalysis and Psychoanalytic Islam. Cultural and Clinical Dialogues*, London: Routledge.

Mehta, Pratap Bhanu. 2010. "What is Constitutional Morality?," *Seminar*

615, https://www.india-seminar.com/2010/615/615_pratap_bha
nu_mehta.htm.

Mekoa, Itumeleng. 2020. "The Politics and Nuances of Language in South
Africa," *Journal of African Languages and Literary Studies*, vol. 1, no. 1.

Menon, Dilip M., ed. 2022. *Changing Theory: Concepts from the Global
South*, Delhi: Routledge.

Menon, Dilip, Nishat Zaidi, Simi Malhotra, and Saarah Jappie. 2022. *Ocean
as Method. Thinking with the Maritime*, Delhi: Routledge India.

Menon, Nivedita. 1998. "Women and Citizenship," in Partha Chatterjee, ed.,
Wages of Freedom, Delhi: Oxford University Press.

Menon, Nivedita. 2004. *Recovering Subversion: Feminist Politics Beyond the
Law*, Delhi: Permanent Black, and Champaign: University of Illinois
Press.

Menon, Nivedita. 2007a. "Outing Heteronormativity: Nation, Citizen,
Feminist Disruptions," in Nivedita Menon, ed., *Sexualities*, Delhi:
Women Unlimited.

Menon, Nivedita. 2007b. "Living with Secularism," in Anuradha Dingwaney Needham and Rajeswari Sunder Rajan, eds., *The Crisis of Secularism in India*, Durham: Duke University Press.

Menon, Nivedita. 2008. "Citizenship and the Passive Revolution: Interpreting the First Amendment," in Rajeev Bhargava, ed., *Politics and Ethics
of the Indian Constitution*, Delhi: Oxford University Press.

Menon, Nivedita. 2010. "Introduction," in Partha Chatterjee, *Empire and
Nation. Essential Writings 1985–2005*, Ranikhet: Permanent Black.

Menon, Nivedita. 2012. *Seeing like a Feminist*, Delhi: Zubaan and Penguin
(updated 2nd ed., 2022).

Menon, Nivedita. 2014a. "Cooking Up Nature: Science in the World of
Politics," in Nivedita Menon, Aditya Nigam, and Sanjay Palshikar, eds.,
Critical Studies in Politics. Sites, Selves, Power, Hyderabad: Orient
Blackswan.

Menon, Nivedita. 2014b. "Narmada Waters for Coca-Cola—really, how
much more development can we take?," *Kafila*, https://kafila.online/
2014/09/15/narmada-waters-for-coca-cola-really-how-much-more-
development-can-we-take/.

Menon, Nivedita. 2019a. "Environment and the Will to Rule. Supreme
Court and Public Interest Litigation in the 1990s," in Mayur Suresh and
Siddharth Narrain, eds., *The Shifting Scales of Justice: The Supreme Court
in Neo-liberal India*, Hyderabad: Orient Blackswan.

Menon, Nivedita. 2019b. "Law versus faith, female activists versus male devotees and other strange creatures at Sabarimala," *Kafila*, 6 February, https://kafila.online/2019/02/06/law-versus-faith-female-activists-versus-male-devotees-and-other-strange-creatures-at-sabarimala/.

Menon, Nivedita. 2020a. "Hindu Rashtra and Bollywood: A New Front in the Battle for Cultural Hegemony," *South Asia Multidisciplinary Academic Journal*, https://journals.openedition.org/samaj/6861.

Menon, Nivedita. 2020b. "NEP 2020: Elitist and Corporatized Education under Hindu Rashtra," *Kafila*, 9 September, https://kafila.online/2020/09/08/nep-2020-elitist-and-corporatized-education-under-hindu-rashtra/.

Menon, Nivedita. 2022. "Oishik Sircar's Violent Modernities" (Review Essay), *Law and Other Things*, https://lawandotherthings.com/oishik-sircars-violent-modernities-review-by-nivedita-menon/.

Menon, Nivedita. 2023. "Performing the Constitution," in Silvija Jestrovic and Bishnupriya Dutt, eds., *Theatre, Activism, Subjectivity: Searching for the Left in a Fragmented World*, Manchester: Manchester University Press.

Menon, Nivedita, and Aditya Nigam. 2014. *Power and Contestation. India since 1989*, Hyderabad: Orient Blackswan.

Menon, Nivedita, Aditya Nigam, and Sanjay Palshikar. 2014. "Introduction," in idem, eds., *Critical Studies in Politics. Sites, Selves, Power*, Hyderabad: Orient Blackswan.

Mernissi, Fatema. 1987. "The Muslim Concept of Active Female Sexuality," in *Beyond the Veil. Male–Female Dynamics in Modern Muslim Society*, Bloomington: Indiana University Press.

Mernissi, Fatema. 2002. *Islam and Democracy: Fear of the Modern World*, New York: Basic Books.

Mevani, Jignesh. 2018. "Will Ask PM to Choose Between Manusmriti and Constitution," *The Quint*, 11 January, https://www.thequint.com/news/india/mevani-will-ask-pm-to-choose-between-manusmriti-and-constitution.

Mies, Maria, Claudia von Werlhof, and Veronika Bennholdt-Thomsen. 1988. *Women: The Last Colony*, London: Zed Books.

Mignolo, Walter D. 2011. *The Darker Side of Western Modernity*, Durham: Duke University Press.

Mignolo, Walter. 2017. "Interview," *E-International Relations*, 1 June, https://www.e-ir.info/2017/06/01/interview-walter-d-mignolo/.

Mills, China. 2014. *Decolonizing Global Mental Health: The Psychiatrization of the Majority World*, London: Routledge.

Miranda, Natalia A. Ramos. 2022. "Explainer: What's in Chile's Proposed

New Constitution?," *Reuters*, 29 July, https://www.reuters.com/world/americas/whats-chiles-proposed-new-constitution-2022-07-29/.

Mirror Now. 2022. "Himachal Polls: EVMs Found in Private Vehicle in Shimla, Polling Party Suspended; Congress Alleges Tampering," *Economic Times*, 13 November, https://m.economictimes.com/news/elections/assembly-elections/himachal-pradesh/himachal-polls-evms-found-in-private-vehicle-in-shimla-polling-party-suspended-congress-alleges-tampering/videoshow/95485750.cms.

Mishra, R. C. 2006. "Indian Perspectives on Cognition," in Uichol Kim, Kuo-Shu Yang, and Kwang-Kuo Hwang, eds., *Indigenous and Cultural Psychology. Understanding People in Context*, Berlin: Springer, 263–84.

Misra, Salil. 2020. "Communalism in Modern India," *Social Scientist*, March–June, vol. 48, no. 3/6 (562–5), 25–54.

Mitchell, Timothy. 2007. "Properties of Markets," in Donald MacKenzie, Fabian Muniesa, and and Lucia Siu, eds., *Do Economists Make Markets? On the Performativity of Economics*, Princeton: Princeton University Press.

Mitta, Manoj. 2023. *Caste Pride: Battles for Equality in Hindu India*, New Delhi: Westland Books.

Mnisi, Sindiso. 2007. "Postcolonial Culture and the South African Legal System: Understanding the Relationship Between Living Customary Law and State Law," *Zeitschrift für Rechtssoziologie*, 28 Heft 2, 241–51.

Mohan J., Anand. 2022. "Arrested Over Gyanvapi Post, DU Associate Professor Ratan Lal Gets Bail," *Indian Express*, 22 May, https://indianexpress.com/article/cities/delhi/du-prof-ratan-lal-bail-gyanvapi-shivling-post-7929316/.

Mohan, Archis. 2019. "Cabinet Nod to Rs 3,941-cr Fund for NPR Update, Rs 8,500 cr for Census 2021," *Business Standard*, 25 December, https://www.business-standard.com/article/politics/cabinet-nod-to-rs-3-941-cr-fund-for-npr-update-rs-8-500-cr-for-census-2021-119122401306_1.html.

Mohanty, Prasanna. 2019. "CAA & NRC III: Who Are 'Doubtful' Citizens NPR Seeks to Identify?," *Business Today*, 24 December, https://www.businesstoday.in/latest/economy-politics/story/caa-nrc-iii-who-are-doubtful-citizens-npr-seeks-to-identify-241445-2019-12-24.

Moorjani, Priya, Kumarasamy Thangaraj, Nick Patterson, Mark Lipson, Po-Ru Loh, Periyasamy Govindaraj, Bonnie Berger, David Reich, and Lalji Singh. 2013. "Genetic Evidence for Recent Population Mixture in India," *American Journal of Human Genetics*, 8 August.

Morse, Michelle Milford, and Grace Anderson. 2020. "The Shadow Pandemic. How the Covid 19 Crisis is Exacerbating Gender Inequality," *United Nations Foundation*, 14 April 14, https://unfoundation.org/blog/post/shadow-pandemic-how-covid19-crisis-exacerbating-gender-inequality/.

Mostov, Julie, and Rada Ivekovic, eds. 2004. *From Gender to Nation*, Delhi: Zubaan Books.

Mouffe, Chantal. 2018. *For a Left Populism*, London and New York: Verso.

Moyo, Sam, and Paris Yeros. 2005. *Reclaiming the Land. The Resurgence of Rural Movements in Africa, Asia and Latin America*, London and New York: Zed Books, and Cape Town: David Philip.

Mundkur, Balaji. 1975. "The Enigma of Vaināyakī," *Artibus Asiae*, vol. 37, no. 4, 291–302.

Mundkur, Balaji. 1980. Response to Gabriella Eichinger Ferro-Luzzi, "The Female Lingam: Interchangeable Symbols and Paradoxical Associations of Hindu Gods and Goddesses," *Current Anthropology*, February, vol. 21, no. 1 45–68.

Muniraju, S. B., and K. Sirisha. No Date. "Local to Global. Promotion of Tribal Products," *NITI Aayog*, https://www.niti.gov.in/local-global-promotion-tribal-products.

Mustafa, Seema, ed. 2020. *Shaheen Bagh and the Idea of India*, Delhi: Speaking Tiger Books.

Nagi, Saroj. 2007. "Nervous Government Now Chants 'Ram Naam'," *Hindustan Times*, 13 September.

Nair, Janaki. 1996. *Women and Law in Colonial India: A Social History*, Delhi: Kali for Women.

Nandy, Ashis. 1985. "An Anti-secularist Manifesto," *Seminar*, October, 314.

Nandy, Ashis, ed. 1988. *Science, Hegemony and Violence. A Requiem for Modernity*, United Nations University, https://www.arvindguptatoys.com/arvindgupta/hegemony-nandy.pdf.

Nandy, Ashis. 1990. "The Politics of Secularism and the Recovery of Religious Tolerance," in *Mirrors of Violence: Communities, Riots, and Survivors in South Asia*, ed. Veena Das, New York and Delhi: Oxford University Press, 69–93.

Nandy, Ashis. 1995a. "An Anti-secularist Manifesto" (Revised and updated), *India International Centre Quarterly*, Spring, vol. 22, no. 1, 35–64.

Nandy, Ashis. 1995b. *The Savage Freud and Other Essays on Possible and Retrievable Selves*, Delhi: Oxford University Press.

Nandy, Ashis. 1997. "The Twilight of Certitudes: Secularism, Hindu Nationalism, and Other Masks of Deculturation," *Alternatives: Global, Local, Political*, April–June, vol. 22, no. 2, 157–76.

Nandy, Ashis. 2003. "The State: The Fate of a Concept," in idem, *The Romance of the State and the Fate of Dissent in the Tropics*, Delhi: Oxford University Press.

Nandy, Ashis. 2014. "A Unique Communal Harmony in Kochi," *The Hindu*, 30 July.

Narasimhan, Vagheesh M., N. J. Patterson, Priya Moorjani, et al. 2019. "The Fomation of Human Populations in South and Central Asia," *Science*, 365 (6457).

Nath, Dipanita. 2012. "The Spirit Eaters and Other Curiosities," *The Indian Express*, 31 January, https://indianexpress.com/article/cities/chandigarh/the-spirit-eaters-and-other-curiosities/.

Nath, Vijay. 2009. *The Puranic World. Environment, Gender, Ritual and Myth*, Delhi: Manohar.

Nayak, Venkatesh. 2019. "EVMs and VVPATs: RTI Reveals Micro-controller Used Is Not OTP Type . . .," *Commonwealth Human Rights Initiative*, 22 May 22, https://www.humanrightsinitiative.org/blog/evms-and-vvpats-rti-reveals-microcontroller-used-is-not-otp-type-as-claimed-by-the-election-commission-bel-and-ecil-refuse-to-reveal-software-audit-reports-citing-national-security-and-commercial-con fidence.

Neelakantan, Anand. 2013. "Preface," in idem, *Ajaya: Epic of the Kaurava Clan*, Mumbai: Platinum Press.

Newbigin, Eleanor. 2009. "The Codification of Personal Law and Secular Citizenship: Revisiting the History of Law Reform in Late Colonial India," *The Indian Economic and Social History Review*, vol. 46 (1), 83–104.

Newsclick Report. 2022. "NFHS Data Shows More Men Eating Non-veg Than Before," *Newsclick*, 17 May, https://www.newsclick.in/NFHS-Data-Shows-More-men-Eating-Non-veg-Than-Before.

Niaz, Noorjehan Safia. 2022. "I Can See the Pitfalls of Supporting Practices Such as Hijab," *The Hindu*, 4 March, https://www.thehindu.com/society/i-can-see-the-pitfalls-of-supporting-practices-such-as-hijab-noorjehan-safia-niaz/article65092300.ece.

Nicholson, Andrew J. 2010. *Unifying Hinduism: Philosophy and Identity in Indian Intellectual History*, New York: Columbia University Press.

Nigam, Aditya. 2014. "'Molecular Economies': Is There an 'Outside' to Capital?," in Nivedita Menon, Aditya Nigam, and Sanjay Palshikar, eds., *Critical Studies in Politics. Exploring Sites, Selves, Power*, Hyderabad: Orient Blackswan.

Nigam, Aditya. 2016. "Violence and the Political," in Kalpana Kannabiran, ed., *Violence Studies I*, Delhi: Oxford University Press.

Nigam, Aditya. 2020. *Decolonizing Theory. Thinking Across Traditions* Delhi: Bloomsbury.

Nigam, Aditya. 2023. "Populism and the 'Nirgun' People," in M. K. Jha and K. N. Choubey, eds., *Indian Politics and Political Processes*, Delhi: Routledge.

Niyogi Committee Report. 1956. *Report of the Christian Missionary Activities Enquiry Committee, Madhya Pradesh. Volume 1*, https://indianculture.gov.in/reports-proceedings/report-christian-missionary-activities-enquiry-committee-madhya-pradesh-1956.

Nyeleni Declaration. 2007. https://nyeleni.org/IMG/pdf/DeclNyeleni-en.pdf.

Nzegwu, Nkiru. 2004. "Feminism and Africa: Impact and Limits of the Metaphysics of Gender," in Kwasi Wiredu, ed., *A Companion to African Philosophy*, Oxford: Blackwell Publishing.

Obama, Barack. 2009. *Inaugural Address*, https://obamawhitehouse.archives.gov/blog/2009/01/21/president-Barack-obamas-inaugural-address.

Oberoi, Harjot. 1994. *The Construction of Religious Boundaries: Culture, Identity and Diversity in the Sikh Tradition*, Chicago: The University of Chicago Press.

Obeyesekere, Gananath. 1990. "The Illusory Pursuit of the Self: A Review of 'Culture and Self: Asian and Western Perspectives'," *Philosophy East and West*, April, vol. 40, no. 2, 239–50.

Obeyesekere, Gananath. 2012. *The Awakened Ones. Phenomenology of Visionary Experience*, New York: Columbia University Press.

Okin, Susan Moller. 1999. *Is Multiculturalism Bad for Women?* Princeton: Princeton University Press.

Okonogi, Keigo. 1979. "Japanese Psychoanalysis and the Ajase Complex (Kosawa)," *Psychotherapy and Psychosomatics*, vol. 31, no. 1/4, 350–6.

Olivelle, Patrick. 2013. *King, Governance, and Law in Ancient India: Kautilya's Arthasastra*, New York: Oxford University Press.

Omvedt, Gail. 2008. *Seeking Begumpura: The Social Vision of Anticaste Intellectuals*, Delhi: Navayana Publishing.

Organiser Web Desk. 2020. "Group of Intellectuals and Academicians Submit Report on Delhi Anti-Hindu Riots to Home Ministry . . .," *Organiser*, 11 March, https://www.organiser.org/Encyc/2020/3/11/Group-of-Intellectuals-and-Academicians-submit-report-on-Delhi-anti-Hindu-riots-to-Home-Ministry.html.

Oyewumi, Oyeronke. 1997. *The Invention of Women. Making an African sense of Western Gender Discourses*, Minneapolis: University of Minnesota Press.

Palshikar, Sanjay. 2014a. "The *Asuras* Through the Ages," in Nivedita Menon, Aditya Nigam, and Sanjay Palshikar, eds., *Critical Studies in Politics. Sites, Selves, Power*, Hyderabad: Orient Blackswan.

Palshikar, Sanjay. 2014b. *Evil and the Philosophy of Retribution. Modern Commentaries on the Bhagavad-Gita*, Delhi: Routledge.

Pande, Mrinal. 2016a. "Guess What? Durga and Mahishasur Actually Share the Same Origin," *Scroll.in*, 27 February, https://scroll.in/article/804263/guess-what-durga-and-mahishasur-actually-share-the-same-origin.

Pande, Mrinal. 2016b. "The Sanjivani Quest: An Uttarakhand Village Hasn't Forgiven Hanuman for Defacing Their Holy Mountain," *Scroll.in*, 31 July, https://scroll.in/article/812802/the-sanjivani-quest-an-uttarakhand-village-hasnt-forgiven-hanuman-for-defacing-their-holy-mountain.

Pandey, Alok. 2019. "Questions Raised Over Movement of EVMs in UP, Bihar After Videos Surface," *NDTV*, 21 May, https://www.ndtv.com/india-news/lok-sabha-elections-2019-questions-raised-over-movement-of-evms-in-up-bihar-after-videos-surface-2040479.

Pandey, Gyanendra. 1990. *The Construction of Communalism in Colonial North India*, Delhi: Oxford University Press.

Pandey, Prashant, and Premankur Biswas. 2016. "Meet the Asurs—A Marginal Tribe that Describes Durga as a Goddess who Enticed Mahishasur," *The Indian Express*, 8 December.

Pandolfo, Stefania. 2018. *Knot of the Soul Madness, Psychoanalysis, Islam*, Chicago: University of Chicago Press.

Parashar, Kiran, and Apurva Vishwanath. 2022. "Karnataka Govt Invokes State Law to Back Hijab Ban: 'Don't Wear Clothes that Disturb Law & Order'," *The Indian Express*, 6 February, https://indianexpress.com/article/cities/bangalore/karnataka-hijab-controversy-clothes-ban-harmony-public-order-7758633/lite/.

Parasher, Archana. 1992. *Women and Family Law Reform in India*, New Delhi: Sage.

Pareek, Harsh. 2016. "The Day Mahishasur Visited Rajya Sabha," *Firstpost*, 26 February, https://www.firstpost.com/politics/the-day-mahishasur-visited-rajya-sabha-smriti-iranis-argument-may-be-misguided-but-its-a-discussion-that-must-be-had-2644370.html.

Parthasarathy, Suhrith. 2020. "'Republic of Religion—The Rise and Fall of

Colonial Secularism in India', Review: Interplay of State and Religion," *The Hindu*, 9 May, https://www.thehindu.com/books/books-reviews/republic-of-religion-the-rise-and-fall-of-colonial-secularism-in-india-review-interplay-of-state-and-religion/article31533693.ece.

Patel, Vibhuti, and Lea Goelnitz. 2020. "Who Cares? Feminist Responses to the Pandemic," *Freidrich Ebert Stiftung*, 20 April, https://asia.fes.de/news/who-cares-feminist-responses-to-the-pandemic/.

Paul, Sonia. 2018. "When Caste Discrimination Comes to the United States," *American University Radio*, 27 April, https://wamu.org/story/18/04/27/when-caste-discrimination-comes-to-the-united-states/.

Payne, Geoffrey, Alain Durand-Lasserve, and Carole Rakodi. 2009. "The Limits of Land Titling and Home Ownership," *Environment & Urbanization*, vol. 21 (2), 443–62.

Pereira, Stacey. 2020. "Two Bengaluru Activists Who Helped Migrants Get Train Tickets Booked After Builders Complain," *News 18*, 9 May, https://www.news18.com/news/india/complaint-filed-against-2-activists-in-ktaka-for-allegedly-assisting-migrant-workers-in-going-home-2612671.html.

Peter, Benoy, Shachi Sanghvi, and Vishnu Narendran. 2020. "Inclusion of Interstate Migrant Workers in Kerala and Lessons for India," *The Indian Journal of Labour Economics*, 12 November.

Philip, Christin Mathew. 2020. "Under Fire, Karnataka Does U-turn, Will Resume Trains for Migrants," *Times of India*, 8 May, http://timesofindia.indiatimes.com/articleshow/75614188.cms?utm_source=contentofinterest&utm_medium=text&utm_campaign=cppst.

Philip, Shaju. 2019. "Organising People on Religious Lines Will Weaken Secular Unity, Says CPM," *The Indian Express*, 23 December, https://indianexpress.com/article/india/organising-people-on-religious-lines-will-weaken-secular-unity-says-cpm-6180283/.

Piketty, Thomas. 2016. "What Unequal Societies Need is Not a 'Basic Income' But a Fair Wage," *The Wire*, 14 December, https://thewire.in/86990/basic-income-fair-wage-piketty/.

Pillay, Suren. 2023. *On the Subject of Citizenship. Late Colonialism in the World Today*, Delhi: Bloomsbury Publishing.

Pinto, Sarah. 2019. *The Doctor and Mrs. A. Ethics and Counter-Ethics in an Indian Dream Analysis (Thinking from Elsewhere)*, Delhi: Women Unlimited.

Pinto, Sarah. 2020. Interview with Shikha Kumar, "Sarah Pinto on the Fascinating Indian Dream Analysis Study that Inspired Her . . .," *Firstpost*,

10 April, https://www.firstpost.com/living/sarah-pinto-on-the-fas
cinating-indian-dream-analysis-study-that-inspired-her-new-book-
exploring-relationship-between-ethics-and-counter-ethics-8243501
.html.

Pirate Care Project. No Date. https://pirate.care/pages/concept/.

Pirate Care Syllabus. 2020. https://www.maddalenafragnito.com/
post/615506149674008576/pirate-care-a-syllabus-we-live-in-a-world-
where.

Poddar, Umang. 2022. "Why is Karnataka HC Deciding if the Hijab is an
'Essential Religious Practice' in Islam?" *Scroll.in*, 24 February, https:
//scroll.in/article/1017822/explainru-why-is-karnataka-hc-deciding-if-
the-hijab-is-an-essential-religious-practice-in-islam#:~:text=In%20
1994%2C%20while%20deciding%20on,anywhere%2C%20even%20
in%20the%20open.

Polga-Hecimovich, John. 2022. "Scenarios in Chile After a Failed Constitution," *GIS Reports*, 24 October, https://www.gisreportsonline.com/r/
chile-constitution/.

Prakash, Brahma. 2022. "Bulldozer Is a Sign that Hindutva is Flat!" *Indian
Cultural Forum*, 23 May, https://indianculturalforum.in/2022/05/23/
bulldozer-is-a-sign-that-hindutva-is-flat/.

Prakash, Gyan. 1999. *Science and the Imagination of Modern India*, Delhi:
Oxford University Press.

Prasad, Chandrabhan. 2018. "'Dalit Capitalism Can Turn the Caste Order':
Activist Chandrabhan Prasad," Interview with Aditi Phadnis, *Business
Standard*, 30 December, https://www.business-standard.com/article/
current-affairs/dalit-capitalism-can-turn-the-caste-order-activist-chan
drabhan-prasad-118122900470_1.html.

Press Trust of India. 2018. "More than 19,500 Mother Tongues Spoken in
India: Census," *The Indian Express*, 1 July, https://indianexpress.com/
article/india/more-than-19500-mother-tongues-spoken-in-india-cen
sus-5241056/.

Press Trust of India. 2018. "British Era Survey Report Says Sabarimala Ban Existed 200 Years Ago," *The Week*, 22 November, https://www.theweek.in/
news/india/2018/11/22/british-era-survey-report-says-sabarimala-ban-
existed-200-years-ago.html.

Press Trust of India. 2019. "Those Indulging in Arson 'Can be Identified by
Their Clothes': Narendra Modi on anti-CAA Protest," *The Economic Times*,
15 December, https://economictimes.indiatimes.com/news/politics-

and-nation/those-indulging-in-arson-can-be-identified-by-their-clothes-narendra-modi-on-anti-caa protest/articleshow/72687256.cms?utm_source=contentofinterest&utm_medium=text&utm_campaign=cppst.

Priyadarshini, Anna. 2020. "How a Coalition of Diaspora Indians in America Aims to Counter the Hindutva Narrative," *Newslaundry*, 25 September, https://www.newslaundry.com/2020/09/25/how-a-coalition-of-di aspora-indians-in-america-aims-to-counter-the-hindutva-narrative.

PTI. 2013. "SC Notice to Govt on Plea Against Constitutional Clause Referring to Sikhs as Hindus," https://www.news18.com/news/india/sc-notice-to-govt-on-plea-against-constitutional-clause-referring-to-sikhs-as-hindus-621554.html.

PTI. 2020a. "Spraying of Disinfectant on People 'Physically and Psychologically Harmful': Health Ministry," *Economic Times*, 18 April, https://economictimes.indiatimes.com/news/politics-and-nation/spray-ing-of-disinfectant-on-people-physically-and-psychologically-harmful-health-ministry/articleshow/75226204.cms?utm_source=contentofin terest&utm_medium=text&utm_campaign=cppst.

PTI. 2020b. "Prasar Bharati Makes it Mandatory for Staffers to Install COVID-19 Tracking 'Arogya Setu' App," *Economic Times*, 15 April, https://economictimes.indiatimes.com/industry/media/entertainment/media/prasar-bharati-makes-it-mandatory-for-staffers-to-install-covid-19-tracking-arogya-setu-app/articleshow/75158606.cms?utm_source= contentofinterest&utm_medium=text&utm_campaign=cppst.

PTI. 2021. "Oil Ministry Proposal to Privatise Biggest Oil Field Upsets Union: Report," *NDTV*, 21 November, https://www.ndtv.com/india-news/ongc-privatisation-news-ongc-privatisation-bid-ongc-shares-oil-ministry-proposal-to-privatise-biggest-oil-field-ongc-upsets-union-report-2619025.

PTI. 2022. "Can Muslims Surpass Hindus in Population Numbers? Experts Say Practically Not Possible," *Deccan Herald*, 24 April, https://www.deccanherald.com/national/can-muslims-surpass-hindus-in-popula tion-numbers-experts-say-practically-not-possible-1103547.html.

Puzhakkal, Dheeshma. 2020. https://www.indiatoday.in/fact-check/story/fact-check-no-kerala-has-not-banned-raksha-bandhan-celebrations-in-medical-colleges-1729207-2020-10-07.

Quraishi-Landes, Asifa. 2022. "Abortion Bans Trample on the Religious freedom of Muslims, Too," *San Francisco Chronicle*, 23 June, https://www.sfchronicle.com/opinion/openforum/article/abortion-bans-religion-17259119.php.

Radhakrishnan, Rajiv. 2020. "Temple-healing in South India," *Indian Journal of Psychiatry*, May–June, vol. 62 (3), 335–6.

Rajamani, Lavanya. 2007. "Public Interest Environmental Litigation in India: Exploring Issues of Access, Participation, Equity, Effectiveness and Sustainability," *Journal of Environmental Law*, vol. 19, no. 3, 293–321.

Rajkotia, Malavika. No Date. "Laws, Patriarchy," unpublished paper.

Ram, Sandhya. 2018. "Ban on Entry of Women in Sabarimala Temple—Just Another Case of an Age Old Prejudice Against Women," *Live Law*, 8 March, https://www.livelaw.in/ban-entry-women-sabarimala-temple-just-another-case-age-old-prejudice-women/.

Ramakrishnan, Venkitesh. 2019a. "'Missing' EVMs," *Frontline*, 9 May, online edition (print edition 24 May), https://frontline.thehindu.com/cover-story/article27056139.ece.

Ramakrishnan, Venkitesh. 2019b. "Missing 'EVMs': EC's Rejoinder and *Frontline*'s Response," *Frontline*, 10 May, online edition, https://frontline.thehindu.com/dispatches/article27093327.ece.

Ramanan, Vrinda, and J. Ramanan. 2017. "Shrine for Duryodhana!," *The Hindu*, 11 May, https://www.thehindu.com/society/history-and-culture/a-temple-for-duryodhana-in-the-himalayas/article18425964.ece.

Ramanujan, A. K. 1973. *Speaking of Siva*, Harmondsworth: Penguin.

Ramanujan, A. K. 1989. "Is There an Indian Way of Thinking? An Informal Essay," *Contributions to Indian Sociology*, vol. 23/1, 41–58.

Ramanujan, A. K. 1995. "The Indian Oedipus," in Lowell Edmunds and Alan Dundes, eds., *Oedipus. A Folklore Casebook*, Madison: University of Wisconsin Press.

Ramaswamy, Sumathi. 2001. "Maps and Mother Goddesses in Modern India," *Imago Mundi*, vol. 53, 97–114.

Ramaswamy, Sumathi. 2010. *The Goddess and the Nation: Mapping Mother India*, Durham: Duke University Press.

Ramdas, Sagari. 2009. "Women, Forestspaces and the Law: Transgressing the Boundaries," *Economic and Political Weekly*, 31 October, 65–79.

Rangarajan, Mahesh, and Vasant Saberwal. 2003. *Battles Over Nature*, Delhi: Permanent Black.

Ranjan, Pramod. 2016. *Mahishasur. A People's Hero*, Wardha, Maharashtra: Forward Press Books.

Rao, Ramakrishna K. 2014. "Positive Psychology and Indian Psychology in Need of Mutual Reinforcement," *Psychological Studies*, vol. 59 (2), 94–102.

Rao, Velcheru Narayana. 1993. "Purana as Brahminic Ideology," in Wendy Doniger, ed., *Purana Perennis. Reciprocity and Transformation in Hindu and Jaina Texts*, Delhi: Sri Satguru Publications, India Books Centre.

Rao, Velcheru Narayana. 2019. "The Concept of Author in Indian Text Culture," https://www.sahapedia.org/interpreting-indian-literatures-velcheru-narayana-rao-concept-author-indian-text-culture.

Rao, Vidhatri. 2022. "Anatomy of Anti-conversion Legislation in India: A Comparative Look at State Laws," *Indian Express*, 16 August, https://indianexpress.com/article/political-pulse/anti-conversion-laws-himachal-up-karnataka-comparison-8092477/.

Rashid, Omar. 2015. "Championing Gond Culture," https://www.thehindu.com/news/national/other-states/on-the-margins-championing-gond-culture/article7686156.ece.

Rashid, Omar. 2021. "54 Arrested in U. P. Under Unlawful Conversion Ordinance So Far," *The Hindu*, 15 January, https://www.thehindu.com/news/national/other-states/54-arrested-in-up-under-unlawful-conversion-ordinance-so-far/article33582567.ece.

Ravishankar, Sandhya. 2015. "India's Mentally Ill: On a Pill and a Prayer," *Al Jazeera,* 31 August, https://www.aljazeera.com/features/2015/8/31/indias-mentally-ill-on-a-pill-and-a-prayer.

Ray, Himanshu Prabha. 2020. *Coastal Shrines and Transnational Maritime Networks across India and Southeast Asia*, Delhi: Routledge.

Raygorodetsky, Gleb. 2018. "Indigenous Peoples Defend Earth's Biodiversity—But They're in Danger," *National Geographic*, 16 November, https://www.nationalgeographic.com/environment/article/can-indigenous-land-stewardship-protect-biodiversity-.

Reich, David, Kumarasamy Thangaraj, Nick Patterson, Alkes L. Price, and Lalji Singh. 2009. "Reconstructing Indian Population History," *Nature*, vol. 461 (7263), 489–94.

Rhouni, Raja. 2010. *Secular and Islamic Feminist Critiques in the Work of Fatima Mernissi*, Leiden: Brill.

Roberts, David. 2020. "Why Rich People Use So Much More Energy," *Vox*, 20 March, https://www.vox.com/energy-and-environment/2020/3/20/21184814/climate-change-energy-income-inequality.

Rocher, Ludo. 1986. *The Puranas*, Wiesbaden: Otto Harrassowitz Verlag.

Rodinson, Maxime. 1966/2007. *Islam and Capitalism*, London: Saqi Books.

Rojas, Carlos. 2019. "Method as Method," *Prism*, vol. 16 (2), 211–20, https://read.dukeupress.edu/prism/article-abstract/16/2/211/165803/Method-as-Method?redirectedFrom=fulltext.

Roopesh, O. B. 2018. "Sabarimala Protest. Politics of Standardising Religious Pluralism," *Economic and Political Weekly*, 15 December.

Roy, Anupama. 2022. *Citizenship Regimes, Law and Belonging: The CAA and the NRC*, New York: Oxford University Press.

Roychoudhuri, Arup. 2020. "India's Top 63 Billionaires Have More Wealth than 2018–19 Budget Outlay," *Business Standard*, 21 January, https://www.business-standard.com/article/economy-policy/india-s-top-63-billionaires-have-more-wealth-than-2018-19-budget-outlay-120012100038_1.html#:~:text=%E2%80%9CThe%20combined%20total%20wealth%20of,its%20report%20released%20on%20Monday.

Rugh, Peter. 2013. "How Murdoch, Bill Gates and Big Corporations Are Data Mining Our Schools," *The Indypendent*, 30 April, https://indypendent.org/2013/04/how-murdoch-bill-gates-and-big-corporations-are-data-mining-our-schools/.

S Mahendran v. The Secretary Travancore. 1991. https://indiankanoon.org/doc/1915943/.

Saaliq, Sheikh, and Adrija Bose. 2018. "Documenting Violence Against Dalits: One Assault at a Time," *News18*, https://www.news18.com/news/immersive/documenting-violence-against-dalits-one-assault-at-a-time.html#dalitmap.

SabrangIndia. 2019. "Post 370 Abrogation, August 5, the Forest Advisory Committee of J & K Has Cleared 125 Projects on Forest Land," *Sabrang*, 19 October, https://www.sabrangindia.in/article/post-370-abrogation-august-5-forest-advisory-committee-j-k-has-cleared-125-projects-forest.

SAFSC. No Date. South African Food Sovereignty Campaign, https://www.safsc.org.za/.

Saglio-Yatzimirskya, Marie Caroline, and Brigitte Sebastia. 2014. "Mixing Tirttam and Tablets. A Healing Proposal for Mentally Ill Patients in Gunaseelam (South India)," *Anthropology and Medicine*, October.

Sahaney, Ranee. 2022. "Bastar Dussehra: Riddles of Antiquity," *Outlook Traveller*, 2 October, https://www.outlookindia.com/outlooktraveller/explore/story/71521/how-dussehra-is-celebrated-in-bastar.

Said, Edward. 1978. *Orientalism*, New York: Pantheon Books.

Said, Edward. 2014. *Freud and the Non-European*. London: Verso.

Sakai, Naoki. 2010. "Theory and Asian Humanity: On the Question of Humanitas and Anthropos," *Postcolonial Studies*, vol. 13, 441–64.

Sakthidharan, A. V. 2019. *Antigod's Own Country. A Short History of the Brahminical Colonization of Kerala*, Delhi: Navayana.

Salleh, Ariel. 1997. *Ecofeminism as Politics: Nature, Marx and the Postmodern*, London: Zed Books, and New York: St Martin's Press.

Samaddar, Ranabir. 1999. *The Marginal Nation: Transborder Migration from Bangladesh to West Bengal*, Delhi: Sage Publications.

Samarthan. 2012. "Recognition of Community Rights Under Forest Rights Act in Madhya Pradesh and Chhattisgarh. Challenges and Way Forward," http://www.undp.org/content/dam/india/docs/DG/recognition-of-community-rights-under-forest-rights-act-in-madhya-pradesh-and-chhattisgarh-challenges-and-way-forward.pdf.

Sampath, G. 2017. "The Hidden Agenda of Benevolence," *The Indian Express*, 31 January.

Sampath, Vikram. 2018. "Savarkar Wanted to Smash Caste System, Cooked Prawns and Didn't Worship the Cow," *The Print*, 10 December, https://theprint.in/opinion/savarkar-wanted-to-smash-caste-system-cooked-prawns-and-didnt-worship-the-cow/161016/.

Samrat, X. 2021. "Why Ramakrishna Mission's Stance on Hindu Culture Matters in Bengal Election," *Newslaundry*, 2 April, https://www.newslaundry.com/2021/04/02/why-ramakrishna-missions-stance-on-hindu-culture-matters-in-bengal-election.

Sandhu, Amandeep. 2021. "Left, Khaps, Gender, Caste: The Solidarities Propping Up the Farmers' Protest," *The Caravan*, 13 January, https://caravanmagazine.in/agriculture/left-punjab-haryana-caste-gender-solidarities-farmers-protest.

Sangari, Kumkum, and Sudesh Vaid. 1989. *Recasting Women: Essays in Colonial History*, Delhi: Kali for Women.

Santhosh, Hyma. 2018. "Denouement of Marginalization through Priesthood: A Study of the Myth and Stigmatization in Malanada Duryodhana Temple," *Journal of Arts, Culture, Philosophy, Religion, Language and Literature*, vol. 2, issue 4, September–December, 208–10.

Saran, Bedanti. 2021. "Pathalgadi Movement Gets More Refined, Demands Implementation of Rules," *Hindustan Times*, 19 March, https: //www.hindustantimes.com/cities/ranchi-news/pathalgadi-movement-gets-more-refined-demands-implementation-of-rules-10161617 2925508.html.

Sarkar, Sumit. 2001. "Indian Democracy: The Historical Inheritance," in Atul Kohli, ed., *The Success of India's Democracy*, Cambridge: Cambridge University Press.

Sarkar, Sumit. 2014. *Modern Times: India 1880s–1950s*, Ranikhet: Permanent Black.

Sarkar, Tanika. 2022. "The Birth of a Goddess," in idem, *Hindu Nationalism in India*, Ranikhet: Permanent Black.

Sarkar, Urvashi. 2023. "Why Nuclear Industry's Comeback Hopes Rest on Very Thin Ice," *Newsclick*, 12 January, https://www.newsclick.in/Why-Nuclear-Industry-Comeback-Hopes-Rest-Very-Thin-Ice.

Satgar, Vishwas, and Jane Cherry. 2019. "The Food Sovereignty Alternative," https://www.wits.ac.za/news/latest-news/opinion/2019/2019-11/the-food-sovereignty-alternative.html.

Saumya, Uma, and Niti Saxena. 2021. "Juxtaposing 'Honour' with Women's Agency. Rights and Wrongs of Anti-conversion Law(s)," *Economic and Political Weekly*, vol. 56, no. 1, 2 January.

Savarkar, Vinayak Damodar. 1923. *Essentials of Hindutva*, http://savarkar.org/en/encyc/2017/5/23/2_12_12_04_essentials_of_hindutva.v001.pdf_1.pdf,

Savarkar, Vinayak Damodar. No Date. "Seven Shackles," http://savarkar.org/en/encyc/2017/5/22/Seven-shackles.html.

Sawariya, Meena. 2021. "Caste and Counselling Psychology in India: Dalit Perspectives in Theory and Practice," *CASTE: A Global Journal on Social Exclusion*, April, vol. 2, no. 1, 189–201.

Schmitt, Carl. 1985. *Political Theology: Four Chapters on the Concept of Sovereignty*, trans. George Schwab, Chicago: University of Chicago Press.

Scott, James C. 1998. *Seeing Like a State. How Certain Schemes to Improve the Human Condition Have Failed*, New Haven: Yale University Press.

Scott, James C. 2009. *The Art of Not Being Governed. An Anarchist History of Upland Southeast Asia*, New Haven: Yale University Press.

Scott, Joan. 2018. *Sex and Secularism*, Princeton: Princeton University Press.

Scroll Staff. 2020. "J&K: Those Living for More Than 15 Years Now Eligible for Domicile Under New Rule, Says Centre," *Scroll*, 1 April, https://scroll.in/latest/957868/j-k-those-living-for-more-than-15-years-now-eligible-for-domicile-under-new-rule-says-centre.

Sebag-Montefiore, Poppy. 2019. "Touch," *Granta 146*, 14 February.

Sekher, Ajay. 2011. "Buddha as Krishna: Kilirur Temple and Kerala History," https://ajaysekher.net/2011/12/29/2041/.

Sekhsaria, Pankaj. 2022. "Nicobar Project Gets Assent for Diversion of 130 sq km of forest," *The Hindu*, 8 November, https://www.thehindu.com/sci-tech/energy-and-environment/great-nicobar-project-gets-in-principle-clearance-for-diversion-of-130-sq-km-of-forest/article66111489.ece.

Selvam, Nivedha. 2022. "Tamil Fishing Communities Set Example of Interfaith Coexistence," *The Federal*, 24 February, https://thefederal.com/states/south/tamil-nadu/tamil-fishing-communities-set-example-of-interfaith-coexistence/.

Sen, Amartya. 2006. *Identity and Violence. The Illusion of Destiny*, New York: W. W. Norton & Company.

Sen, Amiya P. 2019. *Chaitanya. A Life and Legacy*, Delhi: Oxford University Press.

Sen, Nabaneeta Dev. 1997. "Rewriting the Ramayana: Chandrabati and Molla," *India International Centre Quarterly*, vol. 24, no. 2/3, 163–77.

Sen, Nabaneeta Dev. 2021. "When Women Retell the Ramayan," *Manushi*, 16 February, https://www.manushi.in/when-women-retell-the-ramayan/.

Sengupta, Shuddabrata. 2022. "When Kaali Descends: A Poster, a Cigarette, a Film," *The Wire*, 8 July, https://thewire.in/culture/kaali-poster-smoking-history.

Shah, A. P., and S. Muralidhar. 2009. "Naz Foundation vs Government of NCT of Delhi And Others," https://indiankanoon.org/doc/100472805/.

Shani, Ornit. 2022. "The People and the Making of India's Constitution," *The Historical Journal*, vol. 65, 1102–23.

Sharma, Indrajit. 2018. "Tea Tribes of Assam. Identity Politics and Search for Liberation," *Economic and Political Weekly*, vol. 53, no. 9, 3 March.

Sharma, Mukul. 2017. *Caste and Nature: Dalits and Indian Environmental Politics*, Delhi: Oxford University Press.

Sharma, Nandita. 2020. *Home Rule: National Sovereignty and the Separation of Natives and Migrants*, Durham: Duke University Press.

Sharma, Suresh. 1996. "Savarkar's Quest for a Modern Hindu Consolidation," *Studies in Humanities and Social Sciences*, vol. ii, no. 2, 189–215.

Shastry, Kishen, and Vijeta Ananthkumar. 2022. "Time for Temple Freedom in India. Release Them From HRCE Act, Bring Market Economics," *The Print*, 11 January, https://theprint.in/opinion/time-for-temple-freedom-in-india-release-them-from-hrce-act-bring-market-economics/799829/.

Shayara Bano Interview. 2016. "Same Laws for Hindus, Muslims, End Triple Talaq . . ." *Times of India*, 26 April, https://timesofindia.indiatimes.com/blogs/the-interviews-blog/same-laws-for-hindus-muslims-end-triple-talaq-shah-bano-denied-justice-i-got-postal-divorce-muslim-women-exploited/.

Shiva, Vandana. 1988. "Colonialism and the Evolution of Masculinist Forestry," in idem, *Staying Alive. Women, Ecology and Survival in India*, Delhi: Kali for Women. (Rpntd in Nivedita Menon, ed., *Gender and Politics in India*, Delhi: Oxford University Press, 1999.)

Shukla, Suhag. 2018. "Equality Labs' Social Hierarchy Survey Misdirected at Hindus," *Hindu American Foundation*, 21 April, https://www.hinduamerican.org/blog/equality-labs-social-hierarchy-survey-misdirected-at-hindus/.

Siddiqui, Sabah. 2016. *Religion and Psychoanalysis in India. Critical Clinical Practice*, London and New York: Routledge.

Siddiqui, Sabah, and Bhargavi Davar. 2018. "Devi Possession: At the Intersections of Religion, Culture and Psychoanalysis," in Manasi Kumar, Anup Dhar, and Anurag Mishra, eds., *Psychoanalysis from the Indian Terroir. Emerging Themes in Culture, Family and Childhood*, New York, London: Lexington Books.

Sierra Club. No Date. "What is a Green New Deal?," https://www.sierraclub.org/trade/what-green-new-deal.

Singer, Natasha. 2014. "InBloom Student Data Repository to Close" *The New York Times*, 21 April, https://bits.blogs.nytimes.com/2014/04/21/inbloom-student-data-repository-to-close/#:~:text=After%20parents%20in%20Louisiana%20discovered,student%20data%20from%20the%20database.

Singh, Madhur. 2007. "India's Debate Over Sacred Geography," *Time*, 18 September, http://www.time.com/time/world/article/0,8599,1663025,00.html.

Singh, Pritam. 2015. "Institutional Communalism in India," *Economic and Political Weekly*, vol. 50, no. 28, 11 July.

Singh, Pritam. 2019. "Guru Nanak's Message Transcends Time and Space," *The Indian Express*, 12 November, https://indianexpress.com/article/opinion/columns/guru-nanak-dev-guru-purb-sikhism-golden-temple-6115054/.

Singh, Shiv Sahay. 2020. "5 Years After Land Border Agreement, Former Enclave Dwellers in Dire Straits," *The Hindu*, 3 August, https://www.thehindu.com/news/national/5-years-after-land-border-agreement-former-enclave-dwellers-in-dire-straits/article32255788.ece.

Singh, Upinder. 2017. *Political Violence in Ancient India*, Boston: Harvard University Press.

Singh, Upinder. 2021. *A History of Ancient and Early Medieval India: From the Stone Age to the 12th Century*, New Delhi: Pearson.

Singha, Radhika. 1998. "Civil Authority and Due Process: Colonial Criminal Justice in the Banaras Zamindari, 1781–1795," in Michael Anderson and Sumit Guha, ed., *Changing Concepts of Rights in South Asia*, Delhi: Oxford University Press.

Singla, Anmol. 2022. "Karnataka HC Quotes Ambedkar to Conclude Verdict Upholding Hijab Ban," *Mirror Now*, 15 March, https://www .timesnownews.com/mirror-now/in-focus/karnataka-hc-quotes-ambed kar-to-conclude-verdict-uph olding-hijab-ban-article-90218163.

Sinha, Bhadra. 2007. "Ramayana No Basis for Ram Setu Debate: ASI," *Hindustan Times*, 13 September.

Sinha, Rabindra Nath. 2022. "Tribal Outfits Gearing Up to Restart Stir on Sarna Religious Code Issue," *NewsClick*, 15 September, https://www .newsclick.in/tribal-outfits-gearing-restart-sarna-religious-code-issue.

Sinha, Sumant. 2020. "Why India is the New Hotspot for Renewable Energy Investors," *World Economic Forum*, 14 January, https://www .weforum.org/agenda/2020/01/india-new-hotspot-renewable-energy-investors/.

Siqi, Ji, He Huifeng, and Brian Peach. 2021. "What Is 'Lying Flat', and Why Are Chinese Officials Standing Up to It?" *South China Morning Post*, 24 October, https://www.scmp.com/economy/china-economy/article/3153362/what-lying-flat-and-why-are-chinese-officials-standing-it.

Sjaastad, Espen, and Ben Cousins. 2008. "Formalisation of Land Rights in the South: An Overview," *Land Use Policy*, vol. 26, 1–9.

Sonak, Ishani. 2018. "State Govts Acquire Land by Subverting Rights and Bending the Law," *Down to Earth*, 12 December, https://www.down toearth.org.in/news/agriculture/-state-govts-acquire-land-by-subvert ing-rights-and-bending-the-law-62463.

Sonawane, Rakshit. 2022. "What Controversy Over AAP's Rajendra Gautam Attending Buddhism Conversion Ceremony Says About the Political Use of Ambedkar," *The Indian Express*, 11 October, https://indian express.com/article/opinion/columns/aap-rajendra-pal-gautam-at-bud dhism-conversion-ceremony-says-about-political-use-of-ambedkar-8200659/.

Song, Sarah. 2020. "Multiculturalism," in *Stanford Encyclopedia of Philosophy*, https://plato.stanford.edu/entries/multiculturalism/#PosCri.

Sonter, Laura J., Marie C. Dade, James E. M. Watson, and Rick K. Valenta. 2020. "Renewable Energy Production will Exacerbate Mining Threats to Biodiversity," *Nature Communications*, 1 September, https://www .nature.com/articles/s41467-020-17928-5.

Soundararajan, Thenmozhi. 2020. "Caste in the USA, Episode 1: Conversations about Casteism in Indian Diaspora are Vital to Challenging Its Impact," *Firstpost*, 30 October, https://www.firstpost.com/world/caste-in-the-usa-episode-1-conversations-about-casteism-in-indian-diaspora-are-vital-to-challenging-its-impact-8966631.html.

Souter, Anna. 2020. "Run Rewild: Reinstating Nature," *The Architectural Review*, 22 January, https://www.architectural-review.com/essays/books/run-rewild-reinstating-nature.

South African Secular Society. No Date. "Why Secularism is Important," https://www.secularsociety.org.za/why-is-secularism-important-in-south-africa/.

Special Correspondent. 2005. "Equal Rights for Women in Parental Property," *The Hindu*, 17 August, http://www.thehindu.com/2005/08/17/stories/2005081705461200.html.

Srinivasan, Rajeev. 1997. "The Buddhist Connection: Sabarimala and the Tibetans," https://www.rediff.com/news/dec/31rajeev.htm.

Srivastava, Piyush. 2010. "VHP is Real Winner as Ram Lalla's 'Friend'," *India Today*, 6 October, https://www.indiatoday.in/india/north/story/vhp-is-real-winner-as-ram-lallas-friend-83286-2010-10-06.

Srivastava, Prashant. 2021. "Yogi Govt Plans New Law to Regulate Temples, Mosques, Churches . . .," *The Print*, 12 January, https://theprint.in/india/governance/yogi-govt-plans-new-law-to-regulate-temples-mosques-churches-will-keep-tab-on-donations/583376/.

Standing, Guy. 2011. *The Precariat. The New Dangerous Class*, New York: Bloomsbury Academic.

Standing, Guy. 2015. "The Growing Precariat: Why We Need a Universal Basic Income," *SingularityHub*, 30 March, https://singularityhub.com/2015/03/30/the-growing-precariat-why-a-basic-income-is-needed/.

Statement. 2007. *Communalism Watch*, 23 September, https://communalism.blogspot.com/2007/09/condemn-killings-condemn.html.

Statement of Support. 2021. "Dismantling Global Hindutva. Multidisciplinary Perspectives," https://dismantlinghindutva.com/support-letter-4/.

Stott, Michael. 2022. "Chile's Rejection of Populism is an Example for the World," *Financial Times*, 5 September, https://www.ft.com/content/393de88b-c9f8-48cc-af33-d9fe86ee40d9.

Streithorst, Tom. 2015. "How Basic Income Solves Capitalism's Fundamental Problem," *Evonomics*, 20 December, http://evonomics.com/how-universal-basic-income-solves/.

Stuenkel, Oliver. 2022. "Chile's Rejection of the New Constitution Is a Sign of Democratic Maturity," *Carnegie Endowment for International Peace*, 8 September, https://carnegieendowment.org/2022/09/08/chile-s-rejection-of-new-constitution-is-sign-of-democratic-maturity-pub-87879.

Suchland, Jennifer. 2021. "Locating Postsocialist Precarity in Global Coloniality. A Decolonial Frame for 1989?," in Redi Koobak, Madina Tlostanova, and Suruchi Thapar-Björkert, eds., *Postcolonial and Postsocialist Dialogues. Intersections, Opacities, Challenges in Feminist Theorizing and Practice*, Abingdon: Routledge.

Sukhdeve, Harishchandra. 2020. "Did Savarkar Believe in and Promoted [*sic*] Untouchability?" *Velivada*, https://velivada.com/2020/10/01/did-savarkar-believe-in-and-promoted-untouchability/.

Sulochana, N. 2019. "Tamil or Sanskrit, Which is Older?" *Times of India*, 3 August, https://timesofindia.indiatimes.com/blogs/tracking-indian-communities/tamil-or-sanskrit-which-is-older/.

Sundar, Nandini. 2018. "Pathalgadi is Nothing But Constitutional Messianism So Why Is the BJP Afraid of It?," *The Wire*, 16 May, https://thewire.in/rights/pathalgadi-is-nothing-but-constitutional-messianism-so-why-is-the-bjp-afraid-of-it.

Sundaram, Dheepa. 2022. "The Neocolonial Futurism of US Hindutva," *The Immanent Frame*, 23 November, https://tif.ssrc.org/2022/11/23/the-neocolonial-futurism-of-us-hindutva/.

Supreme Court Observer. 2019. "Sabarimala Temple Entry," https://www.scobserver.in/cases/indian-young-lawyers-association-v-state-of-kerala-sabarimala-temple-entry-background/.

Suresh, Haripriya. 2018. "Justice Indu Malhotra's Dissenting Judgement in Sabarimala Case: Key Takeaways," *The News Minute*, 29 September, https://www.thenewsminute.com/article/justice-indu-malhotra-s-dissenting-judgement-sabarimala-case-key-takeaways-89174

Taketomo, Yasuhiko. 1990. "Cultural Adaptation to Psychoanalysis in Japan, 1912–52," *Social Research* , Winter, vol. 57, no. 4, 951–91.

Tamale, Sylvia. 2020. *Decolonization and Afro-Feminism*, Auebec: Daraja Press.

Tan, K. Cohen, and Shuxin Cheng. 2020. "Sang Subculture in Post-reform China," *Global Media and China*, 20 February.

Taneja, Anand Vivek. 2018. *Jinnealogy. Time, Islam, and Ecological Thought in the Medieval Ruins of Delhi*, Stanford: Stanford University Press.

Taskin, Bismee. 2021. "1 Year of UP Anti-conversion law—108 cases, Chargesheet Filed in 72, 'Lack of Proof' in 11," *The Print*, 24 November, https://theprint.in/india/1-year-of-up-anti-conversion-law-108-cases-chargesheet-filed-in-72-lack-of-proof-in-11/770763/.

Taylor, Charles. 1998. "Modes of Secularism," in Rajeev Bhargava, ed., *Secularism and Its Critics*, Delhi: Oxford University Press, 31–53.

Taylor, Charles. 2011. "Why We Need a Radical Redefinition of Secularism," in Eduardo Mendieta and Jonathan Van Antwerpen, eds., *Judith Butler, Jürgen Habermas, Charles Taylor, Cornel West: The Power of Religion in the Public Sphere*, New York: Columbia University Press, 34–59.

Tewary, Amarnath. 2018. "The Pathalgadi Rebellion," *The Hindu*, 14 April 14, https://www.thehindu.com/news/national/other-states/the-pathalgadi-rebellion/article23530998.ece.

Thaker, Aria. 2018. "The Latest Skirmish in California's Textbooks War Reveals the Mounting Influence of Hindutva in the United States," *The Caravan*, 7 February, https://caravanmagazine.in/vantage/califor nias-textbooks-war-reveals-mounting-influence-hindutva-united-states.

Thapar, Romila. 2020. *Voices of Dissent*, Kolkata: Seagull Books.

Tharoor, Shashi. 2018. *Why I Am a Hindu*, Delhi: Aleph Book Company.

The Hindu Data. 2019. "Just 26% of Indians Speak Hindi as Mother Tongue," *The Hindu*, 17 September, https://www.thehindu.com/data/just-26-percent-of-indians-speak-hindi-as-mother-tongue/arti cle29439701.ece.

The Hindu Data. 2021 "Fertility Rates Decline Across Religions in India, Sharpest Drop Recorded Among Muslims," *The Hindu*, 23 September, https://www.thehindu.com/data/data-fertility-rates-decline-across-re ligions-in-india-sharpest-drop-recorded-among-muslims/arti cle36625885.ece.

TNM Staff. 2020. "Images of Lathi-wielding RSS Workers Checking Vehicles in Telangana Ignites Row," *The News Minute*, 12 April, https://www .thenewsminute.com/article/images-lathi-wielding-rss-workers-check ing-vehicles-telangana-ignites-row-122401.

TNN. 2007. "Scholars Divided on Setu Issue," *Times of India*, 18 September, https://timesofindia.indiatimes.com/scholars-divided-on-setu-is sue/articleshow/2378645.cms.

TNN. 2014. "Mela to Protest Against Burning of Ravana's Effigies," http:// timesofindia.indiatimes.com/articleshow/44340759.cms?utm_source= contentofinterest&utm_medium=text&utm_campaign=cppst.

Toynbee, Polly. 2020. "Once Again, Care Work Has Been Exposed as the NHS's Poor Relation," *The Guardian*, 11 May, https://www.theguard ian.com/commentisfree/2020/may/11/care-work-nhs-pandemic-cash.

Tripathi, Rahul. 2020. "NE Delhi Violence: There Were Warning Signs Before Rioting Began," *The Economic Times*, 27 February, https://econo-mictimes.indiatimes.com/news/politics-and-nation/northeast-del hi-violence-there-were-warning-signs-before-rioting-began/article show/74328478.cms?utm_source=contentofinterest&utm_medium= text&utm_campaign=cppst.

Tripathi, Shailaja. 2012. "Work in Progress," *The Hindu*, 3 February, https://www.thehindu.com/features/metroplus/work-in-progress/ article2857092.ece.

Tripathy, Harshvardhan. 2019. "How New India Developed its Own Lynch Culture in Just Five Years," *The Citizen*, 30 March, https://www.thecit izen.in/index.php/en/NewsDetail/index/2/16590/How-New-India-Developed-its-Own-Lynch-Culture-in-Just-Five-Years.

True Nature Foundation. No Date. "What is Rewilding?," https://truena turefoundation.org/what-is-rewilding/.

Tuckey, Sarah. 2020. "Mother's Day and the Importance of Unpaid Care Work during the COVID-19 Pandemic," *Oxfam*, 8 May, https://poli ticsofpoverty.oxfamamerica.org/mothers-day-and-the-importance-of-unpaid-care-work-during-the-covid-19-pandemic/.

UNESCO. 2021. "Durga Puja Inscribed on the UNESCO Representative List of the Intangible Cultural Heritage of Humanity," https://www.un esco.org/en/articles/durga-puja-inscribed-unesco-representative-list-in tangible-cultural-heritage-humanity.

Us Salam, Zia, and Uzma Ausaf. 2020. *Shaheen Bagh: From a Protest to a Movement*, Delhi: Bloomsbury India.

Vahali, Honey Oberoi. 2019. "Explorations and Reflections: On Envisioning the Psychosocial Clinical Programmes at the School of Human Studies, Ambedkar University Delhi, India," *Journal of Psychosocial Studies*, July, vol. 12, nos 1–2, 129–44.

Vanita, Ruth. 2002. "Whatever Happened to the Hindu Left?," *Seminar*, no. 512, https://www.india-seminar.com/2002/512/512%20comment .htm.

Vanita, Ruth. 2022. *The Dharma of Justice in the Sanskrit Epics. Debates on Gender, Varna and Species*, Delhi: Oxford University Press.

Vansintjan, Aaron. 2019. "Degrowth vs. the Green New Deal," *Resilience*, 2 May, https://www.resilience.org/stories/2019-05-02/degrowth-vs-the-green-new-deal/.

Variyar, Mugdha. 2020. "Coronavirus: Govt Asks Social Media Platforms to Promote Aarogya Setu App," *CNBCTV*, 18 April 13, https://www.cn

bctv18.com/technology/coronavirus-govt-asks-social-media-platforms-to-promote-aarogya-setu-app-5664061.htm

Varma, Vishnu. 2022. "'Come Here, You're Not Different': A Theyyam Artist's Comforting Words to Muslim Woman Draw Cheers," *The Indian Express*, 24 February, https://indianexpress.com/article/india/kerala/theyyam-artist-comforting-words-to-muslim-woman-is-drawing-cheers-7787740/.

Veltmeyer, Henry, and James Petras. 2014. *The New Extractivism. A Post-neoliberal Development Model or Imperialism for the Twenty-first Century?* London and New York: Zed Books.

Veluthat, Kesavan. 2013. *Brahman Settlements in Kerala: Historical Studies*, New Delhi: Cosmo Books.

Venkatesan, V. 2008. "Sethusamudram Case in the Supreme Court: Soli Sorabjee's Submission," *Law and Other Things. A Blog About Indian Law, the Courts, and the Constitution*, http://lawandotherthings.blogspot.com/2008/05/sethusamudram-case-in-supreme-court.html.

Venkateswar, Sita, and Emma Hughes. 2011. *The Politics of Indigeneity: Dialogues and Reflections on Indigenous Activism*, London: Zed Books.

Venkatramanan, K. 2022. "What is the Essential Practice Test?" *The Hindu*, 13 February

Venugopal, Vasudha. 2020. "Buddhist, Ambedkarite Bodies Say UP Law that Penalises Mass Conversions is a Move to Quell Dalit Resistance," *The Economic Times*, 3 December, https://economictimes.indiatimes.com/news/politics-and-nation/buddhist-ambedkarite-bodies-say-up-law-that-penalises-mass-conversions-is-a-move-to-quell-dalit-resistance/articleshow/79550748.cms?from=mdr.

Verma, Lalmani. 2021. "In Kumbh Crowd Management, a First: RSS Workers as Special Police Officers," *The Indian Express*, 15 April, https://indianexpress.com/article/india/in-kumbh-crowd-management-a-first-rss-workers-as-special-police-officers-7274131.

Vijaisri, Priyadarshini. 2015. *Dangerous Marginality. Rethinking Impurity and Power*, Delhi: Primus Books/ Indian Council of Historical Research.

Vijaisri, Priyadarshini. 2023. "Notes on Oxymorons: Matsyanyaya and Vadho Avadhah," in idem, *Sacrifice, Pollution and Madness: Essays on Caste Violence*, Delhi: Bloosmbury.

Vink, Markus P. M. 2007. "Indian Ocean Studies and the 'New Thalassology'," *Journal of Global History*, vol. 2, 41–62.

Visvanathan, Shiv. 1997. *Carnival for Science*, Delhi: Oxford University Press.

Viswanathan, Gauri. 2007. "Literacy and Conversion in the Discourse of Hindu Nationalism," in Anuradha Dingwaney Needham and Rajeswari Sunder Rajan, eds., *The Crisis of Secularism in India*, Durham: Duke University Press.

Viswanathan, Manoj. 2020. "Kerala Restores Sabarimala Curbs for Women," *The New Indian Express*, https://www.newindianexpress.com/states/kerala/2020/dec/03/state-restores-sabarimala-curbs-for-women-2231074.html.

Vinea, Ana. 2021. "Diagnostic Dilemmas," in *Africa is a Country*, https://africasacountry.com/2021/06/diagnostic-dilemmas.

Vombatkere, S. G. 2007. "Letter to President, PM, Sonia Gandhi on Ram Setu and Sethusamudram Project," *Mainstream*, vol. 45 (40), 26 September, https://www.mainstreamweekly.net/article334.html.

Wankhede, Harish. 2022. "The Atrophy of the Neo-Buddhist Movement in India," *The Hindu*, 8 October, https://www.thehindu.com/opinion/op-ed/the-atrophy-of-the-neo-buddhist-movement-in-india/article65980690.ece.

Weber, Max. 1905/1930. *The Protestant Ethic and the Spirit of Capitalism*, trans. Talcott Parsons, London & Boston: Unwin Hyman.

Weber, Max. [1918] 1946. "Science as Vocation," in *From Max Weber: Essays in Sociology*, trans. and eds. H. H. Gerth and C. Wright Mills, New York: Oxford University Press, 129–56.

Weeks, Kathi. 2011. *The Problem with Work*, Durham: Duke University Press.

Weeks, Kathi. 2016. "A Feminist Case for Basic Income: An Interview with Kathi Weeks," Interview with Katie Cruz, *Critical Legal Thinking*, 22 August.

West, Cornel, and Suraj Yengde. 2017. "A Shared History of Struggle Should Unite India's Dalits and African Americans in the Fight for Equality," *The Root*, 12 June, https://www.theroot.com/a-shared-history-of-struggle-should-unite-india-s-dalit-1795973401.

Whitlock, Robin. 2020. "YouTube Removes Controversial Michael Moore Film Planet of the Humans After Copyright Infringement Complaint," *Renewable Energy Magazine*, 29 May, https://www.renewableenergymagazine.com/panorama/youtube-removes-controversial-michael-moore-film-planet-20200529.

Wig, N. N. 2004. "Hanuman Complex and Its Resolution: An Illustration of Psychotherapy from Indian Mythology," *Indian Journal of Psychiatry*, vol. 46 (1), 25–8.

Williams, F. E. 1995. "Oedipus in Papuan Folklore," in Lowell Edmunds and Alan Dundes, eds., *Oedipus. A Folklore Casebook*, Madison: University of Wisconsin Press.

Winch, Peter. 1987. *Trying to Make Sense*, Oxford: Wiley-Blackwell.

Winternitz, Maurice. 1981. *History of Indian Literature Vol. 1*, trans. from the German by V. S. Sarma, New Delhi: Motilal Banarsidass (rpntd 2010).

Wintour, Patrick. 2019. "Kashmir: Labour Shifts Policy After Backlash by Indian-heritage Voters," *The Guardian*, 12 November, https://www .theguardian.com/politics/2019/nov/12/kashmir-labour-shifts-poli cy-after-backlash-by-indian-heritage-voters.

Withanage, Hemantha. 2008. "Sethusamudram: Who stand for Sri Lankan Interests?," http://hwithanage-sethusamudram.blogspot.com/.

Witzel, Michael. 1993. "Towards a History of the Brahmins," *Journal of the American Oriental Society*, April–June, vol. 113, no. 2.

Witzel, Michael. 2005. "Indocentrism," in Edwin Bryant and Laurie L. Patton, eds., *The Indo-Aryan Controversy. Evidence and Inference in Indian History*, Abingdon: Routledge.

Wu Guanjun. 2014. *The Great Dragon Fantasy: A Lacanian Analysis of Contemporary Chinese Thought*, Singapore: World Scientific.

Wyeth, Grant. 2022. "Do Australian Politicians Know the Difference Between Hinduism and Hindutva?" *The Diplomat*, 17 May, https://thediplomat .com/2022/05/do-australian-politicians-know-the-difference-between-hinduism-and-hindutva/.

Xinting, Liu. 2020. "Why are Contemporary Youth Increasingly 'Unhappy?' Focus on the Living Conditions of China's Youth," trans. Freya Ge and David Ownby, https://www.readingthechinadream.com/liu-xinting-contemporary-youth.html.

Yamaguchi, Susumu, and Yukari Ariizumi. 2006. "Close Interpersonal Relationships among Japanese. Amae as Distinguished from Attachment and Dependence," in Uichol Kim, Kuo-Shu Yang, and Kwang-Kuo Hwang, eds., *Indigenous and Cultural Psychology. Understanding People in Context* Berlin: Springer, 163–74.

Yoffee, Norman. 2007. *Negotiating the Past in the Past: Identity, Memory, and Landscape in Archaeological Research*, Tucson: University of Arizona Press.

Yuval-Davis, Nira. 1997. *Gender and Nation*. London: Sage.

Zahan, Syeda Ambia. 2019. "Rs 1,220-cr and 10 Years Later, NRC Leaves

Group Favouring Exercise Dissatisfied, Raises Doubts Over Migrant Numbers in Assam," *FirstPost*, 3 September, https://www.firstpost.com/india/rs-1220-cr-and-10-years-later-nrc-leaves-group-favouring-exercise-disastified-final-list-raises-questions-false-claims-on-migrants-7271991.html.

Zavos, J. 2001. "Defending Hindu Tradition: Sanatana Dharma as a Symbol of Orthodoxy in Colonial India," *Religion* (Academic Press), vol. 31, no. 2, April, 109–23.

Zhang, Jingyuan. 1992. *Psychoanalysis in China. Literary Transformations 1919–1949*, New York: East Asia Program, and Ithaca: Cornell University.

Zia, Afiya Shehrbano. 2022. "Pious, Populist, Political Masculinities in Pakistan and India," *South Asian Popular Culture*, vol. 20, no. 2, 181–99.

Index